THE CRADLE KING

Hostage to Fortune:
The Troubled Life of Francis Bacon 1561–1626
(co-authored with Lisa Jardine)

Philip Sidney: A Double Life

THE CRADLE KING

The Life of James VI & I,
the First Monarch of a United Great Britain

Alan Stewart

ST. MARTIN'S PRESS ❧ NEW YORK

www.stmartins.com

Library of Congress Cataloging-in-Publication Data

Stewart, Alan, 1967–
    The cradle king : the life of James VI and I the first monarch of a United Great Britain / Alan Stewart.
        p. cm.
    Originally published: London : Chatto & Windus, 2003.
    Includes bibliographical references and index.
    ISBN 0-312-27488-2 (alk. Paper)
    1. James I, King of England, 1566–1625. 2. Great Britain—History—James I, 1603–1625. 3. Great Britain—Kings and rulers—Biography. 4. Scotland—History—James VI, 1567–1625. 5. Scotland—Kings and rulers—Biography. I. Title.

DA391.S79 2003
941.06'1'092—dc22
[B]   2003058635

First published in Great Britain by Chatto & Windus, an imprint of Random House

First U.S. Edition: December 2003

10 9 8 7 6 5 4 3 2 1

Contents

Acknowledgements

Work on this book started at the Folger Shakespeare Library in Washington DC and finished at the British Library in London, and I am indebted to the librarians and staff of both these great institutions. I am immensely grateful to the Folger for giving me a Short-Term Fellowship in 2000, and to Tom Healy and my colleagues at Birkbeck for allowing me generous research leave. Maggie Pearlstine and John Oates at Maggie Pearlstine Associates encouraged me throughout. At Chatto & Windus, Rebecca Carter was a supportive and challenging editor.

I could not have written *The Cradle King* without the insights of those scholars who have broadened and deepened our knowledge of all things Jacobean since D.H. Willson's 1956 biography of James. I learned particularly from the work of (in alphabetical order) G.P.V. Akrigg, Leeds Barroll, David Bergeron, Caroline Bingham, Antonia Fraser, Jonathan Goldberg, Maurice Lee Jr., Roger Lockyer, Maureen Meikle, Stephen Orgel, Curtis Perry, David Stevenson, Roy Strong and Jenny Wormald. For ideas, suggestions, comments and help of many kinds, I am grateful to Tom Betteridge, Warren Boutcher, Tricia Bracher, Jerry Brotton, Stephen Clucas, Erica Fudge, Donna Hamilton, James Knowles, Gordon McMullan, Steven May, David Norbrook, Alex Samson, James Shapiro, Bruce Smith, Sue Wiseman, Heather Wolfe and Elizabeth Wood.

Finally, my sincere thanks go to the friends who saw me through: Patricia Brewerton, James Daybell, Will Fisher, Eliane Glaser, Andrew Gordon, Lisa Jardine, Simon Lloyd-Owen, Lloyd Meiklejohn, Kirk Melnikoff, Chris Ross, Richard Schoch, Goran Stanivukovic, Garrett Sullivan and especially Tyler Smith.

List of Illustrations

Prologue

IN 1603, JAMES I, King of England, made a visit to one of the most southerly of his new possessions, Beaulieu, in the New Forest. All the local nobility and gentry turned out to get their first glimpse of the King of Scots who had just become their own sovereign. Among them was the eighteen-year-old John Oglander, a son of the local landed gentry. Over fifty years later, Oglander jotted down his memories of that royal visit.[1] By then, his life was consumed by the fight to save James's son, the embattled King Charles. But his image of James was far from complimentary. 'King James I of England was the most cowardly man that ever I knew,' he started. When James came to Beaulieu, he recalled, 'he was much taken with seeing the little boys skirmish, whom he loved to see better and more willingly than men.' The pantomime of juvenile combat suited the King far better than the real, very bloody thing. 'He could not endure a soldier or to see men drilled, to hear of war was death to him, and how he tormented himself with fear of some sudden mischief may be proved by his great quilted doublets, pistol-proof, was also his strange eyeing of strangers with a continual fearful observation.'

Why would Oglander, a staunch royalist, write such a thing? His other notes on the King were positive enough. 'Otherwise', he wrote, James was 'the best scholar and wisest prince for general knowledge that ever England had, very merciful and passionate, liberal and honest.' He was 'a great politician and very sound in the reformed religion'. He 'spoke much and as well as any man, or rather better.' And he was 'the chastest prince for women that ever was, for he would often swear that he had never known any other woman than his wife.' Although he was known to be 'excessively taken with hunting' — indeed, he was notorious for it — 'he did not, or could not', according to Oglander, use much 'bodily action', so that 'his body for want of use' grew 'defective'. In Oglander's eyes, this was a King for whom theory and rhetoric were never matched by practice. 'If he had but the power, spirit and resolution to have acted that which he spoke, or done as well as he knew how to do, Solomon had been short of him.'

For Oglander, the answer to this paradox lay in the King's 'fearful nature'. Throughout his life, James was noted, and lampooned, for his fear of war, weapons, loud noises and unexplained strangers. He referred to them, in his usual grandiose style, as his 'daily tempests of innumerable dangers'. Speaking to the English Parliament after he survived perhaps the greatest threat of all, the Gunpowder Plot of November 1605, he made his own diagnosis as to the cause of his 'fearful nature'. They could be traced and dated, he told the Parliament, 'not only ever since my birth, but even as I may justly say, before my birth: and while I was in my mother's belly'.[2]

CHAPTER ONE

Nourished in Fear

S COTLAND LOOKED FORWARD to a great marriage. Mary, although a widow, was still a young, captivating Queen, only twenty-three years old, a tall, auburn-haired woman. She came from ruling the sophisticated French court as the wife of King François II, and preferred to speak, read and write in French. The groom, Henry Stuart, Lord Darnley, by all accounts was an equally fine-looking man, taller than his bride, blond and elegant, and just nineteen. The French ambassador reported that 'it is not possible to see a more beautiful Prince, and he is accomplished in all courtly exercises'.[1] On Sunday 29 July 1565, very early in the morning, they were married in the Chapel Royal in the Palace of Holyroodhouse in Edinburgh.[2]

But the ceremony almost didn't happen. As one observer noted, less than a month before the wedding, Henry did not think himself sufficiently honoured by the prenuptial arrangements Mary proposed. He wanted to reign alongside her as King, to have the 'Crown Matrimonial'; Mary insisted that he should wait until he came of age and had gained the consent of Parliament. But Henry's 'insolent temper' prevailed,[3] and on the day after the wedding, Henry got his wish. At Edinburgh's Mercat Cross Henry was formally proclaimed as King of Scots, and the official document dated the event as being 'of our reigns the first and twenty-third years', the ordering of the numbers giving Henry's reign priority over Mary's. But a proclamation could not change men's opinions. As 'King Henry' was proclaimed, the nobility maintained silence, refusing to cheer their new sovereign. Only his father, the Earl of Lennox, chimed in with the usual 'God save his Grace!'[4] It's a mark of how little accepted Henry was as King that to this day historians routinely refer to him as 'Lord Darnley'.

The new King Henry was competing with a wife who had been Queen of Scots for twenty-three years, since she was a week old. The only legitimate child left by James V at his early death in 1542, Mary had spent only the first six years of her life in Scotland, under a regency government headed by James Hamilton, second Earl of Arran. Through the intervention of her French mother, Marie de Guise,

Mary had left for France in 1548 to receive an education: ten years later she married the heir to the French throne. In 1554, Arran stepped aside to allow Marie de Guise to take over as Regent, and Marie did her utmost to strengthen the bond between Scotland and France popularly known as 'the auld alliance'.

But Marie's control on the country was never total. Scotland in the 1550s was witnessing the rise of a new religious movement. Protestants, inspired by the ecclesiastical reformations in Germany and England, began to form themselves into a new Church. They were encouraged by the visit of the Calvinist preacher John Knox, who returned to his homeland in 1555 and preached and celebrated communion across the country. When the Scots Parliament met in December 1557 to approve the marriage of their absentee Queen Mary with the French Dauphin François, the Protestant Lords took the opportunity to draw up a formal 'band', or alliance, pledging to further the Reformist cause in Scotland against the regime of the Regent Marie. Two years later, the same Protestant Lords, known as the Lords of the Congregation, succeeded in persuading Knox to return to Scotland permanently. By now they were beginning to wage war against the Regent and her French-maintained army. Gradually, the Lords of the Congregation, headed by James V's illegitimate son Lord James Stewart, pushed the Regent's forces back to Edinburgh's port town, Leith, which they fortified in preparation for battle. English forces were sent by Queen Elizabeth to support the Protestant Lords, but the looming war never materialised. In June 1560 Marie de Guise died, and the impetus of her campaign was lost. On 6 July of that year, a peace was declared at Edinburgh, whereby both the French and the English were to leave Scotland; the English used their involvement to broker an agreement that Mary and François would give up their claims to the English throne. Mary's half-brother Lord James Stewart took control of the country, and imposed a new Reformation on Scotland, adopting a 'Confession of Faith' which founded a new Kirk (Church), broadly Calvinist in spirit, outlawing the saying of the Mass and rejecting the authority of the Pope.[5]

1560 also saw the death of Mary's husband King François from an abscess in his ear. As his brother Charles ascended the throne, Mary had no reason to remain in France and was forced back to Scotland.

It was not a journey she wished to make. She had been brought up to believe that Scotland was a backward, ignorant, unsophisticated land. At the self-consciously civilised French court, Scotland's social conventions — fierce loyalties to local magnates, peace kept through strong 'bonds' and justice meted out in feuds — were decried as outdatedly feudal at best, barbaric at worst. On reaching Scotland, Mary's policy of government seems to have been to close her eyes and hope her troubles would melt away. Radical differences were ineptly smoothed over rather than forced into resolution. So while Mary steadfastly refused to ratify the Acts of Parliament that installed the new Confession of Faith, the split from the papacy and the forbidding of Mass, she manoeuvred strategically, deciding not to interfere with the new religious polity as long as she was allowed to worship freely in the Roman faith. She signed through a deal by which the new Kirk would receive one sixth of the wealth of the old Church. She crushed one of the leading Roman Catholic noblemen, the Earl of Huntly. And she took as her chief counsellor her half-brother Lord James Stewart, leader of the Lords of the Congregation, whom she created Earl of Moray in February 1562; it was through Moray and her Secretary of State, William Maitland of Lethington, that she ruled the country.

This compromise state of affairs was horribly precarious, and Mary's plans for marriage would ultimately blow it down. After negotiations to marry Elizabeth of England's dashing young favourite Robert Dudley foundered, Mary's eyes turned to the young Henry Stuart, Lord Darnley. It seemed a popular choice. Henry was a Scot, son of Matthew Stuart, Earl of Lennox, whom Mary had recalled from exile the previous year. For Mary, Henry's personal charms were matched by his strategic importance in her political future, for the Lennoxes had a strong claim to the English throne. But Henry was suspected of being a Catholic; in April 1565, Moray left the court in protest, and a month later refused to give Mary a written promise that he would support the marriage, saying that he feared that Henry would not be 'a favourer or setter forth of Christ's true religion'; in reply, Mary gave him 'many sore words'.[6] Soon Moray entered into a 'band' of mutual support with the ex-Regent Arran, head of the Hamiltons and the heir apparent to the throne if Mary failed to produce a child. At Moray's suggestion, Arran declined a summons to court: Mary promptly proclaimed him a traitor, and only spared his life because he agreed to a five-year banishment.[7]

Despite the protests, Mary was adamant on her choice, and on 29 July 1565 she made her second marriage. Now Henry was to feel the hatred Mary aroused. On Sunday 19 August, the King attended a sermon by John Knox at Edinburgh's St Giles' Church that lasted 'an hour and more longer than the time appointed'. Knox did not subscribe to the policy of mutual appeasement between Kirk and Queen. Mary, he thought, should either convert or die. Added to his distaste for the Queen was his firmly held and oft expressed belief that a woman should not rule, the subject of his notorious *The First Blast of the Trumpet against the Monstrous Regiment of Women*. He had even turned down Mary's offer to seek his private counsel. 'If your Grace please to frequent the public sermons,' he retorted, 'then doubt I not that ye shall fully understand both what I like and dislike, as well in your Majesty as in all others.'[8] By now Knox was a shrunken old man who had to be helped into the pulpit by two men, and who started his sermon leaning; but by the time he was done with his sermon, wrote one admiring onlooker, 'he was so active and vigorous that he was like to ding that pulpit in blads [seemed likely to beat the pulpit to pieces] and fly out of it!'[9] Knox's text on this occasion was Isaiah 26: 13–21: 'O Lord our God, other lords than thou have ruled over us.' In it, Knox focused on how wicked princes were sent by God because of the sins of the people, to act as tyrants and scourges to plague them, and more particularly 'that God sets in that room – for the offences and ingratitude of the people – boys and women'. Henry and Mary were tacitly likened to Ahab and Jezebel, with Knox pointing out 'that God justly punished Ahab and his posterity, because he would not take order with that harlot Jezebel'. Moving on, Knox compared Henry to Julian the Apostate, and concluded with a prayer that 'we may see . . . what punishment he [God] hath appointed for the cruel tyrants'. Unsurprisingly, the King was 'so moved at this sermon, that he would not dine; and being troubled with great fury he passed in the afternoon to the hawking', an inappropriate Sabbath activity guaranteed to confirm Knox in his low opinion of the King. The Council ordered Knox to abstain from preaching for 'a season', because 'the King's majesty was offended'.[10]

But John Knox was not the newlyweds' only problem. Mary was no sooner married than she found herself once more under attack from Moray, who launched a rebellion citing Mary's 'danger' to the Protestant religion, supported by the Earl of Argyll, who wielded considerable influence in the west of the country. Failing to answer a summons to appear before Mary, Moray was ritually 'put to the horn', or outlawed, on 6 August 1565, and eight days later his properties were seized.[11] As Moray gathered his forces at Ayr, Mary mustered her troops, and from late August to the beginning of October the rebel and the royal forces (the latter led by the King's father Lennox and Mary's Lord Chancellor James Douglas, fourth Earl of Morton, with Henry and Mary in the rearguard) engaged in a tiresome stand-off in often appalling weather during which the rival troops never met, a non-event aptly dubbed 'the Chaseabout Raid'. Mary, carrying a pistol, and wearing a steel cap, was remarked upon for her fortitude: while 'the most part waxed weary' in the tempestuous weather, 'yet the Queen's courage increased manlike so much that she was ever with the foremost'.[12] After rebel forces were expelled from Edinburgh on 1 September, the royal forces gained the upper hand and forced the rebels south. By 6 October, defeat was inevitable, and Moray fled over the border to seek asylum in England.

Despite her vigour during the Chaseabout Raid, Mary's health was fragile, and it was often reported that the Queen was ill. In November 1565, for example, she took to her bed complaining of a pain in her side, but newsmongers were keen for the newlywed's condition to be something more romantic than her 'old malady'. As the winter drew on, word spread that the Queen was expecting her first child, a report only fanned by her decision to ride in a litter, rather than on horseback as usual, from Edinburgh to Linlithgow in December.[13] While an early pregnancy boded well for the marriage, frequent quarrels suggested that all was not well between the King and Queen. In September, Mary had welcomed back from exile a Protestant nobleman, James Hepburn, the fourth Earl of Bothwell, earlier banished on charges of planning to abduct her. Bothwell, the hereditary Lord High Admiral of Scotland, wielded considerable power in the Borders. Contemporary opinion was remarkably consistent on the Earl: he was, according to the English agent in Scotland Thomas

Randolph, 'a blasphemer and irreverent speaker both of his own sovereign and the Queen my mistress'; another English observer, the ambassador Nicholas Throckmorton, saw him as a '[vain]glorious, rash and hazardous young man'.[14] In the words of Sir John Maxwell, fourth Lord Herries, a loyal supporter of Mary, Bothwell was 'a man high in his own conceit, proud, vicious, and vainglorious above measure; one who would attempt anything out of ambition'.[15]

Mary, knowing that Bothwell nurtured a longstanding enmity towards Moray, wanted him to lead her forces; Henry wanted his father to have the position, but Mary prevailed; she soon came to rely increasingly on Bothwell in military matters.[16] There were other signals of marital tension. In December, a coin reading 'Henricus et Maria' was recalled from circulation, and reissued with the inscription 'Maria et Henricus'.[17] By the end of the year, the change of priority was clear: Randolph reported that 'a while [ago] there was nothing but "King and Queen, his majesty and hers"; but now the "Queen's husband" is more common'.[18] Mary was also upsetting many Scottish lords who saw their traditional influence waning, while that of the Queen's personal entourage, which included several foreign servants who had followed her from France, waxed remarkably. They complained that 'the Queen had now a certain resolution to tyrannise over the country; for what could be more grievous than to mistrust her own subjects, and commit her person to the guard of Italians, strangers, and papists!' Look at her secretary David Riccio, 'Signor Davy', 'one whom the Queen gave greater trust unto than her own husband, one without whose counsel the Queen did nothing. He was an Italian himself, and would make these Italians do what he pleased!'[19] David Riccio had come to the Scottish court in 1561 in the retinue of the ambassador of the Duke of Savoy, and had entered the Queen's Household as a singer, before becoming her personal secretary. This post, one of great intimacy with the Queen, was one to set tongues wagging. When Henry withdrew from court to spend time hunting in Peebles, the Queen's party blamed it on his 'wilfulness' and anger at the curbing of his power and deferring of his coronation. Others, however, claimed that Mary had forced him to retire, openly expressing her distaste for his company. At the same time, according to Lord Herries, 'she raised every day Signor Davy higher in her favour, and used him with greater familiarity than was fit. It was openly said that she took more pleasure in his company than in the King's, her husband's; that she made him sit at table with her, and [he] had free access to her bedchamber, at all hours.' Her friends protected Mary by saying that Riccio was 'witty and faithful' but that 'it was nothing likely that she would fancy his person' since he was 'neither handsome nor well-faced'.[20] (Mary's apologist Adam Blackwood confirms that 'He was a man of no beauty or outward shape, for he was misshapen, evil favoured, and in visage very black; but for his fidelity, wisdom, prudence, virtue and his other good parts and qualities of mind he was richly adorned.')[21] Henry's father Lennox, on the other hand, was certain that Mary was 'using the said David more as a lover than a servant. Forsaking her husband's bed and board very often, liking the company of David, as appeared, better than her husband's.'[22] Whatever the truth of the rumours, Lord Herries concluded, 'they were by her enemies cried out with open mouth, to defame her and incense her husband'.[23]

Henry was soon provoked by more than simply sexual jealousy. In order to prevent her husband handing out gifts without her authority, Mary decreed that all papers had to be signed first by her, with her own hand, and then by Henry – or rather, by Henry's signature. She then had a seal made bearing Henry's signature, and gave it to Riccio.[24] This infuriated Henry. Not content with curbing his role as King–husband, Mary was now handing what was left of it to her Italian secretary – a foreigner and a papist, arrogant and conspicuously extravagant in his dress. Rumour had it that Mary wanted to appoint him as Secretary of State or even replace Morton as Chancellor.

Although Mary had appointed Morton Lord Chancellor, and he had helped lead her forces during the Chaseabout Raid, she had never fully trusted the man, who was a staunch Protestant with family ties to Henry's family the Lennoxes, and with reason. It was Morton who fed Henry's suspicions about Riccio and encouraged his ambitions to assume his full powers as King. Henry should take on sole government of the country, Morton urged, drawing on the deeply ingrained misogyny of the time: it was 'a thing against nature that the hen should crow before the cock; yea, against the commandment of the eternal God, that a man should be subject to his wife, the man being the image of God, and woman the image of man'. If Henry would guarantee to pardon past misdemeanours and restore his estates, Morton would guarantee the support of his faction, and of the English Queen Elizabeth.[25]

Soon a plan to kill Riccio had been devised by Morton, along with Patrick, sixth Lord Lindsay and Patrick, Lord Ruthven, 'to become that way masters of the Court'. The courtier and diarist Sir James Melville claims that it was Morton's cousin, George Douglas, a kinsman and perpetual companion of Henry's, who 'put in his head such suspicion against Riccio that the King was won to give his consent over easily to the slaughter of Signor David'.[26] Also drawn in was the fugitive Earl of Moray, who needed to escape the sentence that the forthcoming Parliament would doubtless pass against him; if Henry were to assume sole government, then the Parliament could be cancelled.

Patrick, third Lord Ruthven, was one of the first men drawn into the plot. In his own account of the affair, written at the end of April 1566, he told of how he had doubts, especially concerning the killing of Riccio in front of Mary's eyes. Several of the conspirators were 'very loath to grant' this, pointing out that this might prompt 'sundry great persons' in Mary's company to intervene, causing considerable bloodshed. It was Henry who insisted on this detail: 'Notwithstanding no reason might avail, but the King would have him [Riccio] taken in her Majesty's presence, and devised the manner himself.'[27]

Although Henry did not sign the bond until 1 March 1566,[28] news of the plot had already leaked by 13 February, when Thomas Randolph reported back to England that 'I know that . . . David with the consent of the King, shall have his throat cut within these ten days.'[29] Randolph was slightly premature, but the planned attack became a matter of urgency when it was announced that Parliament would move to bring about the arrest and trial of Moray and his confederates on 12 March: since the conspirators hoped to avoid this, action had to be taken before then. Sir James Melville claims (perhaps with the pathos of hindsight) that he tried to warn both Riccio and Mary of the dangers to them. The secretary ignored his advice: 'he disdained all danger, and despised counsel'. Mary dismissed the rumours, calmly assuring Melville 'that our countrymen were talkative'.[30]

The events of the evening of 9 March 1566 were so extraordinary that several local observers felt compelled to pen full accounts of the bloody proceedings, including Ruthven and Mary herself.[31] While differing in minor details, as one might reasonably expect in telling such a sudden and violent encounter, these narratives are remarkably consistent in what they tell. The Queen was at supper with Riccio and her half-sister Janet, Countess of Argyll, in a small room leading off her bedchamber. She was mildly surprised when Henry came in and made awkward small talk, but she was astonished when, in full armour and backed by six men with drawn swords, Lord Ruthven burst into the room.

'What strange sight is this, my Lord, I see in you?' she asked. 'Are you mad?'

'We have been too long mad,' Ruthven retorted.

But the secretary knew why they were there. Each account tells how Riccio, terrified, moved away from Ruthven and tried to take refuge behind the Queen, clasping his arms around her pregnant belly. This last detail is crucial. Riccio assumed that his best defence lay in being protected not just by the Queen, but by the unborn heir to the throne. He did not know that, by all accounts, Henry wanted his wife to miscarry, perhaps believing, as many would after him, that the child was not his but Riccio's. Mary took hold of the secretary, and refused to let go until one of Ruthven's men, Andrew Kerr of Fawdonsyde, placed a pistol to her breast. After a struggle Kerr pulled Riccio away, and dragged him to the next room where other conspirators waited. There the Earl of Morton struck the first blow with his dagger: fifty-two more were to follow. The King's own dagger was belatedly thrust into the ruined corpse, to seal his complicity.

Mary was weeping and shaken, but she remained imperiously in control of the situation. What was the cause of this attack, she demanded. Henry was taciturn, only speaking to say that no harm had been intended to her. Incensed, the Queen charged him with contempt and ingratitude towards her – she who had raised him from a private nobleman to a King, and her husband! Henry, seeing no way to defend himself, left the room. Then one of Mary's maids came running in, exclaiming that Davy was dead – that she had seen him dead. The Queen dried her eyes. 'No more tears,' she said. 'I will now think upon revenge!' Their job done, Ruthven and Fawdonsyde came back into Mary's chamber, Ruthven sitting himself down and calling for a drink, which further infuriated the Queen. 'How dare you presume to commit that unreverence?' she demanded, but Ruthven was unmoved. 'Well, my Lord,' said Mary, 'it is within my belly that one day will revenge these cruelties and affronts!'[32]

Despite her words, Mary was in no position to make threats. Under an effective house arrest in her private chambers, she had to look on while Henry took for himself the power that she had denied him. On the following day, he and his allies issued a proclamation, using his royal authority to dismiss the forthcoming Parliament. But Mary still had the upper hand in their marriage, refusing to allow him to join her in bed. And she already had her mind fixed on escape. Allowed to see the Dowager Lady Huntly, she passed a letter to her; suspecting foul play, her captors ordered Lady Huntly to leave, but she managed to secrete the letter before she went. In the afternoon, Mary told her captors that she was about to miscarry: a midwife was quickly summoned, and she confirmed it was likely. The conspirators determined that if Mary kept the child she should be moved to the more secure Stirling Castle, while Henry and the nobles would manage the government of the country from Edinburgh. If any persons tried to rescue the Queen, they decided, 'we will throw her to them piecemeal from the top of the terrace'.[33]

By the evening, Moray had returned from exile and had arrived in Edinburgh. The conspirators met together, and as they talked it dawned on the King that he was no longer safe. 'If you wish to obtain what we have promised you,' they told Henry, 'you must needs follow our advice . . . if you do otherwise, we will take care of ourselves, cost what it may.' The King was instructed not to talk with Mary 'save in their presence', his entourage dismissed and a guard put on him. Henry, scared for his life, tried to reach his wife, but she refused him admission to her room until the morning, when he fell on his knees, much to her discomfort. 'Ah, my Mary,' he said, 'I have failed in my duty towards you . . . The only atonement which I can make . . . is to acknowledge my fault and sue for pardon.' Showing her the bond that the conspirators had signed, he told her that they threatened her life: 'Unless you take some means to prevent it, we are all ruined, and that speedily.'[34]

Later in the day, Moray came to see the Queen. Mary threw herself on him, crying 'Oh, my brother, if you had been here they had not used me thus!'; despite his involvement in the plot, Moray reportedly wept to see his half-sister so moved.[35] The midwife and Mary's physician were allowed to examine their charge and agreed that Mary should be moved 'to some sweeter and pleasanter air'; Henry relayed the message, but the lords distrusted it as 'craft and policy'. In the afternoon, Henry brought Moray, Morton and Ruthven to the Presence Chamber, where they fell on their knees as Mary entered; she agreed to pardon them all, and told them to draw up a deed, which they did. The articles were given to Henry, who requested that the guard be removed and guaranteed that he would 'warrant for all' while they went to supper at Morton's townhouse.[36]

Given this space, Mary threw herself into action, organising horses and an escort to take her to Dunbar. At midnight, the King and Queen quietly left the palace via the privy stairs and the backdoor, crossing the graveyard of the old Abbey of Holyrood, where Riccio had been hastily buried. They rode frantically to Seton, with Henry allegedly shouting at Mary: 'Come on, come on! By God's blood, they will murder both you and me if they can catch us!' When Mary reminded Henry that she was pregnant, he was unabashed: 'Come on! In God's name, come on! If this baby dies, we can have more.'[37] Changing horses at Seton, they completed the thirty-mile ride to Dunbar by dawn.

Safely installed at Dunbar Castle, Mary wrote to her cousin Elizabeth in England, complaining that some of her subjects and members of her Privy Council had shown what kind of men they are 'as first has taken our house, slain our most special servant in our own presence, and thereafter holden our proper persons captive treasonably, whereby we were constrained to escape straitly about midnight out of our palace of Holyroodhouse, to the place where we are for the present, in the greatest danger, fear of our lives, and evil estate that ever princes on earth stood in'. She asked for Elizabeth's help. 'Of truth we are so tired and evil at ease, what through riding of twenty miles in five hours of the night as with the frequent sickness and evil disposition, by the occasion of our child.'[38] From Dunbar, Mary gathered support and returned to Edinburgh on Monday 18 March, accompanied by Bothwell, Huntly and some eight hundred men. It was noted that she was 'yet able to ride on a horse' despite being, by her own account, only six weeks away from giving birth.[39] Faced with Mary's forces, power shifted almost instantaneously in her favour. A proclamation was issued declaring that, while Henry had consented to the return of Moray and other rebels, he had himself played no part in the murder of David Riccio.[40] Morton, Ruthven and Lindsay among others fled to England, where Ruthven died in May; John Knox disappeared to Ayrshire and Henry's father Lennox was banished from court. Mary restored Moray, Argyll and Alexander Cunningham, fifth Earl of Glencairn, a tacit admission that she could not succeed in governing alone.[41]

Once the immediate furore subsided, Mary went to work to ensure that she and her unborn child could never be threatened again. Holyrood was clearly too open to intrusion: Mary set up home instead in Edinburgh Castle. There was a speedy reshuffle of the principal governmental positions: the conspirator James MacGill could no longer be Clerk Register, so Sir James Balfour filled his place; Morton was displaced as Lord Chancellor in favour of Huntly. King Henry's role in the new regime was less assured. Mary and Henry maintained their shared government and appeared together in public, washing the feet of the poor in Holy Week.[42] But there were rumours that Mary had broached Rome about a possible divorce.[43] There could be no trust left in their marriage, and it was soon widely rumoured that Henry was no longer welcome in her bed (perhaps not in itself remarkable, given Mary's advanced pregnancy). As one English ballad put it:

> When this Queen she the chamberlain was slain,
> For him her cheeks she did weete [wet],
> And made a vow for a twelvemonth and a day
> The King and she would not come in one sheet.[44]

Over the next weeks, Mary concentrated on the forthcoming birth. On 4 April she wrote to ask Elizabeth to be 'commere' (godmother) to her child. 'Excuse me if I write so badly,' she begged, 'because I am so *grosse* [fat/pregnant], being well into my seventh month.'[45] After spending a month inside the castle walls, Mary emerged for the last time on 22 April, and 'walked upon her feet a mile out of the town'.[46]

The impending birth alarmed her, and for more than the usual reasons. Being in childbed was a serious problem for a sovereign queen. For days, if not weeks, Mary would be bedridden and physically weakened. She was immensely vulnerable to attack or a political coup, as the events of the past few months had made only too obvious. Already she was nervous. She accused (erroneously) the English agent Thomas Randolph of authoring a book entitled *Maister Randolphes Phantasey*, which was circulating in Edinburgh. The tract was 'written against her life and government'; she was afraid, wrote Randolph, 'lest that it should breed danger to her birth or hurt to herself'.[47]

Mary made her ceremonial entrance into her lying-in chamber, a tiny panelled room that survives to this day, on 3 June 1566. Six days later, she called together her whole nobility to appoint Regents. She had already made her will, 'thrice written': one copy to be sent to France, one kept by herself, and one for her Regents. She and Henry were reported to be 'reconciled' but Mary was not about to give any power to her husband: 'what is contained in the testament [will],' wrote Thomas Randolph, 'he is ignorant.'[48] Indeed, it was later reported that there had been considerable 'ado' about how the baby and the country should be governed if the Queen 'miscarried': Henry and his friends had claimed they should govern according to the custom of marriage in Scotland.[49] In fact, the will stated that if Mary died, and her child lived, the child would be her sole inheritor.[50]

On 19 June 1566, between nine and ten in the morning, after a long labour, Mary gave birth to a son. Sir James Melville was secretly despatched to inform Elizabeth of the happy news and an embargo was put on news of the birth getting out until he was past the border at Berwick.[51] After the Prince's birth was announced, the castle artillery was all shot and some five hundred bonfires were lit across the realm.[52] But the atmosphere was different when King Henry came to visit the new mother.

'My Lord,' she exclaimed brightly, 'God has given you and me a son, begotten by none but you!' Clearly this display of marital fidelity was for the benefit of those assembled in the tiny bedchamber that was serving as the delivery room. Henry blushed but kissed the baby boy. Mary would not let the subject drop. Taking the child in her arms, she brushed aside the swaddling clothes to reveal his face, saying,

'My Lord, here I protest to God, and as I shall answer to him at the great day of judgment, this is your son, and no other man's son! And I am desirous that all here, both ladies and others, bear witness' – but there was a sting in the tail – 'for he is so much your own son, that I fear it be the worse for him hereafter!' Not pausing to let the implications of this sink in, she turned her attention to the Englishman Sir William Stanley, who was in attendance. 'This is the son whom, I hope, shall first unite the two kingdoms of Scotland and England!'

'Why, Madam?' asked Sir William, confused, 'shall he succeed before your majesty and his father?'

'Because,' she said, loud enough for her husband to hear, 'his father has broken to me.'

Her words had the desired effect. 'Sweet madam,' protested Henry, 'is this your promise that you made to forgive and forget all?'

All the fear and bitterness of the night of Riccio's murder came flooding back. 'I have forgiven all, but will never forget! What if Fawdonsyde's pistol had shot, what would have become of him and me both? Or what estate would you have been in? God only knows; but we may suspect!'

'Madam,' Henry protested, 'these things are all past.'

Mary was triumphant. 'Then let them go!'[53]

Elizabeth's ambassador Sir Henry Killigrew initially reported that the birth of a prince and heir had 'bred much joy', that Mary was 'in good state for a woman in her case' and the Prince was 'a very goodly child'. In fact, Killigrew could not get to see the new Prince at once: Mary pledged to grant audience 'as soon as she might have any ease of the pain in her breasts', which was expected to be the following Tuesday or Wednesday. On the afternoon of 24 June, five days after the birth, Mary, still in bed, sent for Killigrew. He reported that she had been 'so bold' immediately after delivery that she had not fully recovered, and the few words she spoke to him were 'faintly with a hollow cough'. The Prince, however, was 'sucking of his nourice [wet nurse]', and Killigrew was allowed to see him 'as good as naked, I mean his head, feet and hands, all to my judgement well proportioned, and like to prove a goodly prince'.[54]

Other accounts had Mary recovering with far greater alacrity. According to Henry's father, Bothwell was now so in favour, 'supplying the place of' David Riccio, and Mary so in love that, 'forgetting her duty to God and her husband, and setting apart her honour and good name, [she] became addicted and wholly assotted unto the said Bothwell. Not only for the lust of the body, but also to seek the blood of her dear husband in revenge for the death of her servant David.' Lennox alleges that Mary left Edinburgh Castle for Stirling 'before her month was out being a green woman' simply so that she could be far from her husband, 'taking her pleasure in most uncomely manner arrayed in homely sort, dancing about the Market Cross of that town'.[55] Even putting aside Lennox's bias, marital relations certainly continued to deteriorate, with Mary showing open contempt for her husband: a shocked Earl of Bedford reported home to England that 'it cannot for modesty nor with the honour of a queen be reported what she said of him'. When Sir James Melville gave Henry a water spaniel, she berated him saying she could not trust a man who would give anything to 'such one as she loved not'.[56] And when the French King's ambassador, Castelnau de Mauvissière, entered Edinburgh on 29 July, bringing with him Joseph Riccio, David's younger brother, Mary immediately appointed Joseph as her secretary.

Meanwhile, Henry's behaviour – including drinking and 'vagabondizing' late at night in Edinburgh, forcing the castle gates to be opened to let him back in, and (scandalously) swimming alone in the sea and lochs – was becoming increasingly embarrassing.[57] Without his knowledge, Mary escaped for a short holiday at the end of July with the Earl and Countess of Mar at Alloa; Henry followed, but soon left when it became clear he was not welcome.[58] On 8 August it was reported that 'the disagreement between the Queen and her husband rather increases'.[59] Moray had noted that Bothwell had insinuated himself into the Queen's favour and decided to use him as the means to a better end. The lords played their old trick once again, playing on Henry's jealousy by informing that the Queen was unnaturally close to Bothwell; Henry started to observe his wife with suspicion, and then Mary was informed that her husband was jealous, and watching her like a hawk. The seed sown, the lords pushed the scenario further. The King was in danger, they informed him: the Queen was plotting his death. The King was jealous, they informed the Queen: noting Henry's reserve towards her, she began to believe them. Soon

Mary was publicly expressing her displeasure with Henry, and showing distinct sympathy to Bothwell at court, using him, it was said 'with more familiarity than stood with her dignity'.[60]

With such marital uncertainty, diplomatic commentators kept a careful eye on the location of the baby Prince. When on 6 September, Mary departed for Edinburgh, she left James at Stirling in the custody of the Countess of Moray, who would, it was reported, have 'the government of the young Prince until the Queen returns to Stirling'; shortly, a Convention of Estates would be called to appoint his more permanent guardians.[61] Henry became suspicious of Mary's closeness to her half-brother Moray, and told her that he was going to kill the Earl 'finding fault that she bears him so much company'.[62] But Mary refused to stand for Henry's tantrums, and not only told Moray what he had said, but forced Henry to admit that the information on which he had based his threat was false. Henry was humiliated, and poured out his woes to his father. Mary would no longer sleep with him, he told Lennox, and had even suggested he take a mistress – the Countess of Moray, perhaps – 'I assure you I shall never love you the worse.' Such a thing was unthinkable, Henry assured his father: 'I never offended the Queen my wife in meddling with any woman, in thought, let be in deed.'[63] Lennox wrote to complain to Mary of her treatment of his son, explaining how Henry's status was so uncertain that he had decided to 'retire out of the kingdom beyond sea, and that for this purpose he had just then a ship lying ready', despite Lennox's urging him to rethink.[64] When Mary received the letter, she tried to raise the subject in bed, but Henry refused to talk. Her wifely charms failing, she used her political power. On 30 September, Mary brought the King before the Privy Council and the French ambassador du Croc, and demanded an explanation of what Lennox had said. In du Croc's account, Henry declared that no grounds had been found for the accusation that he was preparing to leave the country. He left the Presence Chamber, saying to Mary, 'Adieu, Madam, you shall not see my face for a long space.' Despite Henry's claims, du Croc reported that 'He is not yet embarked but . . . still holds to his resolution and keeps a ship in readiness.'[65]

In early October, Mary proclaimed that there would be a court of justice held at Jedburgh, and rode there with her Council. At the same time Bothwell was hurt by a pistol shot during a routine flushing out of thieves in Liddisdaill; as he lay injured at Hermitage Castle, Mary, hearing the news at Borthwick Castle, rode through Melrose and Jedburgh to be with him, and after seeing him and riding back in a single day, fell 'dangerously sick' at Jedburgh. One source states that Mary 'was so heavily vexed with the hot fevers', lying 'from nine hours to an afternoon as she had been dead', that her life was despaired of.[66] Prayers were ordered in churches throughout the realm; on the 28th, the King, who had been 'hawking and hunting' with his father in the west, reached Jedburgh. But even now, 'he was not so well entertained' as he should have been, and he left the next day, heading back to Stirling.[67] William Maitland of Lethington saw the cause of Mary's illness as 'displeasure' and 'the root of it is the King. For she has done him so great honour . . . and he . . . has recompensed her with such ingratitude, and misuses himself so far towards her, that it is heartbreaking for her to think that he should be her husband, and how to be free of him she sees no outgait [way out].'[68] With hindsight, and an ample dose of prurience, later writers – and notably the anti-Marian polemicists Knox and George Buchanan – saw the cause of Mary's illness as an adulterous passion, indulged with Bothwell on his sickbed.[69]

On her recovery Mary went to Kelso with Bothwell. At Craigmillar, on 20 October, Moray, Maitland, Huntly, Argyll and Bothwell urged her to divorce the King, but she refused. Another attempt by Henry to reconcile with Mary at Craigmillar fell flat, with Mary this time commanding him to return to Stirling. Despondent, Henry went to visit his father in Glasgow, where he fell ill with 'a grievous sickness, which kept him long in danger of his life'. As his hair fell out, Mary's enemies spread the word that he had been poisoned.[70]

According to Lord Herries, Moray saw the key to power as 'government of the child': whoever had hold of Prince James held the future of Scotland in his hands. He also realised that if the King and Queen reconciled, he would have no hope of getting hold of the Prince. Henry had to be 'cut away' while Mary was still angry at him, and rumours were flying about her love for Bothwell; the Queen would be blamed for the murder and Moray could take power, reasonably expecting support, under such circumstances, from Elizabeth in

England. Moray and Morton fed Bothwell's ambition, urging that the kingdom would be better off with Henry dead, so that Mary might rule alone, or marry 'one of a higher spirit'. Soon, they were promising that if Bothwell disposed of Henry, he could count on their support in his bid to marry the Queen (and to procure a divorce for himself). 'These jumped right with Bothwell's vainglorious humour,' wrote Lord Herries. 'He thinks himself already King!' A contract of conspiracy was swiftly drawn up; now the plotters waited for their moment.[71]

CHAPTER TWO

The Making of A King

ALL THE TENSIONS of the year of James's birth – the religious fissures, the international feuding, a royal marriage in crisis, and an unwanted King in fear for his life – were on lavish display at the Prince's baptism, which finally took place at Stirling on Tuesday 17 December 1566. The baptism was important to Mary to consolidate her international standing. Relations with Queen Elizabeth in England had deteriorated when Mary's private prediction that her baby would unite the kingdoms of Scotland and England was echoed more publicly. Patrick Adamson, the minister of Ceres in Fife then travelling on the Continent, published a book in Paris praising the birth of 'the most serene and noble prince of Scotland, England and Ireland'. This presumption infuriated Elizabeth who in November 1566 ordered her ambassador to require Mary to have the author arrested and punished, and the book suppressed. Adamson was gaoled for six months and only released when Mary interceded on his behalf.[1]

Shortly after James's birth, Mary had written to the King of France, the Queen of England and the Duke of Savoy (husband of her first husband's aunt Marguerite) to invite them to the baptism of her child. It had taken months to bring the French and English ambassadors to Stirling: despite a last-minute delay of a week, Savoy's ambassador Moretta still didn't manage to get there. But the baptism was to be an occasion of immense opulence, funded by £12,000 taxation, and considerable personal outlay by Mary, who dressed the leading nobles in stunning colours and sent home each ambassador and his entourage with generous gifts. They, of course, had not come empty-handed. Savoy sent a huge fan of feathers encrusted with jewels, worth some four thousand crowns. Charles IX of France supplied a necklace and earrings studded with pearls and rubies. Elizabeth's ambassador, the Earl of Bedford, brought an exquisite gold font for James to be baptised in, 'of two stone weight', and decorated with jewels and enamel, 'designed', as one commentator noted, 'so that the whole effect combined elegance with value'.[2] (Even this gift came with its own chequered history: news of Bedford's valuable booty had leaked out, and there was a botched attempt to steal it en route somewhere near Doncaster.)[3]

James was to be a prince of the Roman Catholic Church. Mary, shaken by rumours of her wavering commitment to Rome, ensured that the baptism provided a very public statement of her orthodoxy – and a great piece of theatre. The French ambassador, the Comte de Brienne, accompanied by Savoy's proxy Monsieur du Croc and Elizabeth's proxy as godmother, her kinswoman the Countess of Argyll, carried the baby boy down from his chamber to the Chapel Royal, through two rows of nobles and gentlemen, each of whom was holding a pricket of wax. There followed a procession in which various noblemen bore the markers of the Roman ritual: the wax candle, salt, the cross, and the ewer and basin. Reaching the chapel door, de Brienne and the Prince were greeted by the officiating priest, Archbishop Hamilton of St Andrews, and his leading bishops in full Roman regalia; and the whole college of the Chapel Royal. At the font, the Countess of Argyll held the baby while Hamilton baptised him 'Charles James' – 'Charles' for his French godfather, and 'James' for 'all the good Kings of Scotland his predecessors'.[4] Only in one respect did Mary depart from the usual service, as James was later fond of claiming: she refused to have 'a pocky priest' spit in her son's mouth (the Archbishop was notoriously disfigured by venereal disease).[5] Heralds thrice proclaimed the baby Prince by his full title: 'Charles James, James Charles, Prince and Steward of Scotland, Duke of Rothesay, Earl of Carrick, Lord of the Isles and Baron of Renfrew.' Singing and organ-playing broke out, and the infant was permitted to remain for a while before being carried back to his apartment.[6]

But the occasion could not disguise Scotland's own deep divisions. Elizabeth's ambassador Bedford was a staunch puritan, and therefore obliged to stand outside the Chapel alongside Moray, Huntly and Bothwell.[7] The Countess of Argyll was rewarded for her service by Elizabeth with 'a ring with a stone',[8] but was forced by the Kirk to do penance for participating in the papist ritual. National honour was also at stake. At supper, Mary sat at the centre of the high table with de Brienne on her right, Bedford on her left, and du Croc at the end of the table, each of them waited on by Scottish nobles. Despite Mary's evenhandedness, there was, according to Sir James Melville, considerable bitterness on the part of the other ambassadors because they thought that the Englishmen were being treated 'more friendly and familiarly used than they'.[9]

National pride was again piqued by the dinner's entertainment. The great humanist scholar (and later archcritic of Mary) George Buchanan provided a Latin masque, but the more memorable *divertissement* was less highbrow. One of Mary's French servants, Bastien Pagès, devised a spectacle in which the meat was brought into the hall 'upon a trim engine, marching as appeared it alone, with musicians clothed like maidens, playing upon all sorts of instruments and singing of music'. This was preceded by several men dressed as satyrs 'with long tails and whips in their hands, running before the meat'. But, claimed Melville, the satyrs went too far: they 'put their hands behind them to their tails, which they wagged with their hands, in such sort as the Englishmen supposed it had been devised and done in derision of them, deftly apprehending that which they should not seem to have understood'. Bedford's entourage, who had wanted to dine in front of the Queen so 'that they might see the better the whole order and ceremonies of the triumph', now changed their minds: seeing the satyrs 'wagging their tails or romples', they sat themselves down on the bare floor behind the table, so that 'they should not see themselves scorned'. One of Bedford's retinue, Christopher Hatton, told Melville that 'if it were not in the Queen's presence and hall, he should put a dagger to the heart of that French knave Bastien' – and Bastien was only doing it for spite, because the Queen made more of the English then she did of the French. Ultimately only Bedford's diplomatic intervention managed to calm tempers.[10]

Most conspicuous by his absence was the proud father. King Henry was indeed at Stirling, and costumed by his wife all in gold, but his pride would not allow him to attend. He knew well that Elizabeth did not recognise his title and so her ambassador Bedford would not be allowed to greet him as King of Scots, only as Lord Darnley; he refused to be thus degraded in front of Mary. His fears were not unfounded: one English gentleman who happened to bump into Henry, taking the air, was severely reprimanded by Bedford for addressing him as King.[11] It was not only England that refused to acknowledge Henry. On the very day of his son's christening, Henry tried three times to summon Savoy's proxy du Croc to his chamber: each time du Croc refused. Finally, the diplomat was forced to send a message to make the position cruelly plain: since he saw that Henry 'was in no good correspondence with the Queen' he had been told from his own master 'to have no conference with him'. Moreover, Henry should know that du Croc's chamber had two doors: if Henry came in one, he would be forced to leave by the other.[12] And so the King of Scots spent the day of his son's christening in his chamber.

Mary herself, according to the French ambassador de Brienne, 'behaved herself admirable well all the time of the baptism', but failed to hide an underlying unhappiness. Answering a summons on 22 December to see the Queen, du Croc found her 'laid on the bed weeping sore', complaining of a 'grievous pain in her side', as well as the effects of an accident sustained on setting out from Edinburgh, when Mary 'hurt one of her breasts on the horse, which she told me is now swelled'.[13] Despite any personal unhappiness, Mary continued to consolidate her power against her husband. Seven days after the baptism, on 24 December 1566, she pardoned Riccio's murderers – with the pointed exception of Andrew Kerr of Fawdonsyde and George Douglas, whom she continued to claim had threatened her own life. The men Henry had betrayed to save his skin were thus back in royal favour; his life could not be safe again. Without taking leave of his wife, he left Stirling for his father's home at Glasgow. A mile out of town, he fell suddenly sick with 'very great pain and dolour in every part of his body'. By the time he had reached Glasgow, blue blisters had broken out and, according to Lord Herries, 'his hair fell off' causing the inevitable rumours of poison (modern biographers tend, perhaps equally inevitably, towards a diagnosis of syphilis).[14]

Mary spent what was left of the year with her son, now approaching six months old, at Stirling, leaving him for two days to celebrate the New Year with her Comptroller Sir William Murray at his Perthshire estate of Tullibardine.[15] On returning to Stirling, however, she received disturbing news. A servant of Archbishop Beaton named William Walker asked to be admitted to her presence, and told her, as she later relayed to Beaton, that it was 'openly bruited' (rumoured) and backed by reliable sources 'that the King, by the assistance of some of our nobility, should take the Prince our son and crown him; and being crowned, as his father should take upon him the government'. Pushed to reveal his sources, Walker named the town clerk of Glasgow, William Hiegait, who had told him, 'If I had the means and credit with the Queen's Majesty that you have, I would not omit to make her privy of such purposes and bruits that pass in the country' – 'bruits' like the rumour the King would not abide some of the noblemen who formed Mary's court. Taking the threat seriously, Mary sent for Hiegait and put him in front of the Privy Council. Abruptly he changed his tune, denying that any such conversation had occurred, and relaying instead another 'bruit', that the King was going to be put in prison, naming as *his* source a servant of the Earl of Eglinton named Cauldwell. Cauldwell was instantly summoned and flatly denied Hiegait's story, just as Hiegait had denied Walker's. 'In fine,' wrote Mary in exasperation, 'we find no matter of concordance, every one disagreeing on the whole purposes spoken.' To Beaton she admitted her worries about the intentions of Henry and his father, but concluded, 'God moderates their forces well enough, and takes the means of execution of their pretences from them: for, as we believe, they shall find none, or very few approve of their counsels and devices imagined to our displeasure or misliking.'[16]

As the New Year dawned Henry again fell ill, this time felled 'full of the smallpox'. Mary finally attended to her husband, sending her physician to Henry on 9 January 1567. On 14 January she travelled to Edinburgh, carrying James and accompanied by 'the whole nobility'; six days later, she set off for Glasgow,[17] taking an empty horse litter to bear Henry home. Henry greeted news of her arrival with satirical ennui: 'If she come it shall be to my comfort and she shall be welcome. If she tarry, even as it pleaseth her so be it. But this much you shall declare unto her, that I wish Stirling to be Jedburgh, Glasgow to be the Hermitage, and I the Earl of Bothwell as I lie here, and then I doubt not that she would be quickly with me, undesired.'[18] Asking why she had brought the litter, Mary explained that it was intended to make his journey more gentle than it would be on horseback. A sick man shouldn't travel in such cold weather, he responded. Mary insisted that she would accompany him to take the waters at Craigmillar 'to be with him and not far from her son'. Henry vetoed the Craigmillar suggestion, and insisted on returning to Edinburgh, a slow journey which took them four days, reaching the city on 30 or 31 January. Mary claimed that Holyroodhouse was not a suitable venue due to its bad air — which had not deterred her from placing James there, however — so Henry was lodged at the Old Provost's House at Kirk o' Field, an estate on Edinburgh's south side, on higher ground, 'a place of good air, where he might best recover his health', as Sir James Melville put it.[19] Henry was unhappy about his lodging, but the Queen insisted he stay there, pointing out its handsome furnishings, many of them imported specially from Holyrood.

While Mary lodged with her son at Holyrood, she was a frequent visitor to Kirk o' Field, sitting for hours at Henry's bedside and often spending the night in a room below her husband. For ten days, the King and Queen seemed happier than they had ever been: on 7 February, Henry wrote to his father, celebrating the return of 'my good health' which he attributed to 'the good treatment of such as hath this good while concealed their good will, I mean my love the Queen. Which I assure you hath all this while and yet doth use herself like a natural and loving wife. I hope yet that God will lighten our hearts with joy that have so long been afflicted with trouble.' As Henry finished the letter, Mary read it over his shoulder, put her arm around his neck and kissed him. But, as later Lennox wrote, Mary 'kissed him as Judas did the Lord his Master This tyrant having brought her faithful and most loving husband, that innocent lamb, from his careful and loving father to his place of execution, where he was a sure sacrifice unto Almighty God.'[20]

By Sunday 10 February, the King had been given a clean bill of health. He expected to resume his full public life the following day. That morning, Mary visited Henry at Kirk o' Field in the afternoon, and then returned to Holyroodhouse to attend the marriage festivities of her musician servant Bastien Pagès and Margaret Carwood, her principal bedchamber woman. After retiring for the night, Mary, along with most of Edinburgh, was shaken awake by a huge explosion, which appeared to come from Kirk o' Field. 'The blast was fearful to all about,' wrote Herries. 'Many rose from their beds at the noise, and came in multitudes to looke upon the dead corpses, without knowing the cause.'[21] The bodies of King Henry and his man William Taylor, who shared his bedchamber, were found in the garden of the house.

It was obvious to all, from the state of the bodies, that the two men had been killed before the explosion, probably by strangulation.

In time, it would become clear that the murder was indeed Bothwell's doing, although the precise sequence of events remains unclear. In one account, Bothwell and two associates strangled the King and his servant in their beds, carried the corpses down to the garden, and then fired some gunpowder stored under the King's bedchamber, to make it appear that the house was blown up by accident, and the two corpses flung over the wall by the force of the explosion. But, as Herries notes, 'neither were their shirts singed, nor their clothes burnt (which were likeways laid by them), nor their skins anything touched with fire'.[22] Another scenario had the King awakened by the sound of the conspirators laying the explosives under his chamber, and attempting to escape through the window, only to meet his death outside.

Bothwell volunteered to the Queen to investigate the noise, and on his return, was the one to break the news of the King's death. 'The Queen was suddenly taken with grief,' reports Herries.[23] Writing to Beaton in Paris, Mary claimed that the attack was evidently aimed at her personally: 'We assure ourself it was dressed always for us as for the King; for we lay the most part of all the last week in that same lodging, and was there accompanied with the most part of the lords that are in this town that same night at midnight, and of very chance tarried not all night, by reason of some masque in the Abbey.' Her decision to leave Henry's lodging must have been heaven-sent: 'we believe it was not chance but God put it in our head.'[24]

The English ambassador Sir Henry Killigrew was not allowed audience with Mary until 8 March, when he delivered letters from Elizabeth. 'I found the Queen in a dark chamber, and could not see her face; but by her words she seemed very doleful.'[25] Elizabeth wrote to express her sorrow for the 'horrible and abominable murder of your late husband and my killed cousin', but also to advise Mary more pragmatically. 'I cannot conceal that I grieve more for you than him,' she wrote. As 'a faithful cousin and friend', she urged Mary to be seen to preserve her honour rather than merely 'look through your fingers at revenge'. Mary should 'take this matter to heart, that you may show the world what a noble princess and loyal woman you are.

I write thus vehemently not that I doubt, but for affection.'[26] Elizabeth's advice was timely: Killigrew sensed 'a general misliking among the commons and others which abhor the detestable murder of their King, a shame as they suppose to the whole nation. The preachers say, and pray openly to God, that it will please Him both to reveal and revenge; exhorting all men to prayer and repentance.'[27]

Early searches ordered by Edinburgh's magistrate 'for any suspicious people' had only turned up one Captain William Blackature, who had been drinking wine in the house of William Henderson at the Trone. It was alleged that Blackature, on hearing the explosion, 'run out and left the wine undrunk', a detail that in itself was alleged to be suspicious behaviour for a captain; Blackature was arrested and hanged, 'although no clear proof was brought against him'. Official investigations continued, with interrogations of 'mean people' who lived near the Kirk o' Field, and of Henry's servants. But these were largely irrelevant: 'the streets were strown [strewed] full of libels and pamphlets, that divulged the contrivers and actors, with all the circumstances' – namely, that Moray and Morton had planned it, and Bothwell carried out the act. Moray's departure on the morning before the murder to see his heavily pregnant wife at St Andrews was denounced as a ruse.[28]

Mary may not have been strictly complicit in the murder, but at the very least it seems probable that she had foreknowledge of the conspirators' plans: her recorded attempt to persuade Moray to stay on the morning of the murder suggests that she understood this to be a signal that the act was imminent. Now, however, the dangers to herself and to her baby son were clear. On 19 March Bothwell decreed that Prince James should be returned to Stirling Castle, and he was conveyed there by Argyll and Huntly. The Earl of Mar, 'a trusty man', according to Herries,[29] was removed from Edinburgh Castle and presented with the governorship of Stirling Castle: James could now be raised by Mar at Stirling. Such an upbringing was by no means abnormal for a future King of Scots. Life expectancy of Scottish sovereigns was low: since the accession of Robert III in 1390, every monarch had come to the throne a minor. The upbringing and educating of Scottish heirs to the throne away from their parents was therefore an old, honourable and politically wise practice, to ensure the crown's succession. Mary's directions to Mar, dated 29 March 1567, have survived. James, 'our dearest son, your natural Prince', was to be placed in Mar's hands 'to be conserved, nursed and upbrought' in Stirling Castle 'under your tutill and governance'. Mar was expressly commanded to 'suffer nor permit no noblemen of our realm or any others, of what condition soever that they be of, to enter or come within our said Castle or to the presence of our said dearest son, accompanied with any more persons but two or three at the most.'[30] Such regulations would appear on the surface to be merely precautionary, and highly sensible: that no sizeable armed force should be allowed anywhere near the body of the young and highly vulnerable Prince. But there was another implication to these guidelines, as Mary well knew. For a nobleman to be accompanied by no more than 'two or three at the most' was deeply insulting, as nobility was often vouchsafed by a performance of strength in numbers. Mary's rules meant that anyone wishing to be granted access to her son would have to humble themselves in a highly visible manner.

Bothwell, shaken by the unanimity of public opinion that laid the murder at his door, urged Moray and Morton to procure Mary's consent to marry him. Moray and Morton, according to Herries, saw how this might redound to their favour: 'three strokes shall be given with one stone!' – attention would be deflected from their involvement, Mary would be defamed, and Bothwell (who had the power to reveal their complicity) ruined. In the meantime, however, Henry's father Lennox was waging an insistent campaign of 'continual cries, expostulations and petitions' to bring Bothwell to justice. Moray and Morton advised Bothwell to submit, to clear his name before proposing marriage. Bothwell and Lennox were summoned to appear in Edinburgh on 12 April, giving only ten days' notice (the usual was forty); moreover, Lennox was commanded to come with only his domestic servants. Lennox could not demean himself to respond so quickly and so meanly, and he sent instead Robert Cuningham as his procurator, who complained that the procedure was contrary to proper practice, especially since Bothwell had brought with him a substantial force that would intimidate and silence hostile witnesses. A panel comprised mainly of 'Bothwell's particular friends' forwarded the verdict that there was no cause to condemn Bothwell, but if anyone later accused him they would have indemnity. Bothwell, absolved by law, still wanted to clear his name, and 'sets up a challenge upon the cross, that if any man (his equal) will say that he is guilty of the King's murder, he was ready to clear himself by his sword'. This challenge was soon answered. An anonymous gentlemen replied that he would take up the challenge, 'if a convenient place were appointed, where he might show himself with security'; of course, no such place existed.[31] A short poem proclaimed

> It is nocht aneuch the pure king is deid
> Bot the mischand murthararis occupand his steid
> And doubell addulltrie hes all this land schamit . . .
> [It is not enough the poor king is dead, but the wicked
> murderers occupying his place and double adultery has
> shamed all the land . . .]

An anonymous libel asserted that 'There is none that professes Christ and his Evangel, that can with upright conscience part Bothwell and his wife, albeit she prove him an abominable adulterer and worse: as he has murdered the husband of her he intends to marry, whose promise he had long before the murder.'[32]

Although popular opinion thought Bothwell guilty, he was now technically cleared, and Morton and Moray urged Mary to consider marriage. She could not govern without a husband, they claimed (a 'fact' often urged on cousin Elizabeth south of the border, now nine years a queen without a husband), and her husband should be a powerful man, and her own subject. Bothwell, they concluded, was 'fittest both for courage and friends'. Mary thanked them for their counsel, and said that she would consider. But events would take the decision out of her hands.

Feeling her popularity slipping, Mary decided to regain control of her most powerful weapon: her son. It was reported on 20 April by a source hostile to Mary that 'The Queen intends to take the Prince out of the Earl of Mar's hands and put him into Bothwell's keeping, who murdered his father.'[33] Observers avidly followed the movements of baby James. On 24 April, Sir William Drury, the Marshal of Berwick, reported to Sir William Cecil in England that 'On Monday the Queen took her journey to Stirling to see the Prince, and this day minds to return to Edinburgh or Dunbar', implying that she would be taking James with her.[34] The following day, Drury confirmed that 'Yesternight the Queen of Scots came to Dunbar well and strongly accompanied, and brought the Prince with her from Stirling.' But in a postscript, he changed his information: 'The Earl Bothwell met her three miles from Stirling. She passed by Edinburgh, sending the Prince into the Castle.'[35] Two days later, he was forced to change his story again, and admit that 'The arrival of the Prince into Edinburgh is untrue. The Queen and Bothwell intended to compass it,' he said in his defence, 'howbeit the Earl of Mar would not suffer it to have effect.'[36] It transpired that Mary had indeed ridden to Stirling on 21 April to see her son, with the intention of taking him back to Edinburgh. Mar 'admitted her to the sight of her son; but suspecting her intention, had so provided that he was master and commander' – simply by following Mary's own orders and allowing her only two ladies-in-waiting in attendance when she was allowed in to see her son.[37] She was therefore unable to seize him by force.

The meeting at Stirling between mother and son gave rise to one story that belongs more to fairy tale than history. The following comes from a serious intelligence report of 20 May:

> At the Queen last being at Stirling, the Prince being brought unto her, she offered to kiss him, but he would not, but put her away, and did to his strength scratch her. She offered him an apple, but it would not be received of him, and to a greyhound bitch having whelps was thrown, who eat it, and she and her whelps died presently. A sugar-loaf also for the Prince was brought at the same time; it is judged to be very ill-compounded.[38]

Already Mary was being demonised as the evil, poisoning mother. The Kirk historian David Calderwood tells of how Mary set out from the castle, but '[a] grievous pain seized upon her within four mile to Stirling. Whether it proceeded of her travel, or grief because she was disappointed, it is uncertain.'[39] Whatever the truth of Mary's encounter with James at Stirling, this was the last time she saw her child.

Continuing on her journey, her small train was intercepted by Bothwell; faced with his customary large, armed escort, she had no choice but to go with him to Dunbar. There, it was alleged, he raped her; Melville records that he had heard the Earl boast that 'he would marry the Queen, who would or would not; yea, whether she would herself or not'.[40] But by this point, the people did not trust Mary, and it was assumed that the 'abduction' was another piece of royal theatre. Within days, Bothwell had obtained a divorce from his wife, Lady Jean Gordon, who was forced to petition citing his adultery with a maid named Bessie Crawford. A decree of nullity was pronounced by Archbishop Hamilton on the grounds that the couple were related and had been married without dispensation, neatly forgetting the fact that the Archbishop himself had provided such a dispensation.[41]

This new turn of events was not liked by all Bothwell's erstwhile supporters, who felt themselves to have been shut out of his latest moves. Now Argyll and Morton joined Atholl and Mar at Stirling, to sign a bond on 1 May resolving to rescue their 'ravished and detained' Queen, to preserve the life of the Prince, and to pursue the murderers of the King – and specifically Bothwell. Their resolve was strengthened by the report of du Croc that, despite his pleas to Mary not to marry Bothwell, 'she will give no ear'.[42] On 15 May 1567, three months after the murder of her second husband, Mary Queen of Scots married the Earl of Bothwell at Holyrood, and created him Duke of Orkney. This time it was a Protestant ceremony. After the marriage, it was reported, the new bride wept inconsolably, and talked of killing herself. There was no honeymoon period for this unhappy marriage. Only a month later, Mary and Bothwell were on a battlefield at Carberry Hill, near Musselburgh. Argyll, Morton, Atholl and Mar, known as the Confederate Lords, had taken over Edinburgh, where they issued a proclamation urging the townspeople to follow their three-article manifesto. Prince James played a major part in their propaganda. As their forces were massed at Carberry Hill, they prominently carried a large banner with a painting of King Henry's half-naked corpse lying under a tree, as it had been found at Kirk o' Field. In one corner, a small child prayed to God for divine vengeance, a cartoon scroll from his lips pleading, 'Judge and avenge my cause, O Lord.' While the eleven-month-old child slept at Stirling, the image of Prince James was at war.[43]

There was to be no fighting. After a day-long standoff, Mary surrendered to the Confederate Lords on the condition that Bothwell be allowed to flee. Although the Queen was well treated by the lords to whom she surrendered, she had to endure an angry, jeering mob as she was led back to Edinburgh. The Confederate Lords imprisoned Mary in Lochleven Castle, on an island in Kinross-shire, under the supervision of Moray's half-brother, Sir William Douglas of Lochleven, and their mother, the Lady of Lochleven. There, in July, apparently five months into a pregnancy, she miscarried twins.[44] Shortly after, on 24 July, she was forced to sign a 'voluntary demission' — in effect an abdication — although she maintained for the rest of her life that such a document, signed under extreme duress, had no legal standing.[45]

Five days later, on 29 July 1567, King James VI was crowned in the parish church of Stirling, processing in Mar's arms from the church back to his chamber. The child who had baptised into the Roman Church only seven months earlier, was now given a Protestant coronation. The oath was taken on his behalf by Morton, who swore to 'rule in the faith, fear, and love of God, and maintain the religion then professed in Scotland'.[46] John Knox preached a sermon on 2 Chronicles, 23: 20–21, in which the child Joash was crowned King of Judah, and his mother Athaliah was slain with the sword. The significance was not lost on any of the congregation. On 11 August, Moray returned to Scotland, visiting his half-sister at Lochleven. On the 22nd of that month, he was proclaimed Regent of Scotland.[47] Under Moray's government, the Acts of Parliament which had established the Scottish Reformation were finally ratified.[48]

But Mary had not given up hope. Gradually she won round Moray's half-brother, George Douglas, and another kinsman, Willie Douglas. With their help, she escaped from her island prison on 2 May 1568 and was quickly joined by an impressive array of supporters — perhaps six thousand men led by nine earls, nine bishops, eighteen lords, twelve commendators, and the might of the Hamiltons.[49] Mary, Melville alleges, 'was not minded to fight, nor hazard battle', but wanted to capture Dumbarton Castle, where she might draw back 'by little and little', the support of her subjects.[50] But Mary's forces were met at Langside, near Glasgow, on 13 May by Regent Moray's men. The battle was short and decisive. Determined to avoid the kind of humiliation that met her after Carberry Hill, Mary rode ninety miles south to the Solway Firth, spending the night of the 15th at Dundrennan Abbey. The following day, sailing on a fishing boat from Abbeyburnfoot to England, she left Scottish soil for the last time.[51]

CHAPTER THREE

A Cradle King

THE FIRST DECADE of James's life was one of the most bitter and bloody periods in Scottish history. Ancient dynastic rivalries were played out in the Council chamber and on battlefields; the King would live under no fewer than three Regents before he reached the age of five.[1] But James himself was sheltered from the realities of Scottish politics, by his age, naturally, but also by a series of strategic moves that ensured his insulation from the very real danger of attack. Stirling Castle was chosen as the young King's home for good reason. A good distance from Edinburgh, it perched above its town, rendered inaccessible from one side by a sheer rockface. Compared with other potential royal residences, Stirling was easily defensible, and the Privy Council made sure that those defences were shored up by a limited and closeknit royal household.

The list of members of that royal household, dated 10 March 1568, provide us with a glimpse into James's daily life as an infant.[2] It was headed by 'Imprimis [first], My Lady Mar', Annabella Murray, Countess of Mar, and it was she who had primary responsibility for James in his early years. Writing in February 1572, Queen Elizabeth praised the Countess for 'the universal good report that we hear of your carefulness and circumspection in the bringing up and nourriture of the young King', which echoed the Countess's own progress reports written to Elizabeth. Elizabeth urged her 'not for any respect to forbear your good usage of him in these his young years, both for the increase and conservation of his health, and for the instruction of him in good manners and virtues agreeable to his years and capacity whereby hereafter he shall be thankful . . . to you for his education'.[3]

In the female sphere, the Countess was followed by James's wet nurse, Helen Little — whom he later accused of being a drunkard[4] — and her daughter Nanis Gray, her woman servant Helene Blyth and her manservant Gilbert Ramsay. Seven ladies were appointed as rockers of the King's cradle, with two more responsible for the King's clothes. It was down to the 'master household', John Cunningham, to ensure that the 'prescribed order' was kept to the letter, that every household member attended 'the ordinary preaching and prayers', provided by minister John Dunkeson, and used the kind of 'godly and honorable conversation' that would serve as a model for his Majesty, who should be shielded by 'ungodly and light behaviour' that might 'do hurt to his Highness's tenderness'.[5] Andrew Hegy acted as 'provisour', or steward. Victualling the King and his household were pantryman James Cawbraith, and the kitchen team: master cook John Lyon, foreman James Murray, William 'keeper of the weschell [vessel]', Cristell Lamb, 'gallepyn [turnspit] in the kitchen' and porter Jock Slowan. Jerome Boy kept the wine cellar, and brothers George and John Boig the ale cellar. The laundry was headed by Margaret Balcomie. Three men, William Murray, William Brokkes and Alexander Fargison slept in the King's chamber with him. Also listed are John Acutrie, a 'Frenchman and his wife', perhaps hired to encourage James's early acquisition of French; James Marscell, 'keeper of the Laidnar [Larder]', William Fairbarne, who supplied the household with coal, an essential position given the extreme cold of the winters, and a pastry chef, Patrick Rannald. James even had his own string quartet, made up of four brothers, the 'violaris' (fiddlers) Mekill (Big) Thomas, Robert, James and William Hudson, with their servant William Fowlartoun. The household was kept small and tightknit for a very practical reason: to lessen the risk of James's abduction. On 1 May 1568, Regent Moray wrote from Glasgow to require Mar 'to remove all persons out of the Castle of Stirling, except those of his own family and retinue and such as upon life, honour and heritage will answer to the Regent'. Steward Andrew Hegy was to provide only those named in the roll. The reason for this clamp down, Moray wrote, was 'to the present state of the country and the utmost necessity of circumspection for the safety of the King's person and house of Stirling'.[6]

Mary's departure eliminated one source of tension, but the fighting continued. The Hamiltons now provided the focus for the anti-Regency forces; among their adherents were the Earls of Argyll and Atholl, Eglinton, Cassillis and Huntly. On 22 January 1570, only eighteen months after his victory at Langside, Moray was dead, killed by a shot fired from the steps of Archbishop Hamilton's Linlithgow house by another Hamilton, James Hamilton of Bothwellhaugh.

Moray's death came as a body blow to James's guardian, the Earl of Mar. On hearing the news, he immediately wrote to Elizabeth in England, pressing on her the new danger this action posed to the King of Scots, and asking for her assistance.[7]

The Regency passed to James's grandfather, the Earl of Lennox, and in October 1570 measures were taken to heighten the security of the King. They confirmed Mar's guardianship at Stirling, but ordered that 'all confluence and multitude of people be restricted and helden forth of' the castle. James was to remain at home, and 'no ways be transported forth of the said Castle of Stirling to any other room within the realm or outwith'. Mar was commanded 'to keep the said Castle of Stirling straitly and diligently as he will answer upon his honour and allegiance'. No armed persons should be allowed into the castle, and nobody except those who had pledged allegiance to James and Lennox. An earl or bishop might enter with a maximum of three servants; a lord two, and a baron one, and all 'without armour'. The 'provost, baillies, council and inhabitants of the burgh of Stirling' were required 'to keep watch and ward at the command-ment and ordinance of the said Earl of Mar, and constable of the said Castle in his absence, at all times needful', and 'to search, seek and apprehend all suspect persons haunting and repairing within the said burgh and freedom of the same as well of the inhabitants thereof as others that has [sic] resisted his Highness' authority, and to take order and surety with the said persons by warding, banishment, taking caution of them or otherwise'. In order to allow this, Lennox granted licences to Mar, and his extended family, friends and servants, exempting them from a litany of dangerous gatherings they might be expected to attend: 'sundry oistis, armies, raids, weirs, wapinshawingis and assemblies' (armed confrontations, armies, forays, wars, musters and assemblies).[8]

The feuding continued, but fortunes slowly changed: Lennox managed to take the Hamilton stronghold of Dumbarton Castle, in the process sending the Roman Catholic Archbishop Hamilton to the gallows. Alarmed by this turn of events, three major Hamilton followers, the Earls of Argyll, Eglinton and Cassillis, defected. Now, the Hamilton party was left with only one major stronghold: Edinburgh Castle, held by Maitland of Lethington and Kirkaldy of

Grange. Lennox concentrated his strategy on capturing Edinburgh, with Morton leading the King's forces at Leith, but for months there was a standoff, with effectively two Scottish governments.

On Tuesday 28 August 1571, James made his first public appearance since his coronation, at the opening of the Parliament in Stirling. Sitting in his chair of honour, and wearing 'his robe royal', the King 'spake these words with his own mouth' and, according to one observer, 'without any abashment': 'My lords, and ye other true subjects, we are convened here as I understand to minister justice; and because my age will not suffer me to do my charge by myself I have given power to my gudschir [grandsire] as Regent, and you to do, as ye will answer to God and me hereafter'.[9] A less obviously scripted moment came later in the proceedings when James spotted a hole in the 'boardcloth' on the table where he sat. Fidgeting, he 'pressed to attain to the hole with his finger', and asked the lord next to him where they were. 'The parliament house,' the lord answered. 'Then there is a hole in this Parliament,' he exclaimed.[10]

'Whether God inspired the babe with prophecy at that time or not, I will not dispute,' wrote one commentator. 'But in very deed, the chief leader of the Parliament was stopped with such a hole within these five days after this saying, that it conveyed him even to the death.'[11] On 3 September 1571, a group of nobles from the Hamilton faction launched a surprise offensive on Stirling itself. Their plan was to capture some of the lords surrounding the King, but the plot misfired farcically. Having succeeded in holding a few men loyal to the King, including Morton, the rebels started looting Stirling's merchants. Thus distracted, they were easy prey for a counter-attack by the Earl of Mar, who had planted men in an unfinished mansion he owned. Nevertheless, as they were driven from the marketplace, the rebels, realising they had nothing to lose, shot Lennox. The Regent, 'shot in his entrails', was carried into Stirling Castle in the early morning of 4 September, calling for a physician, 'one for his soul, another for his body'. James, just five years old, looked on at his dying grandfather: later he was to claim he could never forget the sight.[12]

Another Parliament was called, this time to decide the Regency: Mar, Morton and Argyll were the key candidates, with Mar carrying the day. Elizabeth wrote to congratulate him, assuring him 'that surely we think none could have been named in that realm more plausible to that nation, nor more meeter [suitable] for the charge; although we know well yourself of good wisdom would have forborn it'. James's welfare was all the more important now, she wrote, since various 'pernicious practices' of the one-time Queen of Scots had come to light. After her escape to England, Mary had thrown herself on the mercy of the English Queen, but Elizabeth refused to meet with her cousin until she had cleared herself of the accusations against her concerning Henry's murder. A commission, headed by the Bishop of Ross, was set up to hear the case, with Regent Moray providing the most damning evidence against Mary, in the form of the so-called 'casket letters', which appeared to prove Mary's involvement in the plot against her husband. From February 1569, she was held in fairly relaxed captivity in a series of English country houses, in the charge of the Earl of Shrewsbury. Mar could now rest assured that Elizabeth would not treat on Mary's behalf.[13]

Morton returned to the battle against the Hamiltons, fighting through to the summer of 1572, when a temporary truce was called. The Hamiltons knew their luck was running out. One by one, their leaders left Edinburgh Castle, and soon Morton was able to occupy the town. Mar travelled to Edinburgh to call a Privy Council meeting, according to Sir James Melville, 'to show them the calamities that civil wars produced'. While waiting for the Council to assemble, he spent time at Morton's estate at Dalkeith, where he was 'nobly treated and banqueted'; but then 'shortly after . . . he took a vehement sickness'. Leaving hastily, Mar rode back to Stirling, but died there on 28 October 1572. Once again, rumours of poison flared. 'Some of his friends and the vulgar people spoke and suspected he had gotten wrong.'[14]

Whatever the rumours, Morton was now the obvious choice as Regent, and he presided over the Hamiltons' ultimate surrender in February 1573, when with the 'Pacification of Perth' they finally acknowledged James as King. Morton recruited English aid to capture Edinburgh Castle, and Elizabeth sent the Marshal of Berwick, Sir William Drury, with artillery and troops for a siege; the castle finally fell on 29 May. Its defenders, Grange and Lethington, were sentenced to death; Grange was hanged in public, but Lethington 'took a drink and died as the old Romans were wont to do'.[15] Morton's regime was secure.

There are very few eyewitness accounts of James in his earliest years. From the writings of Theodore de Mayerne, the French physician who treated the King late in life, we learn – presumably from James's own recollections – that 'between the second and fifth year he had small-pox and measles. In his fifth year for twenty-four hours he had suppression of urine, nevertheless no sand or slime was ejected.' He also recorded that 'the King to the sixth year of his age was not able to walk, but was carried about, so weak was he from the bad milk of his drunken nurse.' This would tally with reports that James suffered for the rest of his life with a very poor gait, and a tendency to keep walking rather than stand still – perhaps to ease pain in his legs. In 1623, at the age of fifty-seven, James was said to suffer from 'weakness of his knee-joints'; his legs, noted Mayerne, 'seem not strong enough to sustain the weight of his body'.[16]

The Countess of Mar would have been responsible for James's health in his early years, but she did not hold her dominion at Stirling for long. Perhaps as early as 1569 and certainly by 1570, when James was three or four years old, the Stirling household was augmented by men who served as the King's principal 'preceptors', or tutors: George Buchanan, Peter Young, 'his pedagogues for his instruction in literature and religion',[17] and David Erskine and Adam Erskine, the Commendators (lay abbots) of Dryburgh and Cambuskenneth, who were put in charge of his physical and social training.[18] The King shared his schoolroom with at least three other boys: Mar's son John, the Master of Erskine, to whom James quickly gave the nickname 'Jocky o' Sclaittis [Slates]';[19] his cousin William Murray of Abercairney, a nephew of the Countess, who became Lord Invertyle; and Walter Stewart, later Lord Blantyre and Lord Treasurer of Scotland.

We know a remarkable amount about James's education, thanks to a manuscript in the British Library (Add. MS 34,275) that, in its inventory of books acquired during the 1570s, details James's curriculum. It was a basic (if somewhat outdated) classical humanist education, but heavier than most in Greek, history and politics.[20] Peter Young was charged with collecting a library for the King, often having to resort to begging to procure money to buy books. Too often, he complained to Lord Justice Clerk, his requests for further reading were met with 'What needs his Majesty so many books, has he not enough already?'[21] Elsewhere Young recorded an average day in the life of the schoolboy King, when James was probably in his early teens. First thing in the morning, James would practise his Greek by reading Isocrates, Plutarch and the New Testament. After breakfast he would move on to Latin: perhaps Cicero, Livy or some more modern historian. In the afternoon, it was time for logic, rhetoric and composition exercises, and − time permitting − arithmetic or cosmography.[22]

In the margins of the inventory manuscript are recorded the young James's wise words transcribed by Peter Young. Although James apparently complained about being forced to learn Latin before he knew the tongue of his kingdom − 'Thay gar me speik latin ar I could speik Scotis'[23] − it is clear from Young's sketches that the King's first language in the schoolroom was French. From Young's admittedly doting notes, James seems to have had a gift for languages, and many of his prized witticisms hinge on multilingual puns and wordplay, moving between Scots, French, Latin and Greek, and quoting lines *extempore* from Terence, Xenophon and Virgil to comment on current political situations. In his precociousness there is often a cruel streak: coming across the word 'vivifico', James quips that it is 'a word made by some stammerer − vi-vi-fi-co'.[24] After the hapless Captain Cockburn had 'telled a long tale with many gestures and earnestness', James informed him, 'I have not understood a single word of what you've said, and it seems to me that what Monsieur Le Regent [Morton] said is true, that your French is good for nothing, and your Scots scarcely any better.'[25]

The fruits of this upbringing were put on display to the English envoy Henry Killigrew when he visited Stirling in June 1574. James, he reported to Sir Francis Walsingham, was 'well grown in body and spirit' since Killigrew had last visited. 'He speaks the French tongue marvellously well' and, surprisingly to Killigrew, 'he was able *extempore* to read a chapter of the Bible out of Latin into French, and out of French into English, so well that few men could have added anything to his translation'. This was evidently a practised party piece. Buchanan and Young, Killigrew reported, challenged him to select any chapter he liked for the King to translate, so that he knew 'it was not studied for'. These 'rare' tutors also 'made the King dance before him', which he also managed 'with a very good grace'. James 'seemed very glad to hear' from his cousin Elizabeth, 'and could use pretty speeches, as how much he was bound to her majesty, yea, more than to his own mother'. When Killigrew left, the King 'prayed him to thank her majesty for the good remembrance she had of him, and further desired him to make his hearty commendations to her'. James, Killigrew concluded, was 'a Prince sure of great hope if God send him life'.[26]

George Buchanan was one of the leading Scottish humanists of the sixteenth century, steeped in classical and modern continental literature on politics and religion. By the time he came to tutor James, he was already an elderly man, troubled by intermittent poor health, but he was still an imposing figure. Even on a brief visit, it was evident to Henry Killigrew that there was a tension between James's male tutors and the women of his household: 'his schoolmasters are desirous to have him from the handling of women, by whom he is yet guided and kept, saving when he goes to his book.'[27] The difference in relations between James and his mother figure, the Countess, and James and the pseudo-father figure, Buchanan, is shown vividly in the earliest surviving letters by the King. To James, the Countess is 'Lady Minny', an affectionate Scots word for 'mother'.

Lady Minny,
This is to show you that I have received your fruit and thanks you therefore, and is ready for mee [more] when ye please to send them, and shal gif [give] as few by me as I may. And I will not trouble you farther till meeting which shall be as shortly as I may, God willing. And so fare ye well as I do, thanks to God.

James R.[28]

The letter to Buchanan refers to him as 'pater' (father) but the letter is in Latin, the sentences formal, the emotions expressed as if by rote.

King James to his most worshipful teacher,
George Buchanan, greeting.
Since, O my father, nothing can be more profitable or more

welcome to me than your presence and, on the other hand, nothing can happen more unfortunate or more regrettable than your absence, I beseech you again and again that you will not allow me any longer to lack so great a good or to be distressed by this misfortune. Wherefore please be so good as to do your utmost, as soon as those matters are finished on account of which you set forth, to free yourself therefrom and to hasten to us; and may you come no less safe and sound than you are longed for. Farewell![29]

Although Privy Council records the name Buchanan, along with Peter Young, as tutors only in 1570,[30] Buchanan was manoeuvring to take this position even before the child-king was crowned. At the 14th Assembly of the Kirk, held at Edinburgh on 20 July 1567, six days before James's coronation, the ministers subscribed articles agreeing to 'defend and maintain' the Prince, and to 'defend the true religion, and set forward the work of Reformation'. But their agenda reached wider. The education of youth was a top priority. The fourth article urged 'That none be instructers of youth, publicly or privately, but [except] these that are admitted by the Superintendents and Visitors of Kirks, being found both sound and able', claiming education within the Kirk's jurisdiction. The ninth article then stated 'That wise, godly, and learned men have the charge of the education of the Prince, that coming to majority he may be, by the blessing of God, a comfortable instrument of God, being virtuously educated.' Interestingly, this Assembly was conducted under Moderator George Buchanan.[31]

It was not only the Scottish Kirk that was intent on moulding James into a beacon of reformed Christianity, the perfectly educated Christian prince. The eyes of Europe were upon James as a possible successor to the Protestant Elizabeth. In 1580, when the Geneva-based Calvinist Théodore de Bèze [Beza] published *Icones*, a collection of portraits of exemplary Protestant activists, James seemed the natural dedicatee. An icon of the King in profile served as a frontispiece, with James, in armour, carrying a drawn sword in one hand, an olive branch in the other. 'In vtrunque paratvs' read the motto under the portrait, signifying that James was ready for war or peace. The dedicatory letter that followed offered a prayer that God would bring to perfection the faculties that James possessed for the good of his own subjects and those of many nations, and made flattering references to the two superlative Scotsmen – friends and correspondents of Beza himself – who served as the royal tutors, 'Domino Georgio Buchanano' and 'Domino Petro Junio'. Among the other Scots whom Beza praised were those who had visited Geneva, John Knox and Andrew Melvill.[32]

Buchanan possessed very clear ideas on how a prince should behave, and published extensively on the subject. Like John Knox, he promoted the idea that a people could take up arms against a tyrant, or a ruler who didn't follow the proper religion. Scottish history, he argued, contained a plethora of examples of bad kings who had been so dealt with by the Scottish people. These ideas were most extensively promulgated in his books *De jure regni apud Scotos* (1579) and *Rerum Scoticarum historia* (1582), both of which works were dedicated to his young charge. Among the very worst of princes, he wrote, was James's mother Mary, who emerges in his writings as a vain, shallow, proud, ignorant, devious, conniving papist whore. This was the vision of Scotland and of his own family with which James was force-fed during his formative years. In accounts of Buchanan's relations with James, the distaste of the tutor for his student's family is palpable. On one occasion, James decided that he wanted to have a tame sparrow that belonged to his fellow pupil, the Master of Erskine. When Erskine refused to give it up, the two boys started 'a struggling', and in the scuffle the sparrow was killed, setting Erskine crying. When Buchanan discovered what the rumpus was about, he gave the King a box on the ear, and told him, 'That what he had done, was like a true bird of the bloody nest of which he was come.'[33]

As this incident indicates, Buchanan did not refrain from demonstrating physically that the King was not above the law. Several anecdotes of James's education found their way into George Mackenzie's 1722 life of Buchanan, passed on, he claimed, from the Earl of Cromarty, who heard them from his grandfather, Lord Invertyle, James's fellow scholar.[34] These stories usually involve some physical punishment being doled out by Buchanan to James. Even at the time, Sir James Melville commented that, in his teaching methods, 'Master George was a stoic philosopher, and looked not far before the hand';[35]

and Francis Osborne famously records that, in later life, the King used to say of a high-ranking official with whom he had to deal, 'that he ever trembled at his approach, it minded him so of his pedagogue'.[36] By comparison, Peter Young was 'gentler and loathe to offend the king at any time', according to Melville, and allegedly allowed James a whipping boy, the supposed surrogate for the kingly buttocks who absorbed any wrath against their master; but Buchanan clearly didn't indulge his charge this way.[37]

Buchanan was, in Melville's words, 'a man of notable qualities for his learning and knowledge in Latin poesie, much made accompt of in other countries, pleasant in company, rehearsing at all occasions moralities short and fecfull [forceful], whereof he had abundance, and invented where he wanted [lacked].' Although 'of good religion for a poet', Buchanan in his old age was easily influenced by whoever he was with, which led to him becoming increasingly factious in his writings and conversations, and vengeful to those who offended him.[38] Certainly, some of the teaching techniques Buchanan employed with the King were quite cruel. According to one anecdote, published by his own editor Nathan Chytraeus in 1600, Buchanan decided to quash early in life James's tendency to grant whatever favour was asked of him, often without paying attention to what it was that was being requested. So he went to James holding two books of requests, one of which included a supplication that James might give him permission to be King for a fortnight and have complete control over Scotland. James blithely signed all the requests as usual. Buchanan spent the next two weeks telling everyone that he was King of Scotland, and one day asked James to confirm this. James was amazed. But then Buchanan showed him his signature on the petition. '"Well," he said, "here is the letter signed in your hand in which you have handed the kingdom to me." And he began to reproach the King, as a tutor reproves his pupil sternly, instructing him that he could not grant whatever was requested without careful deliberation, otherwise considerable damage to him might follow. In future, therefore, he should not grant someone his wish, unless he was fully aware of what was involved, and knew who would be the beneficiary.'[39]

What is most remarkable about James during these years is the degree to which he attempted to resist Buchanan's indoctrination – although whether this was due to other influences in his life (perhaps the Countess of Mar?) or to an innate intelligence is impossible to determine. One day, for example, Buchanan set James a theme for study: the history of the so-called Lauder Bridge conspiracy that took place during the reign of James III, when the nobles were conferring secretly in Lauder Kirk about how to remove evil favourites from the King. Archibald, Earl of Angus, told the conspirators the fable of some rats that decided to attack a cat, and elected to tie a bell around its neck so that they would be able to hear it coming. But one old rat raised an objection: which of them was brave enough to put the bell on the cat? Angus proclaimed that he would 'bell the cat', in the process earning himself the nickname 'Bell the Cat'. Buchanan clearly intended the story to demonstrate how a sovereign's supposedly absolute rule and the sway of his unsuitable favourites can be successfully challenged. But this tale left a different impression on James's mind. Late one afternoon, James was playing with the Master of Erskine, and making too much noise for his schoolmaster's taste. Buchanan told the King to 'hold his peace'. When this proved of no avail, Buchanan told James 'that if he did not hold his peace, he would whip his breech'. James retorted 'that we would gladly see who would bell the cat' – identifying with the cat, James III, and mocking those who would challenge his authority. Buchanan understood that he had a student who would not passively receive all his teaching. 'In a passion', he threw down his book and whipped the King 'severely', all of which commotion roused the Countess. Hearing her charge cry out, she ran to the King and took him up into her arms, asking what the matter was. James told her that the master had whipped him, and she turned on Buchanan, asking how he dared 'put his hand on the Lord's anointed'? Buchanan replied, calmly: 'Madam, I have whipped his arse, you may kiss it if you please.' Here we have James's insistence that he, as King, is beyond Buchanan's power – who would dare bell the cat? who would dare whip the King? – and the painful realisation that his supposed kingly immunity, in fact, does not exist. It might stand as a metaphor for much of his life as King.

Perhaps realising early that James would be a difficult student, Buchanan sought to protect his own reputation. Dedicating to James a printed edition of one of his early works, *Baptistes*, in November

1576, Buchanan explained that the work strove to provoke youth 'to the imitation of antiquity and to the study of piety'. It 'peculiarly' applied to James, however, 'because it sets forth lucidly the tortures of tyrants, and even when it seems they flourish most, their miseries'. It was not only profitable for James to understand this but a matter of necessity: 'so that you may begin to detest mature what you must always flee. Moreover, I want this little book to be a witness to posterity, if ever at any time impelled by evil counsellors or by the license of rule overcoming right education you act otherwise, that must be attributed for a fault not to your teachers but to you, who will not have conformed to their admonishing correctly.'[40]

In later life, James had some praise for his difficult schoolmaster. Speaking with a group of Scottish academics in 1617, the King berated English scholars for their bizarre pronunciation of Latin. James claimed to owe his superior skills to Buchanan: 'All the world (said he), knows that my master, Mr George Buchanan, was a great master in that faculty [speaking Latin]. I follow his pronunciation both of the Latin and Greek, and am sorry that my people of England do not the like; for certainly their pronunciation utterly spoils the grace of these two learned languages; but ye see all the University and learned men of Scotland express the true and native pronunciation of both.'[41] Buchanan also provided a grounding in Latin verse composition, again in a style different from the English grammar school: the poet and playwright Ben Jonson later said to James that 'his master G. Buchanan had corrupted his ease when young and learned him to sing verses, when he should have read them'.[42] Buchanan's teaching was not wasted on James – but time would show that his main achievement was to provide the King with a philosophy of the proper place of a king against which he could fight.

While he was Regent, Morton's regime, though harsh, brought at least the illusion of stability to Scotland. After Henry's murder, Mary's abdication, the assassinations of Moray and Lennox, and Mar's death (or murder, as some would have it), Scotland finally enjoyed a few years of relatively consistent rule. Laws were restored and enforced. Relations with England sweetened. Morton dealt with the perennial decline of Scotland's finances by seizing back Queen

Mary's jewels from the Countess of Argyll (Moray's widow, who had now remarried).

But the unity was deceptive. Storms were brewing in the Kirk. Although a committed Protestant, Morton was not about to let the Kirk get all its demands. In 1574, the minister Andrew Melvill returned to Scotland after several years on the Continent, most recently and influentially in the heart of Calvinism, Geneva. He set about reforming the Kirk along the lines of the Geneva ecclesiastical polity, giving power to a series of Church courts, headed by the General Assembly of the Kirk, while insisting on a flattening out of Church hierarchy. The victims of this were those in the upper echelons of the Church, the bishops, for whom there was now no place in the Kirk. When Morton tried to force the appointment of a new Bishop of St Andrews, he clashed with John Knox, and (according to Melvill's nephew James) shouted angrily that 'There will never be quietness in this country till half a dozen of you be hanged or banished!'[43] But in practice, relying on Parliament not to ratify the Kirk's anti-episcopal policy, Morton allowed Melvill a pretty free hand, and in 1578 the General Assembly, as expected, condemned episcopacy altogether.

Throughout these years, James's name was often invoked, although his person was kept away from political and religious battles, safely ensconced at Stirling. But as he approached adolescence, there was official recognition that the King was no longer a child. The Privy Council registers for 1577 record the order that 'Our Sovereign Lord the King's Majesty, whom God preserve . . . being come to the twelfth year of his age and daily increasing by the favour of God to greater perfection and activity, as well in his person and ability of body as in his spirit and learning . . . in time coming shall be served and attended upon in his chamber with men, committing the care thereof to Alexander Erskine of Gogar', the younger brother of the late Regent Mar.[44] This appointment was to become significant because Erskine of Gogar truly disliked Morton. His opposition to the Regent, combined with his *de facto* control of the King's body, meant that James's Stirling household took on a new potential to those opposed to Morton.

The first to make use of this was the Earl of Argyll. In early 1578, Argyll was feuding with the Earl of Atholl. Morton intervened and summoned them both before the Council to answer charges of levying private war, and ignoring his summons to lay down arms. Incensed at this trespass into what they considered strictly their own business, Argyll and Atholl promptly forgot their feud and turned their combined anger on the Regent. Morton realised that much of the nobility was now against him, and decided to resign his office into the King's hands, although 'whether he did this upon a plain intention to denude himself, or upon plain hypocrisy' is unclear. On 4 March 1578, he was granted an audience with the eleven-year-old James at Stirling.[45] There he laid out his case, pointing out the burdens of the office, not least that all his predecessors had 'been violently murdered'; the 'great oppression and rebellion' in the realm; the 'age and weakness' of his body; and, most importantly, that it was expected that James would 'embrace the government upon your own person'.[46] According to Peter Young, James responded to the protestation of his advanced age by quipping, 'I wish to God that you were as young as the Earl of Angus, and as wise as you are.'[47] For his part, Morton drew attention to James's age. 'Since I perceive increase of wisdom to grow daily in your Majesty, and that ye have, praised be God, the dutiful favour of all your subjects at this hour, I am most willing to demit my charge in your Majesty's own hands, presently.' James's immediate reaction was reluctant. He was too young to govern, he said, 'and if I were, I know not to what place I should make my resort'. Morton replied that James would 'be well lodged in the Castle of Edinburgh, both for the good situation of the house, the pleasant sight of the fields, and the sight of the sea and frequency of ships'. This seemed to cheer the King, who agreed that he 'would willingly condescend to that charge, providing his keepers should have the maintenance of that Castle'.[48]

By the time the Regent had returned to Edinburgh, intelligence of the meeting had reached Atholl and Argyll. They hurried to the King at Stirling, and as soon as they arrived James told them of Morton's offer 'to demit his office'. They encouraged him to accept 'such a lawful petition', to write to the nobility and 'declare unto them how willing he was for to accept the regiment upon his own person'. At the age of eleven, James decided to assume government, perhaps taking as his guide his grandfather James V, who had been declared to be of age at twelve. Before Morton knew what was happening, the nobility had 'conspired in minds and bodies against him, and voted all that the King should accept the regiment'. On 12 March 1578, his 'acceptance of the government' was proclaimed in Edinburgh and James directed his commissioners that 'from thenceforth they should acknowledge no other authority but of his Majesty'.[49] Government would now be conducted in the King's name by a Council; Morton's Regency was over.

Morton had always claimed that 'As soon as ever His Majesty shall think himself ready and able for his own government, none shall more willingly agree and advance the same nor I.' In practice, he was not willing to accept the invitation, and from his forced retirement at Lochleven plotted his return to power. His tool this time was James's schoolroom friend Jocky o' Sclaittis: John Erskine, now the Earl of Mar.[50] When his father, the Regent Mar died in 1572, John was only fourteen, and so his uncle, Alexander Erskine of Gogar had been appointed guardian of his estate and Keeper of Stirling Castle – and hence of the King – during John's minority. Now, however, Mar was twenty years old and chafing at his uncle's rule. Morton and he came to an arrangement: Morton would support Mar's claim to the guardianship of Stirling and James on condition that Morton would be allowed to hold sway in government. On the morning of 26 April 1578, Mar rose early at Stirling, supposedly to go hunting, and called for the keys, so that he could leave the still fiercely secured castle. When Erskine of Gogar brought the keys, he was seized by Mar's men and pushed outside the castle gates, during which scuffle a son of the guardian was killed. For James, it was another moment of intense panic: woken by the noise, he rushed from his chamber, tearing at his hair. Hearing of the news at Edinburgh and realising what was afoot, several lords raced to Stirling to stop Morton gaining control but Mar, in the name of safeguarding the King, skilfully refused to let more than one of them enter the castle at a time. Foiled by this strategy, the lords reluctantly agreed that Mar could take charge of the King until Parliament met.

In the meantime, Morton arrived at Stirling and proposed that he should be appointed First Lord of the Council; a meeting of pro-Morton nobility agreed to move the next Parliament from Edinburgh to Stirling. On 6 July, the Privy Council issued a proclamation denying rumours that James was being held at Stirling against his will.[51] When Parliament opened on 15 July, Mar was permitted to carry the sword, and confirmed as the guardian of Stirling Castle and James, but with the caveat that four of the new Council should always be in attendance on the King. This smelled bad to Morton's enemies. They demanded that Morton be required to return to his 'own dwelling-place', and that James be returned to the custody of Erskine of Gogar, this time at Edinburgh Castle. It was Robert Bowes, the English ambassador, who arbitrated an agreement that Mar should maintain his custody of the King at Stirling, but that the Council should include more of the anti-Morton faction. This compromise was signed by James on 15 August.[52] Mar's powers were confirmed in March 1579 when the Council decreed that nobody should be allowed to enter Stirling Castle armed while the King was in residence, and that Mar should be allowed to make arrangements for attending the King while he was hunting.[53] The traumatic attack on Stirling unsettled James, and from that date he was understandably uncertain of Morton. In the months following, he turned instead to the Council's second lord, the Earl of Atholl. But their friendship was shortlived. In April 1579, Mar threw a banquet for the King and all the nobility as a gesture of their reconciliation. But when Atholl returned home from the banquet, he suddenly died, prompting, once again, the inevitable rumours of poison.[54]

In the summer of 1579, Morton's ruthless scheme of suppression finally reached the apparently invincible Hamiltons. He invoked the 'Pacification of Perth' which granted a pardon to those fighting against the King, but then declared it was invalid against those implicated in the assassination of Moray. The estates of Lords Claud and John Hamilton were seized, and the young men fled the country; their father, Châtelhérault, was already dead. His widow was taken into custody, and Morton took great delight in blasting the Hamilton strongholds. Of most immediate importance to James, though, the suppression of the Hamiltons had ramifications for the succession of the Scottish throne, which now passed to the Lennoxes, the family of James's father King Henry. Henry's brother Lord Charles Stuart, who had become Earl of Lennox after his father's death in 1572, died after four years, leaving one daughter, Arbella. The ex-Regent's younger brother, Robert, Bishop of Caithness, was created Earl of Lennox in June 1578; despite being over sixty and a lifelong bachelor, he married in January 1579, hoping to father a child. But if the marriage were childless, the male line would be traced to the children of the Regent's youngest brother John Stuart, Lord d'Aubigny, who had settled in France. First among them was Esmé Stuart, Sieur d'Aubigny, and in the late summer of 1579, inspired by the defeat of the Hamiltons, he arrived in Scotland to stake his claim.[55]

CHAPTER FOUR

The Phoenix

ESMÉ STUART, SIXTH Sieur d'Aubigny, arrived at Leith on 8 September 1579 and was promptly escorted to Edinburgh where he was warmly welcomed by the town's magistrates.[1] When thirteen-year-old James met him for the first time one week later in the Presence Chamber of Stirling Castle, Esmé prostrated himself before his cousin 'desiring the King of Heaven to bless his Majesty with perpetual felicity'. Esmé was thirty-seven years old and married with four children. He was also decidedly handsome, 'a man of comely proportions, civil behaviour, red-bearded, and honest in conversation'.[2] For James, who had been betrayed by one after another of his supposed friends, Esmé seemed the perfect ally. According to a contemporary account, 'No sooner did the young King see him, but in that he was so near allied in blood, of so renowned a family, eminent ornaments of body and mind, [he] took him up and embraced him in a most amorous manner.'[3]

James was smitten, but the Kirk was dismayed. It stood to reason that, as a Gentleman of the Bedchamber to Henri III of France, d'Aubigny must be a staunch Roman Catholic. Secret intelligence had it that d'Aubigny was 'furthered, and sent with instructions, by the Guisians', the faction clustered around the ultra-Catholic Duc de Guise. It was said that before d'Aubigny had embarked for Scotland he met privately with the exiled Catholic Bishops of Glasgow and Ross, planning a campaign to undo the friendship with England, revive relations with Queen Mary, and ultimately to reinstate the Roman faith in Scotland. Indeed, had he not spent six hours with the Duc de Guise himself on the very ship that was to bring him to James? And where did his money come from? His lands were heavily mortgaged, but somehow he contrived to bring 40,000 gold pieces, that could have come from nowhere but the Pope, the King of France and the Guisians, and for no other reason than to corrupt the nobility.[4] His retinue did nothing to dissipate the rumours. With him came 'a Monsieur Mombirneau, a subtle spirit, a merry fellow, very able in body, and most meet in all respects for bewitching of the youth of a Prince'. Together, wrote the Kirk man James Melvill, 'they within few days insinuate themselves so in favour of the young King'.[5]

With d'Aubigny's arrival, and perhaps not coincidentally, came James's first entry into public life. On Tuesday 29 September, James left Stirling for the first time in eight years, headed for Linlithgow and from there on to Holyroodhouse. It was a grand procession, the King accompanied by d'Aubigny, Morton, Angus, Argyll, Montrose, Mar, and some two thousand horsemen. The Humes and the Kers with three hundred horse welcomed him at Corstorphine to the west of the city. Edinburgh burgesses stood in full armour in the Long Gate, where he dismounted and saw the castle cannons shot. After the salute, since the pageantry was unfortunately not quite ready, the King processed around the city in great pomp to Holyroodhouse.[6]

James made his formal entry into Edinburgh on Friday 17 October at the West Port. He was welcomed by the town's magistrates, and about three hundred citizens in their finery, under a magnificent purple velvet canopy. There he watched a performance based on the judgement of Solomon, deciding which of the two women claiming to be a baby's mother was telling the truth: Solomon was later to become one of James's favourite scriptural characters, after whom he consciously fashioned himself. After listening to a harangue in Latin by John Sharp, he progressed to the old port of the Strait Bow, where a globe hung, opening artificially as he passed to reveal a young boy who presented to the King a pair of silver keys to the town. Singers, accompanied by viol-players, sang the twentieth psalm. At the Tolbooth, which was decorated with the craft guilds' standards, were four 'fair young maids' representing the cardinal virtues of Justice, Temperance, Fortitude and Prudence, all of whom made an oration. A firework Wheel of Fortune was ignited. As James processed to the Great Kirk, he was invited in by 'Dame Religion' to hear a sermon by James Lawson on Psalm 2: 10, exhorting James and his subjects 'to do their duty, to enter in league and convenant with God'.

Further up the High Street at the Mercat Cross, a man in a 'painted garment' and a garland of flowers represented Bacchus, sitting on a puncheon, a large beer cask. He welcomed James 'to his own town', quashed several glasses and threw them into the crowd. According to eyewitness accounts records, some three puncheons – over two hundred gallons — of wine were used. The Salt Throne was the scene for a representation of the genealogy of the Kings of Scotland, a trumpet fanfare, and a cry of 'Well fare to the king!' The Nether Bow boasted a representation of James's horoscope, 'the conjunction of the planets, as it was in the time of his nativity', with 'Ptolemy' conveniently on hand to describe the future happiness described in his stars. At the abbey, the town of Edinburgh presented James with a cupboard worth six thousand marks. The glamour of the day's festivities overshadowed the injuries caused to several spectators by the overcrowding in the narrow streets.[7]

While Edinburgh looked eagerly to the King, James only had eyes for d'Aubigny. It was not long before the King's affection for his French cousin, unguardedly and physically displayed, was public knowledge. Sir Henry Woddrington recorded how James was 'persuaded and led by him, for he can hardly suffer him out of his presence, and is in such love with him, as in the open sight of the people, oftentimes he will clasp him about the neck with his arms and kiss him'.[8] The very openness of his affections prompted some observers to suggest that their relationship contained something more personal and intimate, or 'inward' in the language of the times. The clerk to the Privy Council, David Moysie, wrote how 'his Majesty, having conceived an inward affection to the said Lord Aubigny, entered in great familiarity and quiet purposes with him'.[9] Later commentators, with the dubious benefit of hindsight, have seen James's affection for Esmé as the prototype for a whole string of relationships with men which would become a lifelong pattern. A typical example is John Hacket who wrote of 'the sweetness of this King's nature' that caused 'from the time he was fourteen years old and no more [in fact he was thirteen], that is, when the Lord Aubigny came into Scotland out of France to visit him, even then he began, and with that noble personage, to clasp some one *gratioso* [favourite] in the embraces of his great love, above all others'.[10] But Hacket was not born until 1592, thirteen years after the Lord Aubigny came into Scotland, and he was accused of 'filching' his information from the historian William Camden, himself not familiar with Scottish affairs of this period. Moreover, James's love for d'Aubigny was different in kind from the passions that dominated his adult life. His later loves were typically callow young men whom James attempted to mould, acting as a teacher, or father figure; but in this relationship it was d'Aubigny who played the sophisticated older man. From him, James learned of the culture of the French court, a world that his mother had been part of and different indeed from the fortress existence at Stirling. D'Aubigny seems to have reciprocated James's love, tenderly calling James – who had been taught to fear Buchanan as *his* 'master' – 'mon petit maistre'.[11]

While d'Aubigny's love may have been sincere, it was all too easy for opponents to see his influence as corrupting and they were only confirmed in their view by events at the Parliament that began in Edinburgh on 20 October 1579. The Kirk ministers in particular were none too happy with the direction in which James's emotions were led. While the Parliament reiterated the act made in the first year of James's reign concerning the Confession of Faith, establishing the Kirk, they were dismayed when, shortly after the Parliament, d'Aubigny purchased a dispensation to hold markets in Tranent on the Sabbath, and a *supersedere* to prevent him from 'being troubled for a year for religion', effectively an immunity from the pressures of the Kirk to conform. As 'crafty fellows' flocked 'under his wings', d'Aubigny's powers grew. At the Parliament, he was appointed commendator of Arbroath, a post forfeited by Lord John Hamilton; soon after, he became Keeper of Dumbarton Castle – this appearing particularly sinister to the Kirk, since Dumbarton's strategic position in the Firth of Clyde meant the castle could be used as a base to 'allure the King, and transport him to France at his pleasure, or receive forces out of France'.[12] Not all observers were so negative. The writer of a 'Memorial of the present state of Scotland', written on 31 December 1579, believed that the Kirk ministers were 'resolved of Monsieur d'Aubigny's good inclination to religion'. He confirmed James's intimacy with d'Aubigny, but claimed that d'Aubigny had worked to consolidate Anglo-Scottish relations by telling James of the 'idle and licentious life' of the French King, which made Henri 'odious' to him. Significantly, the 'Memorial' also records an early instance of what was to become James's abiding passion – to 'delight the fields in hunting and riding', although it also noted that his relative poverty meant that he had only a handful of horses to ride.[13]

In March 1580, James put pressure on Robert Stuart to resign as

Earl of Lennox and gave the title to d'Aubigny. Bowing to the Kirk, James persuaded Lennox to come to Edinburgh in April 'to be instructed by the ministers who mean to labour on him till the first of June', to ensure his proper conversion to Protestantism; the King himself helped the worthy cause by giving Lennox copies of the Scriptures in French. By June 1580, the ministers and the Scriptures had done their work: Lennox wrote to the General Assembly announcing his conversion, and declaring that God had called him to a knowledge of his salvation. At the same time, and clearly as a reward, James admitted Lennox to the inner circle of government, the Privy Council.[14] But Lennox had his most lasting impact in his rearrangement of James's household, drawing on his experience of the French court of Henri III. He invented for himself a new and powerful office: Lord Great Chamberlain and First Gentleman of the Chamber. As Chamberlain, Lennox undertook the role of the Master Household, organising and provisioning the King's household, while as First Gentleman of the Chamber he ensured his continued intimacy with the King. Lennox thus had a hand in government, control over the King's household *and* the King's ear: a remarkable concentration of power.[15]

Many felt threatened by the Frenchman, but it was Morton who was most at risk. Lennox became a magnet for his enemies, most notably Argyll, and Morton, feeling increasingly marginalised at court, disappeared to his country estates. The court soon descended into fearful whispering. Argyll let James know that Morton planned to kidnap him and take him to England; James was scared enough to leave his hunting and seal himself up in Stirling Castle again in February 1580. Lennox had enough influence to persuade the King to go riding to Doune a month later, but by now James had developed a decided nervousness at the sight of weapons, and just the sight of armed men among Lennox's retinue was enough to send James galloping back home to Stirling. With endearing bluster, James recounted these incidents to the English ambassador Robert Bowes, not as examples of fear, but of incisive judgement. He would escape future attempts, he declared, and even if he did fall into enemy hands, he'd display such 'inconstancy, perjury and falsehood' that they'd regret ever seizing him.[16]

By the spring of 1580, James had regained his confidence enough to venture away from Stirling again. On 20 May, he set out on the first of what was to be become an annual ritual: a 'progress' through his country, moving this year through Fife and Angus before returning to Stirling in mid-August. The progress was good for James's personal standing in Scotland since it gave his people the chance to see him in the flesh — an opportunity they had been denied for thirteen years — but it served an additional, more practical purpose: James had been informed by his Lord Treasurer that he was in debt to the tune of £40,000 to the Treasury, and since the entertainment of the King and his retinue on the progress was paid for by his lucky hosts, it was a welcome chance to save money.[17]

An odd incident occurred when the progress reached St Andrews in July. As the spectators were waiting for an entertainment to be played at the New Abbey, a 'frenetic man' known as Skipper Lindsey stepped into the empty performance space, and 'paceth up and down in sight of the people with great gravity, his hands on his side, and looking loftily'. Lindsey was 'rough with hair', great tufts on his brows and 'upon the neb of his nose', and his bizarre appearance provoked the crowd to laughter. But when he started to speak, he gained their attention, as if he had been a preacher, as one observer put it. With a 'mighty voice', he spoke of how God had rescued him from his previous wicked, riotous and abusive life, and concluded that 'God would not be miskenned by the highest'. Then, looking up to the window where James and d'Aubigny stood watching, with Morton underneath them, Lindsey warned Morton that 'his judgement was drawing near, and his doom in dressing [was in preparation]'. Morton was reportedly 'so moved and touched at the heart, that, during the time of the play, he never changed the gravity of his countenance, for all the sports of the play'.[18] Skipper Lindsey's words were to prove oddly prophetic.

The Kirk was still not convinced by Lennox's protestation of faith. In July, he sent a letter to the fortieth General Assembly convened at Dundee, offering 'free and humble offer of due obedience, and to receive your will in anything it shall please you I do'.[19] These, as the Kirk chronicler David Calderwood admitted, were 'fair offers' but they covered 'deep designs, as time declared afterward'. The ministers were particularly concerned that, even if Lennox were sincere in his conversion, his household was a sanctuary for staunch papists. Later in the session, Lennox tried to dislodge this fear by having one of the servants, Henry Kerr, make a passionate confession of how he had 'lain long in blindness' but now acknowledged the Protestant religion 'to be the only true religion'. The ministers remained unsatisfied. When the General Assembly met again in Edinburgh in October, it presented a petition to James requesting, among other matters, 'That order be taken with papists in the King's house', and Henry Kerr had to appear again to explain why there had been a delay in securing a French-speaking minister for Lennox's household, as the Kirk had commanded.[20]

By the end of the year, the more hard-line of the ministers had lost patience with Lennox and his household. On 7 December 1580, Walter Balcalquall, the minister of St Giles', gave a sermon condemning the French courtiers and what he dubbed their 'evil fruits'. Under their wings lurked papists, he preached; papists were defended both in town and in the country. The King's ears were polluted by a French ruffian (meaning Lennox's servant Mombirneau); the Canongate and some houses in the High Town were defiled with whoredom, and plagued with great vanity in apparel, foolish pastimes and syphilis – or the 'French pox' as it was conveniently dubbed. He condemned 'the whoredoms and adulteries of your courts; the murders, the oppressions, the cruelties, and all the rest of the vices that are in your courts' and feared that they would repent that the French court ever came to Scotland. Unless the congregation repented, he continued, 'it shall be easier for Sodom and Gomorrah in the day of the Lord's judgements, than it shall be for you'. Every lord must reform their own persons and their houses and court, and they must 'travel and see that the King's house be well reformed, that no profane nor mischant persons be found there, but such as fear the name of God'. Balcalquall had gone too far. He was called before the Privy Council, and required to submit written copies of his sermons: Balcalquall insolently provided only 'copies of that part of [his] sermon whereof he supposeth, that either the Earl of Lennox, or any of his dependers, may take any occasion of offence', compounding the offence; moreover, he challenged the authority of the secular Privy Council to hear such an ecclesiastical case at all. Eventually, James was forced to remit the matter back to the General Assembly of the Kirk, which unsurprisingly felt that no action was necessary.[21]

Just as Lennox came under the strongest attack from the Kirk, he accelerated his campaign against Morton. He sought out the support of Captain James Stewart of Bothwellmuir, the second son of Lord Ochiltree. Stewart was a well-educated and much travelled man who had spent some time fighting against the Spanish in the occupied Netherlands; he had returned to Scotland in 1579, and in October 1580 became one of the Gentlemen of the King's Bedchamber.[22] On 31 December the Privy Council was in full session when Stewart burst into the Council chamber, threw himself on his knees in front of the King, and accused Morton of having been 'art and part' in the murder of King Henry. Since this intervention was in fluent and passionate Scots, Lennox could pretend to be in complete ignorance of what was happening. Despite his earnest protestations of innocence, Morton was arrested and imprisoned, first in Edinburgh Castle and then later in Dumbarton.[23] With Morton's fall came the rise of his accuser, James Stewart, who was appointed to the Privy Council in February 1581 and then advanced to the Earldom of Arran on 22 April 1581. Lennox and Arran together were a significant force, and soon acquired an influential party including John Maitland of Thirlestane, Lord Maxwell, Lord Seton, Ker of Ferniehurst and Robert Melville of Murdocairnie.[24]

The influence of Lennox and Arran changed James's opinions on many subjects – and most notably started to undo the indoctrination attempted by Buchanan, now ill and unable to regain his hold over the Prince. James Melvill wrote that 'it was a pity to see so well a brought up Prince till his bairnhead [childhood] was past, to be so miserably corrupted in the entress of his springal age [as he entered his adolescence], both with sinistrous and false information of all proceedings in his minority, and with evil and most dangerous grounds and principles in government of Kirk and Commonweal'. The King's attitude towards the Kirk ministers was the most obvious casualty. 'Then was he made to think worst of the best men that ever served in this Kirk and Country,' wrote Melvill, 'to think the whole manner of Reformation of Religion to have been done by a privy faction, turbulently and treasonably; to suspect the noblemen and whole ministry that stood for the cause of Religion and his crown against his mother's faction; yea, to take course against them, and put at them as his unfriends [enemies].' Significantly for James's long-term political beliefs, Melvill writes, the newly promoted Arran 'put the opinion of absolute power in his Majesty's head'. This notion was promulgated for him by the sympathetic Bishop of St Andrews, Patrick Adamson, who pronounced, 'That a Christian King should be the chief governor of the Kirk, and behoved to have Bishops under him, to hold all in order, conform to antiquity and most flourishing estate of the Christian Kirk under the best emperor, Constantine.' The discipline proposed by the Kirk of Scotland, he continued, was incompatible 'with a free kingdom and monarchy, such as was his Majesty's in Scotland'.[25]

In this attitude lay the seeds of a war of attrition between King and Kirk. When in 1582 the Kirk commissioners led by Andrew Melvill, delivered their 'griefs and articles' to the King and his Privy Council, they found a new and vocal opponent in Arran. When the articles were read, Arran (or 'Captain James' as James Melvill insists on calling him) threatened 'with thrawin brow, and boasting language': 'What! who dare subscribe their treasonable articles?' Andrew Melvill answered, 'We dare, and will subscribe them, and give our lives in the cause!', and seizing the pen from the Council Clerk, signed the articles, as did all the other ministers. When Lennox and Arran saw this 'boldness', they understood 'that the Kirk had a back, and became afraid; and, after some calmer language, dismissed them in peace'.[26]

As the King's new regime found opposition in the Kirk, it also came under attack from England. Elizabeth lobbied vigorously for Morton's release and tried to turn James against Lennox. The previous September, the English ambassador Robert Bowes had refused to deliver his commission to the King and Privy Council unless Lennox left the room, on the grounds that Lennox was 'a stranger' (foreigner).[27] At that point, James was in no mood to hear anything against his friend, and Bowes's attempts failed. Now Elizabeth tried sending another envoy, Thomas Randolph, to secure Morton's release, but again to no avail. When Randolph requested that Morton be properly tried, James pointed out sharply that 'he meddled not with the

Queen of England and her subjects, nor execution of justice upon them'.[28] Despite the unwelcome response, Randolph was reluctantly impressed by the boy's skill. 'Though he be young,' he wrote home, 'he wants neither words nor answers to anything said to him.'[29]

But for all James's bravado, Scotland was afraid of England. Rumours, almost certainly without foundation, of an English threat started to circulate. On 11 February, a proclamation called all men between the ages of sixteen and sixty to prepare themselves for war. The following week a convention of estates (a Parliament-like gathering with tax-granting but limited judicial powers) granted a tax of £40,000 if war broke out. The official reason given was to repress thieves, wrote Calderwood, 'but the true intent was, to be in readiness, if there were any invasion made by England'. While fears were heightened, Lennox sealed the King off. The outer gate of the Abbey Close was guarded by a troop of men led by Arran, and the numbers of men allowed in strictly limited. The nobility muttered angrily that Lennox was controlling them, and that he had turned the King's palace into a 'warhouse'. But all the security was not enough to stop the usual proliferation of libels. Calderwood recorded how, on 1 February, 'libels were spread in the King's chamber, and other places' attacking Argyll, Lord Robert and others, and displaying particular venom against Lennox, who was 'called a feeble sow, that saw his wife deflowered before his eyes', a clear impugning of the Earl's masculinity that at once feminised and cuckolded him.[30]

In February 1581, at the Convention of Estates, Elizabeth's ambassador Randolph formally presented her complaints to the King. The Pope, she wrote, had decided that Scotland was the key to his plan to bring England back to popery, first by sending 'Monsieur d'Aubigny' – Elizabeth did not acknowledge him as Earl of Lennox – 'a professed Papist, into Scotland, under colour of his kinred [kinship] to the King, that these twenty years past never offered any service to the King, when as he had most need'. This d'Aubigny worked 'partly by dissimulation and courting with the King, being young, and of a noble and gentle nature, and partly by nourishing and making factions among the nobility', but especially by opposing those nobles known to be pro-English in their views. In this way he would 'make some ready way, by colour of division and faction, to bring strangers, being

Romanists, into the realm, for his party, and, consequently, by degrees, to alter religion, yea, in the end, to bring the person of the young King in danger'. This would be 'very easy', wrote Elizabeth, pointing out that James had appointed d'Aubigny as 'his principal chamberlain, and possessor of his person' on the basis of no service whatsoever. D'Aubigny's final aim, she alleged, was 'to get the crown also, in the end, to himself'.

The Queen then turned to herself. As d'Aubigny's influence had increased, Elizabeth had noted 'some alteration and diminution' in James's friendship towards her, although she ascribed this 'not of the King's own disposition', but to him being abused by others; there had been an upsurge of violence in the Borders; Morton had been wrongly accused, and taken away without trial to a remote castle, under d'Aubigny's custody. All of this, she concluded, was 'sufficient to confirm the just suspicions of Monsieur d'Aubigny's intention to become the principal minister of the Pope and his adherents, for to reduce that realm to the servitude of Rome, whereof himself from his birth had been a professed vassal'. Even though now, for reasons of pragmatism, d'Aubigny 'affirmed by words, to be somewhat otherwise changed', she pointed out, 'some of his company brought with him, and yet secretly cherished by him, do remain still Papists'. Given this danger, she called on the Scottish nobility to preserve 'the young King, her dear brother' from 'the dangerous practisings and seducings of all cunning Papists', and offered her aid in money and men against the influence of Monsieur d'Aubigny.[31]

Unable to retaliate against Elizabeth, Lennox and his followers attacked her ambassador. On 13 March, Randolph found a libel affixed to his gate, allegedly from 'We, the King's Majesty, barons, nobility, boroughs, and commons.' It complained that Elizabeth and Randolph brought the King 'in contempt of his subjects, alleging him to be misruled and misguided by certain particular counsellors, and not willing to obtemper [comply with] the Queen's Majesty your mistress' desires'. Elizabeth had for counsellors the Earl of Leicester and Sir Christopher Hatton, it pointed out, neither of whom was so closely related to her as Lennox was to James. As for Lennox's alleged papism, was not Elizabeth herself negotiating a marriage with the very Catholic brother of the King of France? It also accused Randolph of having secret and seditious nocturnal meetings with the pro-English Earls of Angus and Mar, turning them into 'howlets and nightingales, who converse with you in the night'. Randolph gained audience with James, and complained that he knew the libel to have come from certain courtiers, because some of them had said similar things to him, but James gave him short shrift: Randolph should go and find the author himself.[32] However, when a harquebus shot two bullets through the window in the ambassador's bedchamber, aimed directly 'at a place where he commonly use to sit', it was the last straw: Randolph fled to Berwick.[33] From there on, Scottish relations with England continued to deteriorate. They reached a new low point in the spring of 1582 when James refused to receive a letter from the English Queen which he knew would be full of unwelcome advice. This constituted a serious breach of etiquette: Elizabeth was furious when she heard of it, and James was forced to pen a lame letter of apology.[34]

In the late spring of 1581, Morton was officially charged on various counts, including 'taking of the King' in Stirling in April 1580; conspiring to take the King and slay Lennox in Holyroodhouse in November and December 1580, 'when his lodging was furnished with weapons'; and again on 1 January 1581, the day after he was accused in Council. Perhaps aware that these charges were unlikely to stick, James instructed that they all be dropped except one: the concealing of his father's murder. In time Morton confessed that he had fore-knowledge of Henry's murder and had concealed it, but continued to deny that he was 'art and part'. When two ministers visited him the night before his execution, they asked why he had concealed the information. 'Whom to should I have revealed it?' he asked, 'To the Queen? She was the doer thereof. I was minded, indeed, to [tell] the King's father [i.e. Henry], but I durst [dared] not for my life; for I knew him to be such a bairn, that there was nothing told him but he would reveal it to her again.' Morton was executed in Edinburgh on 2 June 1581. He spent his last night writing, and in the morning sent some ministers to the King with his letters. James 'would not look upon them, nor take heed what they said', it was reported, 'but ranged up and down the floor of his chamber, clanking with his finger and his thumb'. Morton's body was left on the scaffold until 8 p.m. and then carried to the Nether Tolbooth, where his head was set on a spike.

David Calderwood wrote of Morton's passing: 'So ended this nobleman, one of the chief instruments of the reformation of religion; a defender of the same, and of the King in his minority, for the which he is now unthankfully dealt with.' Echoing Knox, he continued, 'We may see how absurd it is to commit the reins of government to the hands of a child, who cannot govern himself.'[35] With Morton dead, Lennox's power was complete. On 8 August, James made Lennox 'the second person' of the kingdom, giving him the only dukedom in Scotland as Esmé was 'proclaimed solemnly Duke of Lennox, Lord Darnley, Lord Torbowton, Dalkeith and Tantallan, Great Chamberlain of Scotland, Commendator of Arbroath'.[36]

It was during Lennox's time at court that James developed an association with a coterie of court poets known as 'the Castilian Band' or 'the brethir [brethren] to the sister nine', the Muses.[37] They took as their leader Alexander Montgomerie, ten years the King's elder, whom they dubbed the 'master poet'. At various times, the coterie included Alexander Scott, Alexander Hume, James's Master Household, Sir Patrick Hume of Polwarth, the musician brothers Robert and Thomas Hudson, who had served the King since his infancy, James's distant cousin John Stewart of Baldynneis, William Fowler and the female poet Christian Lindsay. Together they tried to master poetic forms, especially the difficult sonnet, attempted translations of continental works, and debated the merits of various poetic theories. James himself developed some 'Revlis and Cavtelis of Scottis poesie' to guide the way in which Scottish verse should develop, quoting examples from the efforts of Montgomerie. From the few glimpses of the coterie we have, it appears to have been a serious but also highly humorous gathering, in which James seems to have taken real pleasure.

The King would set tasks for his fellow aspiring poets. James suggested William Fowler translate Petrarch's *Triumphs*, and a sonnet by the King praising his attempts survives. At dinner once, James opined that not only the Greek of Homer and the Latin of Virgil but also the high-flown French of Guillaume Salluste du Bartas were inimitable in English. Hudson begged to differ, 'whereupon it pleased your Majesty to assign me *The Historie of Judith* as an agreeable subject to your Highness to be turned by me into English verse', 'corrected by your Majesty's own hand'.[38] Du Bartas, a Huguenot writer connected to the Navarre court, was perhaps James's favourite contemporary poet, and he translated several pieces of his work. Some of the fruits of the coterie were published by the Huguenot printer Thomas Vautrollier in Hudson's *The Historie of Judith* (1584) and James's *Essayes of a Prentise in the Divine Art of Poesie* (1584) and *His Majesties Poeticall Exercises at Vacant Houres* (1591).[39] With a few exceptions, the poetry is not remarkable, but there is at least a suggestion here that James's young life was not always the political and religious maelstrom that it can easily appear.

Despite his supposed conversion, Lennox was keen that James establish contact with his mother, still imprisoned in England; his own early advances towards Mary had been rebuffed by the Queen, who said she didn't trust him. Influenced by Lennox, James started to write to Mary in French, assuring her that 'it was not with my goodwill' that her previous letters had been returned unanswered. 'I beg you very humbly to believe that I have never had nor will have other will than to recognise you as my mother and as the one from whom all the honour that I can receive in this world will come.'[40] He begged his 'good mother' to 'be helpful to me and to give me your good counsel and advice, which I wish to follow to the end to render you more certain that, in every matter wherein it pleases you to command me, you will always find me your very obedient son'.[41] Early in 1581, buoyed by this new correspondence, Mary proposed to James an 'act of Association'. Under the terms of this, she and James would be joint sovereigns of Scotland, although James would be titled King and he would rule on behalf of both of them. In October 1581, she formulated a set of instructions for the Archbishop of Glasgow to negotiate the Association.

Rifts had begun to show in the relationship between Lennox and Arran. In the formal procession to Parliament in October 1581, as Lennox carried the crown, Arran griped publicly that *he* might have carried the crown. Later that month, Arran commanded Sir John Seton to stand back while James was mounting his horse; when Seton did not obey, Arran threatened 'to cast a baton at him, or to strike his horse on the face'. The Setons, father and sons, were 'commanded to keep their lodging', and Lennox, in protest at their treatment, refused to ride with the King to the Tolbooth the following day. It took two months for James to patch up the quarrel between the erstwhile friends, which he believed to have been confected by enemies of the Association.[42] At the same time, Arran was becoming increasingly unpopular. He had embarked on an affair with the married Countess of March; when she got pregnant, a divorce was procured on the grounds of her husband's alleged impotence, so that she and Arran could marry and 'cover this adulterous fact'. On 14 March 1582, at the urgings of the Kirk, he made repentance for the illegitimate son born of the union, at Holyroodhouse in the presence of the King. A week later, James rode to Stirling to attend the child's baptism, giving the final seal of royal approval.[43] But this did not stop the murmurings against him, and, indeed, the ascendancy of Lennox and Arran was about to end.

Lennox was the first to fall. In the late summer of 1582, Lennox and James were apart, the King hunting in Atholl while Lennox presided over the Court of Justice in Edinburgh in his capacity as Lord Chamberlain. It was perhaps with this separation in mind that, on 22 August, the Kirk prepared a final supplication against Lennox and Arran, almost desperate in tone, for presentation to the King:

> Sir, for the dutiful reverence and obedience we owe to your
> Highness, and for that we ever abhorred to attempt anything might
> seem displeasant to your Excellency, we have suffered now about
> the space of two years such false accusations, calumnies, oppres-
> sions and persecutions, by the moyen [means] of the Duke of
> Lennox, and him who is called Earl of Arran, that the like of their
> insolencies and enormities were never heretofore borne with in
> Scotland. Which wrongs, albeit they were most intolerable, yet for
> that they only touched us in particular, we comported them
> patiently, ever attending when your Highness should put remedy
> thereto. [But now they] have entered plainly to trouble the whole
> body of this common wealth . . .[44]

Although they did not know, by the time the ministers finished work on the document, the King was in no position to listen. Those nobles dissatisfied with Lennox, including Gowrie, Mar, the Master of Glamis and the Master of Oliphant, had bonded together, calling themselves the 'Lords Enterprisers': with Lennox away from the King, they saw their chance.[45] On 22 August, the same day that the Kirk prepared their supplication, as James was riding south to Perth he was met by Gowrie, who invited him to spend the night at Ruthven Castle. James accepted (although one contemporary report has it they 'took him unwilling') but when he tried to depart the next morning he was prevented from leaving, and moved forcibly from Ruthven to Perth. 'With great difficulty' his captors extracted a proclamation from him, dated 30 August, declaring that he was not being held their prisoner, and that he had chosen to reside in the burgh of Perth until the present commotion was pacified. No one was to think that he remained in Perth 'to be forced or constrained, for fear or terror, or against his will', nor should they answer any 'seditious and contrary reports' to call to arms.

Hearing of the capture of the King in what became known as 'the Ruthven Raid', Lennox decided he would be safer in Edinburgh. Stripping the 'whole tapestry and plenishing, or what was worthy to be carried' from his residence at Dalkeith, he transported it with sixty-four horse in attendance. In Edinburgh, he convened the Town Council, claiming himself innocent of any ill doing, and pressed them to find out the King's views on the situation. But Lennox could not win over the Kirk. Despite the Provost of Edinburgh's pleas for the minister 'to be sparing in his sermon', James Lawson delivered a stinging lecture on 26 August. He declaimed against Lennox, Arran and their counsellors as 'violators of discipline, annullers of excommunication, setters forth of proclamations to traduce the best of the nobility and ministry, setters up of Tulchan [false, titular] bishops through insatiable covetousness'.[46] Lennox was singled out for his 'raising of uproars in the Kirk, troubling of the common wealth, the introducing of prodigality and vanity in apparel, superfluity in banquetting and delicate cheer, deflowering of dames and virgins, and other fruits of the French court, and vexing of the commons of the country with airs'. But his worst crime was that Lennox 'made the King the author of all these faults, and laboured to corrupt him'.[47]

On 30 August, James was moved again, this time to Stirling. He hoped that his captors would allow him to ride to Edinburgh the following day, and prepared to do so, putting on his riding boots.

But as he was about to depart, the lords came to him and said that 'it was not expedient that he should ride at that time, till farther order were taken with things out of order'. They gave the King a stark choice: either Lennox left Scotland, or they would. James moved to leave the room, but when he reached the door, the Master of Glamis put his leg in the King's way. He did not break down as he so often did when crossed but, Calderwood recorded, 'the King laid these things up in his heart, and took them heavily'.[48] The Lords Enterprisers drew up a list of charges against Lennox, dated 17 September 1582, claiming that they had taken possession of the King in his own best interest: 'Whereas the King of Scots' good nature and virtuous education are now plainly understood to have been abused, and his royal qualities . . . are now obscured by the craft, subtilty, and treason of Esmé d'Aubigny and his complices.'[49] Their aim was to 'show his Majesty how all things went wrong by the misgoverning of that new counsel come lately from France'. James needed to banish his present counsellors, and 'take him[self] to be counselled by his old nobility'.[50]

From his stronghold of Dumbarton Castle, Lennox issued a proclamation of his innocence on 20 September, but it was greeted with contempt. 'Blessed be God,' came the answer, 'that hath so humbled that proud Pharaoh, now, in the eyes of all, that he is compelled to offer amendment to them whom before, when with humility they craved reformation, disdainfully he called "Pultrons, Mischants, False Prophets," and shamefully handled, stroke, banished, and put oft in hazard of their lives. But I fear, if Pharaoh were freed of his plague, he should return to his wonted hardness, and do as a dog in his old vomit.'[51] On 14 September an English embassy, headed by Sir George Cary and Robert Bowes, met with James at Stirling, and once again pushed the case against Lennox; two days later, letters from France were shown to the King, showing how Lennox was in league with the French. The letters told Lennox that he would be thought a coward and lose all honour if he left Scotland; he had the King's heart still, they assured him, and would not want for assistance in Scotland. On 17 September Lennox was granted a few extra days to leave the country. James confessed to Cary and Bowes that Lennox was 'not wise', that he had 'been urged to many things against his will', and the lords' action at Ruthven 'was honest'. But, he added, 'Three sorts of men

have enterprised it: one meaning well, another for their own particular, the third to avoid punishment.' The ambassadors asked if they
could assure Elizabeth that Lennox would leave the country: James
said they might. But James was still by no means free from attack.
On Wednesday 19 September, John Craig rebuked James in a sermon
for subscribing to a 'slanderous proclamation'. James, it was reported,
was reduced to tears and complained to Craig that he might have told
him that privately. Craig retorted that he had often been told, but to
no purpose. The Kirk's General Assembly, meeting from 9 October
in Edinburgh, was ambivalent towards the new state of affairs: they
approved the enterprise of those guarding the King, but refused either
to condemn or ratify the lords' printed declaration of its causes.[52]

The next few weeks witnessed a tedious cat-and-mouse game.
Lennox tried to buy time, while the Council urged James to hasten
his departure with threats: that Lennox would be denounced as a rebel,
that he would be charged with treason. As Lennox rode to Callander
and Blackness, there were wild rumours that he intended to seize
Holyroodhouse, where James was now residing, and take Edinburgh.
But the rumours came to nothing. By 14 December, patience was
running out. The Council passed an act charging Lennox to depart,
and James strengthened it by composing a sharp letter, accusing the
Duke of 'inconstancy and disloyalty' in disobeying his orders to leave
Scotland.[53] On 16 December Lennox replied, protesting that 'I feel
myself to be the most unhappy man in the world on seeing the bad
opinion which your majesty has conceived of me, and because the
persuasions of those who are now about you have made you believe
that I have any other intention than to render you the obedience and
fidelity which I owe you . . . I would never have thought that your
majesty would have wished to write such words to me.'[54] Two days
later, he wrote again:

Whatever may befall, I shall always be your very faithful servant,
and although there might be still this misfortune, that you might
wish to banish me from your good graces, yet in spite of all you
will always be my true master, and he alone in this world whom
my heart is resolved to serve. And would to God my body could
be cut open, so that there should be seen what is written upon my

heart; for I am sure there would not be seen there those words of inconstancy and disloyalty, but, indeed, those of 'fidelity' and 'obedience' . . . I have such extreme regret that I desire to die rather than to live, fearing that that has been the occasion of your no longer loving me. For if this disgrace befell me, truly the punishment would be to me much greater and more grievous to bear than death, for which ever since I wish and shall wish, even until at length I know that the proof which you have of my obedience has taken from you all the bad opinions which you formed of me.[55]

Finally realising the King was powerless to help him, Lennox departed for France. He fully expected to return to Scotland: on 1 May 1583, Robert Bowes reported that 'it is verily looked that Lennox shall be in Scotland before August next', and on the 29th updated his report that the Duke planned 'to visit the King and Scotland as soon as his body may endure travel'.[56] But by the time Bowes wrote this, Lennox was already dead. On 26 May, 'at seven of the clock', the Duke 'caused to write a writing to the King's grace, showing his grace the estate he was at, desiring him to be good to his bairns, and to take upon his Grace the defence of them'. Declaring himself a Protestant, he refused the ministrations of Catholic priests — a consistency of behaviour *in extremis* that would have confounded his critics — and died that night. Ignoring his wishes, his widow Catherine, a staunch Catholic, had him buried with full Roman rites. But one part of Lennox escaped that fate. The night he died, his attendants set about performing his last wish: 'he was bowelled, the same night, his heart taken out, the body put in a leaden kist, and after in a coach, and on the morn conveyed away secretly.' The heart was kept, 'to send away to the King, not suddenly, for his death will make the King's grace melancholic'[57] — and indeed James was said to be 'much perplexed' by the news of Lennox's death.[58] He often blamed the Duke's early demise on the harsh conditions in which he had been held in his last months in Scotland: before Lennox went to sea, Sir James Melville wrote, 'he was put to as hard a diet as he caused the Earl of Morton to use there, yea, even to the other extremity that he had used at court: for, whereas his kitchen was so sumptuous that lumps of fat was cast in the fire when it soked [smouldered]', now he was 'fain to eat of a maigre [lean] goose, skowdrit with bar stra [scorched with barley straw]'.[59] In June 1583, unbeknownst to his widow, Lennox's embalmed heart was sent to James.[60]

There can be little doubt that James's love for Lennox stood firm even as, either under pressure or for political expediency, he hastened his departure. The grief that he felt is painfully evident in a poem written after Lennox's death, and published in 1584. While sharing the unpolished execution of his previous sonnets and translations, it was undoubtedly striking in its portrayal of his relationship with Esmé.[61] 'Ane Metaphoricall Invention of a Tragedie called Phoenix' opened, somewhat pretentiously, with a 'column of 18 lines serving for a preface', in which James set out the argument in the shape of an implausible diamond-shaped votive column or urn – although there is no attempt to ally the form to the content, as there is with most 'shaped poems'. The argument is then reprinted as a sixteen-line stanza in which first and last letters of each line spell out 'ESME STEWART DWIKE [duke]', leaving no doubt as to the true identity of the poem's eponymous 'Phoenix'/Lennox. The narrative analogy of the poem is clear enough. An exotic foreign bird – the French d'Aubigny – lands in Scotland, and attracts a great deal of admiration. In time, this admiration turns into envy led by three birds, the Raven, the Stainchell, and the Gled, perhaps standing for Angus, Gowrie and Mar.[62] Their vicious attacks on the Phoenix mirror Lennox's experiences in 1582; when the Phoenix takes refuge between the poet's legs, they also attack the poet – the Ruthven Raid. The poem ends with the Phoenix's flight and self-immolation: Lennox's departure for France and eventual death. More remarkable is James's casting of the Phoenix as female, allowing a more obvious love narrative to emerge – and the way in which he sexualises the 'sheltering' of the bird: the Phoenix 'betwixt my legs herself did cast', and the envious birds 'made to bleed | My legs'. But for all the love that is expressed, James also registers his frustration with the Phoenix, whose death here becomes a suicide. Perhaps in order to cope with his loss or through simple pragmatism, James felt the need to blame Lennox for his own death, rather than blaming the ravenous fowl in whose clutches he remained.

* * *

Lennox's departure had been greeted gleefully by the Kirk, who, according to Melville, did 'rejoice in God, and thank him for delivering King, Kirk, and Commonweal of such counsel, as set themselves plainly to pervert all'.[63] But their joy was shortlived. Even as he mourned the Phoenix, James the poet had a happy announcement: 'Part of my tale | Is yet untold. Lo, here one of her race, | A word bred of her ash: Though she, alas | . . . be brunt [burned], this lacks but plumes and breath | To be like her, new gendered by her death.'[64] On 16 November 1583, Esmé's son Ludovic landed at Leith. Intelligencers reported that his entourage included some forty Scots and Frenchmen, 'who are reported altogether to be addict to papistry'. James immediately called for Ludovic to come to Edinburgh, 'and greatly doth esteem for him, showing to take great care for his bringing up'.[65] Ludovic was to have a long and distinguished career in James's inner circle, but his success was largely due to James's continued devotion to his dead father. Within a few months, James had issued a proclamation prohibiting men, on pain of death, from speaking of Lennox as anything other than a true Christian. The phoenix had risen from the ashes.

CHAPTER FIVE

A True Son of His Mother

ALTHOUGH THE RUTHVEN Raiders achieved their immediate objective of ejecting Lennox from Scotland, they were in truth a ragtag coalition with too many internal differences to sustain rule for long. Even during the autumn of 1582, before Lennox departed the country, James was attracting a group of noblemen who were willing to help him escape the clutches of Gowrie's faction. This new group was led by Huntly, Atholl, Bothwell, Montrose and Seton who subscribed a bond to 'remain with his Majesty until the abuses and enormities of the commonwealth should be redressed'.[1]

Their chance came in June 1583. James was at Falkland Place in Fife, and for once not heavily guarded. He turned to the trusted courtier Sir James Melville, and begged him to help him escape, a commission that Melville found 'very unpleasant'. When James persisted, however, saying that he was determined 'to liberate himself fully or die in the attempt', Melville gave in and agreed to provide what assistance he could. The plan was for James to journey to St Andrews: the Earl of March could be persuaded to invite him there on the pretext that the King would eat his 'wild meat and other fresh fleshs that would spoil in case his Majesty came not to make good cheer with him'. Sympathetic lords would be told to meet him there.[2] On 27 June, the King and Melville rode out from Falkland, and were met by March and the Provost of St Andrews at Dairsie. James was elated. 'Meeting them,' recalled Melville, 'His Majesty thought himself at liberty, with great joy and exclamation, like a bird flown out of a cage, passing his time in hawking by the way, after the said meeting, thinking himself then sure enough.' Melville was not so sanguine. 'I thought his estate far surer when he was in Falkland.'[3]

In time, realising that the bird had flown, the Lords Enterprisers followed in pursuit but were halted by a proclamation forbidding them to approach the King's person: James was turning against them the very machinery that had facilitated his continued captivity at Ruthven and Stirling. Gowrie, however, was admitted into the royal presence:

there, kneeling, he humbly asked for the King's pardon, particularly for his words and deeds against Lennox.[4] James started to berate Gowrie, but he soon pardoned him. In the weeks that followed, James appointed a new Privy Council, including the young Earl of Huntly, Crawford, Argyll and Montrose, as well as John Maitland of Thirlestane and Robert Melville of Murdocairnie. But it was Arran who established himself as the figurehead of the new regime. Now, as ever, he polarised opinions. To the English ambassador Sir Edward Hoby, the Earl 'carrieth a princely presence and gait, goodly of personage, representing a brave countenance of a captain of middle age, very resolute, very wise and learned, and one of the best spoken men that ever I heard'. To Sir James Melville, who knew Scottish politics much better, 'the Earl of Arran was a scorner of religion, presumptious, ambitious, greedy, careless of the commonwealth, a despiser of the nobility and of all honest men.'[5] A measure of Arran's steady assumption of power can be found in the fate of the Earl of Mar. Coming to court in August 1583, he failed to reconcile with Arran and was commanded to leave the country. Argyll, to whose custody he was committed, convinced him to give up Stirling Castle to Arran – but this was not enough to assuage Arran, and in January 1584 Mar was banished from England, Scotland and Ireland. By this time, he had already fled the country, but by March he had defied his banishment and was back in Edinburgh, plotting to regain control of the King.[6]

Hearing of yet another new regime north of the border, Elizabeth was concerned enough to despatch one of her most senior councillors, Principal Secretary Sir Francis Walsingham, to investigate. Refusing to speak with Arran, Walsingham used his time with James to hammer home the English Queen's disapproval of what she saw as the King's rash action in switching counsellors without consulting her. James fell into what Walsingham described to Elizabeth as 'some kind of distemperture [sic], and with a kind of jollity said he was an absolute King, and therefore prayed Your Majesty that he might take such order with his subjects as should best like himself, and that Your Highness would be no more curious to examine the affection of his councillors than he is of yours'.[7] Hearing this, Elizabeth needed no further encouragement to lend her support instead to the Lords Enterprisers. On 17 April 1584, Mar, backed by Glamis, Angus and the Lords John and Claud Hamilton, asserted his personal claim to Stirling Castle.[8] With Arran at his side, James mustered some twelve thousand men and advanced on Stirling; the castle capitulated immediately, and the King hanged the captain of the garrison there as a warning. But the lords had already disappeared, fleeing to the Borders, and from there into England.[9] Arran had, however, managed to capture Gowrie (who was not part of the conspiracy), and had him executed on 3 May 1584, supposedly for past crimes.

This success against the Lords Enterprisers provided James with a new confidence, and he set about consolidating his regime. Arran was appointed as Chancellor with Maitland of Thirlestane as Secretary. James also started to exorcise some ghosts of his childhood: all copies of Buchanan's despised *De jure regni* were called in, 'to be revised and reformed' by the new Secretary, 'upon pain of imprisonment and forfeiture of £200' to anyone who was found with a copy.[10] He also dealt with the Kirk. The preacher Andrew Melvill was summoned before the Privy Council to answer for a seditious sermon he had given; when he refused to acknowledge the jurisdiction of the Council, he was forced to flee into England. It was only the start of James's campaign. In May 1584 Arran's government passed what the Kirk dubbed 'the Black Acts'. These declared James head of Kirk and state, confirming his power over both spiritual and temporal estates, insisted on the authority of bishops within the Kirk, and forbade the meeting of presbyteries (which it didn't recognise') and General Assemblies without the King's consent.[11] This was a newly assertive King James.

During the summer of 1584, M. de Fontenay, ambassador of Henri III of France, spent some months in James's court. Like every other ambassador, his first task was to send home a pen-portrait to his paymaster — but Fontenay possessed a rare insight into James's character. His observations reveal to us not only the eighteen-year-old James, but the James of the next forty years. His opening remarks were wholly admiring. 'He is, for his age, the first Prince who has ever been in this world. He has three parts of the soul in perfection. He grasps and understands quickly; he judges carefully and with reasonable discourses; he restrains himself well and for long. In his demands he is quick and piercing, and determined in his replies.' Fontenay was particularly impressed by James's lack of bias in debates – a characteristic that was to be of great significance later in his career when he frequently entered into public controversies. 'Of whatever thing they dispute, whether it be religion or anything else, he believes and maintains always what seems to him most true and just, so that in several disputes on religion I have seen him take the cause for Monsieur de Fentray [a Roman Catholic] and defend him constantly against his adversaries, although they were of the same belief as he. He is learned in many languages, sciences, and affairs of state – I daresay more than all those of his kingdom. In short he has marvellous spirit – for the rest full of virtuous glory and good opinion of himself.' Although generous, he wrote, James was highly competitive, and if he 'saw himself surpassed in exercises he abhors them ever after'. Somewhat prudish, the King 'hates dancing and music in general, as likewise all wantonness at court, be it in discourses of love or in curiosity of habits' – with one particular phobia: 'not being well about to see above all earrings'.

Fontenay did have, however, some reservations. James, he wrote, did not often 'dare to contradict the great lords', and yet 'he likes very much to be considered brave and to be feared'. This he put down to the King's 'having been nourished in fear' – a phrase that beautifully captures James's cowed existence through the first eighteen years of his life. 'His ways for want of being well instructed are very rude and uncivil in speaking, eating, manners, games, and entertainment in the company of women' – perhaps inevitable in one raised in a remote castle full of men.

Fontenay was also one of the first to recognise and comment on James's disability. 'He never stops in one place, taking a singular pleasure in walking, but his gait is bad, composed of erratic steps, and he tramps about even in his room.' This feature, remarked upon throughout James's life, has never been properly explained – if we discount the 'drunken wet-nurse scenario' – but might have been exacerbated, if not caused, by a riding accident. As Fontenay notes, the King 'likes hunting above all the pleasures of this world, remaining there at least six hours together chasing all over the place with loosened rein. He has a weak body, but is in no wise delicate. In short, to tell you in one word, he is an old young man resembling the sirens of Socrates.'

In his assessment of James's grasp of government, Fontenay proved to be almost prophetic. 'I have only noticed in him three things very bad for the preservation of his state and the government of the same. The first is his ignorance and lack of knowledge of his poverty and his little strength, promising too much of himself and despising other princes. The second, that he loves indiscretely and inadvisedly in spite of his subjects [against his subjects' better interests]. The third is that he is too lazy and too thoughtless over his affairs, too willing and devoted to his pleasure, especially hunting, leaving all his affairs to be managed by the Earl of Arran, Montrose, and the Secretary. I know well that this is excusable at his young age, but it is to be feared that continuance will confirm him in this habit.' Indeed, by the time James reached England twenty years later, the habit was unbreakable. Fontenay felt so strongly about this issue that he challenged James on the matter. James replied 'very secretly' that 'he would guard well against such misfortune, because no affair of importance ever happened of which he did not know, although he did not seem to. And although he spent much of his time hunting he could do as much business in one hour as others would in a day, because simultaneously he listened and spoke, watched, and sometimes did five things at once.' Moreover, James boasted, 'nothing was done secretly by the lords that he did not know, by means of having spies at the doors of their rooms morning and evening, who came and reported everything to him'.

In conclusion, Fontenay wrote, 'he is a true son of his mother in many things, but principally in that he is weak in body and cannot work long at his affairs, but when he gives himself to it he does more than six others together' – indeed 'sometimes he has wished to force and keep himself six days continually at accounts, but that immediately after he never fails to be ill. He told me that on the whole he resembled the jennets [small horses] of Spain, who have only a brave course, otherwise the continuation carries them away.' In one aspect, however, James's sympathy for his mother was less than total: 'At one thing only I am astonished,' confided Fontenay: 'he has never inquired anything of the Queen of her health, or her treatment, her servants, her living, and eating, her recreation, or anything similar, and never-theless I know that he loves and honours her very much in his heart.'[12] Fontenay had reason to worry about James's affection for Mary, as the months ahead would prove only too dramatically.

Once James's new regime had consolidated its success at Stirling, Elizabeth had no choice but to deal directly with the King. In August 1584, she sent Henry Carey, first Lord Hunsdon to negotiate an alliance. England felt her position to be increasingly precarious: rela-tions with Spain were collapsing; the Spanish ambassador had been expelled from London in January; and war with Spain was now perilously near. Hunsdon met Arran at Fouldon Kirk, near Berwick, and the groundwork was laid for future negotiations. With channels of communication to England open again, James had less time for the proposed Association with his mother. He was encouraged in this stance by a new influence in his life, Patrick, the Master of Gray, who had become friendly in France with Mary's agent, the Archbishop of Glasgow, and soon become a trusted part of Mary's international circle. Despite his intimacy with the Queen, Gray was a staunch Protestant, and on returning to Scotland in 1583 he started passing on intelligence about Mary to James, intelligence that inevitably lessened James's support for his mother. In the autumn of 1584, James cut off contact with Mary.[13] The next English ambas-sador to Scotland, in spring 1585, was Sir Edward Wotton. Now Elizabeth was talking money, offering James a pension of £4,000 per annum. It was enough to make James renounce the Association plan entirely, much to the distress of his mother, who felt betrayed. There was another effect of this shift in priorities: as James turned towards Gray and England, Arran fell out of favour. As Fontenay wrote, 'I do not know what to say of Monsieur de Arran for fear of lying. Everyone hates him like the Devil.'[14]

Soon Arran found himself sacrificed to Anglo-Scottish relations. A perennial source of tension between England and Scotland were the persistent Border disputes. On 27 July 1585, Scottish and English representatives met to settle the disputes, but instead violence flared. Sir Thomas Ker of Ferniherst, the Scottish Warden of the Middle March, fell into a quarrel, shot and killed Lord Francis Russell, the son of the English Earl of Bedford. Since Ker was an Arran appointee, it was easy enough for Arran's enemies to point the finger at Arran, and several accused him of arranging the killing to scupper relations with England. In truth it was probably an accident; but Wotton's reaction turned it into an international incident. Desperate not to let relations with Elizabeth suffer, James wept publicly and imprisoned Arran at St Andrews. The imprisonment lasted only a week, but the damage to the Earl was done: the King had shown that he would sacrifice him if necessary. Gray hinted at this to England, and in October 1585 Elizabeth ordered the exiled lords back into Scotland, where they headed straight for Arran who was with the King at Stirling. Without time even properly to provision the castle, James was highly vulnerable. On 2 November, a considerable army appeared in front of Stirling, headed by Mar, Glamis, Angus and Lords John and Claud Hamilton. Inside, Arran accused Gray of plotting the return, but Gray managed to persuade James of his innocence. Realising he was beaten, Arran fled the following morning.

The same day, James received the rebel lords into his presence in Stirling's Great Hall. Both sides knew that they had to negotiate. The lords fell on their knees and protested their loyalty. The King answered their supplication with good grace and agreed not to enforce so strictly 'the Black Acts', although they would remain on the books. He allowed exiled Kirk ministers to return to Scotland; Andrew Melvill, though, was singled out to be despatched to the north of Scotland on a wild goosechase to seek and convert Jesuits. James gave in to demands that Arran should be stripped of his chancellorship and his earldom; in return the lords agreed not to pursue him. But it was the end of Arran. Reduced once again to plain 'Captain James Stewart', he disappeared from public view, meeting his end in 1596 when he was murdered by a nephew of Morton, as part of a vendetta.[15]

The formal treaty with England was finally signed on 5 July 1586. Since the first draft contained nothing pertaining to the succession, James proposed a clause that read 'That the Queen should in no way directly or indirectly prejudice the King's title, or at any time give declaration of any other to succeed her in her crown and realms.' Elizabeth replied that she did not find such a clause 'convenient' in the treaty, but she agreed to write a letter 'under her hand and seal', provided that 'title' was replaced by 'pretended title'.[16] Ultimately she agreed the wording 'that nothing shall be done to the prejudice of any title he may pretend unto this crown, unless by the said King's unkind usage towards her Majesty, which God forbid, he shall justly deserve the contrary'.[17] But even as it was being signed, another simmering scandal was about to boil over. On 11 August 1586, Mary Queen of Scots was arrested on charges of conspiring to kill the Queen of England.

Among the many facets of English Secretary of State Sir Francis Walsingham was a flair for intelligence. Recruiting a team of expert cipherers, linguists, agents and double agents, he could probe into virtually any underground network, even into private households. Most of his energies went into tracking down Catholic conspiracies – many of which were often supported by Spain, Rome or the Jesuits – and he knew well that Mary was a highly attractive martyr-cum-saviour figure for these plotters. For years he had been unable to implicate Mary in any particular conspiracy. Then his team unearthed the Babington Plot. Anthony Babington, a Roman Catholic, Derbyshire landowner, had once been a page in the household of the Earl of Shrewsbury, Mary's gaoler between 1569 and 1585. He concocted a remarkably inept scheme that would culminate in the death of Elizabeth. Having detected the conspiracy, Walsingham swung into action, intercepting and reading correspondence between Babington and Mary before allowing it to continue to its intended destination. In this way the plot progressed, while English intelligence knew of every move.

Mary usually avoided committing her plans or views to paper, but this time she let her guard slip. Perhaps her lack of caution was in reaction to the harsher regime to which she had been subjected since early 1585, under the strict guardianship of Sir Amias Paulet. In July 1586, Mary expressed approval of the Babington Plot in a letter. At the beginning of August, the conspirators were arrested and interrogated; Mary was arrested while in Tixall Park on a staghunt – one passion she shared with her son – and her confinement was made more secure, by denying access to her secretaries, Mary's route to the outside world.[18]

James's reaction was not sympathetic. He had just signed the Treaty with Elizabeth, and Mary's actions cast him in a bad light. The resident French ambassador in Scotland, Monsieur de Courcelles, reported James as saying that 'the Queen, his mother, might well drink the ale and beer which herself had brewed'.[19] Nevertheless, it would not look good for him to be in support of his mother's execution, should that possibility arise. Anxious to know how to play the situation, James sent a representative to England, one Archibald Douglas, a kinsman of the late Regent Morton. Douglas had fled south in 1581, fearing retribution for his part in both King Henry's murder and Morton's execution. In England he had found gainful employment acting as an intelligencer for Walsingham until the spring of 1586 when he was repatriated and, in a widely condemned farce of a trial ('the filthiest inquiry that was heard of in Scotland'),[20] found not guilty of both murders. Now Douglas met Walsingham, who suggested that James should not intercede for his mother: if he did, it might be thought he approved of her actions. At the same time though, Gray told Douglas that 'the King is very instant [importunate] for his mother' and intended to send Gray down 'with a commission to that effect'.[21]

James's show of concern for his mother was a political necessity in Scotland. North of the border, Mary was popularly regarded as a victim of English oppression, even by those who had not liked her during her years in government. Ignoring Douglas's advice, James decided to send another ambassador to plead for her life, and chose William Keith of Delnies, a young member of his household. On 20 October, Keith carried a letter from James to Douglas, who was representing the King in London. The letter betrays James's desperation that his mother should not die – but for *his* sake, not hers. 'Think not that any dealing will do good if her life be lost, for then adieu with my dealing with that estate [England]; and therefore if ye look for the continuance of my favour spare no pains nor plainness in this case . . . and in this request let me reap the fruits of your great credit there either now or never.'[22]

By this time Mary's trial was underway. Her judges included several senior English Privy Councillors gathered at Fotheringay Castle in Northamptonshire. Mary had refused to accept that the commissioners could judge her, since they were not her peers, or that she could be charged with treason against Elizabeth, since she was not Elizabeth's subject. 'As an absolute Queen I cannot submit to orders,' she declared, 'nor can I submit to the laws of the land without injury to myself, the King my son, and all other sovereign princes.'[23] Her protests notwithstanding, the trial had gone ahead. Mary initially denied any knowledge of the conspiracy, or having corresponded with Babington. But when the confessions of Babington and others were read, along with those of her two secretaries, she admitted that she had tried to bring about her own escape, and to support the cause of the Roman Church. News of the trial reached James at the end of September along with a letter from Douglas recounting a conversation with Elizabeth. The Queen had suggested that if she 'did justice against the mother' the net effect was 'nothing else but [to] advance the son'. Douglas replied to Elizabeth that James 'could not be forgetful of his own honour, whatsoever she [his mother] was', and that he was under instructions to let Elizabeth understand that James's 'good nature' would shine through despite his mother's 'ingratitude'. Elizabeth retorted abruptly by pointing to Mary's past treachery: 'if the half of that good nature had been in his mother that I imagine to be in himself, he had not been so soon fatherless'; a woman 'that could not for his good bearing spare the father, how can any be persuaded that she will spare the son that she plainly affirms in her letters hath done her wrong?'[24]

Reassembling in Westminster's Star Chamber on 25 October, the commissioners declared Mary guilty of 'compassing and imagining since June 1st matters tending to the death and destruction of the Queen of England'. On 5 November, Keith arrived in London, bearing James's letter, and he and Douglas secured an audience with the Queen on the 10th; Elizabeth was noncommittal, as was her wont, but promised an answer within a few days. On the 12th, however, the English Parliament urged the Queen to order the execution; four days later, Elizabeth despatched two messengers to inform Mary that she should prepare to die. Douglas reported back that the Queen was 'in extreme danger of her life'.[25] In Scotland, James was criticised for his apparent inaction: some of his councillors urged him to understand 'what an injury it should be, if the Queen of England did put her hand in his blood; the reproach it would be to him among all Christian princes; the small account he should seem to make of his mother's honour, and his own natural duty'. James responded 'that he loved his mother as much as nature and duty bound him, but he could not love her conditions; for he knew well that she bare him no more goodwill than she did the Queen of England'. He knew that Mary had often tried to dethrone him and replace him with a Regent. With his own eyes, he declared, he had seen a letter from Mary to the French envoy Fontenay in which she asserted that if James did not 'conform himself to her will, and follow her counsel and advice, that he should content himself with the Lordship of Darnley, which was all that appertained unto him by his father'. It therefore 'behoved him to think of his own affairs'. Mary must stop her 'practices and intelligences', and 'in truth, it was meet [suitable] for her to meddle with nothing but prayer and serving of God'. The bottom line, he told George Douglas, was that 'it was not possible for him to agree with her, being of a religion contary to his'. When Douglas pointed out that Mary retained the religion she had been brought up in, just as he did his, James retorted that 'he had been brought up among a company of mutinous knave ministers, whose doctrine he had never approved; but he knew his religion to be the true religion'.[26]

As the likelihood increased that Mary would be executed, Scotland was in uproar. It had been generally thought that Mary would simply be imprisoned more securely, and her secretaries – her route to the outside world – taken from her.[27] 'The King nor no man ever believed the matter would have gone so far,' wrote Gray from Holyroodhouse to Archibald Douglas in London. 'I never saw all the people so willing to concur in anything as in this same . . . They that hated most her prosperity regret her adversity.'[28] In late November the French ambassador Courcelles had an audience with a rather lachrymose James. 'His mother's cause was the strangest that ever was heard of,' he said. Had Courcelles ever read of a sovereign prince that had been detained prisoner for such a long time without a cause, by a neighbour prince, who in the end would put her to death? His mother had just cause to say, as she had at her arraignment, that she had never had a good day since his birth. But, he said, brightening, he didn't believe Elizabeth would put her hands in Mary's blood.[29]

These thoughts were uppermost in James's mind when he wrote a letter to Keith in London, evidently intending that Keith should show the letter to Elizabeth.

> I perceive by your last letter the Queen my mother still continueth in that miserable strait that the pretended condemnation of that Parliament has put her in. A strange example indeed, and so very rare, as for my part I never read nor heard of the like practice in such a case. I am sorry that beyond my expectation, the Queen hath suffered this to proceed to my dishonour, and so contrary to her good fame, as by subjects' mouth to condemn a sovereign prince descended of all hands of the best blood in Europe. King Henry VIII's reputation was never prejudged in anything but in the beheading of his bedfellow, but yet that tragedy was far inferior to this, if it should proceed as seemeth to be intended; which I can never believe, since I know it is the nature of noble princes at that time chiefly to spare when it is most concluded in all men's minds that they will strike . . . Fail not but let her see all this letter: and would God she might see the inward parts of my heart where she should see a great jewel of honesty towards her, locked up in a coffer of perplexity, she only having the key which by her good behaviour in this case may open the same. Guess ye in what strait my honour will be in, this unhap being perfected; since, before God, I already dare scarce go abroad for crying out of the whole people; and what is spoken by them of the Queen of England, it grieves me to hear, and yet dare not find fault with it except I would dethrone myself, so is whole Scotland incensed with this matter.[30]

When the letter was read by Elizabeth on 6 December, according to Douglas, the Queen flew into such a 'passion as it was a great deal of work to us all . . . to appease her'. It was the King of Scots' reference to her parents, Henry VIII and his 'bedfellow', Anne Boleyn (whom he executed), that most upset her. Elizabeth let Keith know that if he 'had not delivered unto Her Majesty so strange and unseasonable a message as did directly touch her noble father and herself', she would have agreed to Keith's request to delay Mary's execution until two Scots noblemen had arrived and pleaded for her. Now, however, not only would she not promise to delay the execution but she would not receive two noblemen, but two commoners instead – to whom, it was implied, she would not have to pay so much respect or attention.[31]

James found two commoners in Sir Robert Melville of Murdocairnie and the Master of Gray (who though a senior counsellor was technically not a peer), and they were promptly despatched. His instructions to Gray were designed to map out a new situation in which Mary might be allowed to survive without constituting a threat to Elizabeth. If none of James's suggestions appealed, then Gray and Melville were to press Elizabeth to propose some 'form of security' that suited them.[32] But James was playing a double if not a triple game. While Gray and Melville laid out the 'official' Scottish line on Mary's dilemma, James wrote simultaneously to the Earl of Leicester, one of Elizabeth's senior councillors, severing his ties with his mother. He denied having had any contact with his mother since the previous autumn – before the treaty with England was concluded. 'I am honest,' he insisted, 'no changer of course, altogether in all things as I profess to be.' If he ever supported his mother's claim to the throne, then men could judge him 'fond and inconstant'. 'My religion ever moved me to hate her course although my honour constrains me to insist for her life.'[33] Douglas interpreted the letter more bluntly for Leicester's benefit: James would not sever diplomatic relations if Mary were executed.

Gray and Melville were received by Elizabeth at a social occasion on 6 January 1587. They reported that the English Queen was infuriatingly vague about Mary's fate, claiming she had no idea whether Mary were still alive or not. An embassy member named George Young wrote to Secretary Maitland in Scotland on 10 January that Elizabeth 'directed out the warrant long ago and wished not to be made privy to the day of execution. Since then all our intelligence assures us she is gone. We are in a despair to do any good in the errand we came for, all things dishearting us on every side, and every hour giving us new advertisement that we deal for a dead lady.'[34] Two days later, Gray and Melville made a last-ditch attempt to persuade Elizabeth to save Mary's life. They asked for a reprieve of fifteen days, eight days – 'Not for an hour!' exclaimed the Queen. She ended their audience with an instruction: 'Tell your King what good I have done for him in holding the crown on his head since he was born; and that I mind to keep the league that stands now between us, and if he break, it shall be a double fault.' Gray wrote miserably to James: 'Your Majesty sees we have delivered all we had for offers. But all is nothing, for she and her Council has laid a determination that they mind to follow forth.'[35] Perhaps the reasons for their apparent failure lay in another messenger from Scotland. Alexander Stewart, who had been sent as part of the Gray/Melville embassy but 'with more express and secret charge than they had', told Elizabeth from James that he had sent formal ambassadors only because he couldn't be seen to 'neglect his mother, and the duties he owes her'; Elizabeth should not take it 'in ill part'. But then Stewart added a message, perhaps of his own devising: that if Mary died and James 'at first showed himself not contented therewith', the English 'might easily satisfy him, in sending him dogs and deer'. Hearing of this, James was allegedly furious, and raged that when Stewart returned he would 'hang him before he put off his boots, and if the Queen meddled with his mother's life, she should know, he would follow somewhat else than dogs and deer'.[36] Despite the rhetoric, it is perhaps instructive as to James's true state of mind that he didn't punish Stewart at all.

Intelligence came from Douglas that Elizabeth no longer trusted James, and that her Council had advised her to resort to threats: that she would deprive him of the succession by Act of Parliament on the grounds that he had assisted 'one that sought her death', and look instead at one of the Earl of Hertford's sons as her successor. James pronounced himself unimpressed. He should have little courage, he declared, if he were intimidated by an old woman, ill-beloved by her own subjects, weary of her government, in perpetual fear of her own servants – even more than James, who was so fearful himself, he joked, that he had his beard shaved with burning coals, 'fearing lest the barber should cut his throat'. Whenever Elizabeth saw anyone she did not recognise, 'she runs away like one undone'. This must be a great scourge and torment to her. Though he was a mean king with small ability, he protested, he would not change fortunes with her: he'd rather live 'surely among his subjects' than, as she did, seeking the blood of his own people just because they happened to have a contrary religion.[37]

Though James blustered against Elizabeth, she had good reason to be wary of him as a successor. A contemporary memorandum in the Salisbury papers at Hatfield House gives a vivid idea of the 'reasons for which the King of Scots is unacceptable to the people of England'. It lists 'many horrible, detestable, and cruel facts committed in Scotland since the reign of this King, which hath so far alienated men's hearts in England from him that were well bent unto him, which by all just, reasonable and convenient means must be repaired, or that credit which he had will never be recovered, either by league, letters, or fair promises'. The heinous deeds piled up. First, the death of his own father, committed by his mother, with Bothwell and supporters who now were 'of counsel and near about the King's self'. Second, the murder of Regent Moray, 'many yet living and accessory' to the fact. Third, the slaying of Regent Lennox, his grandfather: 'few or none executed for the same.' Fourth, the unjust execution of Morton through the false accusations of Captain James Stewart, who was then raised to be Earl of Arran. Fifth, the death of the Earl of Gowrie and other innocent men, again through Arran's accusations. Last, 'that which most concerneth and grieveth all Englishmen, was the murder of the Earl of Bedford [in fact, the Earl's son] upon the Borders, at a day of true [truce], against all law, justice, and honour, to the perpetual shame of that whole nation, if extreme justice be not ministered upon the offender'. That was not to mention the bullets fired into Randolph's window, and the appalling treatment of the embassy of Secretary Walsingham, 'a blot into that country so long as the memory thereof remaineth'. All these things taken together, it concluded, 'bear such show of an inward mind full of cruelty and mortal hatred to all those of this nation that bear goodwill to England, as, without great show of an altered mind appear in him, the hearts of all honest men in England will never be recovered as beforetime he had them'.[38] James would have his work cut out to win England over.

The embassy of Gray and Melville seems to have ended in some confusion. One source has it that they had to leave because a trumped-up charge of plotting against the Queen's life was threatened.[39]

Certainly they were back in Scotland by 8 February 1587, when the Council made them a formal vote of thanks. The Council did not know that on the same morning, in the Great Hall at Fotheringay Castle, Mary Queen of Scots was beheaded.

CHAPTER SIX

Sole King

WITH THE QUEEN of Scots finally dead, all eyes turned north to see how her son would react. James heard the news on 14 February 1587, six days after the event. Each report of James's reaction tended to reflect what the writer wanted to see. According to David Moysie, James received the news 'in great displeasure and went to bed without supper', riding off to Dalkeith the following morning, 'desiring to be solitaire'.[1] One English source reported that James took the news 'very grievously and offensively, but also gave out in secret speeches that he could not digest the same or leave it unrevenged, as should appear by such goods as they [the English] should receive at his hands'.[2] But Ogilvy of Powrie wrote that 'the King never moved his countenance at the rehearsal of his mother's execution, nor leaves not his pastime and hunting more than of before'.[3] The Kirk chronicler David Calderwood, noting how 'outwardly he seemed to be sorrowful', perversely interpreted that as a sign of 'inward joy. Yea,' he continued, Maitland 'was so ashamed of his behaviour that night, that he caused ish the chamber [made the courtiers void the chamber], that there might be few or no spectators. He said that night to some few that were beside him, "I am now sole king."'[4] But according to Moysie, when he was given a vivid description of Mary's very bloody execution by one of the court ladies, he 'was very sad and pensive all that day and would not sup that night'.[5]

For the benefit of his Scottish audience, James maintained a cold and absolute silence towards England. All communication with England was cut off. Even Elizabeth's personal ambassador, her kinsman Sir Robert Carey, was halted at the border. George Young, Clerk of the Privy Council, was sent to declare to him on 22 February that if the King's mother were alive, and Carey could assure him of it, then Carey 'should be right welcome, and he would be glad to hearken to any accord'; if Mary were dead, on the other hand, Carey could go home and tell his Queen that she should stick at doing him that one injury, rather than seeking to do another 'in bringing him to accord with the price of his mother's blood'. It was, like most of

James's posturing, an act, but one he maintained, uncharacteristically, for several weeks. In private, however, James could not help remarking privately to Courcelles that he was impressed by Elizabeth's choice of messenger, whom he 'esteemed and loved well', 'being furnished with diverse gentlemanly qualities' whom he had previously met during Walsingham's embassy: indeed, he had requested Carey as a resident ambassador, but Elizabeth had 'sent him only old doting Randall [Randolph]'. Courcelles, sensing that the King was weakening, urged him to stand firm: James 'could not but blemish his honour greatly, by treating with those, whose hands were yet red with his mother's blood as was likely'; Elizabeth had sent a messenger 'whom she knew he had a liking of' so that the news might be softened somewhat.[6]

Finally, on 4 March, via Archibald Douglas, the Scottish court received a full and gory written account of Mary's execution. According to Courcelles, 'the King would not abide to hear [it] read out', and 'would not seem to believe it' until he received news from Carey. When Young returned with official confirmation of the execution the following day, James sent him back immediately to fetch Elizabeth's letters, and retired to Dalkeith, 'with very small company, greatly grieved with the death of his mother, which he taketh infinitely at heart', in Courcelles' words. After a hasty trip to Edinburgh to pass on Carey's confirmation of the fact, Young returned to Berwick to tell Carey that James 'was not to receive any strangers at this time, but if he had any letter from her Majesty', he would accept it passed through his courtiers. Carey, however, had instructions to hand over the letters only directly to the King.[7] He sent an agent to Scotland who reported that 'as yet the King would receive no ambassador, partly by reason of his heaviness and sorrowing for his mother, and also for that he is not resolved that the Queen is as sorry for his mother's death as he was informed she was'. Moreover, the agent reported, James claimed he would be unable to control the vengeful instincts of the Scottish people, who were 'wickedly bent and evilly given'.[8] When cries of protest came from England, James denied that he had refused to receive Elizabeth's letter, for it would be against equity and law, he added barbedly, to 'refuse to admit a trial' or to 'condemn a person unheard'. 'As for any proofs she has given of her innocency yet,' he continued, 'we remit it to her own judgement whether she has yet satisfied the world to her honour in that matter, or not.'[9]

Eventually, a meeting with Carey was fixed at Foulden, near Berwick, on 14 March, with Sir Robert Melville representing James. Carey presented Elizabeth's letter, now a month old. The Queen wrote of 'the extreme dolor that overwhelmeth my mind for that miserable accident which far contrary to my meaning hath been befallen'. She claimed 'how innocent I am in this case . . . if I had bidden do it I would have abiden by it.' She was 'not so base-minded' to deny something she had done. 'I am not of so base a lineage nor carry so vile a mind; but as not to disguise fits most a king, so will I never dissemble my actions, but cause them show even as I mean them.'[10] Carey was left to make Elizabeth's excuses: that, despite the 'daily persuasions of her Council', she had 'never thought to put the Queen your mother to death'. However, she had 'news every day both out of Spain and France, of ships and men preparing for the overthrow of her Majesty and the delivery of your mother'; rumours in her own court of men landing in various parts of the realm, followed by reports that Fotheringay had been 'broken open and the Queen escaped away'. All these 'bred jealousy in her Majesty's head' and led her 'to suspect the worse'. So she ordered a warrant to be made, sealed and delivered and handed it to her Secretary, Francis Davison; but Davison showed it to some others who 'without more questions asking, called the whole Council together, straight determined her death, and sent present expedition for the performing of it'. Davison was now in the Tower of London 'and will hardly escape her high displeasure'. Carey reported all this is writing, 'which if I could declare unto your Majesty so well, and set it down so lively as I heard her speak it with so heavy a heart, and so discontented a countenance, I think verily you would rather pity her unpleasant life (which ever since she hath endured) than blame her for the fact, which she never consented unto'.[11]

James's reply to Elizabeth was short and to the point. Since, he wrote, 'ye purge yourself of yon unhappy fact', and considering her 'rank and sex, consanguinity and long professed goodwill to the defunct', and her oft-protested innocence, he dared not wrong her by judging dishonourably her 'unspotted part' in the affair. Not everyone would make such a generous interpretation, he hinted, hoping that her 'honorable behaviour' in times to come might 'fully persuade the whole world of the same'. For his own part, he looked to her for 'a full satisfaction' which would 'be a mean to strengthen and unite this isle, establish and maintain the true religion, and oblige me to be, as of before I was, your most loving and dearest brother'.[12] Elizabeth's Lord Treasurer Burghley complained to Carey of James's 'strange course', and let it be known that Elizabeth thought these a 'strange kind of speeches', so 'repugnant' from the previous friendship between the two sovereigns, that she intended not to reply, but to wait until the King reverted to his usual tone. The King of Scots, Burghley continued, appeared to intend 'to suspend his former manner of intelligence until he may be better satisfied of her Majesty's innocency', implying that the English Queen, who was answerable to no one but God, was somehow on trial. Surely, Burghley persisted, 'the word and writing of a Christian prince uttered with a free conscience in the sight of God' was enough?[13] Secretary Walsingham weighed in, writing a long discourse to Maitland, now Chancellor, that argued strongly that James should not consider revenge or allying with France or Spain.[14] Burghley hoped, in a letter to Archibald Douglas, that James should not listen to counsel from 'passionate pleasing men' that would lose him 'the hearts of great numbers living', that is, the English, would vouchsafe for him 'more good than his mother's life could have done if she had continued'. After all, the Lord Treasurer pointed out, Mary 'by nature was to die before him, and cannot be recovered'.[15]

An outbreak of trouble on the Borders, which James did little to quell, increased English fears. Time and again, rumours of an immediate invasion made the rounds in Berwick, which prepared itself for an assault.[16] Elizabeth sent one of her most senior advisers, Henry Carey, first Lord Hunsdon (father of Sir Robert Carey who had brought the news of Mary's death) to attempt to salvage the broken relationship. In July, James made his demands: he wanted a formal letter, signed by Elizabeth, acknowledging him as 'lawful and nearest successor to the Crown, failing her bodily succession'. In addition, as a token 'to remove all kind of suspicion of her evil meaning, specially after the infernal proceeding against his dearest mother', she should make him a donation of 'some lands in England, chiefly in the north parts, of ample and sufficient revenue, with the title of Duke'.[17] He also demanded the right to be consulted about the marriage of Arbella

Stuart, the daughter and heir of his uncle, Lord Charles Stuart. Arbella was his nearest rival to the English throne, and although as the daughter of a younger son her claim was clearly subordinate to his as son of an elder son, she had the crucial advantage of having been born and bred in England, which many argued was a prerequisite for an English sovereign.[18] James felt that Elizabeth needed to exonerate herself from 'yon unhappy fact', but his chosen penalty – material benefits to himself – compromised his moral highground. Using Douglas in London as a secondary channel of communication, he intimated that, as an alternative, he could so very easily seek revenge for his mother's death, and take up the many offers of support from Catholic states overseas. Douglas informed the English that James was held back only by moral constraints, 'but ye may be sure he cannot be long restrained'. James's every move was watched. Hunsdon maintained that James had 'no good meaning' towards the English Queen, and that troops from France and Spain were expected in Scotland. At the close of the Scottish Parliament on 29 July, Maitland made a speech before the King and the nobility calling for 'a revenge for the death of the Queen'; all the lords made a solemn vow on their knees 'that they would always be ready to aid and assist him, both with the hazard of lands, lives, and goods, whensoever his Majesty should command them in that action'.[19] In London, Archibald Douglas was forced to face English protests about the Parliament, and answered questions to the satisfaction of the Privy Council. Sir Lewis Bellenden, the Scottish Justice Clerk, asked for understanding in interpreting James's actions – he had to show Scotland that he had neither abetted nor acquiesced in Mary's execution.[20] By November, Hundson was reporting that James was to receive money from Spain which would provide for a simultaneous Scottish and Spanish assault on England. Even Hunsdon, though, did not rule out the possibility of a positive end to this troubled period 'in this dangerous time'. He advised that Elizabeth should send a letter through him – since James could not accept an openly friendly letter from England – and the letter should offer an increased pension.[21]

England was right to suspect that James was looking to Catholic princes. In addition to his tetchy diplomatic ballet with Elizabeth's councillors, James was in contact with the Duc de Guise, and Henri

III of France, using Mary's death to encourage funding for Scotland.[22] This was bad news to Spain who believed that James was a hopeless heretic, lost to the Catholic cause, and better off supplanted. King Philip quickly set about sabotaging James's new Catholic overtures. With beautiful timing, Philip discovered that in fact *he* was the heir to Elizabeth's throne, with two clean bloodlines leading back to Edward III's son, John of Gaunt. And if that claim failed to convince, Philip announced that James's mother had named him her heir in her last will and testament. Angry with her son in May 1586, Mary had indeed intimated to the Spanish agent Bernardino de Mendoza that she intended to make her throne over to Philip: 'I have made the decision that in the case that my son does not conform to the Catholic religion before my death (which, I must tell you, I have little hope of as long as he remains in Scotland) to cede and give my right, by will, in the succession of this crown, to the King.'[23] The will itself, much talked of, never came to light – presumably because it never existed. As Mary died, Philip urged his claims on Pope Sixtus V asking for his support in a crusade to supplant the 'young heretic' James and to place his daughter, the Infanta, on the Scottish throne.[24]

It was only in later years that James started to exhibit a real defensiveness towards the memory of the mother whose death, in all probability, he had done his share to bring about. In 1596, when Edmund Spenser brought out the second part of his epic poem *The Faerie Queene*, James made a formal objection to Elizabeth concerning the character Duessa, the murderous, treacherous, adulterous, impious woman whom many read to represent Mary, demanding that 'Edward [sic] Spencer for his fault, may be duly tried and punished'.[25] When James reached England in 1603, one of his first acts was to send a velvet pall to cover the tomb of his mother in Peterborough Cathedral; ten years later, at his order, Mary's body was exhumed and reburied in Westminster Abbey, where her monument faced that of Elizabeth. 'Our dearest mother,' James wrote to the Dean of Peterborough, should be 'in our Church of Westminster, the place where the kings and queens of this realm are usually interred.'[26]

England was further discouraged by the latest rising star in James's court, whose ascent was aided by the fall of the Master of Gray. Soon after his return from England, Gray had been accused by Sir William Stewart that he had confessed that he and Maitland had been involved in the action at Stirling in November 1585. Gray denied ever having said this, but he was nonetheless warded in Edinburgh Castle and in May 1587 formally accused of a series of crimes, including trafficking with Spain and the Pope; planning the assassination of Maitland; counterfeiting the King's stamp, and attempting to use it to prevent the King's marriage; and for consenting to Mary's death in return for rewards in England. Gray confessed to sedition, and of trying to impede James's marriage, but at James's intervention was saved from death and financial ruin by being permitted to enjoy the profits from his estates, while being banished from the realm.[27] A sole exception to the Gray estates was the abbacy of Dunfermline, most of which the King gave to George Gordon, Earl of Huntly. Huntly was four years older than the King, and had been sixth Earl of Huntly since 1576 after his father 'deceased suddenly one afternoon coming from the football'.[28] As early as 1579, he had been identified as the key to Roman Catholic hopes in Scotland – in the words of the exiled Catholic Bishop of Ross, the Earl, then only eighteen years old, was the man on whom hopes should be pinned to 'restore the worship of God in Scotland, one of these days'.[29] As the prime landed magnate in the north, with influence in the burgh of Aberdeen and on the Moray Firth, with their deep-water ports, Huntly was seen as strategically placed to forward Catholic hopes; years spent in France only consolidated his Francophile and Catholic leanings, and his value rose as in time he became one of James's favourites.

The Kirk was dismayed, letting the King know of their 'grief that sundry papists of great calling are promoted to offices and benefices; and that such, and others of high rank within the country, take upon them the maintenance of Papists and idolators' – Huntly's name headed the list of the guilty parties.[30] At the July 1587 Parliament, Huntly, now a Privy Councillor, bore the sword at the opening ceremonies, and was made one of four Lords of the Articles.[31] By mid-August, an anonymous 'advertiser in Scotland' was informing Walsingham that 'My Lord of Huntly is indeed a great courtier and knows more of the King's secrets nor [than] any man at this present doth';[32] Ogilvy of Powrie reported that Huntly 'now remains ordinarily at court, and that by his Majesty's special command'.[33]

Whatever his motivation, James's sudden show of favour towards Huntly turned out to be a canny move. With Mary dead, Scottish Catholics may have gained a perfect martyr, but they had lost a living figurehead: Huntly was the most obvious choice as successor, but by entering James's circle, his potential danger might be significantly diluted. James now held the disaffected Kirk and the disaffected Catholics in an uneasy balance, made all the more tenuous by the perennial insecurity of Huntly's relationship with the King. Scotland's state papers of the period are littered with conflicting accounts of James's favour towards the Earl, and Huntly's irritation with James's insistence on maintaining positive relations with England. More than once, Huntly made a show of leaving court to express his anger and disappointment with the King. Nevertheless, Huntly's position at court was shored up when, on 21 July 1588, he married Lady Henrietta Stuart, one of the daughters of James's beloved Esmé, shipped over from France at a cost of five thousand marks, voted by the Privy Council.[34] James himself contributed verses to an entertainment at the wedding festivities featuring men portraying Mercury, nymphs and zani.[35] At their marriage, Huntly and his wife publicly renounced Roman Catholicism and embraced the reformed faith. Thomas Fowler wrote that 'The King, desiring to have him his familiar in court, persuaded him from papistry, and, as he thought prevailed.' At Huntly's subscription to the Kirk, James 'rejoiced exceedingly', and the Earl was subsequently 'lodged in the King's chamber, and had place in the King's favour above all others'. Huntly's *modus operandi* was very different from that of his predecessor Lennox, however. The Earl, Fowler observed, 'never meddled in matters of state'; instead, he 'followed [the King] in all pastime and would flatter and feed his humour in whatever exceedingly'. Indeed, continued Fowler, Huntly was 'shallow witted. But he hath shrewd counsellors about him whose advice he follows.'[36]

These shrewd counsellors understood that, Catholic sympathies aside, Huntly could be the invaluable linchpin of an anti-Maitland party. Maitland's rise — as Secretary in 1584, Vice-Chancellor and Keeper of the Great Seal in 1586, and finally Chancellor in 1587 — had been seen as a triumph for those committed to Protestantism and good relations with England, but there were many who opposed some, if not all, of these supposed achievements. Round Huntly there now coalesced a *de facto* opposition, politically conservative, supportive of the nobility against what they saw as the lower-born Maitland's advances on their privileges, and generally drawn to France rather than England. There was indeed a Catholic tinge to the Huntly faction, which included Errol, Lennox, Crawford, Seton and Maxwell, but its politics also drew Protestants such as Atholl, Montrose and Lord John Hamilton; certain courtiers, including Bothwell, Glamis and Gray vacillated between Maitland and Huntly.[37]

James neatly balanced his intimate favour for Huntly with a display of his orthodox Protestantism. As part of his campaign to keep the Kirk sweet, James spent the winter months 'in commenting of the Apocalypse and in setting out of sermons thereupon against the Papists and Spaniards'.[38] The former was *A Fruitful Meditation*, published in early 1588 and expanded to five times its length as *Paraphrase upon the Revelation of the Apostle S. John* in 1616; it marked the King's first entry into theological writing, which was later to become a passion.[39] James also put his grasp of Church doctrine to public test by challenging to a debate a leading Jesuit, Father James Gordon – Huntly's uncle, no less. The encounter turned into a marathon five-hour scholarly exchange, in which James, tellingly, displayed none of the vehemence or tantrums he was prone to when debating with Kirk ministers. At the end, the two men praised each other graciously and generously, with Gordon conceding that no man 'use his arguments better nor quote the Scriptures and other authorities more effectively' than James.[40] In his chamber, however, according to Bernardino de Mendoza, James declared 'that Gordon did not understand the Scripture, which is a fairly bold thing to say'. What could be expected though, Mendoza sneered, from a King who had 'the assurance to translate Revelation and to write upon the subject as if he were Amadis de Gaule himself'.[41]

In the spring of 1588, James was forced to turn his attention to more pressing matters. Rumours reached James that Huntly, Crawford and Montrose in the north, and Maxwell and Lord Claud Hamilton in the south were plotting to bring a Spanish army to Scotland, and to force his conversion to the old faith. In fact, Spain was not interested in Scotland, but the rumour served to bolster those still faithful to Catholicism, and to rally troops at Dunfermline and Linlithgow.

At the beginning of May, Maxwell 'passed through the country with a plaid about him, like a wayfaring man';[42] the King denounced him as a rebel, but friends still flocked to him. James soon showed himself 'earnest to proceed against Maxwell', and levied one hundred horse and two hundred footmen, but rumour had it that he had also ridden to Calder for secret negotiations with Maxwell and Lord John Hamilton, a charge strenuously denied by James's entourage.[43] As James advanced, Maxwell's castles surrendered one by one until only Lochmaben remained, holding out until 9 June, when the royal forces seized the castle, hanging the captain and five garrison men, and bringing Lord Maxwell back to Edinburgh as a prisoner.[44] The incident demonstrated to James that he should not be too complacent about his neutralisation of the Catholic threat, and from then on he was more careful: when Huntly invited him to attend a banquet at Dunfermline, James accepted readily enough; but then he panicked during the night, and left secretly and in great haste before dawn. The old nervousness, of the King 'nourished in fear', was back.

While the Scottish Catholics was countered with relative ease, a greater threat was on the horizon. In July, England braced herself for the Spanish Armada that her intelligencers had long reported was being prepared for an attack on her shores. At this most crucial moment, the new English ambassador in Scotland, William Asheby opted, without any authority, to offer James whatever was needed to keep him on the side of the English – promises that included an English dukedom, funds to keep a royal guard and to police the Borders, and a yearly pension of £5,000. James, predictably fired with a new enthusiasm for England, wrote to Elizabeth: 'In times of straits true friends are most tried, now merits the thanks of you and your country, who kithes [shows] himself a friend to your country and estate; and this time must move me to utter my zeal to the religion how new a kinsman and neighbour I find myself to you and your country.' He had therefore offered her 'my forces, my person, and all that I may command to be employed against your strangers on whatsomever fashion and whatsomever mean as may best serve for the defence of your country. Wherein I promise to behave myself not as a stranger and foreign prince, but as your natural son and compatriot of your country in all respects.' Calling for commissioners to confirm

Asheby's offer, he continued 'I protest I desire not for that I would have the reward to precede the deserts, but only that I with honour, and a[ll] my good subjects with a fervent good will may embrace this your godly and honest cause, whereby your adversaries will have ado not with England but with the whole Isle of Britain.'[45]

Unfortunately for Asheby and James, by the time these offers were rashly made and enthusiastically accepted, the international political situation had altered beyond recognition. The Spanish fleet set sail from Corunna on 12 July and were in English waters within a week; England's fleet, commanded by the Lord Admiral Howard of Effingham, engaged them on the 21st. For the next ten days, the two fleets were consumed in battle, but on the night of the 28th, the Armada suffered grievous losses from English fireships, and on the following day the battle of Gravelines made England's victory clear. The Spanish ships fled northwards, and started a slow and costly return to the homeland by circumnavigating the British Isles.

On 11 August, Asheby received two letters, portentously written in Sir Francis Walsingham's own hand, informing him that he had committed a 'great oversight' 'in the offering to the King, it being done without commission.' In replying, Asheby threw himself on Elizabeth's mercy, but even as he grovelled, he reiterated the urgency of an Anglo-Scottish pact: 'What danger and utter ruin must needs follow if the minds of these two princes be not firmly knit together, all the world doth foresee.'[46] From Paris, the disgraced Master of Gray saw James's position with clearer eyes. 'I am sorry to know from Scotland,' he wrote to Archibald Douglas, 'that the King our master has of all the golden mountains offered received a fiddler's wages.'[47]

The Armada may have been crushed, but the Kirk still saw papists under every trundlebed. In January 1589, the ministers presented petitions to the King and the Council urging vigilance, and urging the King 'to purge his house, Council, and Session, and to retire his power of lieutenantry, wardenry, and other his authority whatsomever, from all and whatsomever person avowed or suspected to be Papists'. Their insistence seemed vindicated on 27 February. James was sitting with the Lords of the Session at the Tolbooth, about to rise as usual at twelve, when a packet was presented to him by the English ambassador

Asheby. He was informed that it contained matters from the Low Countries, but on retiring he discovered it was in fact a set of letters, intercepted by English agents, from Huntly and Errol among others, to King Philip II of Spain and his commander the Duke of Parma, all of them expressing regret that Philip had not thought to use Scotland as a landing point for the Armada, and requesting men and money to help invade England. Also implicated were Crawford, Maxwell, Lord Claud Hamilton, and the Protestant Bothwell.[48]

The mere fact of correspondence between Scotland and Spain was hardly shocking: James himself had written to Parma only two months earlier.[49] But these letters laid open a treacherous negotiation of some three years' standing with one Robert Bruce (decidedly *not* to be confused with the Kirk minister) acting as their intermediary – indeed, in early 1587, Bruce had negotiated with Parma to smuggle Spanish-paid soldiers into Scotland in the hulls of thirty grain ships. Moreover, the letters contained evidence that Spain had been funding Huntly's party.[50] What really mortified James was that the treachery had been uncovered by English agents, allowing their Queen to rub salt in the wound, and indeed, Elizabeth's covering letter made no attempt to conceal her glee. She had told him before, she reminded him, that she would be his 'faithful watch, to shun all mishaps or dangers'. Now these letters 'of high treason to your person and kingdom' are nothing more or less than 'as in a glass, the true portraiture of my late warning letters'. If only he had followed her advice, instead of just reading it, 'you might have taken their persons, received their treason, and shunned their further strengthening'. Instead, their strength 'hath grown daily by your too great neglecting and suffering of so many practices which, at the beginning, might easily have been prevented'. 'Good Lord!' she continued, 'methink I do but dream: no king a week would bear this! Their forces assembled, and held near your person, held plots to take your person near the seaside; and all this wrapped up with giving them offices, that they might the better accomplish their treason!' Now he must listen to reason. 'Of a suddenly [immediately] they must be clapped up in safer custody than some others have been, which hath bred their laughter.'[51]

Under such pressure, James had to be seen to take action against Huntly, but the action was so mild as to be laughable. The Earl was held in Edinburgh Castle, his own choice of prison, to await trial, but his wife, servants and friends were given free access and, within a day, James and Maitland were seen going to the castle to dine with Huntly, where, according to the English agent Thomas Fowler, the King 'entertained Huntly as well and kindly as ever, yea he kissed him at times to the amazement of many' exclaiming that 'he knew he was innocent'. Huntly's friends were 'in fury' at his imprisonment, reported Fowler, and using 'threatenings and proud words to many, specially to Englishmen', who blamed James directly through his 'fond dealing'. 'It is thought,' he concluded, 'that this King is too much carried by young men that lies in his chamber and is his minions.'[52] As if to mourn the loss of his favourite, James refused to go hunting while Huntly was imprisoned, and visited him every day until his release on 7 March, on which night Huntly slept in James's bedchamber.[53]

Yet James's displays of affection for Huntly were not without a political motive. James's immediate objective was precisely to maintain the factionalism that proved so supportive of his own position. James, it seems, understood Huntly's machinations to have less to do with designs against the King, and more to do with challenging the power of Chancellor Maitland. The conspirators claimed that the intercepted letters were devised by Maitland and sent into England deliberately to be intercepted, or that they were part of an English plot devised to set the Scots 'together by the ears', at each other's throats.[54] So James welcomed Huntly into his bedchamber, but when Maitland objected to the restoration of Huntly to the captaincy of the royal guard (which had been taken from the Earl for a few days), James was quick to climb down, and reinstate the penalty, commanding Huntly to retire to his country estates. More immediately important to the King than appeasing England was keeping his very different favourites in line – not necessarily with each other, but with him. Maitland and Huntly had equal but different calls on the King's love and favour. As the English intelligencer Thomas Fowler put it, 'The King hath a strange, extraordinary affection to Huntly, such as is yet unremoveable, and thereby could persuade his majesty to any matters to serve his own particulars of friends.' Maitland, on the other hand, 'is beloved of the King in another sort, for he manages the whole affairs of the country. He sees he cannot be without him; he finds his whole care for his well-doing, and yet hath flattered the King too much. The King hath had a special care to make and keep these, his two well-beloved servants, friends, but it never lasted forty days without some suspicion or jar.' Recently, Fowler reported, Maitland had abandoned all politic flattery, and now dealt with James 'most plainly and stoutly', telling him that if he continued to support Huntly as he did, then 'he would not have a protestant in Scotland to follow or acknowledge him'. Nevertheless, Fowler continued, if James had his way, 'he will have Huntly in court again within a month . . . When Huntly or his solicitors come in place he forgets all, and many say they doubt him bewitched.'[55]

James stayed with Maitland for a fortnight in early March, and the Chancellor took the opportunity to press home what he should do: Huntly must be banished, he urged, and James accepted.[56] Before going north to his estates, Huntly invited James to hunt and dine with him one last time on 13 March. When they met, Huntly claimed that he had heard rumours that Edinburgh was in 'tumult', the citizens 'in arms' and likely to turn against him, and that a plot by Maitland's party was planned for that afternoon. (In fact, it seems that the Provost of Edinburgh had secretly told the town's burgesses 'to have their armour and weapons in their booths, ready for whatsomever adventure, because he had heard that there was a variance among the nobility.') Errol then appeared with a dozen horsemen, and he, Huntly and Bothwell spent an hour urging the King to go with them 'to some neuter place' but James refused, threatening 'if they attempted any such thing against his heart, they should never have his heart, and if ever he find his time, to be revenged'.[57] Finally, the King returned to the planned banquet; Huntly, presumably believing himself vulnerable to attack, rode instead to his house at Dunfermline, and from there via Perth to Strathbogie. James, 'in a great brangle' and 'melancoly' at Huntly's departure, was forced by Maitland to discharge Huntly's guards but continued to send the Earl regular and 'very friendly' posts.[58]

Before long, Edinburgh was buzzing with rumours that Huntly was 'convening . . . his faction'. Errol, on the other hand, claimed that the accusations against him were the work of Maitland, 'behind my back', and urged that he should be heard before his King and his peers. Maitland received word from the Master of Glamis that Huntly had assembled his followers at Brechin, and planned to march to Edinburgh. When news of this reached James, he rode posthaste from Haltoun to Edinburgh, at two in the morning on 5 April, to sleep in his Chancellor's lodging for safety. Loyal forces were commanded 'to repair to the King', while Bothwell, with men from the Borders, reached Dalkeith on 6 April. Bothwell offered himself up to James, saying he was willing to answer any accusation in any place – 'except where Chancellor Maitland was'. For his part, he had three points of treason with which to charge the Chancellor. James would not listen.[59]

Huntly, Errol and Crawford passed through Perth on 10 April, capturing the Master of Glamis in his house at Kirkhill and leading him in disgrace past his own Glamis Castle. News of this indignity reportedly 'irritate[d] his Majesty very much',[60] and Huntly was forced to write to James, assuring him that he had acted only to reveal his enemies' intention, for his own security.[61] James, however, was by now deeply hurt by Huntly's constant betrayals. 'What further trust can I have in your promises,' he wrote in a letter, 'confidence in your constancy, or estimation of your honest meaning?' Every time he gave the Earl a chance, only to be bitterly disappointed. 'Are these the fruits of your well conversion? Is this a likely purgation of your letters intercepted by England? Or is this a good proof of your honest course in my service?' Huntly had 'offended two persons in me, a particular friend and a general Christian king'. To satisfy the particular friend, the Earl had 'willingly (without irking) to be content with whatsomever form I shall please to use you in. To remit fully to my discretion your contentment in all things. To use yourself in whatsomever thing as I shall direct you . . . Never to trust hereafter but such as I trust. And finally to repent you of all your faults, that in heart and mouth with the forlorn [prodigal] son ye may say' – misquoting the book of Luke – 'Peccavi in caelum et contra te [I have sinned against heaven and against you]'.[62]

On 9 April, James rode to Linlithgow with 140 horse; at his request, Edinburgh sent a further two hundred. Perth was the meeting point for Huntly, Errol, Crawford, Bothwell and Montrose. As James gathered strength, he advanced from Linlithgow to Stirling to Perth, whence the lords had recently departed for Aberdeen. By the time he reached Dundee, James had two thousand men to move to Brechin, and thence to Cowie. By now James had taken on the role of military leader. Warned that the enemy might attack while they slept, the royal forces kept watch for two nights, at Brechin and Dunnottiris. 'His Majesty would not so much as lie down on his bed that night, but went about like a good captain encouraging us,' wrote John Colville on 18 April.[63] A few days later, English agent Thomas Fowler confirmed this verdict: 'The King hath marched already almost six score miles, and means to go forward three or score miles further. It hath been very painful to him already, but not as it will be. Never was prince more willing than he in this journey against these false ingrateful traitors who have deceived him.' The demands on James's time and energy were immense. 'This people must have free access to the King's presence: if there were no more but the continual disquiet of such a throng from morning to night and their entertainment, it were too much toil for any prince; but he must visit their watches nightly, he must comfort them, be pleasant with them passing from place to place, that in effect day or night the good King has little quiet and less rest. He hath watched two nights and never put off [taken off] his clothes.'[64]

As the King reached Cowie, Huntly, Crawford and Errol came to the Brig o' Dee with three thousand men. By this time, James had hardly one thousand of his own, but the simple knowledge that he was present had a strange effect on the rebel earls' men. As Calderwood tells it, Huntly had 'made many to believe' that he had a royal commission to muster forces – an assumption that James's presence clearly proved to be false. Unsurprising, then, that 'fear seized upon the most part of Huntly's faction when they heard the King was in person in the fields.' While Errol was keen to fight on, Huntly was reluctant, and as their men deserted, and many northern barons defected to the royal troops, their situation became untenable. On 20 April, despite the sorry state of his troops, James entered Aberdeen without opposition. Since Huntly had not surrendered, James 'purposed to go forward to his lands, to demolish his castles and houses, and specially Strabogie [Strathbogie]'. In secret, however, Huntly was told that if he threw himself on the King's mercy his punishment would be mild. As James reached Terrysoule, Huntly finally 'came in', and was committed to prison, without being allowed to see the King. His work done, James returned to Edinburgh; Crawford later turned himself in on 20 May, claiming that Huntly had misled him, by implying that he had a commission to levy forces.[65]

While James was in the north, Bothwell and his men had been marauding through Cannongate, Edinburgh, Leith and Dalkeith 'living dissolutely'. On the King's return, Bothwell used his influence with some of James's close attendants to gain access to him on 11 May, as the King strolled in the garden of the house where he was staying. Bothwell 'meanly apparelled' in 'a long black cloak', 'in a wet alley fell on his knees to the King', craving pardon and 'protesting that he had no intent to do evil to his Majesty nor to the religion'. This time James was not listening, and 'suffered him to sit a long time upon his knees without any answer', committing him to the attention of the new Captain of the Guard, William Hume.[66] Under examination, Bothwell denied that he had made any attempt against the King or the true religion, and insisted that he had gathered men only to support him in his ongoing feud with Maitland. Both Bothwell and Crawford were convicted of treason: Bothwell warded in Tamtallon, and Crawford in the Castle of St Andrews. Huntly, whose punishment was left to the King, was sent to Borthwick Castle. But as Calderwood noted sourly, James 'meant no great harm to the convicted, for they were soon after set at liberty'. The return from England, around the same time, of the Master of Gray with Lord Hunsdon only added to the general disillusionment with the King's performance of justice – 'banishment was but only for the fashion'.[67]

CHAPTER SEVEN

The New Rib

J AMES WAS SOON to have an all too brief respite from the factionalism riddling Scottish politics. In 1589, the King turned twenty-
three, by contemporary standards a dangerously advanced age for
a reigning sovereign to remain unmarried and, more pertinently,
without an heir. There had long been rumours of possible brides, of
course. When James was still considered a potential convert to Rome,
there was talk of a marriage to the Pope's niece. Since at least 1583,
rumours had persistently come from Spain that James was about to
turn Catholic and marry a daughter of King Philip:[1] as late as 1588,
Lord Burghley thought it worthwhile routinely to interrogate any
captive Spaniards on the subject.[2] But in the search for a Protestant
bride, two courts were looked to by the King's counsellors: Huguenot
Navarre, and Lutheran Denmark.

A Danish match, building on the centuries-old trading links between
the two countries, was mooted as early as 1582;[3] in the summer of 1585
a Danish embassy was received in Scotland. By October 1586, the
possibility had been brought to the attention of Elizabeth and it was
noted that 'The Queen is not much pleased with the King of Scots'
match with Denmark.'[4] But it was only after Mary's death that James
made serious steps towards finding a wife, 'while as yet the memory
of the execution of his mother was recent in men's minds', as David
Calderwood put it.[5] On 26 March 1587, emissaries were sent to both
Navarre and Denmark, 'to treat upon a match to the king'. The Navarre
reconnaissance mission found a likely bride in Catherine de Bourbon,
sister to King Henri of Navarre, to whom all Protestant France looked
(and who would in 1589 become Henri IV of France). This was a
match that would have pleased George Buchanan: his correspondence
includes two letters from 1580 in which friends at the Navarre court
urged him to forward the match, although by that date his influence
over James had severely declined.[6] James's other tutor Peter Young was
despatched to Denmark in March 1587 alongside Sir Patrick Vans of
Barnbarroch, with a remit to express interest in either of King
Frederick's two daughters, Elizabeth and Anna, but with no commit-

ment and no discussion of money and the vexed question of sovereignty over the Orkney islands (which Scotland then had as part of a messy marriage bargain in the fifteenth century). This mission was not particularly successful – access to the Danish king was difficult, and the elder daughter was suddenly contracted elsewhere – and the men returned home in August.

The pendulum swung towards Navarre in June when James's idol, the poet Guillaume Salluste du Bartas, visited the Scottish court as an unofficial envoy from Henri, accompanying James to hear a theology lecture by Andrew Melvill at St Andrews. In September, James sent William Melville of Tongland (brother of Sir James Melville) to report on Catherine; Melville brought back 'a good report of her rare qualities' and a portrait of the princess.[7] In September 1588, James wrote a flattering letter to Catherine referring to his 'intentions'[8] but Catherine replied in December saying his letter was 'too much care and remembrance of me from so far away', and could only be inspired by James's friendship for her brother the King.[9] Meanwhile, Danish hopes had been kept alive by Colonel William Stewart, the Prior of Pittenweeme. In February of 1588, acting very much on his own initiative, he travelled to Denmark to gain assurances that Anna would be available should James ask. King Frederick finally died in April, just as the Convention of Estates voted to grant James a tax of £100,000 over the next three years, making a marriage financially viable. Another Scottish embassy to Denmark, ending in November, produced further assurances about the size of the dowry.

With the options well matched, there was also the matter of age to be considered: Catherine was thirty-one while Anna was fourteen. Some urged that 'it is much better for the King to match with a wise staid woman than with a child, considering his careless disposition';[10] others saw greater child- and heir-bearing potential in Anna than in Catherine, 'old, cracked and something worse if all were known'.[11] It was in early 1589, according to Sir James Melville, that James finally put his mind to the question of which to choose. 'His Majesty determined first to seek counsel of God by earnest prayer, to direct him where it would be meetest for the weal of himself and his country. So that after fifteen days' advertisement and devout prayer, as said is, he called his Council together in his cabinet and told them how he had been advising and praying to God the space of fifteen days to move his heart the way that was meetest, and that he was resolved to marry in Denmark.'[12] But there may have been a more pragmatic reason. On 28 May, there was a riot in Edinburgh led by local officials against Maitland, apparently because they believed that Maitland was opposed to the Danish marriage – which they wanted in order to guarantee and further Edinburgh's trade with Denmark. It seems unlikely that the riot was instigated by James himself, as Sir James Melville suggested, but it certainly strengthened the case for a match with the Danish princess.[13] For a few weeks, James kept up the pretence that he was still considering Navarre. By the summer, Henri had heard rumours that Scotland was looking elsewhere. James quickly wrote to reassure him, asking to be commended to his sister and apologising that he had not had sufficient leisure – 'as the present scrawling will bear sufficient witness – and you know that it doesn't do to present anything other than *l'exquis* to the ladies' – and assuring him that 'in spite of all contrary reports that might have come to your ears', he remained his greatest supporter.[14] But by now the decision was already made.

On 18 June, an embassy led by George Keith, fifth Earl Marischal, left Leith for Denmark. This time negotiations proceeded smoothly: Anna was wedded by proxy to James on 20 August, and set sail for her new home.[15] In Scotland, elaborate plans were developed dictating 'the manner how to receive the Queen'. Despite the pomp, there was a touching concern for young Anna's sensibilities. Peter Young's formal 'harangue in Latin' was to be executed 'as briefly as may be'; everywhere she was to walk was to be 'laid with Turkey tapis or tapestry'; there was to be 'no working in the ships foreanent [outside] her lodging, during her remaining in Leith, nor nothing on the bounds within the two new ports that may unquiet her'; there was to be 'no shooting . . . while the Queen be in her chamber'.[16]

But three weeks later, and there was still no sign of the ship carrying Anna. On 12 September, Lord Dingwall landed at Leith, and reported that 'he had come in company with the Queen's fleet three hundred miles, and was separated from them by a great storm: it was feared that the Queen was in danger upon the seas'.[17] For some sixteen or seventeen days James stayed with Robert, sixth Lord Seton, at his home, Seton House, which afforded him a view of the Firth of Forth and any Leith-bound ship.[18] When none appeared, the King 'very impatient and sorrowful for her long delay',[19] ordered a fast to be held to ensure Anna's safe arrival.[20] As September turned into October, Colonel Stewart was 'directed to Norway, to see what was word of the Queen'.[21] He took with him a letter from James, written in French, and headed 'The King to the Queen of Scotland in Norraway':

> Only to one who knows me as well as his own reflection in a glass could I express, my dearest love, the fears which I have experienced because of the contrary winds and the violent storms since you embarked, the more especially since the arrival here of some ships which put to sea after your own and came without word of you. My resultant anguish, and the fear which ceaselessly pierces my heart, has driven me to despatch a messenger to seek for you, both to bring me news of you and to give you the same of me . . . Praying you therefore to give credence to all that he will say to you on my behalf, I make an end praying the Creator (my only love) with all my heart to grant you a safe, swift and happy arrival in these parts so that you can make proof of the entire affection of him who has vowed to you alone all his love.[22]

He also composed a serious of marvellously overwrought sonnets, in one of which all possibility of romance was obliterated by an overly graphic account of the torments James felt:

> O cruel Cupid what a ruthless rage,
> What hateful wrath thou utterest upon me;
> No medicine my sickness may assuage
> Nor cataplasm cure my wound I see.
> Through deadly shot alive I daily die,
> I fry in flames of that envenomed dart
> Which shot me sicker in at either eye
> Then fastened fast into my hoalit heart.
> The fever hath infected every part,
> My bones are dried their marrow melts away,
> My sinnows feebles through my smoking smart

And all my blood as in a pan doth play.
I only wish for ease of all my pain,
That she might wit what sorrow I sustain.[23]

As the English ambassador William Asheby noted, James was playing to the hilt the role of 'a true lover' who 'thinketh every day a year till he see his joy and love approach'.[24]

Colonel Stewart arrived in Norway on 4 October, and learned what had happened. A flotilla, led by Anna on the *Gideon*, left Copenhagen on 5 September, but had only been able to stagger as far as Elsinore. There, accident piled on accident. That evening, a naval gun back-fired, killing two gunners. The next day, another gun fired in tribute to two visiting Scottish noblemen exploded, leaving nine of the crew injured, and another gunner dead. Once at sea, gales put the ships under immense stress, and one report had Anna's ship missing for three days and three nights. On the 10th, the *Gideon* was found to be leaking dangerously, and had to anchor at Gammel Sellohe in Norway to make repairs. In high seas, two of the other ships in the flottilla, the *Samson* and the *Josua*, collided, taking the lives of two more sailors: soon the *Samson* too was unusable, stuck in Flekkerø harbour. Ostensibly repaired, the *Gideon* set out once again on 28 September; once again sprung a leak; and once again the fleet returned to Norway, this time to Flekkerø. By now it was Michaelmas, 1 October, and the Danish sailors firmly believed that the foul weather would continue until Christmas. With boats damaged, and too many friends maimed and killed, they had no intention of going any further. By the time Colonel Stewart arrived on 4 October, the leaking *Gideon* was no longer safe (it took sixteen men to pump it as it made a final journey to Varberg in Denmark), and it was decided by Stewart and the Earl Marischal that Anna's Scottish entrance would have to be delayed until the spring. Glad to be on dry land, after a month of seasickness, Anna, with the Earl Marischal and her tiny court, rode to Akershus in Oslo.[25]

James was informed of the decision not to travel by a letter dated 7 October – a letter that ironically managed to reach him at Craigmillar Castle, near Edinburgh, in just three days. In his own account, the news upset him to the point that he 'could [not] sleep nor rest', and he made a snap decision: 'ay, upon the instant, yea very moment resolved to make possible on my part, that which was impossible on hers':[26] if his Queen could not come to Scotland, then he would go to her in Norway. In his absence, James appointed the Duke of Lennox, still only fifteen years old, as President of the Council, with Bothwell to act as his deputy, while as a strategic move to neutralise the Kirk, minister Robert Bruce was brought into the Council. Rather than risk a backlash against Maitland, James resolved to take him with him. James informed his Council to expect him back within twenty days, but he cannot really have believed he would return so quickly. These preparations made, late in the evening on 22 October, the King, Maitland, and a retinue of some three hundred, set sail from Leith.[27]

James set down his reasons for going in a letter to the Scottish people, to be read after his departure. It is a fascinating document. He knew well, he wrote, that 'the motion of my voyage at this time will be diversely skansit upon [looked upon]', resulting in 'my great dishonour' as well as 'the wrangous blame of innocents'. He therefore wanted to make it clear that he kept his plans 'generally close [secret] from all men' – including Chancellor Maitland, the man to whom he usually entrusted 'any secrets of my weightiest affairs'. He wrote this because James knew if he had confided in him, Maitland would have 'been blamed of putting it in my head', since Maitland was daily accused of leading the King 'by the nose as it were, to all his appetites, as if I were an unreasonable creature [a creature without reason] or a bairn that could do nothing of myself.' James did not want to be the cause 'of the heaping of further unjust slander upon his head'. And he proclaimed this now as much 'for my own honour's sake, that I be not unjustly slandered as an irresolute ass who can do nothing of himself'.

But the letter also gave his reasons for the marriage.

As to the causes, I doubt not it is manifestly known to all how far I was generally found fault with by all men for the delaying so long of my marriage. The reasons were that I was alone, without father or mother, brother or sister, King of this realm and heir apparent in England. This my nakedness made me to be weak and my enemies stark [strong]. One man was as no man, and the want of hope of succession bred disdain. Yes, my long delay bred in the breasts of many a great jealousy [suspicion] of my inability, as if I were a barren stock. These reasons and innumerable others, hourly objected, moved me to hasten the treaty of my marriage; for, as to my own nature, God is my witness I could have abstained longer nor [than] the weal of my patrie [country] could have permitted. I am known, God be praised, not to be intemperately rash nor conceity [flighty] in my weightiest affairs, neither use I to be so carried away with passion as I refuse to hear reason.[28]

It is a shockingly unguarded letter, written by the King in his own hand, and apparently without any advice from his close counsellors. This is no declaration of love for Anna, nor even a political, pragmatic explanation for his marriage. Instead, it testifies to James's fear of ridicule because of challenges to his masculinity. His lack of an heir makes him weak politically, but also damages his virility, as if he were incapable of being a father, not a real man. During his years with James, Lennox was libelled 'a feeble sow, that saw his wife deflowered before his eyes'.[29] More recently, there had been speculation about James's relationship with his new favourite, Alexander Lindsay, spoken of as 'the King's only minion and conceit', 'his nightly bed-fellow', and perhaps James felt the need to prove some kind of masculinity by becoming a husband.[30] But even as he asserts his virility, he admits quite openly that his own nature would not have driven him to marriage – and certainly not at this stage of his life. James was eager to share these feelings with his people, and to place his letter in the Register of the Privy Council for posterity: reading the letter now, it's difficult not to conclude that his much-vaunted romantic yearnings for Anna were little more than the conventional posturings of an amateur poet.

On 27 October James's ships were sighted off the Norwegian coast, and two days later they landed at the island of Flekkerø, where Anna had stayed; with a proper sense of romance, James insisted that he should 'sleep in the same place as she had slept earlier', 'with a poor man' at a small farmhouse.[31] Bad weather delayed James's immediate progress, and Steen Bille, who had been the Danish ambassador in Scotland, departed for Oslo to inform Anna of her husband's arrival.

As Bille left, a salute from the King's ship went awry: the cannon had been fully loaded by mistake, and what was meant to be a gesture of goodwill ended with one of Bille's kinsmen losing his arm, and a boy on another ship losing his life.[32] What James Melvill described as the 'mickle foul weather of a stormy winter'[33] slowed James's progress, and he reached Oslo only after three weeks' trek, making his entrance on the afternoon of 19 November, escorted by assorted Danish, Norwegian and Scottish nobles. To the Danes, James appeared as 'a tall, slim gentleman thin under the eyes [perhaps lean-cheeked, or with deep-set eyes?], wearing a red velvet coat appliquéd with pieces of gold so that there was a row of golden stars and another row where the velvet could be seen. He also wore a black velvet cloak lined with sable.'[34] He processed to the great hall of Old Bishops' Palace to meet his new bride. According to one chronicler, James went straight to Anna, not pausing to take off his boots. 'His Majesty minded to give the Queen a kiss after the Scots fashion at meeting, which she refused as not being the form of her country. Marry, after a few words privately spoken between His Majesty and her, there passed familiarity and kisses.'[35] The half-hour encounter was regarded as 'a joyful meeting on all sides'.[36]

Four days later, they were married in the same venue, 'with all the splendour possible at that time and place'. The hall was decorated with tapestries, and the couple stood on a piece of red cloth, with two chairs covered in red damask. At 2 p.m. the Danes and Norwegians accompanied James from his lodgings to take him to his bride. When the couple arrived, James walked on to the red cloth, standing 'with his hands on his hips'. Anna followed, to stand at his side. After some brief singing,[37] the service, a standard homily on marriage, was conducted in French by the Leith minister David Lindsay, who described the bride as 'a princess both godly and beautiful, as appeareth to all that knoweth her'.[38] After plighting their troth, the marriage was blessed, and the bishop delivered an oration in Danish. As the couple left, the local bishop saluted James in Latin, wishing him good fortune in his new marriage and in his reign. 'Hoc scio te ex corde precari' (I know that you wish it from your heart), James replied. 'Certe ex corde precatur' (certainly he wishes it from his heart), said Maitland. 'Hoc lubens accipio' (then it is dear to me), replied the King.[39] The wedding breakfast was perhaps less than spectacular: 'a reasonable banquet being on such an accident,' as one observer put it sniffily.[40] Leading Nordic scholars such as Jacob Jacobssøn Wolf, Anders Sørensen Vedel, Halvard Gunnarssøn and Jens Nielssøn wrote eulogies in Latin, and were rewarded with lavish gifts.[41] A month of celebrations followed, including a welcome day of hunting on the island of Hovedøya.[42]

On 22 December, the newlyweds set out for Denmark, to spend the first few months of their marriage at Elsinore's then newly built Kronborg Castle.[43] As James left, 'he stood up in the sledge and bade all the people good night not only in Scots but also in Danish'.[44] En route, he was 'well entertained by the way in many of the priests' houses', and, according to David Calderwood (perhaps with wishful thinking), 'he had occasion to consider and to take to heart the poverty of the ministers of Scotland, and to think upon some remeed [remedy]'.[45] On 4 January, at Bohus, the King and his Queen danced, one of the very few times James is known to have indulged since his childhood displays for visiting dignitaries.[46] Finally on 21 January, James and Anna reached Elsinore, sailing there in a small boat sumptuously furnished in red velvet. They were back in the world of courtly ceremony, and they entered the castle in a formal procession, with each Scottish councillor escorted by a member of the Danish Council. James was greeted by his mother-in-law, dowager Queen Sophia, the ten-year-old King Christian IV, Duke Ulrick, and Christian's four regents.

James was to be based at Elsinore until early March,[47] and the pervasive mood was alcoholic. Whether fairly or not, the Danes had gained an international reputation for their drinking, starting the day with the traditional Danish spirits *brændevin*, moving on to German ale, and finishing off with Prussian beer. Ben Jonson claimed that the Danes were seeking to 'drench | Their cares in wine' but more importantly, according to Cornelius Hamsfort, court doctor to Anna's father, Frederick II, drunkenness was deemed a sign of manliness. Frederick had been infamous for his drinking, indulging in a drunken fistfight at his sister's wedding, and falling from his horse into a river: the oration at his funeral frankly admitted that drinking had shortened his life. If James's baptism had spoken volumes about Scotland's factional religiosity and strained international relations, then perhaps

Christian's 1577 baptism had done the same for the Danish national character: in a mock battle between the ancient Israelites and the Philistines, the Danes playing the Philistines were drunk enough to ignore history, and refused to yield to David and his men, instead beating up the Israelites, before the entire nobility piled in.[48] The King of Scots soon acquired the habit, and Sir James Melville was only one of several who remarked on James's increasingly prodigious taste for drink. The King, he recorded, 'made good cheer and drank stoutly till the springtime'.[49]

Slowly, the drunken winter at Elsinore melted into spring. James and his entourage moved on to Copenhagen on 7 March, where more academic pursuits awaited him. He visited the Royal Academy, and imbibed learned discourse from Hans Olufsen Slangerup, the professor of theology, and Anders Christiensen, who, as professor of medicine, was an early teacher of modern practical anatomy. In conversation with the Bishop of Zealand, Povel Mathias, James insisted on his love for matters literary: he assured Mathias that 'From my earliest days I have been addicted to the literary arts [addictus sum litteris] – and I should like to declare that today.' To show his enthusiasm, he sent gifts to the Bishop to be bestowed on the University including seven large books, a gilded cup, and purses of money for some doctors who had given him a book, and for the Copenhagen hospital.[50] From Copenhagen, James moved on to the village of Roskilde on 11 and 12 March, to visit the great cathedral that served as the burial place of the kings of Denmark. James listened to a Latin oration by Mathias, and debated with Niels Hemmingsen, the elderly leading Danish theologian. Much of the doctrinal discussion centred on Hemmingsen's Calvinist-tinged Lutheranism (for which he had been removed from his office of Professor of the University of Copenhagen): a Danish account records that Hemmingsen 'discussed, with acute perception, predestination. For he was completely a disciple of Calvin.' The theologian made a huge impact on James: he confided to a local priest that meeting Hemmingsen stood alongside seeing a monument to Frederick II in Roskilde Cathedral, and witnessing the Danish churches free of idolatry, as one of the highlights of his visit.[51]

Moving on via Frederiksborg and Horsholm,[52] James reached the

island of Hveen in the Sont near Copenhagen on 20 March, home
and laboratory to the great Danish astronomer Tygo (latinised as
Tycho) Brahe. Brahe had become famous for his 1572 tract discovering
the new star in Cassiopeia, and for his lectures at the University of
Copenhagen, where he had promulgated his belief that astronomy
could only improve through systematic and accurate observation.
Anna's father, Frederick II, had sponsored Brahe's research by giving
him the island of Hveen, on which Brahe built his observatory,
Uraniborg. Brahe's home and laboratory was now a popular attraction on the academic tourist circuit. His meteorological diary for 1590
records that, in addition to long-term guests such as the Dutch instrument maker Jakob van Langgren, Brahe welcomed a constant stream
of visitors, both noblemen and academics, from Scotland, Germany,
Denmark and Eastern Europe.[53] James had a particular interest in
Brahe, because the astronomer was a correspondent of both George
Buchanan and Peter Young. Brahe had sent Buchanan his treatise *De
nova stella*, when he learned that Buchanan was composing a poem on
the subject; when Buchanan failed to acknowledge receipt (though the
book in fact had arrived), Brahe sent another copy, this time with a
poem enclosed. Young had met Brahe during the embassy to Elsinore
in 1586, and later sent Brahe a portrait of Buchanan, much to Brahe's
delight, promising to follow it with his 'life' of Buchanan.[54] Brahe's
diary records that the King of Scots visited on 20 March 1590, from
8 a.m. to 3 p.m. According to Brahe, James smiled at seeing a portrait
of Buchanan in his library, although, if true, this presumably suggests
James's desire to please Brahe rather than a love for Buchanan.[55] Reports
tell us that James discussed various scientific matters with Brahe,
including the Copernican system, and was apparently impressed
enough with the Dane to promise him copyright over his writings in
Scotland for the next thirty years (copyright was a pet peeve of Brahe's:
he had already won blanket copyright for his works in the Holy Roman
Empire and France).[56] Three years later, James made this arrangement
formal in a document that praised Brahe's learning, which he knew
not merely from others' accounts or from reading his published work:
'I have seen them with my own eyes, and heard them with my own
ears, in your residence at Uraniborg, during the various learned and
agreeable conversations which I then held with you, which even now

effect my mind to such a degree, that it is difficult to decide, whether I recollect them with greater pleasure or admiration.'[57]

At Uraniborg, Brahe threw a banquet for James, with musicians, entertainers, and plenty of wine, at which the company talked in Latin. James produced three English sonnets on Brahe,[58] and left his mark at Uraniborg, presenting Brahe with two English mastiffs to guard the gates, and setting on the door a Latin epigram: 'Est nobilis era Leonis | Parcere subjectis et debellare superbos. | Jacobus Rex.' (The Lion's wrath is noble | Spare the conquered and overthrow the proud).[59] James wrote the same lines in a hymn book belonging to King Christian's tutor, Henrik Ramel, and it eventually became the motto on his twenty pounds coin.[60] The King also composed a four-line Latin eulogy 'in commendation of Tycho Brahe his works, and worth', which Brahe proudly placed in his printed *Works*. An English version read,

> What Phaeton dared, was by Apolle done
> Who ruled the fiery horses of the sun.
> More TYCHO doth; he rules the stars above
> And is Urania's favourite, and love.[61]

It appears, however, that James's compositions were helped along by his Chancellor Maitland, a much more accomplished Latinist. Maitland too was inspired by the surroundings, and poured out Latin epigrams, on the Armada, the problems of the Pope, the ill fortunes of France, and Parma's scheming with the Scots.[62] He then moved on to another set, this time in honour of Brahe, with one on Uraniborg – 'the Muses' royal castle, jewel of the world, rivalling Olympus, | Nourishing house, your spirit's equal to your name'. Maitland set his poems on the door of James's bedchamber, where they were taken to be James's, and remained for visitors to copy.[63]

Even as he was revelling in the high intellectual atmosphere, James was thinking ahead to his return to Scotland – which he envisioned in glorious terms. 'I pray you,' he wrote from Kronborg to the Kirk minister and Privy Councillor Robert Bruce on 19 February 1590, instructing him to 'waken up all men to attend my coming, and prepare themselves accordingly.' James had his reasons for wanting his homecoming to be spectacular. 'For God's sake, take all the pains ye can to toon our folks well, now against our homecoming; lest we be all shamed before strangers.' He thought the homecoming 'should be a holy jubilee in Scotland'. He asked Bruce to persuade the Provost of Edinburgh to kit out and send three or four ships to take him home, and to set top craftsmen to work getting the royal residences into shape. James signed off from both himself and his wife: 'Thus recommending me and my new rib to your daily prayers, I commit you to the only All-Sufficient.'[64]

Maitland had wanted James to return to Scotland directly after the ceremony and before 'the closing of the seas' in winter, but he had quickly realised he was to be foiled in that ambition. Maitland had then opposed the trip to Denmark, knowing only too well 'what occasion of expenses he should have in a foreign part'. German dukes were due to visit, which would mean 'exorbitant charges' to ensure that the King of Scots were not hopelessly outclassed. Maitland was by no means sure that James should even meet foreign princes: 'interview of princes,' he confided to Robert Bruce, 'produces not oft the expected fruit, but breeds rather emulation, than increase of amity and good intelligence.' Moreover, sailing home from Denmark would be longer and more dangerous than sailing home from Norway would have been. Foiled in all his ambitions, Maitland could now only turn his attentions to a campaign 'to conserve his Majesty's toucher [dowry]' – to prevent James and his retinue from merrily spending all the financial advantage the marriage had brought, although he knew he could not save it all. By December, James had retrenched his retinue to fifty men,[65] but even that was costly. The only remedy was 'to haste his Majesty's returning': Maitland dealt with the Danes to expedite the preparation of the navy, and in mid-February nudged Robert Bruce to encourage the sending of Scottish ships and skilled mariners.[66] By April 1590, the *Gideon* was patched, and it was time for James to present his Queen to Scotland. By now, Anna's arrival was eagerly awaited: it was reported in mid-March that a messenger returning from Denmark reported 'very confidently that the Queen of Scots is already discovered to be with child', although a month later that rumour 'is not so generally embraced as before it hath been'.[67] James's final engagement in Denmark was to attend the much-delayed marriage of Anna's elder sister Elizabeth, his first choice as bride, to Henry Julius, Duke of

Brunswick-Wolfenbüttel, on 19 April.[68] Two days after the wedding, James and Anna, accompanied by a sizeable Danish embassy set sail in thirteen ships. The fleet arrived in the Firth of Leith on 1 May 1590, landing at about 2 p.m.

Scotland was determined to impress her new Queen from the start. James led Anna on to dry land through a 'trance', or covered way, covered with tapestry and cloth of gold, designed so 'that her feet touch not the earth'. Accommodating Anna's lack of Scots, the first oration of welcome was made by James Elphinstoun, a senator of the College of Justice, in French,[69] while great volleys were fired from Edinburgh Castle and the town's ships. At the church of Leith, James listened to a sermon of thanksgiving by Patrick Galloway, and then the couple retired to their lodgings. Since, despite the forewarning, the elaborate celebrations were not fully ready, the couple had to lodge in the 'King's Wark' while the final preparations were made for Anna's state entry into Edinburgh. It was therefore five days before the royal couple rode from Leith to Holyroodhouse. Well aware that Scotland lacked a vehicle grand enough to convey its new Queen, Denmark had sent over with their daughter a coach of silver, dressed with cloth of gold and purple velvet, to be drawn by eight white horses; James, Lennox, Bothwell and Lord John Hamilton rode alongside on horseback. When they reached the palace, James took his Queen by the hand and took her through to the Great Hall, and then to the chambers, which had been newly refurbished with cloth of gold and silver.[70]

Scarcely had he set foot on the soil of his homeland before James was reminded of the rebellious Kirk that he had so happily forgotten during his Scandinavian idyll. Both James and the Danes wanted Anna's coronation and entry to take place on a Sunday, but some Kirk ministers, led by John Davidson, vehemently opposed this use of the Sabbath, alleging that a Sunday coronation would be unlawful. Even more controversial was James's wish for Anna to be anointed Queen. He chose Robert Bruce to perform the ceremony, but predictably the Kirk objected to the anointing, which they regarded as 'popish'. James stood his ground, pointing out that anointing dated back to Old Testament times and that, if they truly objected to Bruce, one of their most prominent brethren, being given the duty, then he could quite easily appoint a bishop to do it. It was a clever tactic. After much soulsearching, the Kirk sanctioned the Sunday coronation, the reasoning being that it was merely a minister's blessing of 'a solemn oath passed mutually betwixt the prince and the subjects, and from both to God'. Even the anointing was justified, not as a minister's duty, but as a 'civil ceremony' that a subject might perform at the command of his King, 'not as a minister, but as a civil person, providing declaration were made by the anointer in time of the action to that sense, that all opinion of superstition be removed'. After much debate, Bruce was allowed to carry out the anointing.[71]

While James's own coronation had necessarily been rushed on account of his infancy, Anna was afforded the full ordeal.[72] The ceremony, which took place on 17 May at Holyrood's Abbey Church, lasted all of seven hours, with sermons and speeches in Latin and French as well as Scots, none of which languages Anna understood well. The anointing was the ritual's centrepiece. The Countess of Mar was selected to open the Queen's gown, and Bruce poured on her shoulder and breast 'a bonny quantity of oil'.[73] Anna received the sceptre from Lord John Hamilton, and her sword of state from the Earl of Angus, and pronounced the Kirk-friendly oath in which she had been carefully coached:

> I, Anna, by the grace of God, Queen of Scotland, profess, and before God and his angels wholly promise, that during the whole course of my life, so far as I can, shall sincerely worship that same eternal God according to his will revealed unto us in the Holy Scriptures, and according to those precepts which are in the same scriptures commanded and directed: That I shall defend the true religion and worship of God, and advance the same, and shall withstand and despise all papistical superstitions, and whatsoever ceremonies and rites contrary to the word of God: And that I shall further and advance justice and equity, and maintain the same, and shall procure peace to the Kirk of God within this kingdom, and to the subjects thereof: so God, the father of all mercies, have mercy upon me.[74]

The ambassadors expressed their 'great admiration' for an oration by Andrew Melvill, and even the King had to acknowledge that Melvill 'had honoured him and his country that day'. He promised never to forget the sermon, and had it rushed to the printer the very next day to be published as *Stephanischion*.[75] James, who had been seen to bestow favour on Lennox and Bothwell since his return, diplomatically passed the matrimonial crown to Maitland for placing on Anna's head, and chose the day for rewarding the Chancellor for all his recent support by creating him Lord Thirlestane.[76]

The following Tuesday, Anna made her formal entry into Edinburgh, entering in her white coach drawn by eight horses at the West Port, preceded by the Scottish and Danish noblemen, and followed by their ladies. The coach was accompanied by the citizens who held a purple velvet sheet over the coach, and the entire procession was headed by twenty-four youths apparelled in cloth of silver and white taffeta, with golden chains around their necks, legs and arms, and visors covering their faces, the intention apparently to 'mak[e] them seem Moors', all 'very gorgeous to the eye'. At the West Port, Anna was greeted by an oration made by John Russell,[77] whose son then appeared from inside a descending globe, which opened to reveal an angel who presented her with keys, a Bible and a Psalm book. As she processed, there were further orations by Hercules Rollock, Master of the Grammar School, and by the young son of the prominent Kirk minister John Craig. On Bow Street, another globe was placed on a table, with a boy sitting representing James, who made an oration. At the Butter Trone, nine women, representing the nine Muses, sang psalms. The Tolbooth presented five boys in women's clothing representing Peace, Plenty, Policy, Justice, Liberality and Temperance.[78] Entering St Giles', Anna heard Robert Bruce deliver a half-hour sermon, which presumably she could not follow, before emerging again into the town. At the Cross, the Queen was greeted by Bacchus 'winking, and casting' wine 'by cups full upon the people', to a musical accompaniment, with the Goddess of Corn and Wine crying out in Latin 'that there should be plenty thereof in her time', while the Cross itself 'ran claret wine upon the causeway' – perhaps a backhanded tribute to the Queen's bibulous motherland. Moving to the Salt Trone, James's genealogy was represented, with one king lying at their feet 'as if he had been sick': Anna's presence revived him, to give a Latin oration, while the Nether Bow had been 'beautified' with an image of 'a marriage of a King and his Queen, with all their nobility about them'. A representation of the seven planets was followed by a more tangible treat. 'There was let down unto her, from the top of the port, in a silk string, a box covered with purple velvet; whereupon was embroidered A. for Anna, her Majesty's name, set with diamonds and precious stones, esteemed at twenty thousand crowns, which the township gave for a present to her Highness.' Anna probably did not know the story behind the generous gift. Protocol required that Edinburgh give Anna a gift, but there was no money available. Finally, it was remembered that James, in need of cash, had given to the city a pledge of 'a tablet of gold in a case with a diamond and an emerald' in return for a loan of £4,000. And thus, with his blessing, James's pawned jewels were presented as Edinburgh's heartfelt gift to their new Queen.[79]

The Danish retinue was not merely decorative. The wedding settlement still had plenty of creases to be ironed out, and there was fierce bargaining going on behind the ambassadorial smiles. On 12 May, the Danes gained Falkland and parts of Fife (symbolised by a stone and some earth, solemnly handed over); on the 13th Dunfermline; and on the 14th Linlithgow.[80] After some final tidying up of the paperwork, the ambassadors were feasted in splendour at Edinburgh's Coinhouse on the 23rd, and finally took their leave on 26 May.[81] Anna was left with only sixteen attendants, instructed by her mother Queen Sophia 'to attend upon her daughter the Queen of Scots, till she might be acquainted with this country and language'.[82] In time the Danes left one by one, being replaced by Scots, although one maid, Anna Roos, was to stay with Anna until the Queen's death.[83]

James was concerned that Anna's household should have a Scottish presence, and sent for Sir James Melville of Halhill, informing him that, to fulfil a promise to Queen Sophia and the Danish Council, he was appointing 'good and discreet company' around the Queen. In Melville's own account, James explained that only one other man had been made privy to the plan but somehow Anna had got wind of it, and supposed that Melville had been placed there to 'inform her rightly' of Scottish court etiquette, and instruct her how she should behave towards the King and each nobleman and woman: in short, 'to be her keeper'. At dinner, in front of the Queen, James talked Melville up, pointing out his long-standing dealings with Denmark, and Queen Sophia's personal approbation of him, with the purpose 'to cause her Majesty [to] take the better liking of me'. The strategy failed. When James presented Sir James to the Queen after dinner, telling her that he would be her 'counsellor and Gentleman of her Chamber', Anna 'took coldly' with Melville. A few days later, she asked him outright 'if I was ordoned to be her keeper'. Melville handled the situation tactfully, pointing out to the Queen that she was 'known to be descended of so noble and princely parents, and so well brought up, that she needed no keeper', only honourable servants. Anna replied Melville had been 'evil done to', and that 'some indiscreet enviers' had taken advantage of her when 'she was yet ignorant of every man's qualities'. Melville assured her that his job was precisely 'to instruct such indiscreet persons' and to give them an example of how to behave with the Queen, and 'to hold them a-back'. In time, Anna appeared 'well content with my service', and Sir James struck up a long-standing relationship with the Queen.[84]

James saw his return to Scotland as a clean start. On Sunday 24 May, attending a sermon by Patrick Galloway at the Great Kirk, he took the opportunity to reinforce his previous promises to 'prove a loving, faithful and thankful king; to amend his former negligence, and to execute justice without feed or favour, and to see the kirks better provided'. He confessed that 'many things had been out of order before, partly through the injury of the time, and partly through his youth'; now, however, 'he had seen more, and being married, he said he would be more staid'. As soon as the Danes had departed, he promised, he would devote all his attentions to proving his promises.[85] But, as Calderwood noted tartly, 'the King soon forgot his promises made in the Great Kirk'.[86] At a General Assembly of the Kirk in August, James paid lip service to various Kirk demands, but failed to satisfy any of his hearers. In a last-ditch attempt 'to please the Assembly', he started to praise God that he had been 'born in such a time of the light of the Gospel, to such a place as to be king in such a kirk, the sincerest kirk in the world'. Even Geneva, he alleged, celebrated the papist holidays of Easter and Christmas. As for 'our neighbour Kirk in England', they celebrated little more than 'an evil said mass in English'. He charged his people 'to stand to your purity' and proclaimed that 'I, forsooth, so long as I brook my life and crown, shall maintain the same against all'. The plan worked, prompting the Assembly to a lengthy 'praising of God' and a quarter of an hour of prayers for the King.[87] It was a rare moment of unity.

CHAPTER EIGHT

Bewitched

WHILE ANNA WAS establishing her place in Scotland, her countrymen were still raking over the strange circumstances of her failed first attempt to depart. Those who had been responsible for conveying Anna to her new home were busy covering their backs. First in the firing line was the admiral of the flotilla that should have transported her, Peter Munk. To defend himself, Munk blamed Copenhagen's governor Christoffer Valkendorf for failing in his duties to keep the navy in proper shape, and took his complaint to the *Herredag*, Denmark's Supreme Court; the *Herredag* found in favour of Valkendorf, laying the blame on the gales. But as Valkendorf pointed out in court, the gales may not have been natural: indeed, trials were even now being held for witchcraft — witchcraft that aimed to stop Anna ever getting to Scotland.[1]

From the fifteenth century onwards, various parts of Europe were subject to a series of 'witchhunts', crazes in which the practice of witchcraft was detected in particular locales, and prosecuted — often with great severity — by the authorities.[2] Several writers wrote learned tracts on witches, developing an entire sub-discipline of 'demonology' that accepted witchcraft as real. According to these theorists, the individual witch made an arrangement with the Devil, a demonic pact. The witches would renounce their baptism, promise their services and ultimately their soul to the Devil, in return for superhuman powers and riches. At midnight, they would meet with the Devil, who appeared in a physical form, to have sex with him and other diabolic spirits, and to receive his orders.[3] In Denmark, witches were frequently accused of causing harm: the fiasco of a Danish naval attempt against Zeeland in 1543, the loss of ships off Visby in 1566, the unexpected death of state councillor Iver Krabbe in 1561 — all these were laid at the witches' door. Eric XIV of Sweden had even allegedly engaged four witches to help his military campaign against Denmark.[4] The witch trials started in May 1590, in Copenhagen, where an alleged witch confessed that sorcery had been responsible for the delay to the fleet; in turn, she named others, and the majority were interrogated, tried and sentenced to death – despite the fact that the supposed witches testified to planning their activities only at Michaelmas, when the ships were already in Norway.[5]

Witchcraft had been on the Scottish lawbooks from 1563, but went virtually unprosecuted until 1590. In the winter of 1590–91, however, there was an explosion of witchcraft investigations and prosecutions in Scotland. Perhaps the Danish visitors suggested witchcraft to the Scottish authorities. Perhaps James himself had been influenced by his discussions with Niels Hemmingsen, a noted demonologist. Whatever the cause, between November 1590 and May 1591 more than one hundred suspects were examined, and in all, more than three hundred witches were said to have gathered at various times and at various locations in Scotland. Among their activities, they were accused of raising the ferocious storms which buffeted the King and Queen at sea; to have attempted to bring about the King's death by burning his effigy in wax; and to have indulged in disgusting sexual rituals in the Kirk of North Berwick in the presence of the Devil. A large number of the one hundred witches examined were executed.[6] James was at first sceptical, and accused the North Berwick 'witches' of lying. According to a publication sanctioned by James, a witch named Agnes Sampson took him to one side and told him 'the very words which passed between the King's Majesty and his Queen at Upslo [Oslo] in Norway the first night of marriage, with the answers each to other, whereat the King's Majesty wondered greatly, and swore by the living God, that he believed all the devils in hell could not have discovered the same, acknowledging her words to be most true, and therefore gave the more credit to the rest that is before declared'.[7]

At the end of January 1591, a further complication emerged. The same Agnes Sampson testified that she had met with nine other witches and the Devil at night near Prestonpans. There a body of wax made by Sampson was wrapped in a linen cloth and delivered to the Devil, being passed around the circle as they chanted, 'This is King James the Sext [Sixth], ordered to be consumed at the instance of a nobleman Francis Earl Bothwell.'[8] Sampson, it was alleged, had 'said that there would be both gold and silver and victual from my Lord Bothwell'.[9] Called before the Privy Council on 15 April, Bothwell denied the charges but was imprisoned in Edinburgh Castle the next day. At first, according to Melville, James was 'not willing to credit [Bothwell's] devilish accusers'.[10] But another witness, Ritchie Graham, was produced to testify that Bothwell had asked how long the King would live, in itself an act of treason. Bothwell thought, probably with good reason, that the witnesses were being primed by his political opponents: to the King and Council he claimed that 'this practice with Graham was devised against him' and 'alleged that this matter grew not only by Graham, but sprang from his enemies'.[11] Two years later, Bothwell explicitly identified Maitland as the leader of these 'enemies'.[12] A correspondent in Durham reported that Bothwell 'stands upon his truth' and begged to be able to settle the matter 'by combat' against his accuser 'however so mean a person', but that this would not happen: 'We say that he shall die.'[13] Presumably fearing this outcome, Bothwell escaped from his gaol on 21 June; four days later the Privy Council issued a proclamation claiming that the Earl had 'had consultation with necromancers, witches and other wicked and ungodly persons, both without and within his country, for bereaving of his Highness's life'. He had given himself 'over altogether in[to] the hands of Satan, heaping treason upon treason against God, his Majesty, and this his native country'.[14] Not everyone was convinced. A letter 'To the Nobility' circulated, defending Bothwell and berating Ritchie Graham's charge as an 'incredible and unnatural accusation led against a noble personage by an infamous person moved by the disposition and humour of his devilish nature'. The court, it continued, was controlled by evil counsellors, who 'in gilded and painted palaces . . . execute their power at the dictates of hatred and favour' and 'obscure that great Majesty that . . . is due unto his sacred person'.[15]

By the time that Robert Bruce admonished the King from the pulpit in June 1591 that he must exercise justice on the witches, 'although it should be with the hazard of his life',[16] James needed no encouragement. As the interrogations and trials progressed he had become fascinated by the witchcraft phenomenon. He took a particular interest in the trial of Barbara Napier, who was arrested for consulting with witches, and was known to be a friend of Bothwell. During her interrogation, she claimed to be pregnant, a strategy that, if successful, would save her from the death penalty. James was unsympathetic. To Maitland in April 1591, he ordered: 'Try by the mediciners' oaths if

Barbara be with bairn or not. Take no delaying answer. If you find she be not, to the fire with her presently, and cause bowel [disembowel] her publicly.'[17] When Napier's jurors allowed her to live, he berated them personally for their verdict. The reasons he gave are telling. Witchcraft was a secondary issue: his main concern was that he as King had been thwarted in his wishes. He believed Napier to be guilty of treason, and he could not believe the presumption of the jury in finding her innocent. 'Yet this I say, that – howsoever matters have gone against my will I am innocent of all injustice in these behalfs, and for my part my conscience doth set me clear, as did the conscience of Samuel, and I call you to be my judges herein. And suppose I be your King, yet I submit myself to the accusations of you my subjects in this behalf, and let any one say what I have done. And as I have this begun, so purpose I go forward; not because I am James Stuart, and can command so many thousands of men, but because God hath made me a king and judge to judge righteous judgement.'[18] He had almost died as a result of this witchcraft, he pointed out – not that he feared death for himself, but he was concerned for 'the common good of this country, which enjoyeth peace by my life . . . as you may collect by mine absence, for if such troubles were in breeding whilst I retained life, what would have been done if my life had been taken from me?'

James felt that what he had learned from the witchcraft phenomenon needed to be understood by a wider audience. In 1591, he commissioned the publication of *News from Scotland*, which outlined the facts of the recent proceedings, presumably for an English audience. But he wanted to write something more scholarly – and to challenge the likes of Reginald Scot's 1584 treatise *The Discoverie of Witchcraft*, which with great scholarship and at great length rubbished beliefs in witchcraft. So James set out to pen his *Daemonologie*, primarily to refute 'the damnable opinion of two principally in our age, whereof the one called SCOT, an Englishman, is not ashamed in public print to deny that there can be such a thing as witchcraft: and so maintains the old error of the Sadducees, in denying of spirits'.[19]

James's *Daemonologie* takes the form of a dialogue between the sceptical Philomathes and the learned Epistemon, who answers Philomathes' questions about withcraft. Its three books deal with magic in general, sorcery and witchcraft in particular, and finally with spirits and ghosts. Witches, Epistemon claims, can harm and even kill by chanting over wax images melted over a fire, and they 'can raise storms and tempests in the air, either upon the sea or land, though not universally, but in such a particular place and prescribed bounds, as God will permit them so to trouble'.[20]

Daemonologie affords us a rare glimpse into the composition of James's writings. In common with many Renaissance authors, the King did not work in isolation.[21] Early versions of two sections of *Daemonologie*, drafted in James's own hand, survive in manuscript form at the Bodleian Library, Oxford.[22] James then authorised a clean copy of his treatise to be made, perhaps by his childhood friend Sir James Sempill: this copy, now in the Folger Shakespeare Library,[23] however, also bears the signs of revisions by two persons, one of whom has been identified as James Carmichael, the Minister of Haddington,[24] and the other as James himself. James made over one hundred amendments to the manuscript, ranging from deletions and insertions of single words, to the addition of entire passages. The longest of these amendments was also the last, as James added in the margin a characteristically gruesome discussion of how witchcraft can be detected by the telltale signs it leaves on the corpses of its victims: 'if the dead carcass be at any time . . . handled by the murderer it will gush out of blood as if the blood was crying to the heaven for revenge . . .'[25] When James finally published his *Daemonologie* in 1597, his belief in witches seems to have been waning: perhaps the fact that Bothwell was by then no longer a threat contributed to his less hard-line attitude. But Scotland had been bitten by the witchcraze bug, and there was a steady stream of accusations, trials and executions, fuelled by eager clergymen and lawyers, well into the seventeenth century.[26]

After Bothwell escaped from his gaol in June 1591, he fled to the Borders eluding capture. Although he was declared an outlaw, there was a great deal of public sympathy for him, and much of the nobility, whatever their qualms about Bothwell personally, saw James's continuing antagonism as a dangerous Maitland-inspired threat to the nobility. This general support allowed Bothwell to roam fairly free, and he was sighted publicly in Dalkeith, Crichton and Leith. His confidence increasing, he turned up at the Canongate, to throw a brave challenge at the Chancellor. Bothwell's unpredictable movements were guaranteed to put James into his customary panic.[27] At the same time, he had to deal with an increasingly obstructive wife. Anna had taken a personal dislike to Chancellor Maitland. Although Queen Sophia had charged Maitland with keeping an eye on Anna's interests,[28] the Chancellor soon found himself torn between the Queen's interests and his own. The quarrel focused on the ownership of Dunfermline Abbey's lordship of Musselburgh, which both Queen and Chancellor claimed. Maitland had been granted the lordship in 1587; when he saw in 1591 that the Danes wanted it, he renewed his charter and starting selling its lands off. Anna was enraged, and displayed her fury by pointedly turning down an offer of hospitality from the Chancellor in April 1591, staying at Dalkeith while James went alone.[29] Perhaps because of this, Anna started to align herself, controversially, with Bothwell, drawn to his grasp of French and of European culture. She went so far as to plead for Bothwell with the King after his escape in July 1591, but her pleas left him 'so moved' with anger that she wisely let the matter drop.[30] It was to be the first of several interventions by the Queen for men who had fallen foul of her husband, her success rate increasing slowly but surely over the next few years.[31] As Melville described her *modus operandi*, 'The Queen's Majesty, according to her custom, whenever she understands that his Majesty by wrong information is stirred up against any honest servant or subject, she procures incontinent for them [forwards their case immediately], and uses great diligence to get sure knowledge of the verity, that she may the boldlier speak in their favour.'[32] As the Queen's influence waxed, Maitland was threatened. He was not helped by his wife, who failed to realise that Anna was by now quite capable of understanding her gossip in Scots which implied that the Queen had been favourable to 'Bothwell's late attempt'.[33] Anna was deeply insulted, and refused to cooperate with the Chancellor. When informed that the 'dryness' and 'heavy countenance' between her and Maitland was hurting 'the King's service', she made an attempt to heal the rift, which was ruined when Maitland again offended her.[34]

On 27 December 1591, James's fear of Bothwell was fully vindicated. In a piece of daredevil bravado Bothwell raided Holyroodhouse at suppertime with about fifty followers. He and his men attacked the doors of the King, Queen and Chancellor; setting fire to the King's door, and taking hammers to the Queen's, in the process killing the King's Master Stabler, John Shaw. James wrote an touching epitaph for his stabler:

> Thy kindness kithed [showed] in loosing life for me
> My kindnesse on thy friends I utter shall;
> My perrill kindled courage into the[e],
> Mine shall revenge thy saikles [innocent] famous fall.
> Thy constant service ever shall remaine
> As freshe with me as if thou lived againe.[35]

Luckily for James, news of the raid quickly reached the Provost of Edinburgh, and his advance, supported with a bevy of townsfolk, was enough to cause Bothwell and all but seven or eight of his men to flee. The incident thoroughly unnerved James, who realised that some-body close to him must be implicated, perhaps even Lennox: Bothwell and his men had entered through Lennox's stables, and Lennox was himself notable for his absence 'till all was ended'. But nothing could be proven against the Duke.[36]

The next day, James went to St Giles' to thank the people of Edinburgh, and spoke of the benefits he had given to Bothwell, and how he showed his gratitude by seeking to kill him, first by poison and witchcraft, and now directly in this attack. But Bothwell still commanded considerable loyalty, and public sympathy for James's predicament was notably lacking. The following day, 29 December, one of the King's own chaplains, the veteran Kirk minister John Craig, delivered a sermon before James in which he claimed that the King 'had lightly regarded the many bloody shirts presented to him by his subjects craving justice', so God 'had made a noise of crying and fore-hammers to come to his own doors'. James insisted that the congre-gation stay after the sermon, so he could purge himself. If he had thought that his feed-servant (meaning the preacher) would deal with him in that manner, James declared, he 'would not have suffered him so long in his house'. But James's grand pronouncement was drowned out by the crowd, and Craig left without hearing it.[37]

A formal proclamation was made against Bothwell on 10 January

1592, officially condemning him as one of the faction of Huntly's Brig o' Dee revolt in April 1589. Three days later, James galloped to Haddington, where a sighting of Bothwell had been made, but succeeded only in endangering his own life, when his horse fell into the Tyne: he was saved from drowning only when a yeoman pulled him out by the neck, his courtiers not daring to dive into the water.[38] Thoroughly spooked, James left Holyroodhouse for Edinburgh, but his popularity had been severely damaged. Matters worsened two months later when James was implicated, probably without foundation, in the vicious murder of one of Scotland's most popular young Protestant heroes, the Earl of Moray, by Huntly, whom James had so long protected. Huntly was caught up in a long-standing feud between his family, the Gordons, and the Morays, dating back to the reign of James's mother. Mary had created her half-brother Lord James Stewart (who later became James's Regent) Earl of Moray, an earldom which the fourth Earl of Huntly had hoped to gain. On Moray's death, the title had passed to James Stewart of Doune, husband of Regent Moray's eldest daughter, and had fuelled his ambition to extend his influence in the north-east of Scotland, which would hit at the Gordons' powerbase.[39] James decided that he had to sort out this squabble once and for all. He ordered that Moray and Huntly should come to arbitration. The enemies made their way south, but arbitration was the last thing on Huntly's mind. On 7 February 1592, Huntly suddenly and unexpectedly crossed the Forth, turning up at Donibristle, Moray's mother's castle, where Moray was temporarily lodging, and put the house to the torch. Moray tried to flee, but ran straight into Huntly's path, and was murdered in a cave. This bloody end soon became the stuff of legend. One account told of how Moray ran towards the river, his hair and the plume of his helmet in flames, and that Huntly killed him with a dagger blow to the face. The handsome Moray allegedly died saying, 'You have spoilt a better face than your own.' Rumour spread that James had ordered the murder, and one ballad embellished it with the suggestion that Moray, 'a braw callant [brave gallant]', was the true love of Queen Anna, and 'micht ha' been a king'.[40] When James went hunting the following day near Innerleith and Weirdie, he caught sight of the fire, but was apparently 'nothing moved'. Unsurprisingly, 'the people blamed him as guilty', citing his hatred of Moray as a supporter of Bothwell, and more generally hating the house 'for the Good Regent's sake'. James's involvement remains obscure: even the ballad claiming Moray as Anna's lover makes it clear that James 'forbade' Huntly to slay Moray, suggesting that the King knew of the plot but did not approve the murder. James called half a dozen ministers to his presence and 'did what he could to clear himself', so that they could spread the message to the people; they replied that if he wanted to clear himself, he should hunt down Huntly. James certainly did nothing substantive against Huntly, writing to the Earl to claim that 'Always I shall remain constant', and indeed the official proclamation insisted only on the King's innocence – James said he was like David, when Abner was slain by Joab – and said nothing of pursuing Huntly.[41]

Whatever the truth, both James and Maitland were encouraged to keep away from Edinburgh, the Chancellor moving to Lethington, while the King wandered the country, pretending to chase Bothwell. In May, in an attempt to win round the Kirk, James called another Parliament, probably at Maitland's instigation. After the promises at his home-coming from Denmark, action against Arran's 1584 'Black Acts', one of which had controversially confirmed the status of bishops, was now long overdue. In its place, the May 1592 Parliament now passed a 'Golden Act' by which the Kirk was finally allowed to develop its ecclesiastical polity, and official recognition was given to their system of Sessions, presbyteries, synods, and the General Assembly. On one level, this bypassing of the episcopacy was a triumph for the Kirk. But James insisted on keeping another of the 1584 Acts which asserted his royal supremacy, and suggested to the Parliament that they pass an Act which would take action against attacks against him in sermons. When Parliament refused, James 'chafed and railed against the ministers'.[42]

Worse was to come: Bothwell was not finished. On 27 June 1592, he launched a midnight attack on James at Falkland Palace. With three hundred men and a battering ram, he attempted to break down the palace gates. James locked himself in a tower, which the Earl continued to besiege until morning, before fleeing again. This time it was self-evident that James had been betrayed by men close to him, a realisation that sent the King into a depression, 'lamenting his estate and accounting his fortune to be worse than any prince living', since he was destined to 'die in himself' – betrayed to his death 'by the means of those who are nearest to him and most trusted'.

One of his Gentlemen of the Bedchamber, a young laird named John Wemyss, was accused of dealing with Bothwell and put under arrest. Wemyss's lover, one of Anna's Danish maids named Margaret Vinstarr, contrived a daring escape for Wemyss through Holyrood's royal bedchamber, 'where the King and Queen were in bed', and let him out at a window 'where she had prepared cords for his escape'. This incident led to James upbraiding Anna, causing her, and himself, to end up in tears,[43] but it was reported that she refused to dismiss Vinstarr, announcing that 'she will rather go to Denmark than part with Mistress Margaret or any others [of] her domestic servants'.[44] Once again, the King's nervousness sent him moving from one residence to another through the summer and into the autumn; still dogged by Anna, Maitland found himself so unpopular by September that he gave up life at court altogether, and retired to the west of Scotland with friends.[45]

The King's lack of action against Huntly was to damage him still further. In the autumn of 1592 another Spanish plot was uncovered. More correspondence with Spain was intercepted, this time blank pieces of paper presigned by Huntly, Errol, Sir Patrick Gordon of Auchindoun and their new ally, the tenth Earl of Angus, a recent convert to Roman Catholicism. A Scottish Catholic named George Kerr was apprehended as he was about to set sail for Spain, and found to be carrying the so-called 'Spanish blanks'; he confessed under torture that a Spanish invasion, of 30,000 Spanish troops joining 15,000 Scots raised by the conspirators, was being planned under the leadership of the Scottish Jesuit Father William Crichton, now resident in Spain, and that the blank pieces of paper were designed to carry details of the plot. The Kirk reacted with horror to the relevations, with most of their alarm directed at the King himself. James had shown himself to be incapable of taking decisive action against Huntly, despite his repeated and proven acts of treason. Perhaps, it was whispered, the King himself was involved? One document among the 'Spanish blanks' seemed to suggest this was a real possibility: a memorandum in which, it appeared, James listed the arguments for and against a possible invasion of England by Scotland in the summer of 1592, concluding firmly

that such a plan was impossible. The reasons given for this impossi-
bility are interesting. The current disorderly state of Scotland, it was
argued, meant that James could not be sure of conquering his own
country, let alone the major power to the south. He certainly could
not leave Scotland to lead an army into England, since he would be
giving the already troublesome nobles *carte blanche* to undermine his
tenuous grip on government. If he were to invade England, it would
have to be some time off in the future, and he would do it with as
little aid as possible from overseas powers. 'In the meantime,' James
wrote, 'I will deal with the Queen of England fair and pleasantly for
my title to the Crown of England after her decease, which thing, if
she grant to (as it is not impossible, howbeit unlikely), we have attained
our design without stroke of sword. If by the contrary, then delay
makes me to settle my country in the meantime and, when I like hereafter, I may in a month or two (forewarning of the King of Spain)
attain to our purpose, she not suspecting such a thing as she does
now, which, if it were so done, would be a far greater honour to him
and me both.' What the memorandum suggests is that James was
willing to give an ear to plans to attack England, and to evaluate them,
not from a moral highground, but from practical exigency.[46]

Once again, James could not bring himself to be anything but
lenient to Huntly, but this time the Kirk was adamant that the King
had to act against this blatant Catholic threat. Accordingly, James
mustered his forces and marched north to Aberdeen in February of
1593, but it was clearly only for show: as soon as Huntly and his allies
retreated towards Caithness, James gave up the chase. A few token
gestures – taking bonds of good behaviour, some garrisons staking
out strategic locations – fooled nobody. When he seized the rebels'
estates, only to hand them over to their friends, the English ambassador Lord Burgh wrote that James had only 'dissembled a confisca-
tion'; compounding this interpretation, the July 1593 Parliament failed
to pass the expected act of forfeiture against Huntly and his followers.
James's lack of real action may have been as much due to fear as to
love of Huntly: James confided to Bowes that Huntly, Errol and Angus
were three of the most powerful nobles in Scotland, and 'if he should
again pursue them and toot them with the horn he should little
prevail'.[47]

Seeing how the Kirk was turning against the King, Bothwell took his chance. In a bizarre turn of events, he now pledged his support to the Kirk, and they reciprocated in kind, minister John Davidson ingeniously explaining that Bothwell was a 'sanctified plague' who had been sent to cause James to 'turn to God', and away from the papists.[48] Elizabeth, too, saw the potential of the rebel Earl as a possible magnet for anti-Catholic activism. Her efforts were not appreciated by her loving cousin, as James made clear to her ambassador, Lord Burgh: 'Touching that vile man,' he said of Bothwell, 'as his foul offences towards me are unpardonable and most to be abhorred for example's sake by all sovereign princes, so we most earnestly pray her [Elizabeth] to deliver him in case he have refuge anymore within any part of her dominions, praying you to inform her plainly that, if he be received or comforted in any part of her country, I can no longer keep amity with her but, by the contrary, will be forced to join in friendship with her greatest enemies for my own safety.'[49] To the Queen herself, he protested that he would rather be a slave in the galleys of the Turk than demonstrate leniency towards a man who had dishonoured him. Elizabeth could hardly think him so ignorant of the honour of a prince, he continued, unless she thought that he, James, had been bewitched by Bothwell and turned into an ass. For once, Elizabeth was moved by the passion of his protest, and wrote a letter in which she partially apologised.[50]

But the threat from Bothwell still remained. At Holyroodhouse on 24 July, James was preparing to dress, when he heard a disturbance in the chamber next to his own. Rushing in, undressed as he was, he was confronted by Bothwell kneeling next to his drawn sword – a sign that Bothwell considered that he had control of Holyroodhouse, but would not use his power to harm the King. James, always nervous of weapons, was reluctant to trust to such a fine distinction. He shouted that 'Treason' was afoot, and rushed to Anna's bedchamber, only to find the door bolted. Turning back to the outlaw, he screamed that Bothwell might take his life, but would not, like Satan dealing with a witch, obtain his immortal soul. He, James, was a sovereign king, only twenty-seven years old: he would rather die than live out his life in captive shame. James believed not only that Bothwell had been helped by the witches of North Berwick, but that Bothwell had satanic powers of bewitchment – to which James was immune. Bothwell flamboyantly offered him his sword, urging him to strike him down – but luckily James's response wasn't required. At the moment, other courtiers entered, and James changed tactic, calming the situation and agreeing to bargain with them. Their discussion ended in a compromise: Bothwell agreed to withdraw from court until he came to trial on the witchcraft charges. The trial, it went without saying, would acquit the Earl; James would then pardon Bothwell for all his other offences, but in exchange, Bothwell would withdraw from court life. Aware of a crowd gathering outside, James appeared at a window to assure them that nothing was amiss.[51]

This dramatic attempt on James inspired him to three sonnets, the self-pitying tone of which can be heard in the following:

> Shall treason then of truth have the reward
> And shall rebellion thus exalted be?
> Shall cloaked vice with falsehood's fained fard
> In credit creep and glister in our eye?
> Shall coloured knaves so malapertly lie
> And shameless sow their poisoned smitting seed?
> And shall perjured infamous foxes sly
> With these triumphs make honest hearts to bleed?
> How long shall Furies on our fortunes feed?
> How long shall vice her reign possess in rest?
> How long shall Harpies our displeasure breed
> And monstrous fowls sit sicker in our nest?
>   In time appointed God will surely have
>   Each one his due reward for to resave [receive].[52]

Bothwell retired from court, as agreed, and James went to work. The outlaw Earl's power had alarmed several major players, and they now came together, overlooking previous differences: Treasurer Glamis, Lord John Hamilton, Homes, Maxwell, several members of the Douglas and Stewart families – and Chancellor Maitland, who returned to court, much to the King's relief. In September 1593, James felt secure enough to declare that he was a free King, and to threaten Bothwell that he had to stick to his side of the bargain.[53] But James still showed little real desire to rid himself of the Catholic earls led by Huntly. In November of 1593, a small convention in Edinburgh passed an Act of Oblivion for all the Catholic earls' illegal acts, on various conditions, including that they should formally submit to the Kirk. James was heavily implicated in this manoeuvre: it was claimed that he had manipulated the nobles at the convention, and tampered with the wording of the Act. The Kirk, predictably enraged, took little notice of the Act: the Synod of Fife excommunicated the earls anyway. Elizabeth taunted James with a letter 'in which she lamented the sight of a seduced King, an abusing Council, and wry-guided kingdom'.[54]

Amends were made in April 1594. Bothwell appeared at Leith, this time with only a small group of men, driving some of the King's horse back to Edinburgh – James himself, according to an unsympathetic Calderwood, 'came riding into the city at the full gallop with full honour'. The King went to St Giles' and appealed to Edinburgh to support him: 'If ye will assist me against Bothwell at this time, I promise to prosecute the excommunicated lords [i.e. Huntly and his followers] so that they shall not be suffered to remain in any part of Scotland.' Bothwell realised that his honeymoon with the Kirk was over, and fled north.[55] Shortly after, James was made aware of yet another Spanish plot involving Huntly and the Catholic earls. This time, having made his promise to Edinburgh, he could not refuse to take proper action. Crucially, he drew his support now not from the nobility, but from the lairds and the burghs. He also appealed to the Kirk for support, but their initial reaction was sceptical, telling James they would pray for him. But then news reached Edinburgh that Huntly was sheltering the fugitive Bothwell. Faced with this dangerous concentration of rebel power they were forced to act.

James's military expedition was ready in September to march to the north-east with the Kirk represented by Andrew Melvill; the advance guard commanded by the young Earl of Argyll soon reached Aberdeenshire. A skirmish on 3 October, rather grandly known as the battle of Glenlivet, saw Huntly defeat Argyll; when James approached, the Earl put up no resistance, but refused to surrender Bothwell. Bothwell again fled for his life to Caithness, but this was to be the last time. The royal forces burned the rebels' houses to the ground.

Either exhausted, or realising his luck had turned, Bothwell fled north.

In dealing with his prisoners, James showed his true colours. To him, Huntly was never a real enemy, as Bothwell was. In March 1595, with official permission, Huntly and Errol left the country, but Huntly returned to Scotland the following year, and was officially received into the Kirk in 1597, rewinning James's friendship and being rewarded in 1599 with the title of Marquis.[56] While Huntly was never again to have the influence over the King that he had enjoyed in the late 1580s, he and James retained a close friendship in future years, cemented when James asked for Huntly's son to be sent to London as a companion to his own son, Charles. Indeed, at the end of his life, James summoned Huntly to London to present him to Charles, who would be his new king, describing him as 'the most faithful servant that ever served a prince, assuring Charles that so long as he would cherish and keep Huntly on his side, he needed not be very apprehensive of seditious or turbulent heads in Scotland'.[57] Bothwell's flight this time took him abroad. He lived on for another thirty years, but never returned to Scotland. Scotland's most seditious and turbulent head was gone.

CHAPTER NINE

Advice to A Son

IF JAMES HAD believed that marriage to Anna would stop the attacks on his masculinity he was truly misguided. Rumours in Scandinavia that Anna had conceived shortly after their wedding proved to be unfounded. The Earl of Worcester, sent by Elizabeth to welcome the new Queen in the summer of 1590, joked that Anna's toothache was evidently 'a token of breeding child', but again no child was born.[1] By the autumn of 1591, there were intimations of resentment on the part of the Scottish people: an anonymous Englishman in Berwick reported their 'great disliking of their Queen, for that she proves not with child'.[2] And in time, the resentment spread to the King.

In the summer of 1592, James sent for several Edinburgh ministers and showed them some harshly mocking 'contumelious verses' that had been sent to him. James thought they must be the work of one Captain Hackerston, one of the leading followers of Bothwell, then the King's principal bugbear. 'Ye may see,' James told the ministers, 'what they mean to my life, that carry such libels about them.' The scurrilous rhymes contained three rumours: 'calling him Davy's son, a bougerer [bugger], one that left his wife all the night *intactam.*' The claim that the King was in fact the illegitimate son of Mary's Italian secretary David Riccio was older than James himself and would never be quashed; but the other two, impugning his masculinity, struck him to the heart. Ever since Esmé Stuart had come into Scotland, it had been suggested obliquely that the King's relations with his male favourites might cross the line into physical expression, and James himself, in his open letter to the Privy Council as he set sail to Denmark, had drawn attention to rumours that he had no desire to marry. But now he had a wife – and yet what had been only hinted at before was now spelled out in the libels. James decided to act, but he had a strange order for the ministers. 'I thought good to acquaint you with these things, that ye may acquaint the people with them, for they have a good opinion of you, and credit you.' And so the Edinburgh ministers were despatched to inform their flocks that the

King was not the illegitimate son of David Riccio, that he did indeed consummate his marriage, that he was not a bugger. Quite what the Edinburgh congregations made of these assurances is not recorded.[3]

It was with great relief, then, when it became clear in late 1593, after over three years of marriage, that the Queen was pregnant. On 19 February 1594, Anna gave birth to her first child, a son, at Stirling. James named him Henry Frederick, Henry after his father, and Frederick after Anna's. The baptism in August was a grand affair, far more lavish than James's precarious finances truly afforded, and attended by representatives of many European courts. As with James's own christening, the festivities were marked by entertainments, this time with James contributing, with William Fowler, to a masque in which he starred as one of the Christian Knights of Malta, doing battle with Moors and Amazons, the latter portrayed in full female dress by several noblemen.[4]

When Henry was only two days old, family tradition was honoured when the Earl of Mar, James's boyhood friend Jocky o' Sclaittis, was appointed as his guardian, with Stirling Castle as his residence. The dowager Countess of Mar, who had looked after James, was still alive, and was called on to undertake the same duties with Henry. The same restrictions of access were imposed — with the interesting addition that no enemy of the prince 'nor their wives, bairns, or servants' should be allowed into the castle.[5] While this state of affairs seemed perfectly natural to James, Anna was firmly opposed to losing her child so early. In March 1595, she asked her husband to transfer to her the keeping of Prince Henry and Stirling Castle. James was dismayed, and demanded to know who had put such a thing into her mind: of all people, Maitland was blamed. 'There ariseth a variance at court,' wrote one commentator. 'The Queen would have had the prince in keeping in the Castle of Edinburgh and Buccleuch [a Border nobleman] to be captain . . . It was thought that the motion proceeded from the Chancellor who was now a great courtier with the Queen.'[6] The King thought the idea 'perilous to his own estate' and refused to yield, angrily swearing 'that if he were about to die he would with his last breath command Mar to retain possession of the Prince.'[7]

Anna refused to let the matter drop. In May, it was reported that 'the Queen speaks more plainly than before and will not cease till she has her son.' Court sympathies split into 'two mighty factions', the King's faction at Stirling – Mar, Thomas Erskine and Sir James Elphinstone, and the Queen's faction, including Maitland, at Edinburgh. The custody of the Prince became a sticking point in the royal marriage. 'No good can come between the King and Queen till she be satisfied anent the Prince,' George Nicolson wrote on 15 July, since there was a 'division of this land into two factions almost to the parting of the King and Queen'.[8] Obviously fearing what his wife might do to get her son back, James wrote to Mar urging him to stick to the letter of his contract, not giving Henry to anyone without permission directly from the King's own mouth, 'because in the surety of my son consists my surety'. He even specified that Anna should not be given custody if James were himself to die: 'in case God call me at any time, that neither for Queen nor Estates' pleasure ye deliver him [the Prince] until he be eighteen years of age.'[9]

Realising that the King would not climb down, Anna tried a more dramatic tactic. James, staying at Stirling, was told that Anna had fallen ill at Edinburgh, and wanted to see him. The King's counsellors were immediately suspicious and advised against his going, in case some sort of attempt was made against him. Anna's party sent her physicians to Stirling to assure James that his wife was indeed ill. James took the bait and decided 'to set aside all occasion of suspicion, jealousy or pleasures' and give 'a proof of his love to his wife' by riding to Edinburgh. Anna turned out to be 'very merry and well disposed', and took advantage of her husband's rare show of concern to ask him once again for her son. This time James 'took it in a more higher sort than before' and replied, 'My heart, I am sorry you should be persuaded to move me to that which will be the destruction of me and my blood.' Anna burst into tears. The following day, James said to Maitland, 'If any think I am further subject to my wife than I ought to be, they are but traitors and such as seek to dishonour me.'[10] Realising she could not win, the Queen abandoned her campaign and publicly reconciled with Mar but it was thought permanent damage had been done to the marriage: 'There is nothing but lurking hatred disguised with cunning dissimulation betwixt the King and the Queen,' wrote John Colville in August, 'each intending by slight to overcome the other.'[11] Nevertheless, the King and Queen knew their duty, and Anna continued to give birth to a succession of princes and princesses: Elizabeth in 1596, Margaret in 1598, Charles in 1600, Robert in 1601, Mary in 1605 and Sophia in 1607; although Margaret, Robert, Mary and Sophia all died in infancy, fears about the succession were calmed.

The death of Maitland on 5 October 1595 eased some of the factional tension. James had relied on Maitland for many years, and wrote a sonnet lamenting his demise, that generously admitted Maitland's contribution to James's writing.

If he who valiant even within the space
That Titan six times twice his course does end
Did conquise old Dame Rhea's fruitful face
And did his reign from pole to pole extend
Had thought him happier if that Greek had penned
His worthy praise who traced the Trojan sack
Then all his acts that forth his fame did send
Or his triumphant trophies might him make.
Then what am I who on Pegasian back
Does flee amongs the nymphs' immortal fair
For thou O Maitland does occasion take
Even by my verse to spread my name all where
   For what in barbarous lead I block and frames
   Thou learned in Minerva's tongue proclaims.[12]

Despite this, it was reported that 'His Majesty took little care for the loss of the Chancellor'. Whatever his personal attitude towards Maitland, James seemed to have little taste for the power of the Chancellorship, and was in no hurry to fill the vacant post. As he pointed out, he was damned whoever he appointed: if a nobleman, then the new Chancellor would very quickly 'be better attended upon than the King himself'; if a commoner, then the new Chancellor would build a faction at court – Maitland, of course, had been a commoner.[13]

Over the next year the dominant court party emerged from a rare attempt on the part of the royal couple to manage their finances. In 1593, James had appointed a council to sort out his Queen's accounts, a group that became known as the 'Octavians'.[14] Their endeavours were not in vain, and Anna was so impressed with their work that she recommended them to her husband. At New Year in 1596, she boastfully let James have a view of the 1000 Scottish pounds that the Octavians' efforts had saved her. Handing over half of it to the King, she pointedly inquired as to when *his* Council would give as much. Stung into action, James dismissed his Treasurer, the Master of Glamis, and other Exchequer officials, and appointed the Octavians to sort out his finances on 9 January, allowing them control of all royal revenues and undertaking not to override their decisions, a tactic that effectively insulated James from any responsibility. This time, however, the Octavians had an impossible job on their hands. They suggested various schemes to reduce expenditure, but James's hangers-on opposed them at every stage.[15]

From England, the factionalism at the Scottish court and within the royal marriage was viewed with dismay. Elizabeth wrote to Anna, and sent her messenger with a more important, lengthy verbal message giving the benefit of her opinion on evil counsellors. These evil counsellors were likely to be papists wanting to draw Anna away from her inherited Lutheranism – and it would be better if Elizabeth knew their names. Anna supplied only one name: it was Maitland who had talked her into trying to win back her son, and yes, he had tried to convert her. But now he was dead, and there was no one else; if such a seducer emerged, she would let Elizabeth know immediately.[16]

Elizabeth's fears of Anna's possible conversion to Catholicism were uttered more widely by those alarmed by what appeared to be a new trend towards the faith in James's government. Although Prince Henry had been placed with the firmly Protestant Earl of Mar, the next three children (Elizabeth, Margaret and Charles) were given to guardians less staunch in their convictions;[17] at the same time, Anna had taken as her confidante a known Catholic, Henrietta Gordon, Lady Huntly; and when James welcomed back into Scotland Huntly and Errol in the summer of 1596, there was an inevitable backlash from the Kirk. In September 1596, a delegation of ministers, led by Andrew Melvill and including his nephew James, were granted an audience with the King at Falkland. James Melvill commenced by informing the King that the commissioners of the General Assembly had just met in Cowper – at which point James broke in, angrily charging that

such a meeting was held without a warrant, and was therefore seditious. This was too much for Andrew Melvill, who attacked the King
'in so zealous, powerful and unresistable a manner' that despite James's
'most crabbed and choleric manner', Melvill 'bore him down'. Calling
him 'God's silly vessel', Melvill took him by the sleeve, and harangued
him: 'Sir, as divers times before, so now again, I mon [must] tell you:
there is two kings and two kingdoms in Scotland. There is Christ
Jesus the King, and his kingdom the Kirk, whose subject King James
the Sixth is, and of whose kingdom not a king, nor a lord, nor a
head, but a member!'

Worse was to come from the St Andrews minister David Black,
who had become infamous for his attacks on Queen Elizabeth's religious purity. In a sermon he now denounced the English Queen as
an atheist, protesting that religion in England was an empty show,
and claiming that the English bishops had persuaded the King of
Scots to reintroduce an episcopal government in Scotland, against the
terms of the Confession of Faith by which the Kirk was founded.
Moreover, he claimed, James had allowed the return of the Catholic
earls Errol and Huntly. 'But what could be expected when Satan ruled
in the court and in the Council, when judges and councillors were
cormorants and men of no religion, when the Queen of Scotland was
a woman for whom, for fashion's sake, the clergy might pray but from
whom no good could be hoped. Were not all kings Devil's bairns?'
Called before the Privy Council, Black refused their jurisdiction,
claiming only an ecclesiastical court could try him; his refusal was
disseminated to every presbytery.

James was determined that Black would be punished, and refused
to waiver. Edinburgh was soon in a state of crisis, with a campaign
from the pulpits that 'pressed forward and sounded mightily' against
the King and his counsellors. On 17 December, a sermon at St Giles'
used the story of the foiling of the evil counsellor Haman from the
book of Esther to incite the congregation; the crowd became increasingly excited and leapt up shouting 'Save yourselves! Armour, armour!
Bills and axes!' Running from the church, they seized arms, some going
to the King in the Tolbooth, some to defend the ministers, shouting
'Bring forth the wicked Haman!' Through the intervention of the
Provost, the riot quickly subsided, but James was furious. The following

day the court moved to Linlithgow, from where the Privy Council declared that the riot had been an act of treason. James levied a force of Borders men, and forced Edinburgh to hand over 20,000 marks to keep the peace.[18]

The riots provided a neat excuse for James to impose new regulations on the Kirk. He gave himself the power to influence the location of General Assemblies, deliberately chose locations such as Perth, Montrose and Aberdeen, knowing that northern ministers were less supportive of Melvill than those in his strongholds of St Andrews and Edinburgh. Difficult ministers were called into James's own cabinet and subjected to a barrage of threats, promises and bribes: James Melvill lamented, 'Alas, where Christ guided before, the court began then to govern all.' Concessions came from the General Assemblies in Perth and Dundee in early 1597: ministers would avoid political themes and attacks on the King in their sermons, unless he was informed first in private; presybteries would deal only with ecclesiastical affairs. In exchange, a commission was set up to advise the King on matters ecclesiastical, to the great suspicion of some Kirk men: James Melvill sneered that they were 'the King's led horse, and usurped boldly the power of the General Assemblies. They were as a wedge taken out of the Kirk to rend her with her own forces, and the very needle which drew in the thread of the bishops.'[19]

The commission did, however, propose that the Kirk should be directly represented in Parliament, instead of being a vociferous lobbying group. James compromised by suggesting that ministers could be appointed to vacant bishoprics, and that these new bishops might sit in Parliament, thus allowing the Kirk parliamentary representation while restoring the episcopacy. Calderwood was disgusted: this was 'nothing better than that which the Grecians used for the overthrow of the ancient city and town of Troy: busking up a brave horse and . . . persuading them . . . to receive that in their honour and welfare which served for their utter wreck and destruction.' Or as one old minister put it, 'Busk, busk, busk him as bonnily as ye can, and bring him in as fairly as ye will, we see him well enough: we see the horns of his mitre.'[20] James got his way, and the first three so-called 'parliamentary bishops' – of Ross, Caithness and Aberdeen – entered Parliament in 1600. The Kirk, sticking to their anti-episcopal line, refused to recognise them as bishops, and treated them as ministers instead.[21]

In the late 1590s, James set about consolidating his status as a learned king. The poetic experimentation that had preoccupied him in the early 1580s had now dwindled to a trickle of occasional pieces; the flush of religious commentary later in the decade had receded. Instead, he concentrated now on issues of greater political import. In 1597, his *Daemonologie*, probably composed around 1591, was finally published.[22] Then, in 1598, he published his two most significant political prose works: *The Trew Law of Free Monarchies* and the *Basilikon Doron*.

The Trew Law of Free Monarchies was published anonymously but by the King's printer Robert Waldegrave; it was quickly recognised as James's work.[23] The tract called for political principles, 'true grounds' with which to avoid the 'endless calamities, miseries and confusions' that Scotland had suffered. He had no intention, he declared, of 'refuting the adversaries', such as 'seditious preachers in these days of whatsoever religion'. Instead to support his analysis of 'the reciproc [sic] and mutual duty betwixt a free King and his natural subjects', James turned to history, reason and above all scripture.[24] One paragraph drawing on the Scriptures in particular lays out the basis of much of his belief-system and behaviour as King:

> Kings are called Gods by the prophetical King David, because they sit upon God's throne in the earth, and have the count of their administration to give unto him. Their office is *to minister justice and judgement to the people*, as the same David saith: *to advance the good, and punish the evil*, as he likewise saith: *to establish good laws to his people, and procure obedience to the same* as diverse good kings of Judah did: *to procure the peace of the people*, as the same David saith: *to decide all controversies that can arise among them*, as Solomon did: *to be the minister of God, to take vengeance upon them that do well, and as the minister of God, to take vengeance upon them that do evil*, as St Paul saith. And finally, *as a good pastor, to go out and in before his people*, as is said in the first of Samuel: *that through the prince's prosperity, the people's peace may be procured*, as Jeremy saith.[25]

Over the rest of his life, James was often to think, speak and write
of himself as a Solomon or a David – and there were plenty of writers
and preachers among his subjects who were willing to support him
in the notion.

Basilikon Doron was a much longer work, subtitled *Or His Maiesties
Instrvctions to his Dearest Sonne, Henry the Prince.* Henry was four years old
when James composed the tract in 1598; the King's own, much amended
draft survives in the British Library.[26] The book's function is set out
in its opening sonnet:

> Lo here (my son) a mirror vive and faire,
> Which showeth the shadow of a worthy King.
> Lo here a book, a pattern doth you bring
> Which ye should press to follow mair and mair [more].
> This trusty friend, the truth will never spare,
> But give a good advice unto you here:
> How it should be your chief and princely care,
> To follow virtue, vice for to forbear.
> And in this book your lesson will ye leare, [learn]
> For guiding of your people great and small.
> Then (as ye ought) give an attentive ear,
> And panse [think] how ye these precepts practise shall.
>   Your father bids you study here and read.
> How to become a perfit King indeed.[27]

Who could he dedicate the book to, he asks Henry, except the person
to whom it most justly appertained, his dearest son? As his natural
father, he was responsible for Henry's 'godly and virtuous education';
as a king, he had to 'provide for your training up in all the points of
a King's Office'.[28] This is meant to be a manual reflecting his hands-
on experience: as a king, he continues, 'it became me best . . . having
learned both the theorick and practick thereof, more plainly to expres,
than any simple schoolmen, that only knows matters of kingdoms by
contemplation'. James goes on to insist that the book was not 'ordained
for the institution of a prince in general' but rather to contain 'particular precepts to my son in special', containing specific discussions of
'the particular diseases of this kingdom, with the best remedies for

the same', making the book of personal relevance to Henry as future King.[29] Indeed, James was later to claim that it was *Basilikon Doron*'s specificity to the situation in Scotland that led to its misinterpretation in England.

James could not be with his son at Stirling, but the existence of the book facilitated a new educational possibility. He cast *Basilikon Doron* as a textual 'preceptor and counsellor', a 'resident faithful admonisher', that could replace the all too flesh-and-blood tutor James had suffered as a child. Unlike a counsellor though, *Basilikon Doron* lacked human failings: 'ye will find it a just and impartial counsellor; neither flattering you in any vice, nor importuning you at unmeet times. It will not come uncalled, neither speak unspeered at [unquestioned]'.[30] It is tempting to think that James must have had in mind the book that he was given in 1579, Buchanan's *De jure regni ad Scotos*, which his schoolmaster presented to him 'not merely as a guide, but also as an importunate critic – one even lacking, at times, in respect' which would not only 'show you the way', but 'check you and draw you back if you would stray'.[31] Whereas Buchanan saw the role of his book as a rudely importunate critic, James presented *Basilikon Doron* as a respectful, silent tutor or counsellor, available when needed, and easy to access – he thoughtfully divided the short tract into three sections.

Basilikon Doron is an intriguing document, stuffed with advice gleaned from James's fairly conventional reading of the classics and scripture, but with occasional examples drawn from nearer home. On marriage, for example, James instructs Henry to 'keep inviolably your promise to God in your marriage', and to avoid 'the filthy vice of adultery'. 'Have the King my grandfather's example before your eyes,' he suggests, 'who by his adultery, bred the wrack of his lawful daughter and heir [Mary]; in begetting that bastard, who unnaturally rebelled [Moray], and procured the ruin of his own sovereign and sister. And what good her posterity hath gotten sensyne [since], of some of that unlawful generation, Bothwell his treacherous attempts can bear witness.'[32] Henry should be 'well versed in authentic histories, and in the chronicles of all nations, but specially in our own histories the example whereof most nearly concerns you', but James qualifies that instruction: 'I mean not of such infamous invectives as Buchanan's or Knox's Chronicles:

and if any of these infamous libels remain until your days, use the Law upon the keepers thereof.'[33]

The strongest condemnation is reserved for the Kirk. The Protestants in Scotland, James writes, were 'clogged with their own passions', so that the Reformation did not progress properly as it did in Denmark, England or some parts of Germany. Some 'fiery spirited men in the ministry' got carried away with their 'guiding of the people', and began to 'fantasie to themselves a democratic form of government'. This notion, 'overwell baited upon the wrack, first of my grandmother, and next of mine own mother, and after usurping the liberty of the time in my long minority', led to them casting themselves as tribunes of the people, 'and so in a popular government by leading the people by the nose' – one of James's favourite images – 'to bear the sway of all the rule'. These ministers were the cause of all Scotland's problems, James continued. All the factions of his childhood and ever since made sure to court the 'unruly spirits among the ministry', as a result of which 'I was ofttimes calumniated in their popular sermons, not for any evil or vice in me, but because I was a King, which they thought the highest evil'.[34]

Basilikon Doron was first secretly printed, in an anglicised version, by Robert Waldegrave in a tiny 1599 edition of seven copies, for private circulation. Somehow Andrew Melvill got hold of a copy, even before the book was through the press. Not surprisingly, he found much to criticise, especially in James's comments about the Kirk. At the Synod of Fife in September of that year, Melvill's criticisms to *Basilikon Doron* were presented by John Dykes, lambasting what he saw as its pro-English, pro-episcopalian, pro-Catholic tendencies, ingeniously dubbed its 'Anglo-pisco-papistical conclusions'.[35] The Synod did not have time formally to censure the book before James had ordered the arrest of Dykes, who fled instead into England.[36] But in time his complaints were drowned out by the overwhelming success of the book. Over the next few years, *Basilikon Doron* appeared in multiple editions that have been estimated at totalling as many as 16,000 copies: James had written one of the runaway bestsellers of the Renaissance.[37]

CHAPTER TEN

A Wild Unruly Colt

O N 6 AUGUST 1600, Edinburgh awoke to some very strange news. A series of letters arrived telling how, on the previous day, the Earl of Gowrie had sent his brother Alexander, the Master of Ruthven, to the King as he was hunting in Falkland Park. Alexander confided that his brother had found a great treasure in an old tower in his house at St Johnstone – a treasure that might be of help to the King, if he came over to see it that day, without fanfare. James continued hunting for a while, but, after a drink, took a fresh horse and rode on with Alexander, dismissing Lennox and Mar, and taking just a few servants. Despite orders, Lennox and Mar followed the King, and en route met the Lord of Inchaffray, who joined the train. At St Johnstone, James was greeted by Gowrie, who took him into his house and gave him a good dinner, before going into dinner with Lennox and the rest of the King's men.[1]

While they were dining, Alexander persuaded the King to go quietly with him to see the treasure. James dismissed his company, and followed Alexander from chamber to chamber, whose doors the young man locked as they progressed. Finally, they came to a chamber containing a man – the man, so the King thought, who had found the treasure. But suddenly Alexander took hold of the King and drew his dagger, exclaiming that he had killed his father, and now he would kill him. James tried to dissuade him, pointing out that he had been very young when Gowrie was executed, and was therefore innocent of the death. Had he not made amends by restoring Alexander's brother to a greater status than he had previously? If Alexander killed him now, he would not escape, nor would he be Gowrie's heir; he was sure that Alexander had learned more divinity than to kill his prince; and he assured and promised him that if he stopped this enterprise he would keep it secret and forgive him. Alexander retorted that his preaching would not help him, and that he should die, and then struck out at the King. James and Alexander fell to the ground, and Alexander called on the other man to kill the King, but his accomplice answered that, though he was a courageous man, he had neither heart nor hand to do it. Despite being unarmed, in his hunting clothes with only his horn, James defended himself against Ruthven, and managed to struggle to the window to shout 'Treason!' His cries were heard by Sir Thomas Erskine, Lord Herries and John Ramsay, who ran up the stairs to him, but found the doors locked. Ramsay, however, discovered another way in: when the King saw him, he shouted out that he was slain, and Ramsay drew his rapier and killed the Master of Ruthven. Gowrie had told Lennox, Mar and the others that the King had left by a main gate, but when they ran out, there was no sign. Gowrie said he would go back and locate the King, and ran up the stairs with eight men, a steel bonnet and two rapiers; he was met by Ramsay, Erskine and Herries, who between them killed the Earl, both Erskine and Herries being injured in the process. Outside, Gowrie's friends and the local townsmen demanded to know where the Earl was. Lennox and Mar were sent to the magistrates to pacify the situation, and the King and his company got away, James thanking God for his deliverance.

An hour after the news of the attack reached Edinburgh, a letter from the King arrived, outlining the story told above, and the ministers were summoned to appear before the Council. There, James's letter was read out, and the ministers were ordered to 'go to the kirk, convene the people, ring bells, and give praise to God' for the King's deliverance. But the ministers were not about to obey the King's orders without considering the case more carefully. Meeting in the East Kirk, they concluded that they could not speak of treason, since the King had not mentioned it, and the reports by various courtiers were contradictory. They announced to Chancellor Montrose that they could not mention treason, but were happy to say 'in general' that James had been 'delivered from a great danger'. The lords objected that all they had to do was read the King's letter, but the ministers said it was better not to read it, in case they doubted it.[2] At that moment, the minister David Lindsay entered, and told the story first hand. The situation seemed to be saved: Robert Bruce averred that if Lindsay was speaking the truth 'as he would [be] answerable to God', then he 'was well content'. Lindsay went with the lords to the Mercat Cross, and delivered the story to the people, who bared their heads and praised God. And then came the usual celebrations: bells, cannon shot and bonfires.[3]

But soon it became clear that the ministers were not the only men suspicious of the King's story. The doubts gave rise to superstitions. Just before the murders, it was said, the sea, which was at low tide, suddenly 'ran up above the sea mark, higher nor [than] at any stream tide, athort [across] all the coast side of Fife, and in an instant retired again to almost a low water'.[4] On the first Sabbath after the event, the shapes of men were seen in the murder room, 'opening and closing the windows with great flaffing [fluttering, flapping], coming to the windows, looking over, and wringing their hands'. The next day, Monday the 11th, 'such mourning' was heard in the air 'that the people about were terrified'. That afternoon, as James sailed from Clanesse (near East Burntisland) across to Leith, it was noticed 'that there was ebbing and flowing three times at that tide; that the water betwixt Leith and Brunitland was blackish; that the ships in Leith haven were troubled with the swelling of the water'.[5] All these were taken as signs that an unnatural act had taken place, that the deaths of the Ruthvens were murderous. James paid no attention. He was greeted at Leith with the usual great bombast of cannon and harquebuses, 'as if he had been new born', remarked Calderwood sardonically. Thanks were given in church for his deliverance, but James notably failed to respond to the preacher David Lindsay's hope that now the King would carry out the vows he had made previously to ensure 'performance of justice'; instead, Calderwood noted that James merely 'smiled, and talked with these that were about him, after his unreverent manner of behaviour at sermons'.[6]

Despite his apparent nonchalance, James realised that he needed to make good the unlikely story he had told of events at St Johnstone. 'Because many doubted of the report that was made by the King and courtiers,' wrote Calderwood, 'many means were used to make good the report, with presumptions and testimonies which were gathered out of the depositions of some persons which were examined.'[7] In this spirit, James processed with several noblemen from the church to the Mercat Cross, which had been draped with tapestry for the occasion, while Patrick Galloway delivered a sermon on Psalm 124, David being freed from the great danger of his deadly enemies, and James himself gave a speech supporting the notion that the Ruthvens had conspired to kill him, and had been slain as they attempted to put their plan into action, the two speeches lasting over an hour.[8] Galloway

took the opportunity to untangle a potential embarrassment to the
Kirk. The dead Gowrie had been a notably staunch Protestant, but
the preacher refused that interpretation: 'let none think, that by this
traiterous fact of his, our religion has received any blot: for one of
our religion was he not, but a deep dissimulate hypocrite, a profound
atheist, and an incarnate devil in the coat of an angel.' Galloway cited
objects and books which had been discovered since the Earl's death,
'which prove him plainly to have been a studier of magic, and conjurer
of devils, and to have had so many at his command'. Gowrie had
suspiciously lived outside the country, 'haunting with Papists; yea, the
Pope himself' with whom the Earl had made 'convenants and bonds'.
Since returning to Scotland Gowrie had 'travailed most earnestly with
the King, and his Majesty has received from him the hardest assault
that ever he did; from him, I say, to revolt from religion; at least, in
inward sincerity to entertain purpose with the Pope'.[9]

In Galloway's account, it was the evil Gowrie who led James, 'a
most innocent lamb, from his palace to the slaughterhouse', in the
expectation of 'dinner, a cold dinner, yea, a very cold dinner, as they
knew who were there'. 'Now, judge ye, good people,' he continued,
warming to his theme, 'what danger your David was in, whom, as an
innocent lamb, he was closed up betwixt two hungry lions thirsting
for his blood, and four locks betwixt him and his friends and servants,
so that they might neither hear nor hearken unto him.' His delivery
against these odds was nothing short of a miracle that could only be
ascribed to God. Galloway had proof. His source was not the King,
but the very man who 'should have been the doer of the turn' – the
mysterious armed man. 'He is living yet, he is not slain, a man well
enough known to this town: Andrew Henderson, chamberlain to my
Lord of Gowrie.' Galloway brandished a letter of confession from
Henderson: 'any man that would see it, come to me, and see if they
can know his hand writ, for their satisfaction.'[10] 'This is the verity,'
concluded Galloway, 'which will satisfy any good subject: for as these
rumours that go, that the King was a doer and not a sufferer, a pursuer
and not a pursued, it is not true nor likely.' Did they really think that,
if James had had such a plan, he would have gone to the very place
where Gowrie was so well liked, with only ten men to keep him
company, men who were all friendly with Gowrie, like Lennox 'his

godbrother' and Mar 'his godfather', who gave him his name when he was baptised. Men who refused to believe the King would 'perish in their incredulity. There are evidences enough of this verity. Now, what am I that speak these things? One, as I protest before God, who loved the Earl of Gowrie better than any flesh in the earth except his Majesty.'[11]

Few were convinced by Galloway – 'partly', as Calderwood writes, 'because he was a flattering preacher', but partly because Henderson was the fourth man to have been unmasked as the 'armed man'. An early proclamation identified him as Oliphant, 'a black grim man'. But later he was named as Leslie, and then again as Younger. Younger was at least a Gowrie servant, but he had been safely in Dundee on 5 August. When he heard that he was implicated, Younger started out for Falkland, but was slain before reaching Edinburgh by an overeager captain named Harry Bruce. Patrick Galloway assured James: 'Now, sir, the man which should have helped to have done the deed, he could not be gotten alive, but there he lieth dead.' Galloway then set up his friend Gowrie's chamberlain Andrew Henderson as the armed man. Unfortunately, Henderson was no 'black grim man', but 'a man of lower stature, ruddy countenance, and brown bearded'. Even James, asked while hunting the day after the attack whether Henderson was the armed man, said 'it was not he, he knew that smaike [ruffian] well enough'.[12]

Within a week, reported George Nicolson, 'it is begun to be noted that the reports coming from the King should differ': the third man in the chamber was given several names, and had apparently disappeared, or been killed; that the mortally wounded Thomas Cranston had signed a declaration clearing the Ruthvens; that Alexander Ruthven was wearing only a silk cut doublet, and that he was unarmed, or found with his dagger still sheathed; that the Earl of Gowrie was found to have no arms on him 'save a rapier or two with him'. 'The matter,' concluded Nicolson, 'is judged to be otherways than the King reports.' The increasing suspicion could only be curbed, he suggested, if the King would give some of the conspirators 'out of his hands to the town and ministers to be tried and examined for the confessing and clearing of the matter to them and the people upon the scaffold at their execution'. If this failed to happen, 'a hard and dangerous conceit will enter and remain in the hearts of the people and of great ones (how fair soever they carried it to the King) of him and his dealings in this matter'.[13] By the end of August, according to Sir Henry Brouncker, 'the suspicion of the King's plot upon this poor Earl increases daily'.[14] Why would the Ruthvens invite the King to their house to murder him — where they would be held responsible? Why did the King not allow someone else to check out the pot of gold story? Why didn't they go immediately to the treasure? If the King suspected treason, why did he go with Alexander? If the Earl knew the King was coming to dine, why did he go to dinner before the King came? Why was there not a better welcome prepared? Why did the King go unarmed, if Alexander had a sword? How could James have pulled Alexander 'that was thrice as strong' to the window, bring him out of the study, and drive him back to the door of the turn-pike? (A miracle, admitted Galloway.) Why was Alexander not kept alive? He could have been taken after the first blow.[15]

The Privy Council was offended by the ministers' reluctance to toe the line, and reported 'hardly of them' to the King.[16] On 12 August, the ministers appeared before James, who demanded that they explain why they had disobeyed his orders. The ministers replied that they could not speak about the particulars about the dangers the King had been in, because they had no proof of them. 'How are ye yet persuaded?' the King asked Robert Bruce. 'Ye have heard me, ye have heard my minister, ye have heard my Council, ye have heard the Earl of Mar touching the report of this treason: whether are ye yet fully persuaded or not?'

'Surely, sir,' replied Bruce, 'I would have farther light, before I preached it, to persuade the people. If I were but a private subject, not a pastor, I could rest upon your Majesty's report, as other do.'

'Are *ye* fully persuaded?' demanded the King, turning to James Balfour.

'I shall speak nothing to the contrary, sir,' Balfour replied.

'But are ye not persuaded?'

'Not yet, sir.'

William Watson made the same answer, and Walter Balcalquall said that 'he would affirm all that Mr David Lindsay preached in pulpit, in presence of his Majesty', which was founded on James's own report.

James was not satisfied. 'Think ye that Mr David doubted of my report?' Lindsay was sent for, and confirmed that he was 'persuaded in conscience' of this treason. Was this enough to persuade Balcalquall, James demanded? 'Sir, I would further time and light', the minister replied.

'Are *ye* fully persuaded?' James asked John Hall. 'I would have the civil trial going before, sir, that I may be persuaded', replied Hall. Peter Hewatt claimed that 'I suspect not your proclamation'. But do you believe it, James persisted? 'The President heard what I said the last Sabbath', replied Hewatt, but James had to hear with his own ears. 'Sir, I believe it', said Hewatt at last.

Thanks to their answers, Hewatt and George Robertson were spared censure. The other ministers were forbidden to preach anywhere in Scotland, required to quit Edinburgh within forty-eight hours and to keep a distance of ten miles from the city, all under pain of death.[17] In time, four of them capitulated, and were allowed to return to Edinburgh, but only after suffering the humiliation of travelling around the country and giving repeated public performances of their submission. Finally, only Robert Bruce – the only Kirk man that James had trusted enough to place on his Privy Council during his sojourn in Scandinavia – stood firm, and that stand led to his permanent banishment from Scotland on pain of death. 'I see, Mr Robert', said the King, 'that ye would make me a murderer. It is known very well that I was never bloodthirsty', he claimed. 'If I would have taken their lives, I had causes enough. I needed not to hazard myself so.'[18]

Against all odds, James turned the bizarre Gowrie incident into his most successful attack on the Kirk. As even Calderwood had to acknowledge, 'This occasion was gripped at to overthrow the minister at Edinburgh' because the Kirk had 'crossed the court in all their evil proceedings, and was a terror to the session, nobility, and others of the land.' Now, after 5 August, 'the King and Council usurped the place and authority of the Kirk'. To James Melvill, it was 'a sacrilegious sentence' that 'usurping Christ and his Kirk's place and authority, deposit [deprived] them from preaching the Gospel within his country for ever; which was a hundred times war nor [worse than] if by form of civil process he had hanged them'.[19]

The Kirk was not the only victim. James had also triumphed over the Ruthvens, whose humiliation did not end with their deaths. James swore 'to root out the whole house and name'.[20] The bodies of the two young men were set upon gibbets, quartered, and subjected to public display at the cross in Edinburgh. As traitors, the Ruthvens forfeited all their estates and honours; Gowrie's sisters were instantly banished from court; and William and Patrick Ruthven fled to Berwick, to seek shelter in England. In November a Parliament decreed that, 'as the name of Ruthven should be extinguished in all time thereafter', so the place that was now unhappily named Ruthven should be reborn as 'Huntingtower'. For saving the King's life, the young John Ramsay was knighted, and later created Earl of Holderness. On the anniversary of the event, any favour Holderness cared to request was granted.[21] Revising his *Basilikon Doron* for publication, James included a new dig at the family: 'virtue or vice will oftentimes with the heritage, be transferred from the parents to the posterity', he had written; 'witness the experience of the last house of Gowrie', he added. To his brother-in-law Christian IV of Denmark in November 1605 he recalled the occasion 'when by the favour of the divine power we on the fifth day of August in the year 1599' – James's chronology seems to have gone astray here – '[we] escaped the impious and wicked hands of traitors bent on our destruction'.[22] Even as late as 1623, James noted in a letter he was writing to his son Charles and his then favourite Buckingham that he was writing 'upon the good fifth day of August' – still a day of public thanksgiving.[23]

Initial reports suggested that the alleged plot brought the King and Queen closer: 'The Queen makes exceeding much on the King and is glad of his happy deliverance', reported Nicolson a week after the attempt.[24] But James's ruthless eviction from her household of two of the ladies 'in chiefest credit' with Anna, Barbara and Beatrix Ruthven, put a different complexion on the case for the Queen.[25] In August, her younger daughter Margaret died, and it was erroneously reported at the same time that she had miscarried her current pregnancy.[26] Sir George Home, who had become 'the only man of all other most inward with the King', took it on himself to advance a theory concerning the Gowrie plot, suggesting that the Queen might have been involved. It was impossible to prove. 'What the Queen's part was in the matter,' wrote Roger Aston, 'God knows. The presumptions were great both by letters and tokens, as also by her own behaviour after the deed was done.' James could not be convinced, and was concerned only, in Aston's words 'to cover her fully. She has now won so far in to the King by her behaviour towards him as no man dare deal in that matter further. She does daily keep the preaching and entertains the King in a more kind and lovinger sort than ever she did before. She now will obey the King in whatsover, and his will shall be obeyed.'[27]

Other reports were less sanguine about Anna's new obedience. By mid-October, according to the deputy governor of Berwick, 'the Queen of Scots is very narrowly looked unto, and a strait watch kept about her'. It was even reported that after she had given birth, 'she shall be kept as a prisoner ever after, and the King will no more come where she is. It is said that the Queen says plainly that she will be utter enemy to all that were at the murder of Gowrie save the King himself.'[28] It was reported that there was 'an open diffidence' between James and Anna, which one correspondent put down to 'the discovery of some affection between her and the Earl Gowrie's brother', Alexander, which had been 'the truest cause and motif of all that tragedy'.[29]

Matters came to a head at the dinner table in late October, in a display of what the Master of Gray called the 'very evil menage' of the King and Queen. Anna burst out that she knew that James intended to imprison her, but warned him to beware what he minded at for she was not the Earl of Gowrie. He responded that he thought she was mad. He would find she was neither mad nor beside herself, she flashed back, if he did what he intended.[30] James laid the blame for her behaviour on her advanced pregnancy.[31] Despite this embarrassing public scene, however, the royal couple were soon reconciled, perhaps as a result of the birth on 19 November 1600 at Dunfermline, of another son, Charles — by a coincidence, Anna was happily not able to witness the hanging and quartering of the Ruthven brothers' corpses in Edinburgh's marketplace the same day.[32]

Anna did not forget her loyalty to the Ruthvens. Two years later, in December 1602, the English agent James Hudson described Anna to Principal Secretary Sir Robert Cecil as 'that violent woman who will not leave till she either restore the last destroyed house or revenge the fall of it'. Hudson clearly believed Anna to be a danger to the King, but 'the gentleman, the husband, is so syllid [beguiled] in love that none dare deal in this matter as they would or should for fear of offense'. Nevertheless, Hudson continued, Anna's perfidy was a public talking point for the Kirk ministers: 'it has been plainly spoken in pulpits and so fervently that it has drawn out many tears from the auditors to hear so much of the peril of his person, and it has been plainly told herself that she must leave such matters and take a better course'.[33] Anna had no intention of leaving such matters. A month later, she managed to smuggle Beatrix Ruthven back into her palace, and there, 'in a chamber prepared for her by the Queen's direction', Anna had 'much time and conference' with Beatrix. When the incident came to James's attention, he saw it as a security breach, and ordered 'all dangerous passages . . . coming near the King's chamber' to be sealed up. But he didn't blame Anna: instead, her servants were summoned to the chapel to be lectured on the necessity of shunning the Ruthvens — no dealing with them 'without the King's and Queen's direction and privity upon pain of death'.[34] In February 1603, when Anna asked Sir Roger Aston how she was regarded in England, he brought to her attention two matters, which he saw as connected: 'the countenance which she had given to the brethren and sestern [sisters] of Gowrie' and 'the suspicion conceived of some late practice that should have been against his Majesty'. While she protested her innocence of complicity in any plot against the King, he reported, Anna 'could not deny' the Ruthvens.[35]

How James and Anna were regarded in England was by the time of the Gowrie Plot perhaps their primary concern. Since the execution of his mother in 1587, James's every move was made with one eye on England, and his claim to the English throne. The succession was no simple matter. By a series of statutes passed between 1533 and 1546, Henry VIII's crown was to pass to his only legitimate son Prince Edward and then, if Edward should die without issue, to his elder half-sisters, first Mary, and then Elizabeth. In the unlikely event that all three should die without children, the statute empowered Henry to direct the succession by letters patent, or by 'his last will in writing, signed with his most gracious hand'. This scenario had indeed come to pass: Edward had died unmarried at the age of sixteen in 1553; Mary Tudor had died childless five years later; and now Elizabeth was past the age of bearing children. According to Henry's last will, written on 30 December 1546, under these circumstances the crown was to descend through the line of Henry's sister Mary. It was a highly pointed dictate. For Mary, Duchess of Suffolk, was only Henry's younger sister; the elder, who one might expect to have priority, was Margaret, who became Queen of Scotland, and who was James's great-grandmother. Henry had passed over the Scottish line completely.[36] However, the document could be challenged. Henry's will was supposed to be 'signed with his most gracious hand', but there were those who claimed a seal had been used. In any case, the document had helpfully gone missing.

Among the dozen or so pretenders, only two apart from James had any real claim. Edward Seymour, Lord Beauchamp, was the obvious heir through the Suffolk line, but the marriage of his parents, Katherine Grey and Edward Seymour, Earl of Hertford, had been secret, and his legitimacy was far from secure. From the line of James's ancestor Margaret, there was another great-grandchild from her second marriage. But Lady Arbella Stuart was female, and her Protestant credentials were dubious: the Pope himself had recommended her to English Roman Catholics as Elizabeth's proper successor. Even so, for those willing to make a negative case, the odds were stacked against James. James owed his claim to the English throne through his mother, but his mother had been executed for treason against the current sovereign of England. James was an alien, and aliens could not inherit a pebble on English soil. Just how strongly this was felt had been seen in the year of James's birth when Patrick Adamson had published his poem welcoming the King of Scotland, France and England. In the English Parliament, a lawyer named James Dalton launched a tirade against Adamson's poem, protesting that he hoped he would never see the day 'that ever any Scot or stranger shall have any interest in the Crown of this realm, for it is against the law that any person other than such as be born the Prince's subjects hold merit in this land'. The matter was calmed by diplomatic interventions by Queen Mary's ambassador and Elizabeth herself, but the point was well made: James was no Englishman.[37]

The King of Scots' case required some support on the ground in England. James may have hoped to enlist as allies the powerful Cecils: father William Cecil, Lord Burghley, Elizabeth's Lord Treasurer and most valued adviser until his death in 1598, and son Sir Robert Cecil, who was officially appointed Principal Secretary of State in 1596 after unofficially fulfilling the duties of the post for several years. James's relations with the Cecils, however, had been fitful: the repeated failures of the English to pay his annual pension could easily be blamed, fairly or unfairly, on the Lord Treasurer.[38] James turned instead to Elizabeth's young, handsome and famously headstrong favourite, Robert Devereux, second Earl of Essex. In 1592, James approached Essex for help in a trivial matter concerning which he had previously approached Lord Treasurer Burghley, but 'always without effect';[39] two years later, he was routinely recommending his ambassadors instead to Essex.[40] The surviving papers of Essex's right-hand man, Anthony Bacon, bear witness to a thriving correspondence between the Essex camp and any number of Scottish informants: Dr Thomas Morison, Edward Bruce, Abbot of Kinloss, John Bothwell, the laird of Holyroodhouse, Dr Herries, Robert Bowes, James Hudson, Roger Aston and James Foulis.[41] James's distaste for the Cecils intensified when he received reports, vehemently denied, that Sir Robert Cecil had met Bothwell during an embassy to Rouen in 1598.[42]

But there were those who thought that Essex himself had designs on the English throne, and might prove a rival to James's claim.[43] In March 1599, Essex set off to Ireland at the head of the English army, and at the height of his power. Realising that James might interpret this as a potential military threat, Charles Blount, Lord Mountjoy, an Essex supporter already in Ireland, sent a messenger to Scotland in the summer of 1599 to assure him that Essex would not challenge his claim.[44] By the autumn, Essex was in no position to challenge anybody's claim: ordered out of Ireland by the Queen, he was held under house arrest in London, and then tried by Star Chamber in November. Mountjoy then proposed a concrete plan in February 1600: James should prepare an army 'at a convenient time' and Mountjoy would provide forces from Ireland. But, sensing that Essex's powers were declining, James was noncommittal, and the scheme withered away.[45] By May 1600, Essex was placing himself in James's hands: 'such as I am, and all whatsoever I am (though perhaps a subject of small price) I consecrate unto your regal throne . . . Neither do I doubt, that the minds of al my countrymen . . . will jointly unite their hopes in your majesty's noble person, as the only center, wherein our rest and happiness consist.'[46] The following month, Essex was brought before a court at York House, dismissed from all his offices of state, and put under house arrest.

It was not until the end of the year that Essex showed signs of regaining his former confidence. On 25 December 1600, the Earl wrote James a long tirade against what he saw as 'this reigning faction', by which he meant Cecil's party, which had 'left no degree, county, nor no man almost of living, courage, or understanding without some complaint against them'. Among their heinous deeds, he alleged, were 'their devilish plots with your Majesty's own subjects against your person and life'. He urged James to beware of the 'reigning faction': 'as they seduce some that are weak and ignorant by their slanderous reports of your Majesty, so they abuse others that are well affected to you by a persuasion that this faction hath a great secret interest in your favor, which doth more advantage them and hurt your Majesty and your friends than any one thing whatsoever'. But he was responding to calls to take on the Cecils. 'Now am I summoned of all sides to stop the malice, the wickedness and madness of these men, and to relieve my poor country that groans under her burthen [burden]. Now doth reason, honor, and conscience command me to be active. Now do I see by God's favor the fairest and likeliest hopes that can be of good success.' To aid this campaign, Essex suggested that James send an ambassador, preferably the Earl of Mar, to London, and gave 1 February 1601 as a deadline. 'And when by God's favor your Majesty shall be secured from all practises here and against all competitions whatsoever, you shall be declared and acknowledged the certain and undoubted successor to this crown.'[47]

James apparently responded to this in a ciphered letter, which has not survived. An embassy was prepared, to be led by Mar and Edward Bruce, Abbot of Kinloss. They were instructed to 'temper and frame all your dealing with the Queen or Council by the advice of my friends there, whose counsel ye shall directly follow in all your behaviour there'. If his friends 'perform their promises on their part', Mar and Kinloss were delegated 'ample power to give them full assurance of my assisting them accordingly'.[48] The embassy was about to leave, a few weeks behind schedule, in mid-February when news arrived from

England. Essex had indeed followed reason, honour and conscience and been 'active', as he predicted, attempting to lead an uprising in the City of London on Sunday 8 February 1601 – precisely one week after he had wanted James's embassy in England. The rebellion failed miserably, as Essex's expected support failed to materialise; there was no doubt in the minds of local commentators that the fiasco must spell the end of Essex's political hopes. James hurriedly revised his instructions to the ambassadors. If James's 'friends' thought it best that his allegiances remain hidden, then they should follow their advice; but 'if they think that your kything [intervening] in it may do good, stand not upon terms and I shall avow you bravely'. If, however, 'as God forbid, it be past redding ere [saving before] ye come there, use then all the means ye can to get me a party there and assure them I can neither with honour nor surety disguise myself any longer'.[49]

The situation was 'past redding' even before Mar and Kinloss finally arrived in London, with Essex and several of his associates already executed. In a series of audiences with Elizabeth, Mar and Kinloss received 'nothing but negative answers, the matters being of so sour nature to the Queen, who loves neither importunity nor expostulation'.[50] Exhausted after a month, the ambassadors complained of the Queen's 'coldness',[51] which they attributed to her continued suspicions about James's connections with Essex. Cecil reported that Elizabeth was 'infinitely distasted' because Mar and Kinloss 'were reserved in confessing the traffic between' James and Essex, 'whom it seemed the King did either believe to be his friend, or thought it wisdom to seem so. For her Majesty, knowing all particulars, took it unkindly.' But, he added, Elizabeth's heart was so far from malice 'though it will never be free from jealousy, as she was contented to lap up all things, and to profess once more a good satisfaction and mutual correspondency'.[52] Elizabeth had good reason to be suspicious: when Essex was arrested, it was said that he'd been wearing James's most recent letter in a casket round his neck. Writing to James in April 1601, Elizabeth signed off with a teasingly opaque reference: 'Remember, that a bird of the air, if no other instrument, to an honest King shall stand in stead of many feigned practices, to utter aught may anywise touch him. And so I leave my scribbles, with my best wishes that you scan what works becometh best a King, and what in end will best avail him.'[53] But at the last minute, Elizabeth added an extra paragraph to her letter, offering an increase in her pension to James, from £3,000 to £5,000 a year — on the condition that it should be 'thankfully accepted and sincerely requited and deserved'.[54]

At the same time, Mar and Kinloss followed James's instruction to 'get me a party' in England, turning inevitably to Sir Robert Cecil, whose influence with Elizabeth was now almost unchallenged. Given that Cecil knew that James had inclined to Essex earlier, the establishing of this new relationship required some fancy footwork, and James rose to the occasion with a letter that demonstrated the slippery evasion of great statecraft. Employing the most rudimentary of ciphers to disguise the leading players, '30' (James) made formal advances to '10' (Secretary Cecil), declaring how 'heartily glad' he was that 10 'hath now at last made choice of two so fit and confident ministers whom with he hath been so honourably plain in the affairs of 30'. The fact that these fit and confident ministers had in fact been sent to deal with Essex was tidily forgotten. Unable to 'speak face to face' with Cecil, James proposed that they use 'his long approved and trusty 3' as their intermediary, 'a sure and secret interpreter'. '3' was Lord Henry Howard, indeed one of Essex's closest followers through the late 1590s, the Earl's eyes and ears at court when Essex was in Ireland.[55] But, as one commentator noted in September 1599, despite his Essex affiliations, Howard was a 'neuter' (neutral party),[56] who also pursued friendly relations with Cecil. At the time, this worked to Essex's advantage: as the same commentator noted, when 'things were far out of square between him and Mr Secretary', Howard 'hath infinitely travelled in his business', and 'by his direction' the Earl and the Secretary seemed 'to be upon better terms'.[57] When Essex started to formulate his plans for the February 1601 uprising, Howard kept his distance. Now Howard was ideal, James argued, because he had urged James 'to take a good conceit' of Cecil, and had tried to bring about a 'conformity' between Cecil and Essex, when Cecil 'mistrusted the aspiring mind of Essex'. For his own part, James protested 'upon his conscience and honour, that Essex had never had any dealing with him which was not most honorable'. As for the Earl's 'misbehaviour', it wasn't James's place to judge it, because, although he 'loved him for his virtues, he was no ways obliged to embrace his quarrels'.[58] But he was pleased that Cecil had broken his silence towards him, for James admitted that it had been 'continually beaten in my ears that your silence did proceed, not of duty to your sovereign, but out of unquenchable malice against me'.[59]

Thus was born a secret correspondence. The true identities of the correspondents were concealed: letters from James were often closed by the seals of other Scottish figures with whom Cecil might legitimately be corresponding; letters from England appear to have been received as being from the Duc de Bohan.[60] Cecil was almost neurotically concerned to keep the correspondence privy: when Edward Bruce once wrote saying he thought a packet had been lost, Howard made sure that Cecil didn't read the news: 'if Cecil had seen [the clause], I protest to God all the course of convoy and intelligence had been ruined for ever . . . upon the multiplicity of doubts his mind would never have been at rest, nor he would have eaten or slept quietly; for nothing makes him confident, but experience of secret trust, and security of intelligence.'[61]

Cecil advised James that the best approach would be to employ 'clear and temperate courses' to win over Elizabeth, who was naturally adverse to 'needless expostulations, or overly much curiosity in her own actions'. He advised him to confine himself to 'a choice election of a few in the present, will be of more use than any general acclamation of many', and he should ignore those who urged him to be 'too busy, to prepare the vulgar beforehand'.[62] 'No!' James snorted contemptuously. He was not 'so evil [poorly] acquainted with the histories of all ages and nations' that he was ignorant of 'what a rotten reed *mobile vulgus* is to lean unto' – although some of Cecil's countrymen had recently learned that lesson the hard way. He would never give Elizabeth 'any just cause of jealousy, through my too busy behaviour'.[63]

As Cecil pointed out, 'the subject itself is so perilous to touch amongst us, as it setteth a mark upon his head forever that hatcheth such a bird'. But, then again, James should be reassured that 'on the faith I owe to God, that there is never a prince or state in Europe with whom either mediate or immediate her Majesty hath entered into speech these twelve years of that subject'.[64] Sir Robert was pleased that 'if it should happen that the veil of secrecy were taken off by error or by destiny, the Queen herself (who were likest to resort to jealousy) should (notwithstanding) still discern clearly, that whatsoever hath passed in this correspondency hath wholly tended to her own repose and safety, without any incroachment upon other liberty than such as divers good physicians do take when they deceive an indisposed patient by giving *salutaria pro soporiferis*'.[65] To James there was soon no 'so worthy, so wise, and so provident a friend as 10 is', not even his childhood friend: 'I trust no more in the fidelity of 20 [Mar] that of a child was brought up with me, than I do in you.'[66] By the autumn and winter of 1602, paranoid secrecy about the succession was beginning to wane.[67] In October of that year, Cecil let the French ambassador know that he supported James as successor to Elizabeth, a move that was noted by other foreign ambassadors.[68] A young Scottish gentleman named Indernyty, passing through England, reported to James on 9 February 1603 'that wherever I passed and lodged they think your Majesty their young lord, which within few years so man durst [dared] speak'.[69] For James's part, he looked forward to the day he could ride south: 'St George surely rides upon a towardly riding horse, where I am daily burstin [burst] in daunting a wild unruly colt.'[70] He did not have much longer to wait. Early in the morning of Thursday 24 March 1603, Elizabeth I died. Eight hours later in London, James was proclaimed King of England.

CHAPTER ELEVEN

Betwixt Both

A S JAMES LOOKED south to his future, he did not forget his past. Making his last 'harangue' to Edinburgh on Sunday 3 April 1603, he made it clear that what was uppermost in his mind was unity between his two realms. 'As my right is united in my person,' he declaimed, 'so my marshes are united by land, and not by sea, so that there is no difference betwixt them. There is no more difference betwixt London and Edinburgh, yea, not so much, as betwixt Inverness or Aberdeen and Edinburgh; for all our marshes are dry, and there be ferries betixt them. But my course must be betwixt both, to establish peace, and religion, and wealth, betwixt both the countries. And as God has joined the right of both the kingdoms in my person, so ye may joined in wealth, in religion, in hearts, and affections.' He assured them that he could not forget Scotland. 'Ye mister [must] not doubt, but as I have a body as able as any king in Europe, whereby I am able to travel, so I shall vissie [visit] you every three year at the least, or ofter [more often], as I shall occasion; for so I have written in my book directed to my son, and it were a shame to me not to perform that thing which I have written. Think not of me, as a king going from one part to another; but as a king lawfully called, going from one part of the isle to the other, that so your comfort may be the greater.'[1]

It had been decided that the royal family should stagger their entry into England. James would be the first to go, followed by Anna with Prince Charles and Princess Elizabeth on 14 May.[2] Prince Henry, now nine years old, would stay at Stirling for the time being. With no time to visit his heir before leaving for England, James wrote a letter to Henry. Although many of the sentiments are banal, James's excitement at his new challenge is palpable:

My son, That I see you not before my parting impute it to this great occasion, wherein time is so precious, but that shall, by God's grace, be recompensed by your coming to me shortly, and continual residence with me ever after; let not this news make you proud or insolent, a King's son and heir was ye before, and no more are ye yet; the augmentation that is hereby like to fall unto you, is but in cares and heavy burdens; be therefore merry but not insolent; keep a greatness but *sine fastu* [without pride]; be resolute, but not wilful; keep your kindness, but in honourable sort; choose none to be your playfellows but them that are well born; and, above all things, give never good countenance to any but according as ye shall be informed that they are in estimation with me; look upon all Englishmen that shall come to visit you as upon your loving subjects, not with that ceremony as towards strangers, and yet with such heartiness as at this time they deserve . . .

With the letter he sent a copy of his *Basilikon Doron* 'lately printed'. 'Study and profit in it as ye would deserve my blessing,' he instructed his son. On matters where the book laid down no specific advice, Henry should weigh the advice of his counsellors against James's general rules, 'mistrusting and frowning upon them that advises you to the contrare. Be diligent and earnest in your studies,' he urged, 'that at your meeting with me, I may praise you for your progress in learning.'[3]

On 4 April 1603, James set off for his new throne, travelling down England through Berwick, Withrington, Newcastle, Durham, York, Doncaster, Newark, Burley, Royston and Theobalds – the journey deliberately filling a whole month so that the formal sadness of Elizabeth's funeral on 28 April could be forgotten by the time he reached London. Each city and town welcomed their new King with fireworks, bonfires, orations, feasting and gifts. In return, James gave a performance of regal generosity: on his command, the gaols were opened, and prisoners set at liberty – excepting those accused of treason, murder, or 'Romish disloyalty'.[4] More controversially, James started to hand out knighthoods to the chief gentlemen of each county, on the recommendation of his Scottish favourites; soon it was rumoured that these favourites were taking bribes from would-be knights in exchange for their support, and the English lawyer Roger Wilbraham noted disapprovingly that 'it grew a public speech that English had the blows and Scottish the crowns'.[5]

James reached the Cecils' estate of Theobalds on 3 May, meeting for the first time his long-time correspondent Sir Robert Cecil, and there too he attended his first English Privy Council meeting.[6] Four days later, as he approached London, James was met at Stamford Hill by the capital's Lord Mayor, its Aldermen and five hundred citizens all in chains of gold, with outpourings of loyalty and gladness. As he made his way to London, James was mobbed. The crowds of people, one observer reported, 'in the highways, fields, meadows, closes, and on trees was so great that they covered the beauty of the fields; and so greedy were they to behold the King that they injured and hurt one another'.[7] With a reputed 40,000 trying to attend court, and some 100,000 extra bodies in London, James was 'swarmed' by well-wishers and suitors 'at every back gate and privy door, to his great offence', reported Wilbraham.[8]

While James was being welcomed in London, Anna was at Stirling for the first time in five years. She knew that the Earl of Mar, Henry's guardian, was riding south with the King: without his opposition, she believed that she could do what she had failed to do eight years earlier – bring her eldest son away with her. But Mar's wife and son easily guessed what the Queen planned. When James entrusted Henry to Mar's care he had specified that, even if he died, Mar was to 'see that neither for the Queen nor Estates their pleasure you deliver him till he be eighteen years of age, and that he command you himself'.[9] Accordingly, the Mars flatly refused to let Henry go out. But Anna was not to be easily swayed. Soon she was joined at Stirling by a small group of nobles, all of them 'well supported'[10] – armed and manned – and perhaps Anna believed that she could use them to take Henry by force. But once again, sticking to the rules of the house, the Mars would not allow anyone in with more than two followers. The Venetian ambassador reported that Anna flew into a violent fury, and four months gone with child as she was, she beat her own belly, so that they say she is in manifest danger of miscarriage and death'.[11] It seems that indeed she did miscarry: according to David Calderwood's account, the Queen 'went to bed in an anger, and parted with child the tenth of May'.[12]

The Earl of Mar arrived back at Stirling two days later, carrying orders from James that the Queen was to join her husband in England. The Queen decided not to allow him to convey the King's commands, not deigning even to 'look upon him', and instead demanding to be given the letters sent from James. Mar refused, saying that he would only do so if she would grant him access to her presence 'to discharge his secret commission'. Once again, Anna and Mar reached an impasse. They both sent letters posthaste to James, Anna accusing her husband of listening to scurrilous rumours about her involvement in Catholic and Spanish plots, of not loving her, and of only marrying her because of her high birth. James responded by sending the Duke of Lennox to mediate, and wrote to Anna protesting 'upon the peril of my salvation and damnation, that neither the Earl of Mar nor any flesh living ever informed me that ye was upon any papish or Spanish course'. 'I say over again,' he pleaded, in a rare moment of apparent emotion towards his wife,

> leave these froward womanly apprehensions, for, I thank God, I
> carry that love and respect unto you which by the law of God and
> nature I ought to do my wife and mother of my children, but not
> for ye are a king's daughter, for whether ye were a king's or a cook's
> daughter ye must be all alike to me, being once my wife. For the
> respect of your honourable birth and descent I married you, but
> the love and respect I now bear you is because that ye are my
> married wife, and so partaker of my honour as of my other
> fortunes. I beseech you excuse my rude plainness in this; for casting
> up of your birth is a needless impertinent argument to me. God is
> my witness, I ever preferred you to all my bairns [children], much
> more than to any subject . . .[13]

Lennox arrived at Stirling on 19 May with what was phrased as a compromise, but was in effect a climb-down on the King's part. Mar, his mother and his friends 'had done good service to the King', Lennox declared, but now he had been ordered 'to transport both the Queen and the Prince' into England. The handing over of the Prince was a delicate business. The Council convened in Stirling and barred the Queen's posse of noblemen from coming within ten miles of Henry; instead, Mar would deliver the Prince to Lennox, and Lennox would hand him over to the Council. The Council then, 'to pleasure the Queen', delivered Henry to Anna and Lennox, who would take him to the King, with a retinue of noblemen from which Mar was excluded, 'to pleasure the Queen'.[14]

Knowing he had lost this battle, Mar departed for England immediately. Anna spent some time convalescing after her miscarriage, and then on Friday 27 May set out for Linlithgow with Prince Henry. The train reached Edinburgh the following evening, and on Tuesday 31 May the Queen and Prince travelled to the Great Kirk in a coach, accompanied by many English ladies in coaches and on horse. 'Great was the confluence of people flocking to see the Prince,' reported Calderwood. The following day, about 10 a.m., Anna and Henry set out for England; Princess Elizabeth, who had been sick the night before, followed two days later.[15] Prince Charles was left in the care of Lord President Fyvie at Dunfermline, where visitors found him to be 'a very weak child'. Fyvie reported at the end of the month that Charles was 'yet weak in body, is beginning to speak some words far better as yet of his mind and tongue nor [than] of his body and feet'.[16] It may well be that the King and Queen did not expect their younger son to live.

Once they were able to observe him close at hand, early English impressions of the King were highly favourable. The verdict of the lawyer Roger Wilbraham was typical: 'The King is of sharpest wit and invention, ready and pithy speech, an exceeding good memory; of the sweetest, pleasantest and best nature that ever I knew; desiring nor affecting anything but true honour.' Before meeting him, the Venetian ambassador Giovanni Carlo Scaramelli had heard 'on all sides that he is a man of letters and business, fond of the chase and of riding, sometimes indulging in play. These qualities attract men to him and render him acceptable to the aristocracy. Besides English, he speaks Latin and French perfectly and understands Italian quite well. He is capable of governing, being a Prince of culture and intelligence above the common.' When he was granted his first audience with the new King at Greenwich in May 1603, Scaramelli provided a vivid portrait of James. 'I found all the Council about his chair, and an infinity of other lords almost in an attitude of adoration. His Majesty rose and took six steps towards the middle of the room, and then drew back one, after making me a sign of welcome with his hand. He then remained standing up while he listened to me attentively. He was dressed in grey silver satin, quite plain, with a cloak of black tabinet [material made of silk and wool] reaching below his knees and lined with crimson, he had his arm in a white sling, the result of a fall from his horse; from his dress he would have been taken for the meanest of his courtiers, a modesty he affects, had it not been for a chain of diamonds around his neck and a great diamond in his hat.'[17]

Others had minor reservations. Although he came across immediately as mentally alert, 'witty to conceive and very ready of speech', in Sir Thomas Lake's estimation, he was surprisingly not given to using 'great majesty nor solemnities in his accesses'. Francis Bacon, an ambitious lawyer and courtier whose brother Anthony had facilitated relations between Essex and James and who hoped to flourish under the new regime, opined that 'His speech is swift and cursory, and in the full dialect of his country; and in point of business short; in point of discourse large . . . He is thought somewhat general in his favours, and his virtue of access is rather because he is much abroad and in press than that he giveth easy audience about serious things.' Bacon's one reservation was that James showed a lack of foresight in calling for advice about 'the time past than of the time to come'.[18]

James's accession was somewhat marred by a terrible outbreak of plague in London necessitating the impromptu rehousing of the royal family in Winchester, at a safe distance from the capital. Although his coronation went ahead on 11 July, the ceremony was much curtailed; the planned public festivities had to be postponed, and ultimately did not take place until 15 March 1604.[19] The City of London prepared for the big day with military precision. 'The streets are surveyed,' wrote the playwright Thomas Dekker, 'heights, breadths, and distances taken, as it were to make fortifications, for the solemnities. Seven pieces of ground, (like so many fields for a battle) are plotted forth, upon which these Arches of Triumph must show themselves in their glory; aloft, in the end do they advance their proud foreheads.'[20] These seven 'Arches of Triumph' – at Fenchurch, Gracious Street, the Royal Exchange, two on Cheapside, Fleet Street and Temple Bar – were the focal points for complex allegorical representations honouring James and Anna, planned and scripted by a team of highly skilled artisans led by the joiner Stephen Harrison, and dramatic poets, including Ben Jonson and Dekker himself.[21] On the day itself, all of London turned out to acclaim the King, Queen and Prince as they rode through the city: 'The streets seemed to be paved with men,' wrote Dekker, 'stalls instead of rich wares were set out with children, open casements filled up with women. All glass windows taken down, but in their places, sparkled so many eyes, that had it not been the day, the light which reflected from them, was sufficient to have made one.'[22] But James was no Elizabeth, who had lapped up the crowds' adulation, and given them what they wanted in return. His reluctance was quickly noticed. As Arthur Wilson recalled, 'He was not like his predecessor, the late Queen of famous memory, that with a well-pleased affection met her people's acclamations . . . He endured the day's brunt with patience, being assured he should never have such another.' There were, of course, other such days to come, but James made less and less effort to play his part. 'Afterwards in his public appearances,' wrote Wilson, 'the accesses of the people made him so impatient, that he often dispersed them with frowns.'[23]

There had been considerable anxiety among the English Privy Council that James would have his own ideas about who should counsel him – or more pointedly, that they find themselves replaced by his Scottish favourites. So there was great relief when it became apparent that for the most part the new King was happy to keep Elizabeth's counsellors about him. Among these, unsurprisingly, Cecil was an early confidant. The French ambassador reported in May 1603 that the Secretary 'begins to grow great with the king, staying alone with him shut up in the *cabinet* [James's personal closet] for three or four hours together.'[24] James elected to retain all the other thirteen of Elizabeth's Privy Councillors, promoting several men who had supported his cause over the last years, including Henry Howard, who now became Earl of Northampton, and Essex's ally Mountjoy, who became Earl of Devonshire. But James did add five Scots to the Council: Lennox and Mar, two long-standing allies; James Elphinstoun, the Scottish Secretary; Sir George Home, who was later to become Earl of Dunbar; and Edward Bruce, who became Lord Kinloss. In practice the influence of these five men in England was negligible. Mar and Elphinstone never lived outside Scotland; Lennox was a familiar and high-ranking presence in court, but without real power; Kinloss, the only Scot to be given high office in 1603 (as Master of the Rolls), died shortly afterwards. Only Dunbar would rise, becoming in turn chief adviser for Scottish affairs, Chancellor of the Exchequer and Master of the Wardrobe.[25]

Despite their relative absence from the top government posts, the Scots made their presence felt in other ways. For James's accession to the English throne produced an important shift in the style of government. Reduced to its most basic components, political influence could be measured by access to the physical presence – and therefore to the ear – of the sovereign. Under Henry VIII, the most intimate space in the royal household was the Privy Chamber, and within the Privy Chamber, there had been the even more private Privy Lodgings centring on the King's Bedchamber. When Elizabeth came to the throne, the fact that the sovereign was now a woman, who had to be surrounded at certain times by other women rather than by her councillors, had meant that the Privy Lodgings, where she spent much of her time, were divided from the Privy Chamber by a Withdrawing Chamber; as a result the Privy Lodgings lost much of their explicitly political tone, and the Privy Chamber became more formal, but also politically influential. With James's accession to the throne, however, there came to the English court what has been dubbed 'the revival of the entourage'. Under the new King, it was not the Privy Chamber, but the Bedchamber and the men it contained, that became the focus of attention. The Bedchamber controlled the more intimate aspects of serving the King, while the Privy Chamber became a more formal, ceremonial space. Whereas attempts were made to keep the Privy Chamber roughly half Scots and half English, the Bedchamber was comprised almost entirely of Scottish courtiers, with the sole exception of Sir Philip Herbert. Lennox was Steward of the Household; Sir George Home, Master of the Wardrobe; John Murray, Keeper of the Privy Purse; and Sir Thomas Erskine, a cousin of Mar, Captain of the Guard. This last appointment was particularly resented, since the post had been confiscated from the popular English courtier Sir Walter Ralegh.[26]

It was the absolute dominance of Scots in James's immediate

household that particularly galled English commentators like Gervase Holles, who wrote of James bringing with him 'a crew of necessitous and hungry Scots' and filling 'every corner of the Court with these beggarly bluecaps', referring to the blue woollen bonnets that the Scots were traditionally reputed to wear.[27] His kinsman Sir John Holles complained in 1610 that 'the Scottish monopolize his princely person, standing like mountains betwixt the beams of his grace and us', urging that the Bedchamber should be 'shared as well to those of our nation as to them'.[28] The exclusion from the Bedchamber had serious administrative implications. Since the household ordinances stated that 'no person of what condition soever do at any time presume or be admitted to come to us in our Bedchamber, but such as . . . are . . . sworn of it, without our special licence, except the Princes of Our Blood',[29] some of James's leading government officials were effectively excluded from the regular access to the King that was constantly enjoyed by his Bedchamber staff. Even Secretaries of State would be granted audiences in the (outer) Privy Chamber or Withdrawing Chamber, with the King emerging from his (inner) Bedchamber for the purpose. In the words of the Venetian agent in May 1603, 'No Englishmen, be his rank what it may, can enter the Presence Chamber without being summoned, whereas the Scottish lords have free entrée of the Privy Chamber, and more especially at the toilette.'[30]

When James made the journey south to London upon his accession in 1603, expectations had been high for his performance as sovereign. 'Our virtuous King makes our hopes to swell; his actions suitable to the time and his natural disposition,' enthused Thomas Wilson, a Cecil protégé, in June. But it was soon discovered that James's 'natural disposition' led him away from what many regarded as his kingly duties. 'Sometimes he comes to Council,' Wilson reported, 'but most time he spends in fields and parks and chases, chasing away idleness by violent exercise and early rising, wherein the sun seldom prevents him.'[31] Or as the Venetian ambassador Giovanni Carlo Scaramelli put it: 'the King, in spite of all the heroic virtues ascribed to him when he left Scotland and inculcated by him in his books, seems to have sunk into a lethargy of pleasures, and will not take heed of matters of state. He remits everything to the Council, and spends his time in the house alone, or in the country at the chase.'[32]

James did not believe himself to be negligent in his style of government. Indeed, he was continuing very much in the way he had for the past two decades in Scotland. But the English had become accustomed, over some forty-five years, to a very different sovereign. Elizabeth had made herself central to decision-making on virtually every level, playing her counsellors and courtiers off against each other as though they were suitors for her affections, while demonstrating an almost pathological tendency towards procrastination. This meant that, no matter how annoying her counsellors may have found her, Elizabeth was always present, always the centre of their attention. But the new King was more often away from court altogether, in the country with his horses and his hounds.

Hunting had been a passion for James since his adolescence. Recommending a range of sports to his son Henry in his *Basilikon Doron*, it was hunting to which he gave special praise, deeming it 'martial' and 'noble', 'specially with running hounds, which is the most honorable and noblest sort thereof', although he acknowledged that he might well be considered 'a partial praiser of this sport'.[33] Not that James was necessarily an adept huntsman: the Lancashire gentleman Nicholas Assheton reported in his journal one afternoon of royal hunting during the August 1617 progress, during which James 'went and shot at a stag, and missed. Then my Lord Compton had lodged two brace. The King shot again, and brake the thigh-bone.'[34] It seems that such a patchy performance was not unusual. To indulge his passion, James established small hunting lodges at Newmarket and Royston within months of his accession to the English throne. These lodges were not far from London, but far enough for him to be notably absent from the mechanics of government. For whereas Elizabeth on her lengthy summer processes had been followed, albeit with reluctance, by her entire court including the Privy Council, James took off for the fields with only what one observer contemptuously dismissed as 'his hunting crew' in tow;[35] a crew the Venetian ambassador described as 'a few persons only, and those always the same, people of low degree, as is usual in that exercise'.[36] It has been calculated that throughout his entire reign in England, James spent about half his time either at his hunting lodges or on progress, and when at the lodges, his household comprised only one or two clerks, the Guard, the Privy Chamber, and, of course, the Bedchamber.[37] This was not the English way, as the Venetian ambassador noted: James was 'more inclined to live retired with eight or ten of his favourites than openly, as is the custom of the country and the desire of the people'.[38]

When challenged, James cited his health as the reason for hunting – it allowed him to escape both the unhealthy environs of London, and the sedentary life it entailed. Two days after the Christmas festivities finished at court in 1605, for example, James took off for Royston. He wrote to his Privy Council to tell them 'that it is the only means to maintain his health, which being the health and welfare of us all, he desires them to undertake the charge and burden of affairs, and foresee that he be not interrupted nor troubled with too much business'.[39] The new Venetian ambassador Nicolo Molin elaborated how James had explained that, after having been nearly three weeks in London, he found 'this sedentary life' very prejudicial to his health. In Scotland, he had been able to spend much time in the country, 'and in hard exercise'; the forced repose down south 'robs him of his appetite and breeds melancholy and a thousand other ills'. Since his health was paramount, he informed the Council, he would come to London 'but seldom', spending most of the time hunting in the country. According to Molin, James went on to conclude 'by announcing that he will approve all their resolutions. In this way the King has virtually given full and absolute authority to the Council, and has begun to put his plan in practice, for many who went to him with petitions and grievances have been told to go to the Council, for they are fully authorized to deal with all business public and private.'[40] 'I shall never take longer vacancy from them,' he told Cecil to assure his Council, 'for the necessary maintenance of my health, than other kings will consume upon their physical diets and going to their whores.'[41]

James may have imagined that he had struck a perfect trade-off: the Privy Council would be given a free hand, and he would be allowed to regain his health. But in practice, things did not work out so simply. As the Earl of Worcester, one of the four councillors who made up James's inner sanctum of government, reported in May 1605, James had been 'very ill' with a heavy cold since coming to the country, thanks to 'the sharpness of the air and wind'. Indeed, everyday the

King went hunting 'he taketh a new cold; for, being hot with riding a long chase, he sitteth in the open air and drinketh, which cannot but continue, if not increase, a new cold'. If his health did not bother him, then his subjects did. Worcester reported how James had been out hunting near Thetford, but 'was driven out of the field with press of company, which came to see him'. The King, he wrote, 'took no great delight' in the intrusion, and 'came home, and played at cards'. Sir William Woodhouse, a local dignitary, was ordered to devise a proclamation 'that none shall presume to come to him on hunting days, but those that come to see him, or prefer petitions, shall do it going forth, or coming home'.[42]

More importantly, it soon became apparent that the Council was not confident of its power to bypass the King and was forced constantly to attempt to win the King's attention while he was on hunting trips – no mean feat. Worcester, attending the hunting crew at Royston in December 1604, complained to his fellow councillor Shrewsbury that

> I think I have not had two hours of twenty-four of rest but Sundays, for in the morning we are on horseback by eight, and so continue in full career from the death of one hare to another, until four at night; by that time I find at my lodging sometimes one, most commonly two packets of letters, all which must be answered before I sleep, for here is none of the Council but myself, no, not a Clerk of the Council nor Privy Signet, so that an ordinary warrant for post horse must pass my own hand, my own secretary being sick at London.[43]

James's absences thus caused huge problems for his principal councillors, especially since he often refused point blank to deal with any official paperwork. It was not long before even Cecil was lamenting the change of regime from that of Elizabeth, which took on a retrospective halcyon glow: 'I wish I waited now in her presence-chamber, with ease at my food, and rest in my bed. I am pushed from the shore of comfort, and know not where the winds and waves of a court will bear me.'[44]

While the Privy Council encountered administrative problems with the King's absences, James's hunting became increasingly notorious among the wider public. An early sign of this occurred in December 1604 when one of James's 'special hounds', Jowler, went missing. When he mysteriously reappeared among the other hounds the following day, Jowler was sporting a paper around his neck. The paper read, 'Good Mr Jowler, we pray you speak to the King (for he hears you everyday, and so doth he not us) that it will please His Majesty to go back to London, for else the country will be undone; all our provision is spent already, and we are not able to entertain him longer.' James took the ingenious petition 'for a jest', but before long the tone of public complaint soured.[45] The Venetian ambassador Molin recorded how James's trips were 'the cause of indescribable ill-humour among the King's subjects, who in their needs and troubles find themselves cut off from their natural sovereign, and forced to go before the Council, which is full of rivalry and discord, and frequently is guided more by personal interest than by justice and duty'.[46] By May 1606, the people were making their feelings felt more forcibly. 'The people desire to see their sovereign,' wrote another Venetian envoy, Zorzi Giustinian. 'The discontent has reached such a pitch that the other day there was affixed to the door of the Privy Council a general complaint of the King, alleging that his excessive kindness leaves his subjects a prey to the cupidity of his ministers.' While the complaint was only what the ambassador called 'a paternal warning not to give his subjects further cause for acting so that he should have to complain of them', James read it 'with some annoyance'.[47]

While those at court condemned his absence, those near him in the country mourned his presence. The royal trampling of local farmers' fields was a constant source of contention. One Thetford farmer, 'highly offended at the liberty his Majesty took in riding over his corn, in the transport of his passion threatened to bring an action of trespass against the King', a threat that led to a permanent withdrawal of royal favour from the town.[48] Samuel Calvert was grateful when the weather denied the King 'his common exercise' and therefore 'somewhat the ordinary complaints of poor country farmers to endure continual wrong, by the hunting spoils, and misgovernment of the unruly train'.[49] The Venetian ambassador Molin noted that 'whenever he goes a-hunting the crops are mostly ruined'.[50] Even

Godfrey Goodman, chaplain to Queen Anna, singled out hunting as an evil in a 1616 sermon, identifying the damage done to the poor tenants of farmland: 'the highways cannot always contain them, but over the hedges and ditches [they go]; here begins the cry and the curse of the poor tenant, who sits at a hard rent, and sees his corn spoiled'.[51]

In December 1604, these murmurings reached the King in a more formal complaint. Matthew Hutton, Archbishop of York, wrote to Cecil charging James with neglecting his duties, undue extravagance and an overliberal use of various royal privileges. At length, he came to the subject of the King's hunting: 'as one that honoureth, and loveth his most excellent Majesty with all my heart, I wish less wasting of the treasure of the realm, and more moderation in the lawful exercise of hunting both that poor men's corn may be less spoiled and other [of] his Majesty's subjects more spared'.[52] While carefully admitting that hunting was technically 'lawful', Hutton gave voice to the complaint of James's people that their crops were being ruined by the King and his entourage galloping across their fields. When James read Hutton's letter, Worcester recorded, 'He was merry at the first but when he came to the wasting of the treasure and the immoderate exercise of hunting began to alter countenance and said it was the foolishest letter that ever he read.'[53] Knowing in advance what the King's reaction would be, Cecil had already drafted a firm response: 'For your last point in your letter concerning hunting,' he wrote to Hutton, 'this shall be my conclusion: that it was a praise in the good Emperor Trajan to be disposed to such manlike and active recreations; so ought it to be a joy to us to behold our King of so able a constitution, promising so long life, and blessed with so plentiful a posterity, as hath freed our minds from all those fears which had besieged this potent monarchy, for lack of public declaration of his lineal and lawful succession to the same, whilst it pleased God to continue to the fullness of days our late sovereign of famous memory'.[54] James praised Cecil for this response: 'I am thoroughly pleased with your answer,' he wrote, 'and specially concerning my hunting ye have answered it according to my heart's desire, for a scornful, answerless answer became best such a senseless proposition.'[55]

Complaints about James's hunting were almost always complaints about James's style of government – or, more pertinently, his failure to govern effectively because of his physical absence from court. At the same time, with what became a characteristic perverse delight in accentuating those traits that most annoyed those around him, James adopted hunting as the overarching metaphor for his activities. In March 1605, he defined his kingly activities as the hunting of 'witches, prophets, puritans, dead cats and hares'. Time was measured by the successfully tracked quarry: James signed off, 'so going to bed, after the death of six hares, a pair of fowls, and a heron'.[56] His new favourites were those who distinguished themselves at the hunt, not at court or in government. It was no accident that Sir Philip Herbert, the first Englishman to be admitted to the Bedchamber, was remarked, in the historian Clarendon's words, for 'his skill, and indefatigable industry in hunting', and that he 'pretended to no other qualifications than to understand horses and dogs very well'.[57]

Continuing the hunting metaphor, Cecil was to James, almost invariably, 'my little beagle'.[58] Thirty-five surviving letters from King to secretary open with the greeting, and in them James elaborated on the theme, praising his 'little cankered beagle', 'my patient beagle', the 'King's best beagle if he hunt well now in the hard ways', 'the little beagle that lies at home by the fire'.[59] James loved to embarrass his councillors with epithets and nicknames: he also had a 'fat Chancellor', a 'little, saucy Constable', a 'tall, black and cat-faced Keeper', who together comprised a 'trinity of knaves'.[60] Cecil himself shifted moniker 'from Beagle to Tom Derry, from Tom Derry to Parrot':[61] when he balked at being dubbed by the King 'my little fool', Worcester reminded him that he was also known as 'a parrot-monger, a monkey-monger, and twenty other names'.[62] Despite his annoyance, Cecil, like the good councillor he was, played along with his master's name-games, dutifully referring to himself as James's beagle, as when he protested to Sir Thomas Lake that the King's 'monkey loves him not better than his beagle, nor his Great Commissioner in Scotland more than his little Secretary'.[63]

While James was off hunting in the country, his Queen consolidated a much more cosmopolitan life. Anna took over Greenwich Palace and then Somerset House in the Strand, which she renovated and renamed as Denmark House. By about 1607, the royal couple were rarely in residence together. The King, wrote the courtier Anthony Weldon, 'was ever best when furthest from his Queen'. Bishop Goodman, Anna's chaplain, added that 'The King of himself was a very chaste man, and there was little in the Queen to make him uxorious; yet they did love as well as man and wife could do, not conversing together.'[64] Others targeted the distance between the couple for political ends: sometime after 1605, James took action against a libeller who had made 'villainous speeches' against him, the Queen and Prince Henry. Although from James's letter on the subject, the exact accusations are unclear, it seems that the libeller was accusing Anna of having been unfaithful to her husband, perhaps suggesting that Henry was illegitimate. He also cast doubt on James's 'pedigree', perhaps repeating the libel that the King was 'Davy's son'; and apparently also imagined that Henry would 'renounce the kingdom of England': as James said, if he did so, the prince would be Richard II, 'successor to Henry VI [in fact, to Edward III], and not to me.'[65]

Anna's household at Denmark House quickly emerged as a court in its own right. It became something of a magnet for those not welcomed by the King, and it was popularly whispered that the Queen harboured Catholics and indeed, that she had converted to the Roman Church herself. While there is no doubt that Anna made little attempt to discourage such rumours, Catholic foreign ambassadors – who would surely have welcomed such a situation – were certain that the Queen was beyond their reach. 'She is a Lutheran,' concluded the Venetian envoy Nicolo Molin in 1606. 'The King tried to make her a Protestant [i.e. an Anglican]; others a Catholic; to this she was and is much inclinded, hence the rumour that she is one. She likes enjoyment and is very fond of dancing and of fetes. She is intelligent and prudent; and knows the disorders of the government, in which she has no part, though many hold that as the King is most devoted to her she might play as large a role as she wished. But she is young and averse to trouble; she sees that those who govern desire to be left alone, and so she professes indifference. All she ever does is to beg a favour for someone. She is full of kindness for those who support her, but on the other hand she is terrible, proud, unendurable to those she dislikes.'[66]

Although Anna had considerable personal freedom and her own court, she does not appear to have intervened so visibly against her husband in factional politics as she did in Scotland, and her support was not often sought. Where the Queen's court came truly into its own was as an artistic salon, as Anna patronised playwrights and poets including Samuel Daniel, John Donne, Ben Jonson, and John Florio, with whom she studied Italian. Her tastes reached beyond the literary, to painters and designers such as Paul van Somer, Isaac Oliver, Constantino de' Servi and Inigo Jones; the Dutch inventor Salomon de Caus who laid out her gardens at Greenwich and Somerset House; the lutenist John Dowland and 'more than a good many' French musicians. Anna and her ladies also famously took part in masques, the court entertainments most often identified with James's regime in England. The allure of these elaborate, expensive pieces of theatre is by no means clear from their surviving scripts, suggesting that their appeal lay instead in the design of their sets and costumes, in their special effects, in their music and dancing, and in the novelty of having royalty and nobility performing on stage. Often filled with topical allusions, properly veiled in classical or foreign settings, they were much liked by the Queen – although apparently not by James, whose standard reaction to being presented with a masque was to yawn and have his glass refilled.[67]

Indeed, James was strangely aloof from many of the phenomena that we now see as peculiarly Jacobean. England had entered the seventeenth century with immense promise. A new world was opening up for English adventurers and merchant venturers, with exciting and exotic new territories from Virginia to Goa. Modern science was being born through the insights of Francis Bacon and William Harvey, both of whom became personal servants of the King. English theatre was at its peak, with William Shakespeare one of James's own acting troupe, the King's Men; Inigo Jones brought the latest European taste to the King's Banqueting House in Whitehall and to his masques at court. But James seemed unimpressed. He mocked colonial exploration, fell asleep during England's most celebrated plays, and showed little interest in momentous scientific advances. Bacon dedicated his landmark work *Novum Organum* to James only to have the King quip that it was like God: 'it passeth all understanding'.[68] The King's energies would be devoted elsewhere, to old-style religious and dynastic politicking. James was at heart a sixteenth-century King of Scots, ill-equipped to be a seventeenth-century King of England; a sovereign who gave his name to the Jacobean age, but who was never truly of it.

Those searching for the true spirit of the age started to look to his heir. From the first, Henry was a popular figure with the English. When on 2 July 1603 he was invested with the Order of the Garter on the Feast of St George at Windsor, courtiers presented professed themselves impressed with his 'quick, witty answers, princely carriage, and reverend performing his obeisance at the altar.'[69] When the state entry into London was made in 1604, after a lengthy delay due to the persistent plague, Henry reacted courteously to the acclamations of the crowd, which he 'saluted . . . with many a bend', 'smiling and over-joyed to the people's eternal comfort', a stark contrast to his father's stiff bearing and gritted teeth.[70] Making his home at Oatlands in Surrey, he soon demonstrated a particular love of horses – but, unlike his father, not of hunting: 'when he goes to it,' reported the French ambassador de la Boderie in October 1606, 'it is rather for the pleasure of galloping than that which the dogs give him.' Unlike his father also, Henry proved himself an avid sportsman, playing tennis, 'another Scots diversion very like mall', tossing the pike, leaping, vaulting and archery: 'he is never idle', concluded de la Boderie admiringly.[71]

But his love of sports did not signal an immaturity. 'None of his pleasures savour the least of a child,' wrote the ambassador.[72] Visitors remarked on his piety and good manners, again very unlike James: Henry even seems to have invented the 'swear box', ordering that boxes be put in all his residences, 'causing all those who did swear in his hearing to pay money for the same, which were after duly given to the poor.'[73] The French ambassador noted that, even at thirteen, Henry was always in company 'with persons older than himself, as if he despised those of his own age.' Perhaps because he spent time with adults and because of his serious mien, Henry was quickly seen as a threat to James's control of state business. 'He is already feared by those who have the management of affairs,' wrote de la Boderie, 'and specially the Earl of Salisbury [Robert Cecil], who appears to be greatly apprehensive of the Prince's ascendant', while Henry, 'on the other hand, shows little esteem of' Salisbury.'[74] Nothing could be further from the increasingly lame James, with his hunting and his minions. Those who lost patience with the King now started to look towards Henry — as the future.

CHAPTER TWELVE

Reformation and Combustion

A S JAMES PASSED near Haddington as he travelled south in 1603, the ministers of the Synod of Lothian fell on their knees and prayed for the King. Among their supplications was for the relief of the good brethren of the ministry of England. The King assured them that 'he would show favour to honest men, but not to Anabaptists'.[1] James's response to the Lothian ministers suggests that he did not have much idea what awaited him in England. Unlike the Kirk, the Church of England in its very foundation posited the supremacy of the state in ecclesiastical affairs; James probably saw this situation, with himself fully accepted both as King and as head of the Church, as a perfect polity. But the Church of England was by no means unified, and the hopes of many subordinate factions rested on James's coming. David Calderwood reported that 'The formalists, the Papists, and the sincere professors, had all their own hopes' of the new King. 'The sincerer sort of professors, were the strongest party in the country, looked for reformation of all the abuses and corruptions of that Church.'

James had already been in contact with various 'sincerer sort of professors', writing to one Puritan minister that his brethren might 'assure themselves, that how soon ever it shall please God lawfully to possess me with the crown of that kingdom wherein they are subjects, I shall not only maintain and continue in the profession of the Gospel there, but withall, not suffer or permit any other religion to be professed and avowed within the bounds of that kingdom'.[2] But such assurances were not enough. Even before James had reached London, he was presented with the Millenary Petition, so named because it was supposedly subscribed by a thousand ministers, though in reality the numbers fell somewhat short. The Petition spelled out the cause of the English Puritans, who looked to James to rescue them from what had become an increasingly unhappy situation during the last few years of Elizabeth's reign, when they were often subject to vindictive assaults by the ecclesiastical establishment.[3] The Church of England, they argued vociferously, was still in vital need of proper reformation. Protesting that they were neither factious nor schismatic men, but James's loyal subjects, they presented to him a list of points on which they felt the Church of England had fallen short of its stated Reformation. They wanted the Church to rid itself of what they believed to be residual Romish features – confirmation, the use of the sign of the cross in baptism, the use of the ring in marriage – and to improve worship by introducing shorter services and more edifying church music. Other grievances concerned the shoddy observance of the Sabbath, the corruption in ecclesiastical courts, the prevalence of sinecures and pluralities, and the generally low intellectual quality of the ministry. They also called for a conference to be held between the Puritans and the leading figures in the Anglican Church.

James's religious sympathies were elsewhere. On coming to England, he had asked to meet Richard Hooker whose work *Of the Lawes of Ecclesiasticall Politie*, a considered response to the English Puritans' call for further Church reformation, he had much admired. When gently informed that Hooker had died in 1600, James expressed his sorrow. 'I shall want the desired happiness of seeing and discoursing with that man, from whose books I have received such satisfaction. Indeed,' he continued, 'I have received more satisfaction in reading a leaf, or paragraph in Mr Hooker, though it were but about the fashion of churches, or church music, or the like, but especially of the sacraments, than I have had in the reading particular large treatises written but of one of the those subjects by others, though very learned men.' In Hooker's works, he observed, there was 'no affected language, but a grave, comprehensive, clear manifestation of reason, and that backed with the authority of the Scripture, the Fathers and Schoolmen, and with all law both sacred and civil.' While other comparable works would soon disappear from view, 'doubtless there is in every page of Mr. Hooker's book the picture of a divine soul, such pictures of truth and reason, and drawn in so sacred colours, that they shall never fade, but give an immortal memory to the author.'[4]

James's reaction to Hooker's writings is telling. First, it indicates James's preferred method of theological debate – he was less concerned to return *ad fontes*, to interrogate the earliest sources of a particular scriptural passage, than to read the scripture in association with its accumulated interpretations: of the Church Fathers, the Schoolmen, and of ecclesiastical and civil lawyers. In practice, this meant that James tended towards an intellectual conservatism, preferring to trust the accretions of debate from the entire Christian heritage over the potentially dangerous findings of radical scholarly excavation. Second, it shows his attraction to Hooker's brand of Anglo-Catholicism. James was a firm Protestant, but he was no Calvinist and rejected Calvin's doctrine of predestination. Instead, his personal preference was nearer to the school now dubbed 'Arminian', after its spiritual founder Jacobus Arminius, which looked to the primitive church from the first five centuries *anno domini*.[5] The English Arminians believed, or hoped to prove, that the Reformed Church of England was directly descended from a primitive Christian church whose true light had been obscured for a millennium by the Church of Rome. However, while that Church had fallen into errors, it was still a channel through which truths and ceremonies were handed down. This meant that, while Puritans tended to dismiss the pre-Reformation Church out of hand, Arminians found much to study in it.[6]

Hooker may have died, but James found plenty to please him in the top ranks of the Anglican Church. These men were scholars, intellectuals and writers: John Whitgift, the Archbishop of Canterbury; Richard Bancroft, then Bishop of London; Lancelot Andrewes, Bishop of Chichester; William Barlow, Dean of Chester; and Thomas Bilson, Bishop of Winchester. He felt the Anglican hierarchy to be properly deferential: there was no danger here of an Andrew Melvill or David Black spitting out his Presbyterian bile and publicly humiliating the King. James was in his element. He had his bishops, who accepted the divine right of kings while keeping watch over the Church. Every church service exalted the King, in abstract and in person; homilies punched home the duty of each subject to the King. The Church of England had rituals and ceremonies that to the Kirk would have smacked soundly of papism, but to James held a great allure. He always protested that he did not dislike Scottish ministers who held personal objections to the ceremonies of the Anglican Church. 'No, I am so far from being contentious in these things (which for my own part I ever esteemed as indifferent), as I do equally love and honour the learned and grave men of either of these opinions. We all (God be praised) do agree in the grounds, and the bitterness of men upon such questions doth but trouble the peace of the Church and gives advantage and entry to the Papists by our division.'[7]

James was secure enough in this new setting that he could allow room for another identifiable church party, sympathetic to continental Calvinism and better disposed to English Puritanism, whose leading figures were brothers George and Robert Abbot, and George Carleton. The fact that in time James would appoint George Abbot as Archbishop of Canterbury suggests something of his canny politicking in dealing with differences within the Church of England. After his years of juggling the Kirk and the nobility, he sensed that it was to his advantage not to let one church faction dominate utterly, even if he were personally predisposed to that side. At first the Puritans were cheered by the King's attitude. James's initial reaction to organised English Puritanism, in the form of the Millenary Petition, had been noncommittal but gracious – a stark contrast to the extremely hostile reactions from the universities at Oxford and Cambridge, Oxford in particular ensuring that the analogy between English Puritanism and Scottish Presbyterianism was made for the King's benefit. In reality, there was a huge gulf between the Presbyterians in Scotland and the Puritans in England, but it suited those opposed to Puritanism to play on James's prejudices – and his deeply held and sincere fears. But as James embarked on a series of conferences, both formal and informal, with the English bishops, he began to gravitate towards this unsympathetic understanding of English Puritanism. A summer campaign of Puritan petitions served only to strengthen his growing belief that the English Puritans possessed a suspiciously Presbyterian-like love of argument over the tiniest details of ritual and doctrine.

By October 1603, James was already worried enough to issue 'a proclamation concerning such as seditiously seek reformation in church matters', which effectively prohibited religious petitions. Ecclesiastical reform fell under the jurisdiction of the King, it asserted, and he was 'persuaded' that both the constitution and doctrine of the Church of England 'is agreeable to God's word, and near to the condition of the primitive church'. The proclamation condemned 'some men's spirits, whose heat tendeth rather to combustion than reformation', through their use of 'public invectives against the state ecclesiastical', and the gathering of 'subscriptions of multitudes of vulgar persons to supplications to be exhibited to us'. Instead, James desired 'an orderly proceeding' without 'all unlawful and factious manner of proceeding'; he threatened punishment for offenders, claiming that 'these reformers under pretended zeal affect novelty, and so confusion in all estates'.[8] He instructed Archbishop Whitgift that those ministers who were using 'new forms not prescribed by authority' in their celebration of divine service, should be 'severely repressed'.[9]

The proclamation also demonstrated, however, that James was willing to entertain one of the ideas of the Millenary Petition: a conference between Anglicans and Puritans. It appealed to his notion of himself as an intellectual. He had already attempted to show off his scholarship to the English, some of whom were less than impressed. Sir John Harington relates the performance he endured when ordered to come for an intimate audience in James's closet. After making his way through the Presence Chamber (where he saw 'the lordly attendants, and bowed my knee to the Prince [Henry]', he waited nearly an hour in an outer chamber before being led by a special messenger up a passage, 'and so to a small room, where was good order of paper, ink, and pens, put on a board for the Prince's [James's] use'. James finally entered into the closet, and after some small talk about Harington's family, started to question him 'much of learning, and showed me his own'. The royal grilling, Harington remarked sardonically, reminded him of his examiner at Cambridge.[10] In religious matters, too, James indulged his intellectual curiosity. He became not only an avid attender of the court sermons every Sunday and Tuesday but actively involved himself in the choosing of preachers for court, and texts for their sermons. Eyewitness accounts of James at dinner in England almost always include a preacher or two standing behind his chair while he ate, debating with him 'concerning some point of controversy in philosophy'.[11] John Hacket, describing mealtime with James as 'a trial of wits', sardonically cast the scene in terms of another of James's hobbies: 'Methought his hunting humour was not off so long as his courtiers, I mean the learned, stood about him at his board. He was ever in chase after some disputable doubts, which he would wind and turn about with the most stabbing objections that ever I heard. And was as pleasant and fellow-like in all those discourses as with his huntsmen in the field.' As with his hunting companions, his learned interlocutors might expect to benefit from the experience in more material terms. 'They that in many such genial and convivial conferences were ripe and weighty in their answers were indubiously designed to some place of credit and profit.'[12]

His bishops were not so keen at the prospect of James displaying his learning in a semi-public setting, and Bilson advised the King not to risk such a conference: 'Content yourself, my Lord,' replied James condescendingly, 'we know better than you what belongeth to these matters.'[13] Originally scheduled for November 1603, the conference was postponed until the New Year, and took place at Hampton Court in January 1604. The royal conference would become a familiar sight over the next two decades. It was not an equal forum. James would preside on his chair of state, flanked by judges, councillors or churchmen, depending on what was to be debated. The plaintiffs (perhaps common lawyers, the Commons or as here Puritan ministers) elected a spokesman to make their case from the floor. James would respond as he saw fit, often peppering his earnest pronouncements with crude jokes. Although on occasion he became bored, he evidently relished these chances to display his intellect and wit.[14]

Our main source for the Hampton Court Conference, as it became known, is the 'official version' by William Barlow, Dean of Chester, blatantly partisan in its portrayal and occasional ridicule of what he calls the 'opponents', the Puritan ministers. But precisely because of its unguarded bias, it provides a wonderful account of a particular moment in English ecclesiastical history, when the leading figures of the Church of England found in their new King not only a champion but apparently a serious and learned champion. By the end of the second day's conference James's 'singular readiness, and exact knowledge' had 'raised such an admiration in the lords' that one of them was heard to say exclaim 'he was fully persuaded, his Majesty spake by the instinct of the spirit of God'. Sir Robert Cecil affirmed 'that very much we are bound to God, who had given us a King of an understanding heart'. As Lord Chancellor Ellesmere passed through the door of the Privy Chamber, he said to Barlow, 'I have often heard and read, that *Rex est mixta persona cum sacerdote* [a king is a mixture of a person and a priest], but I never saw the truth thereof, till this day.' And Barlow himself wrote, 'Surely, whosoever heard his Majesty, might justly think; that title did more properly fit him, which *Eunapius* gave to that famous rhetorician, in saying he was a living library, and a walking study'.[15]

The opening meeting of the conference took place on Saturday 14 January, significantly without the Puritans. James met first with the bishops, deans and the lords of the Privy Council in his Privy Chamber, sitting in his chair. He began with what Barlow called 'a most grave and princely declaration of his general drift in calling this assembly'. It was, he claimed, 'no novel device' but typical of all Christian princes starting their reign who 'take the first course for the establishing of the church, both for doctrine and policy'. Henry VIII, Edward VI, Mary and Elizabeth had, of course, all wanted to change the religious polity; James, he insisted, 'was happier than they' because as yet he saw 'no cause so much to alter, and change anything, as to confirm that which he found well settled already'. This pronouncement, Barlow noted, 'so affected his royal heart, that it pleased him to enter into a gratulation to Almighty God (at which words he put off his hat) for bringing him into the promised land, where religion was purely professed; where he sat among grave, learned and reverend men; not, as before, elsewhere, a King without state, without honour, without order; where beardless boys would brave him to his face'.[16]

However, while James did not intend 'any innovation', 'nothing could be so absolutely ordered, but something might be added afterward thereunto'. In any state, just as in any body, 'corruptions might insensibly grow, either through time or persons', and he had received 'many complaints' since his accession, 'especially, through the dissentions in the Church, of many disorders, as he heard, and much disobedience to the laws, with a great falling away to popery'. He purposed therefore, 'like a good physician, to examine and try the complaints, and fully to remove the occasion thereof, if they prove scandalous, or to cure them, if they were dangerous, or, if but frivolous, yet to take knowledge of them, thereby to cast a sop into Cerberus's mouth, that he may never bark again' – in other words, 'to give factious spirits no occasion, hereby, of boasting or glory'. This is why he had called the bishops in by themselves, without their Puritan opponents, so that if anything *did* need to be redressed it could be done 'without any visible alteration' – James repeated this point three times.[17] He moved on to raise several points from the Petition that he wanted the bishops and deans to address: confirmation, absolution, private baptism and excommunication. When the King had finished, Whitgift knelt down, and said 'how much this whole land was bound to God for setting over us a King so wise, learned and judicious, addressed himself to inform his Majesty of all these points'.[18]

James entered into the discussion enthusiastically, often proffering his views first and then seeking approval from the bishops. Frequently he would call for the Bible to check up on a particular passage. He was not afraid to challenge the opinion of the learned divines. When they reached the matter of private baptism, Whitgift told the King that the administration of baptism by women and lay persons was allowed neither in Church practice nor by 'the words in the Book'. James objected to this, 'urging and pressing the words of the Book, that they could not but intend a permission, and suffering [permitting] of women, and private persons to baptize'. The Earl of Worcester admitted that the words 'were doubtful, and might be pressed to the meaning' but Church practice suggested otherwise. James responded that this was a point on which the primitive Church need not be followed (it was not 'sound reasoning from things done before a Church be settled and grounded, unto those which are to be performed in a Church stablished and flourishing'). It was ironic, he continued, that only fourteen months ago he had been criticising the divines in Scotland 'for ascribing too little to that holy sacrament'. Then 'a pert minister' asked him, 'if I thought baptism so necessary, that if it were omitted, the child should be damned? I answered him no: but if you, being called to baptize the child privately, should refuse to come, I think you shall be damned.'[19]

Barlow was impressed. The session lasted three hours, which flew by since his Majesty handled all the points so admirably, 'sending us away not with contentment only, but astonishment; and, which is pitiful, you will say, with shame to us all, that a King brought up among Puritans, not the learnedest men in the world, and schooled by them: swaying a kingdom full of business, and troubles, naturally given to much exercise and repast, should, in points of divinity show himself as expedite and perfect as the greatest scholars, and most industrious students, there present, might not outstrip him'. Barlow was particularly struck by James's assertion that, despite the fact that 'he lived among Puritans, and was kept, for the most part, as a ward under them, yet, since he was of the age of his son, ten years old, he ever disliked their opinions; as the Saviour of the world said, "Though he lived among them, he was not of them."'[20]

The following Monday, 16 January, the four Puritan plaintiffs were called into the Privy Chamber. Dr John Rainoldes was President of Corpus Christi College, Oxford, and Dean of Lincoln, a fine scholar who had tutored Richard Hooker at Oxford, but had declined to be raised to a bishopric by Elizabeth.[21] Laurence Chaderton was Master of Emmanuel College, Cambridge; Thomas Sparke was a prebend of Lincoln; and John Knewstubs a noted controversialist. James was already seated in his chair, surrounded by the Bishops of London and Winchester and all the deans and doctors, as well as his Scottish chaplain Patrick Galloway. Even ten-year-old Henry was present, 'the noble young Prince, sitting by' his father 'upon a stool'. James made much the same speech to the Puritans as he had to the bishops and deans, ending by saying that since 'many grievous complaints had been made to him, since his first entrance to the land, he thought it best to send for some, whom his Majesty understood to be the most grave, learned, and modest of the aggrieved sort, whom, being there present, he was now ready to hear, at large, what they could object or say'. As the four knelt, Rainoldes, whom Barlow identified as 'the foreman', presented the four heads of their argument: that the doctrine of the Church should be preserved in purity, according to God's word; that good pastors might be planted in all churches to preach that doctrine; that the Church government might be sincerely administered according to God's word; and that the Book of Common Prayer might be 'fitted to more increase of piety'.

Rainoldes had got as far as saying that the Book of Articles of Religion, now some forty years old, needed clarification, when the Bishop of London suddenly cut him off, and falling to his knees, burst into a tirade against the Puritans. They aimed not to reform, he claimed, but to overthrow the Church; they wanted to impose their doctrine of predestination, which was a Presbyterian doctrine; and they only opposed the rite of confirmation because they could not confirm. James by no means applauded this interruption, remarking instead that he might excuse the bishop's passion, but he 'misliked his sudden interruption'. Bancroft should have allowed Rainoldes to have finished, since there could be 'no order, nor can be any effectual issue of disputation, if each party might not be suffered, without chopping, to speak at large what he would'.[22] Although his early intervention had backfired, Bancroft was more successful when he turned to an issue close to James's heart, that of personal attacks in sermons. Pulpits should not become the platform for lampoons and satires, he declared, 'wherein every humorous, or discontented fellow might traduce his superiors'. This naturally appealed to the King who agreed it was 'a lewd custom'; he threatened 'that if he should but hear of such a one in a pulpit, he would make him an example', and admonished the Puritan ministers, 'that every man should solicit and draw his friends to make peace and if any thing were amiss in the Church officers, not to make the pulpit the place of personal reproof, but to let his Majesty hear of it'.[23]

James's contribution to this session was much less constructive. During a discussion of whether only bishops were qualified to perform baptism, Bancroft referred to St Jerome who asserted that view, though he was 'otherwise no friend to bishops'. James did not let the reference pass, and taxed St Jerome for his assertion that a bishop was not ordained by God; his views on the question could be summed up 'with this short aphorism, No Bishop, no King'. As Rainoldes went further with his case, James reverted, as he often did when he was bored, to levity. Rainoldes raised Article 37, 'The Bishop of Rome hath no authority in this land', claiming that it should be augmented to read 'nor ought to have'. At this James 'heartily laughed' and the lords followed suit. 'What speak you of the Pope's authority here?' he asked. '*Habemus iure, quod habemus*, and therefore, in as much as it is said, *he hath not*, it is plain enough, that *he ought not to have*.' According to Barlow, this was one of several motions that seemed 'very idle and frivolous' to the King and the lords, and so they drifted into 'some bye-talk', as someone remembered a quip ascribed to one Mr Butler of Cambridge about a Puritan: 'a Puritan is a Protestant frayed out of his wits'. Rainoldes was not to be put off. When he proposed that a negative assertion ('the intention of the Minister is not of the essence of the Sacrament') James protested that if he put into the book every negative proposition the book would 'swell into a volume as big as the Bible, and also confound the reader'. He recalled how John Craig in Scotland did a similar thing, casting all his beliefs in negative terms: 'who with his *I renounce and abhor*, his detestations and abrenunciations he did so amaze the simplest people, that they, not able to conceive all those things, utterly gave over all, falling back on popery, or remaining still in their former ignorance. Yea,' continued James, 'if I should have been bound to his form, the confession of my faith must have been in my table book, not in my head.'[24] When Rainoldes had finished, James turned to the Puritan ministers. 'Surely,' he said, 'if these be the greatest matters you be grieved with, I need not have been troubled with such importunities and complaints, as have been made unto me. Some more private course might have been taken for your satisfaction.' And he turned to the lords, shaking his head and smiling.[25]

Despite James's attitude to the Puritan ministers, there were some areas of agreement. To the demand that learned ministers be planted in every parish, James expressed his approval in principle. He had complained to Whitgift the previous October that 'in many parts of the realm the parishes are so ill-served with persons not able to instruct in matters of their faith as is very scandalous to those of your degree and given much advantage to the adversary to seduce them'. At that point, he had ordered that bishops should undertake an audit of their dioceses as a matter of urgency;[26] now, however, he was not about to be seen to give in to a Puritan demand, and claimed that a sudden change would be dangerous. In any case, the universities could not afford to put a sufficient minister in every parish, and 'he had more learned men in this realm, than he had sufficient maintenance for' – so maintenance had to come first. In the meantime, young ministers who were ignorant and beyond hope should be removed; older ministers should be allowed to die in post. But 'Jerusalem could not be built up in a day'.[27]

The more violent clashes arose from the demands of the Puritan John Knewstubs. Knewstubs took exception to the use of the sign of the Cross in baptism: this would offend the 'weak brethren', those clergymen who would not accept change, he claimed. 'How long they would be weak?' demanded James, incredulously. Was not forty-five years 'sufficient for them to grow strong?' Indeed, it seemed to him that 'some of them were strong enough, if not headstrong; and howsoever they in this case pretended weakness; yet some, in whose behalf, they now spake, thought themselves able to teach him, and all the bishops of the land'.[28] With his third question Knewstubs truly upset the King: these 'weak brethren' wondered how far James's Church ordinances should bind them 'without impeaching their Christian Liberty?' The King, reported Barlow, 'was much moved'. He said he would not argue the point, but added that 'it smelled very rankly of anabaptism'. It reminded him of 'the usage of a beardless boy', John Black, at the last conference he had had with the Scottish ministers in December 1602. Black had told him 'that he would hold conformity with his Majesty's ordinances, for matters of doctrine, but for matters of ceremony, they were to be left in Christian Liberty, unto every man, as he received more and more light, from the illumination of God's spirit'. More and more light until they go mad with their own light, said James, 'but I will none of that, I will have one doctrine and one discipline, one religion in substance, and in ceremony: and therefore I charge you, never speak more to that point'.[29]

There were moments of humour. When Rainoldes objected to the phrase 'With my body I thee worship' from the Book of Common Prayer's marriage service, James poked fun at the unmarried academic. 'Many a man speaks of Robin Hood, who never shot in his bow,' he said to Rainoldes, smiling; 'if you had a good wife yourself, you would think all the honour and worship you could do her, were well bestowed.' On the matter of 'churching', the service of purification of women after childbirth, James quipped 'that women were loath enough of themselves, to come to Church, and therefore, he would have this, or any other occasion, to draw them thither'. When Rainoldes approved the bishops' wearing of the 'corned cap', James turned to the bishops and said: 'You may now safely wear your caps, but I shall tell you, if you should walk in one street in Scotland, with such a cap on your head, if I were not with you, you should be stoned to death with your cap.' When Rainoldes urged that the Church should abandon the sign of the Cross 'because in the time of popery it had been superstitiously abused', James pointed out that by the same argument they should renounce 'the Trinity, and all that is holy, because it was abused in Popery. They used to wear hose and shoes in popery,' he pointed out to Rainoldes, 'therefore, you shall now go barefoot.'[30]

There was a more serious point to be made about popish abuses. In Scotland, the Presbyterians had tried for years to persuade James that the Roman Church's past use (and therefore abuse) of a particular ritual *de facto* rendered the ritual superstitious. But James now declared that nothing had turned him against the Kirk ministers more than their kneejerk reaction of disallowing anything 'which at all had been used in popery'. To James, a greater danger was needless innovation, of which even the Church of England was guilty. 'For my part, I know not how to answer the objection of the papists, when they charge us with novelties,' he continued, 'but truly to tell them, that their abuses are new, but the things which they abused we retain in their primitive use, and forsake, only, the novel corruption.'[31]

Rainoldes proposed that the clergy should meet every three weeks, first in the rural deaneries, with matters raised, then moving to the archdeacon's visitation, and ultimately to the episcopal synod, 'where the Bishop with his *presbyteri*, should determine all such points, as before could not be decided'. At this request, James was evidently 'somewhat stirred', but answered with admirable calm. They aimed at a Scottish Presbytery, he stated, which agreed with a monarchy as much as God did with the Devil. 'Then Jack and Tom, and Will, and Dick, shall meet, and at their pleasures censure me, and my Council, and all our proceedings. Then Will shall stand up, and say, "It must be thus"; then Dick shall reply, and say, "Nay, marry, but we will have it thus". And therefore, here I must once reiterate my former speech, "le roi s'avisera". Stay, I pray you, for one seven years, before you demand that of me, and if then, you find me pursy [corpulent, short-winded] and fat, and my windpipes stuffed, I will perhaps hearken to you: for let that government be once up, I am sure, I shall be kept in breath; then shall we all of us, have work enough, both our hands full. But Dr Rainoldes, till you find that I grow lazy, let that alone.'[32]

Although James had twice let Rainoldes swipe at his Supremacy without comment, now he could not let the matter go. 'Dr Rainoldes,' he said, 'you have often spoken for my Supremacy, and it is well: but know you any here, or any else where, who like of the present government ecclesiatical, that find fault, or dislike my Supremacy?' Rainoldes replied that he did not. 'Why then,' said the King, 'I will tell you a tale.' After the Roman Catholic Mary Tudor came to the throne in England, it seemed that Scotland might follow suit. John Knox had written to the Queen Regent, Marie de Guise, as head of the Church, and telling her to suppress the dangerous 'popish prelates'. But once the Regent had suppressed the popish bishops, Knox and his regime came in and soon 'began to make small account of her Supremacy, nor would longer rest upon her authority, but took the cause into their own hand, and according to that more light, where-with they were illuminated, made a further reformation of religion'. James spoke passionately of how Mary Queen of Scots had suffered under them. 'How they used that poor Lady my mother, is not unknown, and with grief I may remember it: who, because, she had not been otherwise instructed, did desire, only, a private chapel, wherein to serve God, after her manner, with some few selected persons; but her Supremacy was not sufficient to obtain it at their hands.' And James, the cradle king, had felt the pain. 'How they dealt with me, in my minority, you all know; it was not done secretly, and, though I would [would like to], I cannot conceal it. I will apply it thus.' Putting his hand on his hat, he spoke to the 'lords and bishops'. If they were out of power, he claimed, and the Puritans in place, 'I know what would become of my Supremacy. No Bishop, no King, as before I said.' He had 'observed since my coming into England, that some preachers before me, can be content to pray for James, King of England, Scotland, France and Ireland, defender of the Faith, but as for Supreme Governor in all causes, and over all persons (as well Ecclesiastical as Civil) they pass that over with silence; and what cut they have been of, I after learned.' James rose from his chair, and made his way to his Inner Chamber. 'If this be all that they have to say,' he said as he left the room, 'I shall make them conform themselves, or I will harry them out of the land, or else do worse.'[33]

A third and final day's conference was held on Wednesday 18 January, to give the bishops an opportunity to answer some of the points raised. As the session came to a close, Knewstubs fell on to his knees, and begged the King that 'some honest ministers' in Suffolk be exempted from the newly enforced requirement to wear the surplice, or use the Cross in baptism, since it 'would make much against their credits in the country'. Whitgift started to answer him, but James broke in. 'Nay,' said the King, 'let me alone with him. Sir,' he said, turning to Knewstubs, 'you show yourself an uncharitable man. We have here taken pains, and in the end have concluded of an unity and uniformity, and, you forsooth, must prefer the credits of a few private men, before the general peace of the Church; this is just the Scottish argument, for when anything was there concluded, which disliked some humours, the only reason, why they would not obey, was, it stood not with their credits, to yield, having so long been of the contrary opinion; I will none of that,' he concluded, 'and therefore, either let them conform themselves, and that shortly, or they shall hear of it.' James's message was clear. Rainoldes, Chaderton, Knewstubs and Sparke 'jointly promised, to be quiet and obedient, now they knew it to be the King's mind, to have it so'. Barlow was moved. 'His Majesty's gracious conclusion was so piercing, as that it fetched tears from some, on both sides'.[34]

Barlow presents such a cloyingly rosy Anglican vision of the Hampton Court Conference that it comes as a relief to learn that not everyone was so impressed. Sir John Harington, admittedly never a great admirer of James, had a different take. When the bishops came to the King, he wrote, 'I was by, and heard much discourse. The King talked much Latin, and disputed with Dr Rainoldes at Hampton,' he wrote, 'but he rather used upbraidings than argument; and told the petitioners that they wanted to strip Christ again, and bid them away with their snivelling. Moreover he wished those who would take away the surplice might want linen for their own breeches. The bishops seemed much pleased and said his Majesty spoke by the power of inspiration. I wist [knew] not what they meant, but the spirit was rather foul-mouthed.'[35] Such foul-mouthed repartee could hardly expect to find its way into Barlow's 'official version' of events, but the phrases reported by Harington certainly sound like James, and there is evidence that the King's enjoyment of the conference was not all as highminded as Barlow would have us believe. To the Earl of Northampton James wrote, 'We have kept such a revel with the Puritans here these two days as was never heard the like, where I have peppered them as soundly, as ye have done the papists there; it were no reason that those that will refuse the airy sign of the cross after baptism should have their purses stuffed with any mo [more] solid and substantial crosses; they fled me so from argument to argument without ever answering me directly . . . as I was forced at last to say unto them, that if any of them had been in a college disputing with their scholars, if any of their disciples had answered them in that sort, they would have fetched him up in place of a reply, and so should the rod have plyed upon the poor boy's buttocks.'[36]

However, in all of Rainoldes' suggestions, one struck a chord with the King: that there should be a new English translation of the Bible.[37] England already had an 'official' vernacular version, the so-called Bishops' Bible, but other renderings also circulated, most notably the Geneva Bible, the Puritans' choice. Previous translations, Rainoldes alleged, were 'corrupt and not answerable to the truth of the original'.[38] Here James had some sympathy. He had never yet seen a Bible well translated into English — although the worst was the Geneva Bible. Indeed, he had moved the case for a new Bible to the Kirk three years earlier at the General Assembly at Burntiswood, when 'his Majesty did urge it earnestly', wrote John Spottiswoode, who attended the Assembly, 'and with many reasons did persuade the undertaking of the work, showing the necessity and the profit of it, and what a glory the performing thereof should bring to this Church. Speaking of the necessity, he did mention sundry escapes in the common translation, and made it seem that he was no less conversant in the Scriptures than they whose profession it was'[39]

Unlike other translations, James added, this new Bible was to have 'no marginal notes'. In the Geneva translation — which, he suddenly added, rather implausibly, he had only seen 'in a Bible given him by an English lady' — he had found 'some notes very partial, untrue, seditious, and savouring, too much, of dangerous, and traiterous conceits'. For example (and here James was very specific) the note on Exodus 1: 19, where the midwives opposed the King of Egypt, the marginal note actually allowed 'disobedience to Kings'.[40] At 2 Chronicles 15: 16 the note criticised Asa for merely deposing his idolatrous mother Maachah, 'and not killing her'.[41] These two points, disobedience to kings and not murdering your mother, were close to James's heart.[42] He expressed his wish 'that some especial pains should be taken in that behalf for one uniform translation . . . and this to be done by the best learned in both the Universities, after them to be reviewed by the Bishops, and the chief learned of the Church; from them to be presented to the Privy Council; and lastly to be ratified by his royal authority; and so this whole Church to be bound unto it, and none other.'

By June 1604, the translators, fifty-four in total, had been selected. James himself drew up the instructions for the execution of this massive task. When a word had multiple meanings, then the transla-tors should follow the early Church Fathers where possible. The tone should be simple and avoid complex phrasing. The Bishops' Bible, for all its faults, was established as the base text. Translators were required to follow the established usage of certain words: for the Greek *ecclesia*, for example, 'church' was used instead of 'congregation', the preferred translation for Puritan-leaning believers. The translators were divided into six 'companies', two at Oxford under John Harding, two at Cambridge under Edward Lively, and two at Westminster under Lancelot Andrewes. Puritan scholars were included, among them Rainoldes who worked in the Oxford team until his early death in 1607. The teams worked in isolation, but their work was then subjected to a stringent peer review, and other scholars were encouraged to proffer their comments. A committee of six men, two drawn from each city, met in London to review the work, with the final revisions being done by Bilson and Miles Smith, who later became Bishop of Gloucester.[43] The result, proudly published in 1611, has stood the test of time: although the translation has been officially superseded, to many people, the language provided by fifty-four men of varying doctrinal belief and political allegiance working in three separate loca-tions between 1604 and 1611, the 'King James' language, still is *the* language of the Church of England.

Although James wanted a new translation and his organisational principles were followed through, there is no evidence that he person-ally contributed to the translations or revisions – and he may well have realised that his linguistic capabilities were not equal to the task. But he did make a somewhat desultory attempt to flex his poetic muscles on a new metrical version of the Psalms, designed to be sung. Like many Protestant youths, James tried his hand at translating the Psalms early: in the schoolroom he rendered his first Psalm into English verse and in his 1591 *Poetical Exercises* wrote that if his verses were well accepted, he would go on to publish as many of the Psalms as he 'had perfited [perfected]' and would be encouraged to complete those that remained.[44] At the 1601 General Assembly of the Kirk at Burntisland, he urged the importance of such an endeavour, reciting 'whole verses of the same, showing both the faults of the metre and the discrepance from the text. It was the joy of all that were present to hear it, and bred not little admiration in the whole Assembly.' At that point the Assembly gave the task of revising the Psalms to Robert Pont, but nothing came of it. John Spottiswoode recalled how, once he came to England, James 'set the most learned divines of that Church a-work for the translation of the Bible' while 'the revising of the Psalms he made his own labour, and at such hours as he might spare from the public cares went through a number of them, commending the rest to a faithful and learned servant, who hath herein answered his Majesty's expectation'.[15] The faithful and learned servant was Sir William Alexander, who during James's years in England became an occasional poetic foil for the King, whether in debating the merits of metre, or providing an answering sonnet to one of James's.[46] From Alexander's correspondence it appears that he had a ghostwriting role somewhat similar to Maitland's in the King's literary endeavours: Alexander had to execute the translations himself, or persuade others to do them, and then James took whichever he preferred as his own. This work was still going on in 1620 when Alexander wrote to William Drummond of Hawthornden to acknowledge receipt of 'the psalm you sent, which I think very well done. I had done the same long before it came; but he prefers his own to all else, though, perchance, when you see it, you will think it the worst of the three. No man must meddle with that subject, and therefore I advise you to take no more pains therein.'[47] By the time of James's death, only thirty Psalms were done, but his successor allowed Alexander to finish the sequence and publish it under James's name. This Alexander did in 1631, and the text was adopted, by royal command, as the official Church translation. However, its quality was so poor that there was an outcry from the Church and the translation soon disappeared: a sad end for a grand project.[48]

* * *

The net effect of the Hampton Court Conference was precisely the opposite of what the Puritans wished: the imposition of a stricter orthodoxy within the Church. The Church of England's Convocation passed new canons to enforce conformity, with the threat that ministers would lose their livings if they did not conform, with November 1604 set as a deadline. James instructed his bishops to target only those ministers who showed no sign of reformation, but even so up to a hundred ministers were deprived and suspended.[49] As the deadline of November 1604 approached, James received what he called 'the Puritans' catholic petition', the Royston Petition which hoped to lobby the King to prevent the eviction of noncomformist clergymen, a move that produced precisely the opposite effect: 'ye see,' he wrote to Cecil, 'I have daily more and more cause to hate and abhor all that sect: enemies to all kings, and to me only because I am a king.'[50] When the knights and gentlemen of Northamptonshire joined forces with the local petitioners to argue that thousands would be discontented if ministers were deprived, James felt threatened. The following day he spent eight hours with his Privy Council fuming about the Puritans, pointing out that the revolt in the Low Countries, which was as old as he was and would probably outlive him, began as a petition for matters of religion. So, for that matter, did all the troubles in Scotland. Both he and his mother had been haunted from their cradles by a Puritan devil which he feared would follow him to his grave. Even if he had to hazard his crown, he would suppress those malicious spirits. The Council took the hint, and took action; James expressed himself 'wonderfully well satisfied with the Council's proceedings anent [against] the Puritans', which he characterised as full of 'mercy and judgement'.[51]

The bishops were less resolute that the Privy Councillors. The newsletter writer John Chamberlain, a notable barometer of public opinion in Jacobean England, reported that the churchmen were 'loath to proceed too rigorously in casting out and depriving so many well reputed of for life and learning'. Bishop Montagu urged that the process should be more gradual, a gentle selection 'rather than all without difference be cut down at once'; moreover, those culled in this way, 'the poor Puritan ministers, ferreted out in all corners', might end up being martyrs to a cause. Ultimately, Chamberlain wrote, 'only the King is constant to have all come to conformity'.[52] In seeking conformity, James gave a name and a purpose to nonconformity. Now the Puritans had no choice but to organise elsewhere and turned their attention to the one venue where they were well represented: Parliament.

CHAPTER THIRTEEN

Two Twins Bred in One Belly

I N HIS WRITINGS, speeches, letters and table-talk, James returned
again and again to two images of himself as King: the physician
and the *nutritius*, the nursing father. These speak volumes for
James's ideas about kingship. Based on a line in Isaiah 49: 23 – 'kings
shall be thy nursing father' – the nursing father captured James's belief
that he was a teacher-nurturer to his children-subjects, an extreme
form of paternalism that even appropriated the maternal.[1] In *Basilikon
Doron*, James ends his ecclesiastical counsel to Henry by saying 'cherish
no man more than a good pastor, hate no man more than a proud
puritan, thinking in one of your fairest styles to be called a loving
nourish-father to the Kirk'.[2] The figure of speech did not go unno-
ticed: in a 1604 sermon Richard Eedes preached that 'Princes too be
nurses of the Church',[3] and in 1619 Sir James Sempill dedicated a book
'To the Most Noble and truly sacred Prince; Defender of Christ's
Faith, and Nourish-father of his Church James'.[4]

If the nursing father comforted, the physician administered a
harsher medicine. Employing the familiar analogy of the body politic,
James saw it as his duty to diagnose the state's symptoms, and
prescribe the right medicine. In 1604, he put this policy into action
by publishing a pamphlet attacking the evils of a new vogue: *A
Covnter-Blaste to Tobacco*. This diatribe truly blasted 'the stinking suffu-
migation' of smoking tobacco, denying its supposed medicinal values,
and pointing instead to its origins in baser cultures, and its tendency
to addict its users, bankrupting them (through habits of £300 or
£400 per annum), rendering them useless for anything else, and
reducing them to 'imitate the barbarous and beastly manners of the
wild, godless, and slavish Indians'. This 'shameful imbecility', it
continued, brought men to a pretty pass: they were 'not able to ride
or walk the journey of a Jew's Sabbath, but you must have a reeky
coal brought you from the next poor house to kindle your tobacco
with?' The practice of smoking, it concluded, 'a custom loathsome
to the eye, hateful to the nose, harmful to the brain, dangerous to
the lungs, and in the black stinking fume thereof, nearest resembling

the horrible Stygian smoke of the pit that is bottomless'.[5] Published anonymously, since it was 'too mean for a king to interpone his authority' on 'so base and contemptible a condition', its prefatory epistle nevertheless carried, in James's voice, his views on the country he had just inherited:

> We are of all nations the people most loving and most reverently obedient to our Prince, yet are we (as time hath often borne witness) too easy to be seduced to make rebellion, upon very slight grounds. Our fortunate and oft proved valour in wars abroad, our hearty and reverent obedience to our princes at home, hath bred us a long, and a thrice happy peace: our peace hath bred wealth: and peace and wealth hath brought forth a general sluggishness, which makes us wallow in all sorts of idle delights, and soft delicacies, the first seeds of the subversion of all great monarchies. Our clergy are become negligent and lazy, our nobility and gentry prodigal, and sold to their private delights, our lawyers covetous, our common people prodigal and curious; and generally all sorts of people more careful for their private ends, than for their mother the Commonwealth.[6]

To remedy this state of affairs, the anonymous author continues, it was up to the King, as 'the proper physician of his politic-body' to purge it of those diseases. He should maintain public quiet and prevent commotions 'by a certain mild, and yet just form of government'; to shame the people 'of our sluggish delicacy' through his personal example and that of his court; 'to stir us up to the practice again of all honest exercises, and martial shadows of war'; and by his moderation, 'to make us ashamed of our prodigality'. In particular, the good King should aim to awaken the clergy to be diligent; to try and punish 'partial, covetous and bribing lawyers'; and 'generally by the example of his own person, and by the due execution of good laws, to reform and abolish, piece and piece, these old and evil grounded abuses'.[7]

James thought he could effect this reformation through proclamations, speeches and his writings. But he knew that to change laws he had to turn to Parliament, and on 11 January 1604, just before the

Hampton Court Conference, he called his first English Parliament. He may have thought he understood the mechanics of Parliament – had he not been attending for thirty years? – but, once again, English culture would surprise him. To English eyes, Scotland's Parliament was risibly puny. This was because the King of Scots had a firm grasp on Parliament through the 'Lords of the Articles', a committee that controlled what legislation could reach the Parliament for debate: in 1598, James instructed his son Henry in all seriousness to 'hold no Parliaments, but for necessity of new laws, which would be but seldom'.[8] When James described Parliament as being 'nothing else but the King's great council', and an advisory council at that, he was attempting to transfer his understanding of his first Parliament on to his new one. He demanded that all proposals for laws should be submitted to him twenty days before the opening of Parliament, so that he might select which would be sent on to Parliament. No other legislation would be debated, and even those laws selected by him and passed by Parliament would only become statutes with his final approval: 'and if there be anything that I dislike, they raze it out before'.

Such demands were incredibly insulting to the English Parliament which, by the time of James's accession, was a sturdy body. Henry VIII had come to rely on Parliament to bring about the legislative changes he needed to carry through his Reformation in Church and state, and in the forty-five years of Elizabeth's reign it had consolidated its powers, the members of the House of Commons becoming more affluent, and gaining a sense of their own individual and corporate importance. Although outright battles between Queen and Commons had been avoided, calling a Parliament had become a risky business for Elizabeth: it was a forum in which members' complaints were very publicly aired. By 1604 this pattern was well enough established that the Commons were bound to want to obtain certain concessions from the new King, in particular the redress of grievances arising from outmoded feudal tenures, and from antiquated crown rights such as purveyance (the fixing of prices for supplies to the King's court), monopolies and wardships. Implied in most of these was a decrease in not only the revenue but the authority of the Crown, shifting power to Parliament.

James's priority in the 1604 Parliament, on the other hand, was to bring his two kingdoms of England and Scotland into a Union.[9] Writing to the Privy Council of Scotland in January 1604, he was confident that the case for union did not need to be made. 'For that our equal right to both the crowns mon [must] needs affect us with an equal care to both their weals, and that being now joined together and under one head, as they have been of long time past in one religion and language, and one common habitation in an isle disjoined from the great continent of the world, our princely care mon be extended to see them join and coalesce together in a sincere and perfect union, and as two twins bred in one belly, love one another as no more two but one estate.'[10] In his opening address to the English Parliament, James spoke at length of the natural reasons for the union of the kingdoms, and demanded rhetorically whether it was not 'manifest that God by His Almighty providence hath preordained it so to be? Hath not God first united these two kingdoms both in language, religion, and similitude of manners? Yea, hath he not made us all in one island, compassed with one sea, and of itself by nature so indivisible, as almost those that were borderers themselves on the late Borders, cannot distinguish, nor know, nor discern their own limits?' No sea, no great river, no mountain separated these two countries, 'only small brooks, or demolished little walls' – in fact, England and Scotland were divided 'in apprehension' rather than in 'effect'. They were merely waiting for James who 'united the right and title of both in my person, alike lineally descended of both the Crowns'. Just as Henry VII had brought to an end the Wars of the Roses by uniting the battling houses of Lancaster and York, James, Henry's descendant, would bring about 'the Union of two ancient and famous kingdoms', an 'inward Peace annexed to my person'. This new marriage could not be broken by divorce. 'What God hath conjoined then, let no man separate. I am the husband, and all the whole isle is my lawful wife; I am the head, and it is my body; I am the shepherd, and it is my flock. I hope therefore that no man will be so unreasonable as to think that I that am a Christian King under the Gospel, should be a polygamist and husband to two wives; that I being the head, should have a divided and monstrous body; or that being the shepherd to so fair a flock . . . should have my flock parted in two.'

To split England from Scotland was to split James himself: 'As God hath made Scotland the one half of this isle to enjoy my birth, and the first and most unperfect half of my life, and you here to enjoy the perfect and last half thereof, so can I not think that any would be so injurious to me, not in their thoughts or wishes, as to cut asunder the one half of me from the other.'[11]

While James had no doubt that his cause was just, Parliament had other concerns. Within the opening days of this first Parliament there emerged a dispute which, while relatively minor in its own right, set the pattern for what were to be regular, and perhaps inevitable, show-downs between the King and the Commons. This dispute concerned parliamentary elections. In his proclamation summoning the Parliament, the King had directed that returns were to be sent to the Court of Chancery where they would be checked to ensure that nothing was out of order; if irregularities were detected, then the offending return would be rejected, and a second election would have to take place. The Commons resented this royal intervention because it gave another body the right to determine the membership of the Lower House. This was by no means a Jacobean innovation (the Commons had protested against such a direction eighteen years earlier) but the first Parliament of a new sovereign seemed a good moment to iron out such long-standing anomalies.

The possibility arose when a Buckinghamshire election was contested, in which Sir Francis Goodwin had secured the larger number of votes and was duly returned. But Chancery found a tech-nicality whereby the return was invalid; a new writ was issued and in the second election Sir John Fortescue was returned. Fortescue was well known to be the government's preferred choice as member, and so the Lower House decided to ignore the second election, and on 23 March instructed Goodwin to take his seat. Four days later the matter flared again. The Lords asked, 'for the removal of all stumbling blocks', that they confer with the Commons on the matter; the Commons declined on the grounds that 'it did not stand with the honour and order of the House to give account of any of their proceedings and doings'.[12] At this stage, the King intervened. He 'conceived himself engaged and touched in honour' by the case, he told the Commons, and they should confer with the Lords on the matter. The Commons found this message 'so extraordinary and unexpected' that they asked to discuss the matter with the King himself.[13] For his part, James had not expected this development, but he agreed to a meeting the following morning. There he reiterated that he had no intention to impeach parliamentary privileges, but pointed out that the Commons should realise that they derived all their privileges from him, and he therefore expected that such privileges should not be turned against him. As for the precedents they had offered, these had been taken from the reigns 'of minors, of tyrants, of women, of simple kings' and were not to be given too much credit. They should confer with the judges, and report their decision to the Privy Council.[14]

James's words hit hard at the Commons' sense of themselves as a body. They spent time debating the legal origins of privilege, which James had raised, and sent a lengthy tract to the King to justify the position they had taken. On 5 April, James sent back a message by the Speaker of the House. He had as great a desire to maintain their privileges as ever any prince had – indeed, as they had themselves. Having considered the matter carefully, balancing views of the Commons, his Council and judges, he was 'now distracted in judgement'. So he 'desired and commanded, as an absolute King' that the conference between Commons and judges go ahead, with his Privy Council in attendance. The message was greeted with 'amazement and silence'. In living memory, no one dared to speak to the Commons like this. 'The Prince's command is like a thunderbolt,' exclaimed one member, 'his command upon our allegiance like the roaring of a lion. To his command there is no contradiction.'[15]

The Commons were represented by Francis Bacon, whose performance was also a harbinger of many to come. The Commons, he announced, were ready to reconsider their decision, which they had never done before. James graciously replied that he would not press his royal prerogative against his subjects, but would instead allow free rein to his sweet and kindly nature by confirming their privileges. In return, they should agree to a compromise: both previous elections be voided, a new writ issued. There was hesitation on the part of the Commons' delegates, but they finally accepted. James was happy.

Although the Devil had cast in this bone of contention, he pronounced, God had turned it to good, for he, the King, had witnessed the loyalty of his people, and they had seen his grace and bounty. Everyone was happy. James thought he had established his prerogative; the Commons thought they had established one of their privileges by confirming their right to settle election disputes.[16]

None of this helped James's plans for the Union. The subject was debated from mid-April onwards, but decisions were constantly deferred. Much time was spent on the proposed name of 'Britain'; many members believed that the Union in government should be settled before the Union in name. On 20 April James met a committee on the Union and explained that he proposed two points: 'first that by a Bill or Act there should be recognition that his just possession of the Crowns of both the famous, ancient and honourable nations of England and Scotland whereby they are united under one allegiance should be rightly understood of all men. The second was that commissioners might be appointed to confer with Scottish commissioners for the making of a resolution to be propounded to the next two Parliaments of England and Scotland.'[17] But the Commons found the very name of 'Britain' a sticking point. They could not lose the ancient name of England. If they altered the name of England might they not accidentally abrogate all the laws of England, and force their re-enactment? Would laws passed in future be binding on all of Britain? Furthermore, 'Britain' had negative connotations – were not the Britons savages and pagans? The change in name must wait until the change in government was properly sorted out.

On 1 May, the MP for Launceston, Sir Thomas Lake, James's Latin secretary and Keeper of the Public Records, read to the Commons a letter from the King. Resistance to the Union was nothing more than 'jealousy and distrust', he declared, stirred up by 'the curiosity of a few giddy heads'. They could either yield to Providence and embrace what God was giving them, 'and by the away-taking of that partition wall, which already by God's Providence in my blood is rent asunder, to establish my throne and your body politic in a perpetual and flourishing peace; or else, contemning God's benefits so freely offered unto us, to spit and blaspheme in His face by preferring war to peace, trouble to quietness, hatred to love, weakness to strength, and division to union; to sow the seeds of discord to all our posterities; to dishonour your King; to make both me and you a proverb of reproach in the mouths of all strangers, and all enemies to this nation, and all enviers of my greatness', and to force England to build new fortifications along the Borders.[18] The Commons were not impressed by this bombast, and, ultimately, James had no choice but to agree not to alter his title to 'King of Great Britain'; Parliament did however concede to appoint a commission to look into matters pertaining to the Union.

At the end of the session the Commons drew up an *Apology*, presented by Sir Edwin Sandys, MP for Stockbridge in Gloucestershire and a leading member of the Jacobean Commons, in which they instructed the King how to approach an English parliament. James was furious, and in his final speech to Parliament berated the Commons for their behaviour over the Union bill. In Scotland, he remarked, his counsel had been received graciously; in England, on the contrary, there was 'nothing but curiosity from morning to evening, to find fault with my propositions'. In Scotland, everything emanating from the King was warranted; here everything was suspected.[19]

Parliament was prorogued on 7 July, but James decided that if Parliament would not create the Union then he would create it himself. Over the summer months of 1604, the King took counsel on features that he hoped would make the Union a *fait accompli*: inventing coinage common to both countries; reducing the countries' laws to a single law; designing a composite flag; implementing free trade between England and Scotland; attempting to pacify the Borders.[20] The Venetian ambassador reported that the King was determined 'to call himself King of Great Britain and like that famous and ancient King Arthur to embrace under one name the whole circuit of the island', and indeed on 24 October at the great Cross in Westminster, James was 'in most solemn manner proclaimed King of Great Britain, France and Ireland'.[21]

The Union Commission of forty-eight Englishmen and thirty-one Scots assembled on 29 October 1604, without the King, who was in the country hunting. Their deliberations focused on four points: the repeal of laws in each country that were hostile to the other; the possibility of free trade between the kingdoms; the amelioration of justice in the Border regions, through the extradition of criminals; and the mutual naturalisation of James's subjects. Only the repeal of hostile laws was straightforward. The English were scared of a free trade competition that would allow the Scots to undercut them in both cheap goods and cheap labour, and that raised the spectre of Scots gaining admission to the exclusive English trade guilds. The English also feared for any Englishman who would be extradited and exposed to what they perceived as a brutal Scottish legal system.

But it was on the key question of naturalisation that the debate hinged. James's accession to the English throne in March 1603 had created two sorts of subjects: those born before that date, who were referred to as the 'ante-nati', and those born after, the 'post-nati'. The ante-nati were subjects of the King of Scots, and thus aliens in England. But the post-nati, though born in Scotland, were also subjects of the King of England. These post-nati, it was argued, were already naturalised by the common law throughout all his dominions, and as such they could hold office in England, which the ante-nati could not. James objected to the matter being decided by the law rather than by him. Although he was quite happy to prevent the ante-nati from taking office in England – indeed, he would pledge to do so – he demanded that a clause be inserted that this was part of his royal prerogative.

The matter of the Union came to head in the parliamentary session beginning in February 1607. The Commons made known their view that the post-nati were not naturalised as English subjects by common law. Sir Edwin Sandys asserted that 'Unions of kingdoms are not made by law but by act express', and that a chance royal marriage a few generations back should not be allowed to mean the naturalisation of thousands of children now. Arguments were made on legal technicalities, but what came through the parliamentary debates on Union was a loud and vociferous prejudice against the Scots who were depicted as proud, violent beggars, lean and hungry cattle who would overrun England's rich pastures.[22] On 13 February the MP for Buckinghamshire, Sir Christopher Piggott, 'with a loud voice' and discourteously keeping his hat on, launched into 'an invective against the Scots and Scottish nation, using many words of scandal and

This tender portrait of Mary Queen of Scots and her son James is a work of fiction: it was painted in 1583, by which date they had not met in sixteen years.

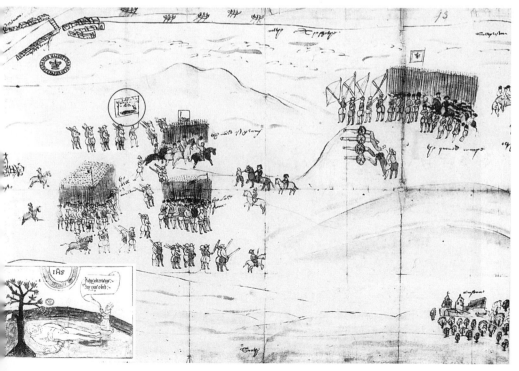

The Confederate Lords confront Queen Mary's army at Carberry Hill in 1567. The Lords (left) carry a banner (*inset*) showing the baby Prince James praying over the body of his father, lying in the garden of Kirk o'Field, with the invocation, 'Judge and avenge my cause, O Lord'.

George Buchanan,
the famed humanist who
became a notably irascible
tutor to the young King.

Esmé Stuart, Sieur
d'Aubigny, later Duke
of Lennox, 'a man of
comely proportions' for
whom James developed
an early passion.

Anna of Denmark, James's young wife who soon proved herself adept at court politics.

IACOBVS · 6 · D · G · R ·
SCOTORVM ·
ÆTA · 29 ·
1595 ·

James, aged 27, when he had finally taken full control as King of Scots.

Robert Carr, Earl of Somerset. Handsome, passionate and petulant, Carr won James's affections and embarked on a meteoric rise at court.

James in a hunting assembly. The scene is more reminiscent of Elizabeth's elaborate hunting trips than James's small, informal parties – and indeed, the image originally depicted Elizabeth: James has been superimposed in the top left-hand corner.

Henry, the new Prince of Wales, typically pictured in a self-promoting allegory with Time as a lancebearer, *circa* 1610.

Hilliard miniatures of
James's children Charles (as
Prince of Wales) and Elizabeth.

George Villiers, later Duke of Buckingham, with his famously long, shapely legs well to the fore.

obliquy'. He claimed to be 'astonished that any ear could be lent for joining a good and fertile country to one poor and barren, and in a manner disgraced by nature; and for associating frank and honest men with such as were beggars, proud, and generally traitors and rebels to their King. There was as much difference between an English and a Scots man as between a judge and a thief.' The inevitable Scots complaint to the King was led by his current favourite, Sir John Ramsay, the hero of the hour at the Gowrie Plot; James summoned his Council and berated them 'very harshly, declaring that he was a Scot himself and that nothing could be applied to the nation in general in which he had not his share'. Piggott was expelled from the House, but he had set the tone: on the 14th Nicholas Fuller proclaimed, in more moderate language, that England had no room for Scots: the universities were overfilled, London was being destroyed by new buildings, merchants had gone three years without profit, and trades were overstocked.[23]

The debates continued into March 1607 with the business being referred to a conference with the Lords, then to the Upper House judges, then back to the Commons, the main point of contention being whether the post-nati should have equal rights in England with the English. The Lower House concluded that neither ante-nati nor post-nati should be naturalised, nor given the rights enjoyed by English citizens. If they enjoyed English benefits, who was to ensure that they paid English taxes, obeyed English law? No: a piece-meal situation was unworkable. The Commons saw only one solu-tion: a single, united legal system with one Parliament and one law, so that practices could not diverge – what they called a 'perfect union'. The King and his government were less idealistic and less patient: James argued that the perfect union would come about over time, a marriage that must be preceded by a courtship – after all two parties could not be put to bed on such short acquaintance (an image that he presumably did not relate to his own marital experi-ence). To advocate a perfect union was to pay lip service, and not to speak from the heart.[24]

Eventually, on 2 May, James spoke to the House somewhat exas-peratedly. What did they need to do? He *was* the Union. 'It is merely idle and frivolous to conceive that any imperfect union is desired, or can be granted. It is no more unperfect, as now it is projected, than a child that is born without a beard. It is already a perfect union in me, the Head.' James was disappointed in his Commons. 'I looked for no such fruits at your hands; such personal discourses and speeches; which of all other I looked you should avoid, as not beseeming the gravity of your assembly. I am your King. I am placed to govern you, and shall answer for your errors. I am a man of flesh and blood, and have my passions and affections as other men. I pray you, do not too far move me to do that which my Power may tempt me unto.'[25] But it was clear that the Commons would not consent to the King's proposals, and the suggestions were postponed.

For James, this was more than a parliamentary defeat. It demonstrated to him that his dreams of a Great Britain were not shared by his Commons, and that they would go out of their way to oppose him when they saw fit. The only success met by the pro-Unionists in James's lifetime was the passing, as late as 30 June 1607, of a bill repealing hostile laws; the passing of the Union would wait for another century.

Bruised by the failure of the Union, the attacks of Puritans, and the increasingly uncooperative Commons, James felt his popularity to be at an all-time low. At the same time, he had to come to terms with the popularity of his heir. Artists and writers portrayed Henry as an emphatically active, martial prince – and it does appear that Henry had a real hands-on interest in all things warlike. One account describes how

> he did also practise tilting, charging on horseback with pistols, after
> the manner of the wars, with all other the like inventions. Now
> also delighting to confer, both with his own, and other strangers,
> and great captains, of all manners of wars, battle, furniture, arms
> by sea and land, disciplines, orders, marches, alarms, watches,
> strategems, ambuscades, approaches, scalings, fortifications, incamp-
> ings; and having now and then battles of headmen appointed both
> on horse and foot, in a long table; whereby he might, in a manner,
> view the right ordering of a battle . . .

He even played host to a Dutch engineer named Abraham van Nyevelt who instructed him in 'all manner of things belonging to the wars'.[26] Whether from his own inclination or from the wishful thinking of others, Henry had become an icon of everything James was not.

There are suggestions that James was not wholly happy with this state of affairs. Henry was less than committed as a scholar, studying 'not with much delight, and chiefly under his father's spur', as the Venetian ambassador Nicolo Molin reported in June 1607. For this, he continued, Henry was 'often admonished and set down'. Molin tells of how one day James taunted Henry that if he did not pay better attention to his lessons he would leave his crown to his brother Charles, a far better scholar. Henry made no reply, out of respect for his father, but later when his tutor tried to make the same point, he said: 'I know what becomes a Prince. It is not necessary for me to be a professor, but a soldier and a man of this world. If my brother is as learned as they say, we'll make him Archbishop of Canterbury.' When this was reported to James, he took it 'in no good part', continued Molin, 'nor is he overpleased to see his son so beloved and of such promise that his subjects place all their hopes in him; and it would almost seem, to speak quite frankly, that the King was growing jealous; and so the Prince has great need of a wise counsellor to guide his steps'.[27]

In time, Henry tired of his rural retreat at Oatlands. On 16 December 1608, the fourteen-year-old Prince declared to his father that he was living too far away from court. James replied that he could make whatever arrangements he liked, and Henry took him at his word, ordering the Earls of Southampton and Pembroke to vacate their lodgings and stables at the palace so that he could move in, and then, when they refused, simply removing their possessions.[28] There were moments when Henry stood up for what he believed. When his servant and friend Phineas Pett was accused of wrongdoing in naval matters, Henry stood by him during his trial, and bitterly attacked his accusers when Pett was ultimately found innocent. He befriended his father's *bête noire*, Sir Walter Ralegh, who had been shut up in the Tower of London since 1603, and was reputed to have said that 'None but my father would keep such a bird in a cage'.[29] Anna's chaplain, Bishop Goodman, wrote that Henry 'did sometimes pry into the King's actions, and a little dislike them . . . and truly I think he was a little self-willed'.[30]

CHAPTER FOURTEEN

A Terrible Blow

FIVE YEARS AFTER the Gowrie Plot, in 1605 James unearthed another conspiracy against his life, although this one was undoubtedly real.[1] The Gunpowder Plot seems to have been the brainchild of an English Catholic gentleman named Robert Catesby who, as early as 1603, was discussing with his friend Thomas Percy the possibility of assassinating the new King. By the spring of 1604, the conspiracy had widened to include three other men: Catesby's cousin Thomas Winter, a friend named John Wright, and a mercenary recently returned from the Low Countries wars named Guy Fawkes. The plot was startling in its audacity – and its simplicity. As James later put it, Catesby and his fellows intended 'not only . . . the destruction of my person, nor of my wife and posterity only, but of the whole body of the State in general; wherein should neither have been spared, or distinction made to young nor of old, of great nor of small, of man nor of woman: the whole nobility, the whole reverend clergy, bishops, and most part of the good preachers, the most part of the knights and gentry; . . . the whole judges of the land, with the most of the lawyers, and the whole clerks'. This they would accomplish in a single blow by planting barrels of gunpowder under the Parliament House in Westminster – poetic justice since Parliament was where 'the cruel laws (as they say) were made against their religion', so 'both place and person should all be destroyed and blown up at once'.[2] Practical planning commenced in May of 1604 with the renting of a house that backed on to the Parliament building; from there the conspirators started to dig a tunnel, a difficult and back-breaking task that necessitated the recruitment of more men. It was only after ten months of toil that they discovered that the house next to their own had a cellar that ran directly under the Parliament building. Once they had rented that house, it was a simple matter to break down the wall between the two cellars, and to move twenty barrels of gunpowder under the relevant chamber. It was Fawkes who carried out this work, covering the barrels with iron bars and faggots.

But Catesby's plans didn't stop at the dynamiting of Westminster.

An explosion at the opening ceremony might carry off James, Anna and Henry, but that still left two heirs to the throne still alive, Prince Charles and Princess Elizabeth. Elizabeth was being raised at the Haringtons' estate at Combe Abbey in Warwickshire, which happened to be only twenty miles from Catesby's mother's house at Ashby St Leger. The plotters resolved to snatch the princess 'by drawing friends together at a hunting' strategically located between the two houses at Sir Everard Digby's at Dunchurch.[3] Thomas Percy would use his position as a gentleman pensioner to abduct Prince Charles, under the pretence of taking him to a safe hiding place.[4] In order to organise all this, more recruits were needed, and, by October 1605, some thirteen conspirators knew about the plot. It was only a matter of time before someone betrayed the elaborate conspiracy.

One Warwickshire conspirator, Catesby's first cousin Francis Tresham, was worried that the blast in Parliament would kill his brother-in-law William Parker, Lord Monteagle, and decided to warn him, while giving the conspirators a chance to escape. Monteagle was at supper at his house in Hoxton, near London, on 26 October when he was passed a note that had been given to one of his servants by a stranger. Monteagle told his servant, Thomas Ward, to read the letter aloud:

> My Lord, out of the love that I bear to some of your friends, I have a care of your preservation. Therefore I would advise you, as you tender your life, to devise your excuse to shift off your attendance at this Parliament. For God and man have concurred to punish the wickedness of this time. And think not slightly of this advertisement [warning], but retire yourself into your country, where you may expect the event in safety. For though there be no appearance of any stir, yet I say, they shall receive a terrible blow this Parliament, and yet they shall not see who hurts them. This counsel is not to be contemned, because it may do you good, and can do you no harm, for the danger is past so soon as you have burnt the letter. And I hope God will give you the grace to make good use of it: to whose holy protection I commend you.[5]

The letter was then taken by Monteagle himself to Sir Robert Cecil, Earl of Salisbury, who was dining with four other Privy Councillors,

Northampton, Nottingham, Suffolk and Worcester. They suspected that 'a terrible blow' might refer to an explosion, but determined to postpone any search, and instead allow the plot to develop.

James was on a hunting trip at Royston until the beginning of November, and it was only on his return to the capital that Salisbury showed him the letter. The King read the message and congratulated himself on breaking its cunning code – plotters had attempted to blow up his own father so the notion did not strike him as far-fetched. Since the opening of Parliament was scheduled for 5 November, he determined that a search should not be carried out until the night before, to give the plot time to mature. Late on 4 November, Suffolk led a search that discovered Guy Fawkes, calling himself John Johnson, standing guard over a pile of faggots. James was informed, and he commanded a more detailed search. At 11 p.m. the gunpowder was discovered, and 'Johnson' was arrested and taken to the Tower. James was awakened and told of developments; he gave thanks to God for his deliverance, and gave instructions that 'Johnson' must not be allowed to kill himself: he was their source for further information. James provided his councillors with a series of questions with which to interrogate 'Johnson', and asked whether they thought a recent 'cruelly villainous pasquil [lampoon]' that had inveighed against James's adoption of the title 'King of Great Britain' might not also be his work?[6] (Fawkes had in fact written a memorandum in July 1603 dealing with the unpopularity of the Scots in James's court.)[7]

Within hours of Fawkes' arrest, the conspirators had fled to Dunchurch, but soon discovered that they had to keep moving. On 6 November, Harington at Combe Abbey received a message from one of his neighbours, claiming that horses had been stolen during the night by armed men whom they believed to be papists. Harington wrote to London for instructions, but as rumours intensified he decided to wait no longer but to take action himself, and whisked Elizabeth to Coventry, placing her in the custody of a merchant there. It was a wise decision: Sir Thomas Edmondes reported that 'popish flight-heads' came 'but two hours too late to have seized upon the person of the Lady Elizabeth's grace'.[8] In truth, however, the Warwickshire conspiracy had fairly much evaporated, and its dregs, led by Catesby, fled west, to what they hoped was a safe house,

Holbeach House, near Stourbridge. There they were captured, Catesby being shot on the spot, the others dying of their wounds, or being taken to London for trial and, ultimately, execution.

James made the most of the opportunity. On 9 November he appeared in Parliament to offer thanks to God 'for the great and miraculous delivery he hath granted to me, and to you all, and consequently to the whole body of this estate'. He begged the members' indulgence to explore a conceit of his: 'That since kings are in the word of God itself called Gods, as being his lieutenants and vice-regents on earth, and so adorned and furnished with some sparkles of the divinity; to compare some of the works of God the great King, towards the whole and general world, to some of his works towards me, and this little world of my dominions.' Just as God punished sin by the 'general purgation' which only Noah and his family survived, James 'may justly compare these two great and fearful Domesdays, wherewith God threatened to destroy me and all you of this little world in me', the Gowrie Plot and this new Gunpowder Plot. He 'amongst all other Kings have been subject' to 'daily tempests of innumerable dangers', 'not only ever since my birth, but even as I may justly say, before my birth: and while I was in my mother's belly', a rare reference to the trauma of the Riccio murder.[9]

James went on to congratulate himself on bringing the matter to light – an uncharacteristic act because he had always believed suspiciousness to be 'the sickness of a tyrant' and tended personally to the other extreme. On this occasion, however, things were different. When Salisbury showed him the letter, he was 'so far contrary to myself' that he 'did upon the instant interpret and apprehend some dark phrases' it contained, namely the 'general obscure advertisment' of 'some dangerous blow'. This interpretation, he continued pedantically, required reading 'contrary to the ordinary grammar construction of them' – the kind of construction that you might expect a mere university divine or lawyer to offer. If he'd interpreted it in any other way, 'no worldly provision or prevention could have made us escape our utter destruction'. In fact, the whole affair showed 'a wonderful providence of God'. It so happened that Fawkes was taken with 'his firework for kindling ready in his pocket': if he'd been apprehended only a few minutes earlier this evidence would not have been there.

Even if the plan had gone ahead, it would have been to James's immortal fame, since future ages could not say that 'I had died ingloriously in an ale-house, a stews [brothel], or such vile place'; instead, 'but mine end should have been with the most honourable and best company, and in that most honourable and fittest place for a king to be in'.[10]

A few months later, upon the publication of the King's Parliament speech of thanksgiving, these self-glorifying notions were developed in an accompanying tract entitled *A Discourse of the Maner of the Discovery of this Late Intended Treason*. Ostensibly written anonymously by a courtier, it describes how, with God's aid, the King discovered the plot, saving his own person and the whole realm. Salisbury and Suffolk are portrayed as possessing no intellectual nous of their own, instead referring the letter to James since they apparently knew of 'his fortunate judgement in clearing and solving of obscure riddles and doubtful mysteries'. In fact, the *Discourse* continues, Salisbury didn't believe the letter to be of importance, but James 'apprehended it deeplier', and ordered the search of the Parliament house, astounding his Secretary. At the same time, the *Discourse* insisted that the King was indifferent to his own harm, 'whereby he had drawn himself into many desperate dangers'; no, his concern derived only from his care for the state. A marvellously sycophantic piece of work, it pleased James enough – if indeed he did not pen it himself – to include it, without comment, in his collected *Workes*, published in early 1617.[11]

The Catesby plot had a severe effect on the royal family. Nine-year-old Elizabeth in particular suffered from the aftereffects of the ordeal. In January 1606, her guardian Harington reported that the Princess was still suffering 'from the fever occasioned by these disturbances': 'this poor lady hath not yet recovered the surprise and is very ill and troubled.'[12] For all his bravado in Parliament, James, too, was deeply disturbed. 'The King is in terror,' reported the Venetian ambassador. 'He does not appear nor does he take his meals in public as usual. He lives in the innermost rooms with only Scotsmen about him. The Lords of the Council also are alarmed and confused by the plot itself and by the King's suspicions.'[13] For James, the Gunpowder Plot, calling to mind only too clearly the attack on Riccio and the Gowrie Plot, was just the last in a line of threats to his life. This was no time for complacency.

＊　　＊　　＊

Most directly, the Gunpowder Plot gave James pause for thought about his policy towards English Catholics. This, after all, was not the first Catholic conspiracy he had encountered in his new country. In his final years in Scotland, James had been informed, primarily by Lord Henry Howard, that Sir Walter Ralegh, one of Elizabeth's favourites, opposed his claim to the throne; James did not forget the advice and as a result Ralegh was one of the few Englishmen to lose out on James's accession, as the new King deprived him of his post of Captain of the Guard, other lucrative posts and licences, and ordered him to leave his house, Durham House in the Strand. On 14 July 1603 he was summoned before the Privy Council and grilled concerning his possible involvement in any plot 'to surprise the King's person', and in particular a plot contrived between the Spanish agent Count Aremberg and Ralegh's friend Lord Cobham. Unable to prove his innocence, Ralegh was imprisoned in the Tower of London three days later. In November, he was brought to trial before a specially appointed, and notably hostile, commission at Winchester. He was found guilty on charges of receiving bribes from Spain; 'compassing and imagining' the death of James and his family, 'the old fox and his cubs'; and of trying to put Arbella Stuart on the throne, to deliver England into the hands of Spain.

Ralegh's alleged co-conspirators, William Watson, George Brooke, Lords Cobham and Grey, were tried and condemned to death. Ralegh himself was due to be executed on 11 December, but the day before Ralegh, Cobham and Grey were reprieved, and sent back to the Tower, where Ralegh was to spend the next fourteen years of his life. According to a published letter, 'written from Master T.M. near Salisbury, to Master H.A. at London, concerning the proceeding at Winchester' but bearing the traces of James's personal involvement, the reprieve was a brilliant *coup de théâtre*, designed to show his kingly clemency. During the trial, James allegedly called fourteen or fifteen Privy Councillors to the nearby estate of Wilton, where he was staying. Warrants for execution were signed, but James secretly wrote a warrant of reprieve in his cabinet, and appointed a Groom of his Bedchamber to deliver it 'even at the instant when the axe should be laid to the tree's roots' – a forgivable dramatisation of the actual event. The letter likened this trick to 'some ancient history, expressed in a well-acted comedy' and applauded 'so many lively figures of justice and mercy in a king, of terror and penitence in offenders, and of so great admiration and applause in all others, as appeared in this action, carried only and wholly by his Majesty's own direction'.[14]

This time, however, James was in no mood to show mercy, even for the sake of his public image. Fawkes had confessed 'that there was no cause moving him or them, but merely and only religion', namely his Roman Catholic faith. What did it mean, asked James, that 'Christian men, at least so called, English, born within the country . . . should practise the destruction of their King, his posterity, their country and all?' On the one hand, it did not follow 'that all professing that Romish religion were guilty of the same'. On the other, 'it is true, that no other sect of heretics, not excepting Turk, Jew, nor Pagan, no not even those of Calicut, who adore the Devil, did ever maintain by their grounds of their religion, that it was lawful, or rather meritorious (as the Roman Catholics call it) to murder princes of people for quarrel of Religion'.[15]

Parliament reacted at the end of May 1606 by passing 'An Act for the better discovering and repressing of Popish Recusants passing tougher laws against Catholic recusants' which included what it termed the Oath of Allegiance. An English Catholic could now be commanded to swear this Oath, which acknowledged James as lawful king, denied the power of the Pope to depose him, and went on to condemn as 'impious and heretical' the 'damnable doctrine' that a sovereign excommunicated from the Roman Catholic Church could lawfully be deposed and murdered.[16] In practice, many lay Catholics chose to take the Oath, justifying it to themselves on the ground that it did not insist that they abjure their faith; Jesuits and priests who refused to take it, however, were banished from the realm.

James's move attracted international opposition. While he saw the Oath as a civil matter, concerning the allegiance of subjects to their sovereign, Rome inevitably viewed it as a matter of spiritual concern that denied papal supremacy, and was thus de facto heretical; this disagreement was made more intense by the death, in 1605, of Clement VIII and his succession by the more hard-line Paul V. The subsequent breakdown of relations with Rome depressed the King. In early 1606, the Venetian ambassador reported, 'His Majesty on Sunday last while at chapel and afterwards at dinner, appeared very subdued and melancholy; he did not speak at all, though those in attendance gave him occasion. This is unlike his usual manner. After dinner, however, he broke out with great violence, "I have dispatches from Rome informing me that the Pope intends to excommunicate me; the Catholics threaten to dethrone me and to take my life unless I grant them liberty of conscience. I shall most certainly be obliged to stain my hands with their blood, though sorely against my will. But they shall not think they can frighten me, for they shall taste of the agony first. I do not know upon what they found this cursed doctrine that they are permitted to plot against the lives of princes. Sometimes I am amazed that when I see that the princes of Christendom are so blinded that they do not perceive the great injury inflicted on them by so false a doctrine." He continued for a whole hour to talk in a similar strain, and those in attendance praised and approved.'[7]

James's newfound passion for debating the false doctrine soon found itself a public form of expression. Paul V put forth two breves, or papal letters (the first on 12 September 1606, the second on 13 August 1607), asserting that English Catholics could not take the Oath 'with safety of their salvation'. Then in September 1607, Cardinal Robert Bellarmine wrote to the English Archpriest George Blackwell, reproving him for taking the Oath, which he claimed was tantamount to abjuring allegiance to the Vicar of Christ. He wrote of how the papacy had the right to take action against secular princes it regarded as heretical. According to his later editor, the cleric and scholar James Montagu, James decided that such challenges must not pass unchallenged, and set about to demonstrate to his Catholic subjects 'that the taking of this oath was so far from endangering their souls, as that it intended nothing but civil obedience, and without touching any point of their conscience, made the State secure of their Allegiance'.[18] He decided to write a formal response to Bellarmine's letter.

What began as an intellectual pastime soon became an obsession. The Venetian ambassador observed that 'The King as a most learned prince embarks right willingly on this subject and shows a kind of rivalry with the Cardinal [Bellarmine], who has here the reputation of being the most learned champion on the papal side.'[19] James set himself merely to sketch out directions for the argument, and appointed Thomas Bilson, Bishop of Winchester, to undertake the writing, but soon got carried away. 'I know not how it came to pass; but it fell out true,' recalled Montagu, 'the King's pen ran so fast, that in the compass of six days, his Majesty had accomplished that, which he now calleth his *Apologie*.' Passing it to Bancroft, now Archbishop of Canterbury, and Andrewes, now Bishop of Ely, the story continues, as 'brief notes' to be expanded, the clerics agreed that James's writing was 'so sufficient an answer both to the Pope and Cardinal', that no further work was needed. James was persuaded to put it in print 'but was pleased to conceal his name'.[20]

In truth, the process was less speedy. James, in the country at Royston and Newmarket, spent most of the winter of 1607–8 cooped up with his books, appearing only at mealtimes. His only reading companions, according to the French ambassador, were Montagu and 'a minister whom he called specially from the city to furnish him with memory and material'.[21] Montagu read out to James all four volumes of Bellarmine's ecclesiastical writings, while the King 'weighed the objections and answers of that subtle author and sent often to the libraries in Cambridge for books to examine his quotations'.[22] By February 1608, the *Apologie* was finished, and promptly published as *Triplici nodo, triplex cuneus. Or An Apologie for the Oath of Allegiance* with translations in Latin and French, for international consumption. James boasted proudly that he had given Bellarmine a sound thrashing. Others were less sanguine: Northampton and Salisbury, it was said, 'wished that he had not printed' the book, and were relieved to be able to dissuade him from another planned book responding to the Jesuit Robert Parsons, who had attacked both James and Salisbury in print.[23] James, well aware that the *Apologie* was bound to elicit a response, resolved that if the Pope and Bellarmine 'would not rest in his answer, and sit down by it', acknowledging the Oath in the spirit it was intended, as 'a point of allegiance and civil obedience', then he would be forced to publish the *Apologie* again, but this time 'in his own name with a preface to all the princes in Christendom; wherein he would publish such a Confession of his Faith, persuade the princes so to invindicate their own power, discover so much of the mystery of iniquity unto them; as the Pope's bulls should pull in their horns, and himself wish he had never meddled with this matter'.[24] Preparing to rebuff the inevitable response, James continued to read and write constantly. The French ambassador de la Boderie wrote in March 1608 of how the King was stockpiling ammunition so he could respond promptly to the criticism he knew his book would receive. 'That will only put the author in his element,' de la Boderie mused, 'for this is the science of which he knows the most and in which he most delights.'[25]

True to form, Bellarmine and Parsons responded enthusiastically, mocking James's efforts and subjecting him to the full blast of their immense learning, Bellarmine in a Latin *Responsio* under the pseudonym of Matthaeus Tortus (one of his chaplains); and Parsons in an English piece entitled *Judgement of a Catholicke Englishman*.[26] The King, reported de la Boderie, was 'extremely irritated';[27] to Henri IV of France, James claimed the books 'were filled with a thousand injuries against my book, but also do not spare my own person'.[28] But he was most irked by that fact that he had been wrongfooted: Bellarmine had included in his *Responsio* something very damaging: a description of a letter ostensibly written in 1599 from James in Scotland to Pope Clement VIII, in which the King suggested that he could still be converted to the Roman Catholic faith.[29]

Although the letter was genuine, a scapegoat was required to clear the King from this heinous imputation, and he chose his Scottish secretary James Elphinstoun, now Lord Balmerino. Balmerino was summoned to Royston, and over the course of two interviews with the King (and, although Balmerino didn't know it, in the presence of concealed witnesses), he admitted, first, that he had himself drawn up the letter but with James's knowledge, and, later, that he had drawn up the letter himself without James's knowledge. The Privy Council were now called in to clear up the only remaining mystery – how the royal signature came to be on the letter. James left nothing to chance in clearing his name. As he protested to Salisbury, 'I pray you to think that never thing in this world touched me nearlier than this doth. God knows I am and ever was upright and innocent. But how the world may know it I look to hear your advice after his examination.' He provided the councillors with the right questions and pleaded with them to come up with the right answer: 'Though ye were born strangers to the country where this were done, yet are ye no strangers to the

King thereof, and ye know if the King of Scotland prove a knave the King of England can never be an honest man; work therefore in this as having interest in your King's reputation.' Finally, Balmerino swore before God and the angels that he had thrust the letters in front of James just as he was about to go out hunting, and the King had signed without knowing what it was. The scenario seemed probable enough: many a Privy Councillor had been forced to do the same. When informed of Balmerino's statement, James suddenly remembered how nine years ago, as he was about to go hunting, papers had indeed been pressed on him to sign. His memory was a miracle, he declared. 'For my part, I may justly say that the name given me of James included a prophetical mystery of my fortune, for' – punning on 'James' as 'Jacobus' in Latin – 'as a Jacob I wrestled with my arms upon the 5 of August for my life [the Gowrie Plot] and overcame; on the 5 of November I wrestled and overcame with my wit [the Gunpowder Plot]; and now in a case ten times dearer to me than my life (I mean my reputation) I have wrestled and overcome with my memory.'[30] And so James satisfied himself that, while his signature was on a letter to the Pope, he himself had never written to the Pope. The sacrificial Balmerino was sent to be tried in Scotland and sentenced to death, but through a secret leniency deal was allowed to die shortly after in peaceful retirement.[31]

James was clear-headed enough to realise that he required assistance for his next foray into religious controversy, even with the mountain of material he had compiled. Officially suppressing Bellarmine's book until his reply was ready for public view, James called on his bishops for assistance, and embarked on a nine-month period of collaborative intellectual endeavour. Lancelot Andrewes compiled a weighty *Responsio ad apologiam cardinalis Bellarmini*. William Barlow parried Parsons with *Answer to a Catholike Englishman (so by him-self entituled)* (Parsons' response did not come into print until after his death). John Barclay was to prepare an edition of his father William Barclay's unpublished manuscript *De potestate papae* on the power of the papacy: Barclay senior had been a Catholic, but his tract argued that the Pope should limit himself to a spiritual jurisdiction, and abandon his claims to temporal power, which were damaging the Church, an argument that was music to James's ears.[32] As for James himself, Montagu writes of how he once again, 'with the like celerity, in the compass of one week, wrote his *Monitory-Preface*'.[33] Certainly, by November 1608 James had reportedly finished a draft of his response, and passed it on to Andrewes to lard with supporting evidence from the Church Fathers.[34] But the King could not leave Andrewes alone, and the Bishop's work turned into a Penelope's web, according to the French ambassador: no sooner had Andrewes finished a portion and shown it to the King, than 'so much is found that must be rewritten that the poor Bishop has more difficulty in making corrections than he had in writing his composition in the first place'.[35] Working on the treatise 'from morning to night',[36] James gradually called in more churchmen and academics for their advice, and he was still redrafting, revising and checking as the work went to the printers in early 1609.

James's apparent perfectionism was all for nought. When the book finally appeared, on 1 April, it was riddled with every kind of error. James, 'infuriated', called for the printer's blood;[37] calming down, he had all copies of the book called back in, by a royal proclamation that blamed the printers for being over-hasty. James now devoted all his attention to the revision of the book, working simultaneously on the Latin, French and Italian translations (the Italian never came to fruition). Four bishops were called in, alongside Sir Henry Savile, the Warden of Merton College, Oxford, Thomas Wilson, the Keeper of State Papers, and John Barclay. As John Chamberlain reported, the King was uncharacteristically 'so wholly possessed and over-careful about his book that till that be finished to his liking he can brook no other sport nor business'.[38] Finally, the revised book appeared in May 1609, but hopes that the 'correcting' of the text would moderate its violence were soon dashed.

The new *Monitory Preface* was in fact longer than the *Apologie* it prefaced. Dedicated to Rudolf II 'and to all other right high and mighty kings, and right excellent free princes and states of Christendom',[39] it aimed to draw the attention of Christian secular rulers to the dangers posed by the temporal power of the papacy. Some of it was temperate enough, reiterating James's willingness to see the Pope as the first priest among priests. But, as ever with James, too much was brought down to the personal level, with a slew of autobiographical references earnestly making the case for his orthodoxy. Elsewhere, though, earnestness was swapped for a mocking, dangerously irreverent humour. James couldn't believe that the Blessed Virgin 'hath no other thing to do in heaven, than to hear every idle man's suit and busy herself in their errands; whiles requesting, whiles commanding her son, whiles coming down to kiss and make love to priests, and whiles disputing and brawling with devils'. Turning to images, he inquires how could we paint God's face, 'when Moses (the man that ever was most familiar with God) never saw but his back parts?' He leaves the question of whether purgatory exists for others – 'how many chambers and anti-chambers the Devil hath, they can best tell that go to him' – but just in case, asks Bellarmine to let him know, whether 'that fair green meadow that is in purgatory have a brook running through it', so that 'in case I come there, I may have hawking upon it'.[40]

James proudly bound his books in velvet and cornered them with gold for delivery to his European brother-kings. But no amount of velvet could muffle the book's shrill carping tone. The Pope, naturally enough, issued a public edict outlawing James's book. The Inquisition of Venice prohibited its publishing there, causing a 'great fray' between the authorities and James's ambassador to Venice.[41] The Duke of Savoy refused to receive his copy; the Grand Duke of Florence gave his to his confessor, who burned it; Count Fuentes had it cut into pieces; and one Italian prince was quoted as exclaiming, 'Vade retro Satana, di tal farina non mangio io pane' (Get thee behind me, Satan, I shall eat no bread of that flour). Even Henri IV of France, once an ally of the King of Scots, dismissed it, throwing his copy on to a table and protesting that bookwriting was no occupation for a king, and James would have better spent his time doing something else.[42] But James had no intention of doing anything else. As late as November 1611 the great scholar Isaac Casaubon, now resident in England, was complaining that 'The King is now so entirely taken up with one sort of book that he keeps his own mind and the minds of all about him occupied exclusively on the one topic. Hardly a day passes on which some new pamphlet is not brought before him, mostly written by Jesuits, some on the martyrdom of Saint Garnett, the sufferings of the English Catholics, or matters of that description. All these things,' he concluded dismally, 'I have to read and give my opinion upon.'[43]

James was no doubt stung by the criticism of his fellow princes, but he continued to debate and write. In February 1617 he brought out a collected edition of his *Workes*, proudly bringing together his political and ecclesiastical works – and even a few pieces he had not written but which redounded to his honour. It would be too easy to dismiss James's writings. In the years following his death, he was not without his admirers: Thomas Hobbes called him 'our most wise' King James, and John Locke saw James as 'that learned King who well understood the notions of things'.[44] If nothing else, while often embarrassingly personal, they are for the most part sincere attempts at rationalising the bizarre and unparalleled position James occupied in the world.

CHAPTER FIFTEEN

Strange Pageantries

JAMES'S FIRM IDEAS on the nature of kingship guaranteed that he would soon have another opponent to place alongside the Scottish Kirk, the English Parliament and the Roman Catholic Church. As far as he was concerned, the King was the lawmaker of his country. Law was an expression of a king's divine right: kings made the law, and kings could alter it at their pleasure. 'Kings are properly judges,' he was to pronounce, 'and judgement properly belongs to them from God, for kings sit in the throne of God and thence all judgement is derived.' All other judges were simply the King's deputies, and the King could sit in judgement in any court of the land. Sadly, this world view was not shared by the English Common Law, and it was not long after his accession before James found himself strangely in battle with a legal system that he believed to be his own.

Technical though they may sound, the fights over the law were perhaps the most acrimonious and bloody of James's encounters with English custom. The first conflict arose over prohibition, the ancient writ whereby Common Law judges exercised substantial influence over the ecclesiastical courts; the serving of the writ of prohibition brought to a halt proceedings in any Church court until the judges were satisfied that the matter being tried did indeed fall within the jurisdiction of the court. This had long been a bone of contention for the Church, and in 1605 the new Archbishop of Canterbury, Richard Bancroft, raised the matter with the King. His argument, designed to appeal to James, was that all judicial authority began in the Crown and flowed down in two great streams, temporal jurisdiction to the Common Law courts and spiritual jurisdiction to the Church courts. This model gave the Crown precedence, and meant that if any dispute arose as to jurisdiction, the Crown, in the form of the King, might intervene. But Bancroft had a formidable opponent, the Lord Chief Justice Sir Edward Coke, a remarkable legal theorist and historian, and stalwart champion of the Common Law courts. Coke argued that the writ of prohibition belonged to the Common Law, and could be altered only by Parliament, not by the

King. Once again, royal prerogative was pitched against parliamentary privilege.[1]

In 1607, a Puritan lawyer named Nicholas Fuller raised the matter again, when he sought a writ of prohibition against the Court of High Commission, doing so in such a hostile and vocal manner that the High Commission summoned him before them. James, recognising the importance of the challenge, saw Fuller as a test case, and wrote to Salisbury: 'I pray you, forget not Fuller's matter that the ecclesiastical Commission may not be suffered to sink, besides the evil deserts of the villain; for this far I dare prophesy unto you, that whensoever the ecclesiastical dignity together with the King's government thereof shall be turned in contempt and begin to evanish [sic] in this kingdom, the kings thereof shall not long prosper in their government, and the monarchy shall fall in ruin, which I pray God I may not live to see.'[2] The judges at first considered defending Fuller by a writ of prohibition, but, perhaps sensing how much this would antagonise the King, decided to let the High Commission deal with him. James was still unsure of the efficacy of this, saying that if the judges denied it, both they and Fuller should be called before the Privy Council for censure, in his presence.[3] The incident made him only the more resolute to prevent the judges from being able to issue prohibitions at will.[4]

In 1608 and 1609 James called more of his formal conferences to debate the matter, but this time he had no real grasp of the subject; he soon became bored, boredom turned into irritation, and irritation into anger. In his *Reports*, Sir Edward Coke recalled one conference at which he informed the King that he could not judge cases 'in his own person' but they had to be 'determined and adjudged in some court of justice'. James replied 'that he thought the Law was founded upon reason, and that he and others had reason, as well as the judges'. 'True it was,' Coke answered, 'that God had endowed his Majesty with excellent science and great endowments of nature; but his Majesty was not learned in the Laws of his Realm of England, and causes which concern the life, or inheritance, or goods, or fortunes, of his subjects; they are not to be decided by natural reason, but by the artificial reason and judgement of Law, which Law is an act that requires long study and experience, before that a man can attain to the cognizance of it.' The Law, he continued 'was the golden metewand [measuring rod] and measure to try the causes of the subjects; and which protected his Majesty in safety and peace'. James, he recalled, was 'greatly offended' with this answer, pointing out that this would mean that he was 'under the Law, which was Treason to affirm'. Coke capped the argument by quoting a legal authority: 'To which I said, that Bracton saith *Quod Rex non debet esse sub homine, sed sub Deo & lege* [that the King should not be under man but under God and the law'.[5]

Another, suspiciously similar, account of a conference in November 1608, casts Coke in a different light. In this version, Coke informed the King that the arguments of the assembled bishops were irrelevant, since only judges could expound the law. The supreme judge was the King, retorted James, and it was for him to judge between rival jurisdictions, although he would defend the Common Law. On the contrary, replied Coke, the Common Law defended the King. This stung James. Coke's words were those of a traitor, he shouted. The King protected the Law, not the Law the King, for the King was protected by none save God. Even the regular line-up of councillors, churchmen and lawyers were shocked by the ferocity of the King's anger: 'His Majesty fell into that high indignation as the like was never known in him, looking and speaking fiercely with bended fist, offering to strike him, which the Lord Coke perceiving fell flat on all fours, humbly beseeching his Majesty to take compassion on him and to pardon him if he through zeal had gone beyond his duty and allegiance.' Whatever the true nature of the encounter between Coke and the King, James's passionate opposition did not cease a steady flow of prohibitions challenging the authority of the ecclesiastical courts through 1609, much to his frustration.

The royal prerogative was also tested in an area where James was more vulnerable: that of his finances. The pecuniary miseries of the court in 1590s Scotland were soon recreated in 1600s England, and once again James's lavish expenditure was singled out for blame. As early as 1605, he had recognised the precariousness of his financial situation. 'I cannot but be sensible of that needless and unreasonable profusion of expenses whereof ye wrote me in your last,' he replied to a letter from Salisbury in October. 'When I consider the extremity of my state my only hap and hope that upholds me is in my good servants that will sweat and labour for my relief . . . otherwise I could rather have wished with Job never to have been than that the glorious sunshine of my entry should be so soon overcasten with the dark clouds of irreparable misery. I have promised and I will perform it that there shall be no default in me . . . my apprehension of this strait (howsoever I disguise it outwardly) hath done me more harm already than ye would be glad of.'[6]

Those who attended the more splendid court functions might well have had reason to doubt the sincerity of James's promises. Sir John Harington provided a 'poor account of rich doings' at the court, when Anna's brother King Christian visited from Denmark in 1606.[7] From the moment Christian was welcomed by James, Henry and a huge retinue at Gravesend on 18 July, until his departure on 1 August, there was 'no lack of good living: shows, sights and banquetings, from morn to eve'.[8] Although one contemporary pamphlet marvelled at the 'good carriage and peaceful modesty' of the Danish King, whom one might expect to have taken 'great delight in drink', it seems that the pamphleteer protesteth too much.[9] Harington wrote, 'I have been well nigh overwhelmed with carousal [carousing] and sports of all kinds. The sports began each day in such manner and such sort, as well nigh persuaded me of Mahomet's paradise. We had women, and indeed wine too, of such plenty, as would have astonished each sober beholder. Our feasts were magnificent, and the two royal guests did most lovingly embrace each other at table.' But there was a down-side to this international cosiness. 'I think the Dane hath strangely wrought on our good English nobles; for those, whom I never could get to taste good liquor, now follow the fashion, and wallow in beastly delights. The ladies abandon their sobriety, and are seen to roll about in intoxication.'

At one feast, the intoxication went too far. Salisbury planned an after-dinner entertainment, which would represent Solomon's Temple – in a gesture to James, the self-styled Solomon – and the coming of the Queen of Sheba. 'But alas!' wrote Harington, 'as all earthly things do fail to poor mortals in enjoyment, so did prove our presentment hereof.' He detailed the fiasco in loving detail. 'The lady who did play the Queen [of Sheba]'s part, did carry most precious gifts to both their majesties, but, forgetting the steps arising to the canopy, overset her caskets into his Danish majesty's lap, and fell at his feet, though

I rather think it was in his face. Much was the hurry and confusion; cloths and napkins were at hand, to make all clean. His Majesty then got up and would dance with the Queen of Sheba; but he fell down and humbled himself before her, and was carried to an inner chamber and laid on a bed of state, which was not a little defiled with the presents of the Queen which had been bestowed on his garments; such as wine, cream, jelly, beverage, cakes, spices, and other good matters. The entertainment and show went forward, and most of the presenters went backward, or fell down; wine did so occupy their upper chambers.' These were indeed 'strange pageantries'. But despite his jocular tone, Harington's reaction was one of disgust, and a rein-vigorated nostalgia for the days of the Virgin Queen. 'I ne'er did see such lack of good order, discretion, and sobriety, as I have now done.' In Harington's view, 'the gunpowder fright is got out of all our heads, and we are going on, hereabouts, as if the devil was contriving every man should blow up himself, by wild riot, excess, and devastation of time and temperance . . . I wish I was at home.'[10]

Although James's first Lord Treasurer, Thomas Sackville, Earl of Dorset, contrived to raise regular Crown revenues (not deriving from parliamentary subsidy) from £247,000 in 1603 to £366,000 five years later, he was forced to work against the King's increasingly profligate expenditure. Throughout his reign, James displayed or feigned a remarkable ignorance about finance. Even if money were successfully raised to clear his debts, he would spend it – but not on the debts. When the question of James's expenditure was raised by his Council, he would claim that he was completely helpless in the matter. If only he could be free of 'this eating canker of want', then he would be as happy 'as any king or monarch that ever was since the birth of Christ'. Inverting his well-worn metaphor of king as physician, he cast himself as 'a poor patient' and his councillors as physicians: he promised to keep 'as strait a diet as ye can in honour and reason prescribe unto me' and to use 'such remedies and antidotes as ye are apply to my disease' – an analogy that would have amused or alarmed anyone who knew of James's customary contempt for the advice of physicians.[11]

In April 1608, the Earl of Dorset dropped dead at the Council table, and was replaced as Lord Treasurer by Salisbury, adding another role to his already bulging portfolio of government posts. By now,

James's outgoings stood at £544,000, an annual deficit of £178,000; often turning to creditors for advances, his personal debts were £597,337.[12] Knowing James as he did, Salisbury recognised that royal expenditure was unlikely to drop, so he should focus on increasing incoming revenue. By selling off £426,151 of Crown lands, he managed to pay off most of James's immediate debts. But in the longer term, Salisbury turned to a more controversial source: impositions. Impositions were customs duties levied by the Crown, over and above the normal schedule of rates authorised by Parliament. Unsurprisingly, they were hugely unpopular with merchants who in 1606 had brought a test case when one John Bate, a merchant trading in currants from the Levant, refused to pay the impositions on his goods. The case went to the Court of the Exchequer which ruled that, since foreign commerce was regulated by prerogative, and impositions were part of that regulation of foreign commerce, the King could indeed levy impositions without recourse to Parliament. Exploiting that ruling, Salisbury speedily placed impositions on overseas trading that he calculated would bring in some £60,000 per annum. These efforts notwithstanding, by 1610 the annual deficit had reached £130,000 per annum, and James's expenditure for the year was projected at some £600,000. There was no alternative but to recall Parliament, and to ask them to authorise a subsidy, a one-off tax on the propertied classes.[13] But by now, this was a dangerous road to take. The Commons were already chafing about the King's insistence on prerogative, his attack on the Common Law, and the new impositions.

The fourth session of James's first Parliament opened on 9 February 1610 and, six days later, Salisbury first presented the King's case, which he elaborated over the course of the following weeks. The Parliament had been called for two reasons — first, to authorise the creation of Prince Henry as Prince of Wales and Earl of Chester, and second, 'to demand some supply of treasure'. The first, a popular move, was clearly a sweetener for the second. A quick fix was not enough. Instead of a simple subsidy, the Crown needed a consistent source of revenue. Salisbury acknowledged that the need for a subsidy called Parliament into existence, and this subsidy provided Parliament with the chance to importune for grievances: Salisbury could hardly expect the Commons to give up their only hold on the King. Instead, he proposed what became known as 'the Great Contract'. The Commons would grant a permanent annual revenue of £200,000 'for the maintenance of the King, the Queen, the Prince, the Duke [of York, Charles], and Lady Elizabeth' in return for which James would abandon certain of his more controversial rights, including wardship and purveyance; he would exempt English shires from jurisdiction of the Council of Wales; and he would protect those who purchased crown lands against any losses brought by technical flaws in their titles – all matters of pressing concern to the Lower House.[14]

On 21 March 1610, James addressed Lords and Commons in a two-hour speech in which, he said, he made them a present 'a fair and a crystal mirror' through which 'you may see the heart of your King'. He started with a further iteration of his familiar philosophy of monarchy: that 'kings are justly called Gods, for that they exercise a manner or resemblance of divine power upon earth'. 'The state of monarchy is the supremest thing upon earth,' he pronounced, 'for kings are not only God's lieutenants upon earth, and sit upon God's throne, but even by God himself they are called gods.' After all, 'in the Scriptures kings are called gods, and so their powers after a certain relation compared to the divine power. Kings are also compared to fathers of families, for the king is truly *parens patriae*, the politic father of his people. And lastly, kings are compared to the head of this microcosm of the body of man.'

The analogy was quite proper, James continued, warming to his theme. Kings were justly called gods because they exercised a 'resemblance of divine power upon earth'. Just as God had certain powers, so did kings: 'they make and unmake their subjects; they have the power of raising, and casting down; of life, and of death, judges over all their subjects, and in all causes, and yet accountable to none but God only. They have power to exalt low things, and abase high things, and make of their subjects like men at the chess – a pawn to take a bishop or a knight – and cry up or down any of their subjects, as they do their money. And to the king is due both the affection of the soul and the service of the body of his subjects.' However, the King had a duty to use this power in the right way, in the way 'ordained by God, *ad aedificationem, non ad destructionem* [for constructive, not destructive ends]' just as it would be 'a foolish father that would disinherit or destroy his children without a cause, or leave off the careful education of them' or 'an idle head that would in place of physic so poison or phlebotomise the body as might breed a dangerous distemper or destruction thereof', a return to his persona of physician to the body politic.

Moving to the question of Common Law, James outlined its flaws in three areas that needed to be redressed: the language in which it was expressed (medieval 'Law French'); its reliance on reports rather than grounds or maxims, when reports were often no more than opinions of the judge or reporter; and its inclusion of contradictory laws, precedents and reports. These, he said, he wanted remedied by 'some golden law or act of Parliament'. He knew that they would want to hear his opinion concerning prohibitions: 'I am not ignorant that I have been thought to be an enemy to all prohibitions, and an utter stayer to them.' To the contrary, he did not oppose prohibitions in general, but when he saw courts not observe their own limits, but 'the swelling and overflowing of prohibitions in a far greater abundance than ever before, every court striving to bring in most moulture [toll money paid to a mill owner] to their own mill, by multitudes of causes', then he wanted to restrict each court to its own bounds. This need for restraint made him think of the Commons – and to deliver them a lecture on the manner in which grievances should be selected, pruned and presented, rather than 'all thrust up in a sack together, rather like pasquils, than any lawful complaints'.

Finally, he admitted that he would not have called Parliament without 'great cause'. To see how great his wants were, they just had to see what he had bestowed so liberally amongst them. 'It may be thought,' he continued, 'I have given much amongst Scottish men. Indeed if I had not been liberal in rewarding some of my old servants of that nation, ye could never have had reason to expect my thankfulness towards any of you that are more lately become my subjects, if I had been ingrate to the old. And yet ye will find, that I have dealt twice as much amongst Englishmen as I have done to Scottish men.' James put his case for a subsidy. His expenses since coming to the throne had been massive, but 'that Christmas and open tide', when he had to extend his prodigality, 'is ended'. Moreover, unlike other 'barren' princes, he had provided the realm with 'a fruitful progeny and the creation of this gentleman', pointing to Henry, standing close by him. He asked the Commons to follow his advice: 'the greatest neglect of my words that can be is to let it lie dead and not follow my advice.'[15]

As the Commons began their usual parade of grievances, they came to impositions. This struck a nerve with James. Surely to debate impositions was *de facto* to question the King's prerogative to levy them? He could not let this pass in silence, and on 21 May he came to the Lower House to put his case again. As one MP wrote, James 'put us in mind of the long time we had spent in matters impertinent (being about 14 weeks)', and then launched into 'a long speech' in which he informed members that, while they might discuss possible abuses in the collection of impositions, he would not tolerate general discussion of his power to exact them in the first place. But James clearly knew this was a sticking point, because he also offered a compromise. If they ceased to challenge any existing impositions, he would undertake not to levy any more without first obtaining the consent of Parliament. However, the Commons would have to take his word on this, because he refused to 'bind himself or his posterity'.[16]

James could scarcely have devised a more tactless speech. According to John Chamberlain it 'bred generally much discontent to see our monarchical power and royal prerogative strained so high and made so transcendent every way', provoking 'many bold passages' in the Commons, 'and amongst the rest a wish that this speech might never come to print',[17] (True to form, James ensured it did, placing it proudly in his 1617 *Workes*.) Members protested that they were not calling into question the King's prerogative, merely needing to know its limitations; at the same time they asserted their privilege of free debate, and asked permission to continue their debate on impositions. Realising that he had stepped over some invisible line of parliamentary tolerance, James wisely backtracked, and allowed the Commons to debate impositions as they pleased. A four-day discussion followed in which the House came to the conclusion that, without the consent of Parliament, impositions must be illegal.

On 17 July Salisbury brought the Commons and the King to a tentative agreement, although there was some haggling over the exact sum: Parliament offered £180,000 and the King asked for £220,000, with a compromise of £200,000 agreed. James was oddly upbeat about the arrangement, even managing a lame joke: the Commons' first offer of 'nine score thousand pounds' he hadn't liked, he said, because nine was the number of the muses or the poets, and they were always beggars. Eleven would be good because that was the number of Apostles when Judas was away. He'd be happy enough with ten score, since there were ten commandments.[18] Once this was settled Parliament moved on to present their grievances in a document so long that James allegedly quipped he could use it as a tapestry: on reading it, he made a few odd concessions, but on those issues he considered to be matters of personal principle – those of prerogative and the Church – he was not able to waver. This was the state of affairs when Parliament was prorogued on 23 July.[19]

When the Parliament reconvened for its fifth session on 16 October, relations between King and Commons quickly disintegrated. Each put pressure on the terms of Salisbury's 'Great Contract', and it crumbled away, leaving the Lord Treasurer still pushing for finance, without any bargaining chips and without the King, who had disappeared again to Royston. Even when Salisbury did manage to revive part of the Contract negotiations, James would not bite. News of the Commons' actions upset him and increased his intransigence. Sir Thomas Lake wrote to the Lord Treasurer to let him know that 'His Highness wisheth your lordship to call to mind that he hath now had patience with this assembly these seven years, and from them received more disgraces, censures and ignominies than ever prince did endure. He followeth your lordship's advices in having patience, hoping for better issue. He cannot have asinine patience, he is not made of that mettle that is ever to be held in suspense and to receive nothing but stripes, neither doth he conceive that your lordships are so insensible of those indignities that you can advise any longer endurance.'[20] James met with representatives on 31 October at Whitehall, but to little effect, and the Parliament limped on through November. He ignored Salisbury's pleas for him to come to London to consult on parliamentary matters late in the month. For James, the travel and the inevitably difficult meeting with his Council held no allure. As far as he was concerned, the only matters to be decided concerned how and when to dissolve the Parliament, and how to punish that 'lewd fellow' who in a speech had compared him to King Joram, the evil King of the Jews. 'Ye see,' he wrote to his Lord Treasurer, 'there is no more trust to be laid upon this rotten reed of Egypt.'[21] James suggested that the subsidy question should be put to the vote, and the Commons threatened with dissolution; when this was averted, on 29 November James ordered Parliament to be adjourned until 6 December. On that day the Lord Chancellor informed the members that, since Christmas was approaching, the King's pleasure was that they should 'go to their houses and keep hospitality . . . and not lie in London or Westminster'.[22] The following day, James stormed to his Privy Council that 'we are sure no house save the house of Hell could have found so many [complaints] as they have already done'.[23] While the members were still holidaying in the country, James dissolved Parliament on 31 December 1610.

Salisbury felt completely undermined by his sovereign, and told him so. 'You will please so to dispose of me or suffer me to be treated as you shall think may best agree with your service; for when I resolved to serve your Majesty as I have done (in a time of want, of practice, and in a place of envy) I searched my heart and found it well resolved to suffer for such a master all the incidents to such a condition.'[24] James pretended to be surprised and wounded. 'My little beagle,' he wrote as familiarly as ever, 'I wonder what should make you to conceit so the alteration or diminishing of my favour towards you . . . I am sure I never gave you any such occasion, and all that know me do know that I never use to change my affection from any man except the cause be printed on his forehead. It is true that I have found that by the perturbations of your mind, ye have broken forth in more passionate and strange discourses these two last sessions of Parliament than ever ye were wont to do; wherein for pity of your great burden I forbore to admonish you . . . But ye may be sure if ever I had found any ground of jealousy of your faith and honesty, I would never have concealed it from you.' Still, James could not resist a further dig at the Treasurer: 'Your greatest error hath been that ye ever expected to draw honey out of gall, being a little blinded with the self-love of your own counsel in holding together of this parliament, whereof all men were despaired (as I have oft told you) but yourself alone.'[25] Salisbury's reply, although larded with the requisite compliments, was unusually direct: 'I am not a little grieved at my hard fortune when I look back at that rock whereupon I ran, if your Majesty's mislike of my passion and indiscreet freedom to so great a King had wrought also upon your Majesty any such alteration as might have kept you from observing likewise how far I was, notwithstanding my errors, from failing in the least duties which I owe your Majesty.'[26]

Something vital had been lost between James and Salisbury: amongst his senior councillors, the King now turned to Suffolk, Northampton, Worcester or Shrewsbury for advice. As for the little beagle, the 1610 Parliament left him broken. 'I have seen this Parliament to an end,' he wrote to Sir Thomas Lake, 'whereof the many vexations have so overtaken one another as I know not to what to resemble them so well as to the plagues of Job.'[27] The plagues led to a further decline in the Lord Treasurer's health, and serious illnesses ('a continual ague, or, as some will have it, a double tertain, with a great pain in his head and much sweating') afflicted him during the winter of 1611–12. Despite the cooling in their political relations, James visited him frequently in February of 1612 (Anna was said to visit every other day) and was concerned enough to give personal instructions to Salisbury's physicians, and to command 'all men for four days to forbear to speak to his Lordship upon any business'.[28] By March, he seemed to have rallied slightly, but in the following month Salisbury gave up his attempts to govern. He died at Marlborough on 24 May 1612, returning from taking the supposedly restorative waters at Bath. Public reaction was remarkably vicious, with a plethora of libels and verses simultaneously ridiculing the man and celebrating his death. Many played on his small stature and hunched back: 'Here lies great Salisbury though little of stature, | A monster of mischief, ambitious of nature'; 'At Hatfield near Hertford, there is a coffin, | A heart-griping harpy, of shape like a dolphin.'[29] Northampton spoke of the demise of 'the little man for which so many rejoice and so few do as much as seem to be sorry'.[30] John Chamberlain concurred: 'I never knew so great a man so soon and so generally censured.'[31]

While James's reputation was increasingly tarnished, his son and heir was coming into his own. On Twelfth Night 1610, an entertainment known as the 'Barriers' effectively marked the start of his public career.

This spectacle, staged in the Whitehall Banqueting House by Ben Jonson and Inigo Jones, drew on Arthurian themes and lauded England's warlike kings, culminating in the figure of Chivalry being stirred from sleep in her cave to hail Prince Henry. This was followed by the 'barriers' proper, fifty-six 'challenges' with various 'shows and devices' that lasted until dawn. Henry, it was recorded, rose to the occasion with panache, performing 'to the great wonder of the beholders', and parrying thirty pushes of the pike, and 360 sword strokes, 'which is scarce credible in one so young in years, enough to assure the world, that Great Britain's brave Henry aspired to immortality'.[32]

On 4 June 1610, his status was enhanced as he was created Earl of Chester and Prince of Wales, in great state. From that point on, he held court at St James's Palace – a court that often appeared more popular than the King's own, much to James's chagrin: 'Will he bury me alive?,' he was reported to have exclaimed. At St James's, Henry built up significant collections of art, antiquities and books, as well as a winter house and a deer park. A gentleman travelling with the Landgrave of Hesse marvelled at Henry's collection of ostriches, American chickens, pheasants, rabbits, turtle doves, 'a large eagle-owl' (Buhu), parrots, and 'a rare Indian bird called an emu that can devour burning coals'.[33] Henry's intellectual and scientific interests were wide ranging: he asked Ottaviano Lotti, the Duke of Tuscany's agent in London, to obtain for him the plans for Michelangelo's staircase in the Laurenziana Library, Galileo's latest book, a new magnet from Elba, and the recipe for cement that joined terracotta piping so that it could carry water.[34] Henry was also an avid reader of news of foreign affairs. Even as early as 1607, Salisbury had encouraged this by forwarding ambassadorial despatches to him: 'I have sent to you with the last dispatch from Ireland, the reading whereof will every day prove more proper to the Prince of Bretany than Aristotle or Cicero.'[35]

To his father, Henry was a valuable bargaining chip in the European royal marriage game. Throughout the years when he was absorbed in challenging the Roman Church in print, James was in regular negotiations with Catholic princes to further the fortunes of his own family. As the eldest, Henry was the first of James's three surviving children to go on the market. In 1604, when the Constable of Castile visited the English court, Queen Anna was vocal in her support for a proposal that he should marry the Infanta Anne, eldest daughter of Philip III of Spain and heiress to the Spanish throne; negotiations were quickly scuppered when Philip insisted on a precondition that Henry be sent to Spain to be educated as a Roman Catholic, and attempts to revive the proposal foundered in 1605 and again in 1607. For Elizabeth, James had looked initially to France, but the assassination of Henri IV in 1610 spelled the end of his hopes there. James turned his attention fleetingly to other European princes in Germany and Sweden – even the widowed King of Spain. In April 1611, a suggestion came that Elizabeth should marry the Prince of Piedmont, the eldest son of the Duke of Savoy, on the condition that Henry marry the Duke's eldest daughter, but James would not bite. Two more possible wives for Henry were paraded – a Savoyard princess, and the eldest daughter of the Regent of France – but Henry remained noncommittal.

The Prince of Wales had his own ideas about who he and his sister should marry. From the age of ten, Henry had been in correspondence with his first cousin Frederic Ulric, son of the Duke of Brunswick; in the summer of 1611 he petitioned his father to allow Frederic Ulric to marry Elizabeth. James refused this, as he did a simultaneous bid from Otto, Landgrave of Hesse, who visited England for the purpose. Finally, in the summer of 1611 James entered negotiations with the family of Frederick V, Count Palatine of the Rhine, who ruled from Heidelberg. It seemed a good match: the Count Palatine was the most senior secular prince in Germany, and one of four entitled to elect the Holy Roman Emperor; in time Frederick would become the titular head of a Protestant union in the area. His mother was Louisa Juliana, the daughter of the Low Countries hero William of Orange, 'the Taciturn'. Henry liked the idea, it was rumoured, since he harboured secret plans to accompany his sister to Germany, and there to find a wife for himself.

In May 1612, a deputation from the Palatinate came to London to agree the contract for the marriage between their Elector and Princess Elizabeth. James offered a dowry of £40,000 and an allowance; Frederick would give his bride £1,500 per annum, and provide for her retinue of thirty-six men and thirteen women. If she were widowed, Elizabeth would receive an income of £10,000 and be able to live where she chose. The marriage of the couple's children would be subject to the advice and consent of the King of Great Britain. The only sticking point in the negotiations was Queen Anna, who made no attempt to hide her disdain for the match, which she thought to be beneath her daughter's dignity. She teased Elizabeth that she would be known as 'Goody [goodwife] Palsgrave'.[36]

Frederick arrived in England on Friday 16 October. Two days later he was received at the Banqueting House in Whitehall where he was embraced by James, kissed the Queen's hand, and saluted Henry. Elizabeth, demurely, had not looked 'with so much as a corner of an eye towards him'. As the Elector made to kiss the hem of her gown, she made a deep curtsey, and 'with her hand staying him from that humblest reverence, gave him at his rising a fair advantage (which he took) of kissing her'.[37] James pronounced himself pleased with the Elector's 'good and discreet carriage', and even Anna, who was still 'not willing to the match', began to come round to the idea. Over the next few weeks, Frederick avoided the usual young men's pastimes of hunting, hawking and tennis, and spent much of his time in Elizabeth's Whitehall apartments, seeming to 'take delight in nothing but her company and conversation'.[38]

On Thursday 29 October, Prince Henry was noticeably absent from a banquet at London's Guildhall in honour of the Palsgrave, and two days later a scheduled play was cancelled; it was said he was suffering from a fever. This was not surprising. From the beginning of 1612, Prince Henry had been noted to be pale. He attempted to deal with this by forcing his body to the limit, riding hard, playing tennis 'for the space of three or four hours' in his shirt 'as though his body had been of brass', and swimming in the Thames at Richmond; he would 'also delight many times to walk late at night by the river's side in moonlight to hear the trumpets sound an echo, which many suspected, because the dew then falling did him small good'. By the autumn, keeping to his gruelling routine, Henry was visibly weaker with 'dead, sunk eyes', and had started to suffer from a 'continual headache, laziness and indisposition increasing (which notwithstanding . . . he strove mightily to conceal), whereas oft before, he used to rise early to the morning to walk the fields, he did lie abed almost every morning until nine of the clock, complaining of his laziness, and many mornings before his rising, ask the grooms of his Bedchamber, "How do I look this morning?" . . . which they, fearing no danger, would put off with one jest or another'.[39]

Henry's condition quickly worsened at the end of October. He was afflicted by 'a great looseness, his belly opening twenty-five times'; physicians attempted to heal him, first with the usual bleedings, purgatives and enemas, before, in desperation, turning to pearl, the bone of a stag's heart, unicorn's horn, and a poultice of 'warm cocks and pigeons newly killed'. The gravity of the situation was publicly guessed at when neither the King nor the Queen attended Bishop Andrewes' court sermon on 5 November, the anniversary of the Gunpowder Plot, and by the prayers the Bishop offered up for the Prince. In time, Henry's sight faded and he could not endure the candlelight in his chamber. It was claimed that his last words before descending into delirium were for Elizabeth: 'Where is my dear sister?' Elizabeth had tried to visit him, but was not allowed into the chamber since it was feared the Prince's illness was contagious.[40] Henry died at around eight in the evening of 6 November 1612.[41] As with virtually every royal death of the period — and especially the unexpected, early deaths — rumours of foul play swirled. John Chamberlain wrote that it was 'verily thought that the disease was no other than the ordinary ague that had reigned and raged all over England since the latter end of summer', and that Henry had been killed by bad medical practice — he pointed the finger at James's own physician, Mayerne.[42] Latter-day experts have suggested enteric fever, typhoid fever or porphyria,[43] but at the time poison was the most popular explanation — and more than one commentator pointed the finger directly at James, jealous of his son's own popularity. Francis Osborne claimed that 'King James was by fear led into this extreme: finding his son Henry not only averse to any popish match, but saluted by the Puritans as one prefigured in the Apocalypse for Rome's destruction'. Osborne was informed by Primrose, Henry's 'foster-brother' that James 'did dread' his son to the point that 'he would not deny anything he plainly desired'. He tells of how the King's jester Archy once taunted James that he 'did look upon Henry rather as a terror than a comfort to the King'. Although James upbraided Archy for his insolence, those present did not fail to notice that the jester's words had reduced the King to tears.[44]

James was not at his son's deathbed. A few hours earlier, 'apprehending the worst and not enduring to be so near the place', he had secretly left for Theobalds, where he fell seriously ill for three days, missing his son's funeral at Westminster Abbey on 8 November. When he was well enough to travel, he elected to go to Kensington, 'not brooking well the sight of any of his own houses'. Chamberlain noted that Henry's death 'was exceeding grievous' to both King and Queen and 'specially to the King who takes it with more impatience than was expected'.[45] But Anna too was deeply moved. The Venetian ambassador reported that he did not offer the Queen condolences on the death of her son. 'I was advised to act thus, and so have other ambassadors, because she cannot bear to have it mentioned; nor does she ever recall it without abundant tears and sighs.'[46] It may be that Anna never recovered from the loss of her first-born. When Charles was installed as Prince of Wales four years later, she refused to attend, according to Chamberlain, 'lest she renew her grief by the memory of the last Prince who runs still so much in some men's mind'.[47]

Chamberlain's remark was no hyperbole. If he had been popular and admired in his lifetime, then Henry became a legend in the years after his death. Elegies and lamentations in his honour were legion.[48] The lawyer and parliamentarian Simonds D'Ewes later wrote that 'The lamentation made for him was so general, as men, women and children partook of it'.[49] Over the next few years, as James encountered new and major challenges to his rule, Henry came to stand for a glory that England had lost. In the words of the courtier and poet Fulke Greville, to take just one example: 'A man may say of this Prince, as was said of Maecenas, both for wisdom and strength of body, there was not the like to be found among the English.'[50] While allowing that Henry deserved 'the highest epithets belonging to an active, generous, and noble cavalier', Francis Osborne was less carried away. 'The truth is, Prince Henry never arrived at the great test, supremacy in power, that leaves the will wholly to its own guidance.'[51] But the idea of Prince Henry as the embodiment of England's 'Lost Renaissance' is a tradition that has continued to this day.[52]

Elizabeth's marriage was postponed. This was not only out of respect for her dead brother: with only her younger brother Prince Charles between her and the English throne, was not Elizabeth now too grand to marry the Palsgrave? By Christmas, the matter was resolved, and on 27 December 1612, Elizabeth and Frederick were formally affianced and contracted in the Banqueting House in Whitehall in the presence of the King. Anna was absent, 'as they say, troubled with the gout', but widely rumoured still to be set against the marriage. Frederick, who arrived escorted by Prince Charles, wore purple velvet trimmed with gold lace; Elizabeth was in black relieved by only a little silver lace, but with a plume of white feathers on her head 'which fashion was taken up the next day of all the young gallants of the court and city, which hath made white feathers dear on the sudden'. James kissed them both and gave them his blessing, then 'directed them to go down, hand in hand, some twenty paces or more, into the middle of that great room; where was a carpet spread on the floor for them to stand on'. Sir Thomas Lake, filling in the still vacant post of Secretary, read the relevant passages from the Book of Common Prayer, in French for Frederick's benefit; but sadly his Englishman's French was as incomprehensible to the Palsgrave as his English, and the couple dissolved in helpless giggles until the Archbishop of Canterbury stepped in to give the proceedings some gravitas.[53]

The marriage took place in the chapel at Whitehall with the Archbishop officiating on 14 February 1613, in English this time – the groom 'had learned as much as concerned his part reasonable perfectly'. The service was preceded by a firework display and a mock battle of 'a Christian navy opposed against the Turks' staged on the Thames at a cost of over £6,000 – John Chamberlain remained unimpressed, feeling it fell short 'of that show and brags had been made of it', and it had caused the loss of two eyes and three hands among the participants. Chamberlain also opined that the groom was 'much too young and small-timbered' to be a husband, a fear that also seems to have gripped the King. The morning after the wedding, James went to visit 'these young turtles that were coupled on St Valentine's Day, and did strictly examine him whether he were his true son-in-law'; Frederick 'sufficiently assured' the King that the marriage had indeed been consummated.[54] A week of the usual masques and dancing, revels, triumphs, banquets, running at the ring and processions by torchlight followed, and the expenses mounted. James for once made an economy

— by dismissing Frederick's household, which the bride took 'very grievously and to heart; but necessity hath no law'. The couple left Whitehall on 10 April 1613, somewhat diminished in splendour, as Chamberlain had predicted: 'I am of opinion her train will not be so great by many degress as was expected; for we devise all the means we can to cut off expense, and not without cause, being come *ad fundum*, and to the very lees of our best liquor!'[55]

James took leave of his daughter at Rochester on 14 April, making Frederick promise that in future Elizabeth would be given precedence over himself, his mother and all other German princes. From Canterbury, Elizabeth wrote to James: 'I shall, perhaps, never see again the flower of princes, the king of fathers, the best and most amiable father that the sun will ever see. But the very humble respect and devotion with which I shall ceaselessly honour him, your majesty can never efface from the memory of her, who awaits in this place a favourable wind.'[56] Sailing from Margate, they arrived at Heidelberg in June. 'Her Highness's physicians do report that in all appearance she should be with child,' wrote Trumbull, the British resident ambassador in Brussels. 'I pray God they prove true prophets and that with the New Year her Highness may be the joyful mother of a fair Prince.'[57] Right on schedule, Elizabeth gave birth to what she termed 'a black baby', Frederick Henry, on 2 January 1614, James's first grandchild.[58]

After the fiasco of 1610's Great Contract, nothing was less appealing to James than the thought of another Parliament. While some of his counsellors urged that it was the only way that the King could raise funds, there was a strong faction that opposed it vehemently. To call a parliament, advised Northampton, was to call together his enemies, 'for such were those of the Parliament, that would do nothing which he desired, as he had seen by experience'. James later took him aside to reproach him for speaking 'with much freedom', while admitting he spoke 'with as much truth'.[59] Sir Francis Bacon was among the most vocal of those in favour of a parliament. Keen to take his revenge on his first cousin Salisbury, whom he thought had sabotaged his early career, Bacon blamed the shambles of the last Parliament utterly on the late Lord Treasurer. He provided James with a 'memorial' of some points which he thought good to be touched upon during the King's speech to the two Houses. James should explain the financial needs of the crown, and pledge that he would 'not speak to them in the language of an accountant, nor of a merchant, nor of a tyrant' – indeed, that he meant to 'set down a course to myself' whereby there would be 'no more arrears but competent store for that which concerneth privy service'. It was an utterly blatant rebuttal of Salisbury's Great Contract policy four years earlier.[60] Parliament was summoned to meet in April 1614. Sir Henry Neville, advising from the perspective of one who had espoused the popular cause four years earlier, drew up a list of concessions with which James might placate his Parliament. Only a week before the opening of Parliament, the empty post of Secretary was suddenly filled by Sir Ralph Winwood, previously James's ambassador to the Low Countries. It should have been a canny choice since Winwood was a known and vocal ally of the Puritans in the Privy Council. In practice, he was a parliamentary novice and his appointment – made over many competitors – could only bring resentment.

James addressed both Houses on 5 April 1614. He divided his speech into three concerns: soul, person and Exchequer. Under 'soul', he dealt with religion, pointing out the care which he had taken to marry Elizabeth to Frederick 'because he was of the same religion'; if he had not been so concerned, then he could have married her to a greater prince. He desired that the laws against recusants should be observed and enforced by judges who were currently neglecting their duties – perhaps because some were papists themselves, or had wives or kin or friends who were papists; laws not executed, he pointed out, 'were like a dead body'. As a result, 'the papists each day grew in numbers', and he told them 'with much pain' that 'it had come to his knowledge that there was a province in the kingdom with so many Catholics that the governor had no authority and could not find help from anybody to enforce the laws against papists'. He paused for a moment to let this sink in. Implementation of existing laws was important because he had no desire to create new laws and be bloody in persecuting; it was also necessary to be considerate with papists 'on account of the respect due to the princes' who belonged to the Catholic Church. As for 'person', James was concerned about the succession. God 'by his secret judgement' had taken Prince Henry, 'which he understood to mean that God was punishing his faults and sins' or indeed 'that He was chastising those of his people'. But while God had taken away, God had given him a grandson – Elizabeth and Frederick's son – who could if necessary ('may God not permit it') succeed him if Charles were to die – hoping 'that all would appreciate his good judgement in marrying his daughter to the Palatinate'.

Which brought him neatly to 'Exchequer'. James was now in debt, he claimed, because of the expenditure of the marriage and of recent colonial interventions in Ireland, and so he had to ask (but not press) for their help. 'I will not now deal with you by way of a bargain as at our last meeting but will tell you what I will grant you, the which things shall be such fruits as appertain unto a just prince. For if I should, like a merchant, treat with you, where a contract begins affection ceases, and I hold the affections of my subjects to be the best purchase. I covet nothing from you but so much out of your loves as you will grant me regarding necessity of my people; for I leave the quantity of your gift to yourselves.' If he received this, 'he would be contented and would act as the most religious and scrupulous king England ever had.' He wanted to show his affection to his kingdom by giving, but 'it was also just' that his vassals should behave 'as was customary towards kings'.[61] James addressed both Houses again in the Banqueting House on 9 April with a very similar speech. This time he offered a list of eleven acts containing some concessions to the Commons' grievances. 'I deliver them unto you as I told you, supported between two sisters, desiring you will accept of my love in them more than of the things themselves. As the former parliament began with love, so may I desire this may do and not to have it interrupted as before. There is a holy emulation to be had between the King and his people, whether the King love the people or the people love the king better; and as you know we love God the best the more we receive from Him so it makes our obedience the greater for the like is amongst ourselves.'[62]

If he truly expected a Parliament of Love (and it must be doubted that he did), then James was to be disappointed. From the outset there were charges that the Crown had tampered with elections: James was forced to rebut these in his first speech to Parliament, but nevertheless one councillor was expelled and even the right to attend of his key adviser Sir Francis Bacon was challenged. By the beginning of May, matters were not progressing as they should: the Commons were insisting on dealing with their grievances, including impositions, before getting to their 'gift' to the King. James elected to speak to the Lower House on the 4th to reinforce his 'Parliament of Love' idea, and employing his familiar 'king as physician' rhetoric. Eventually, he arrived at impositions. When he came to the Crown, he said, he changed no counsellor or judge that Elizabeth had appointed. So it was Elizabeth's counsellors who persuaded him 'that impositions were a great flower of his prerogative', and Elizabeth's judges – and a judgement in the Exchequer Court – that persuaded him of their lawfulness. 'He would die a hundred deaths before he would infringe his prerogative.' The speech did not help matters.

Soon, certain members were speaking out quite harshly. On 21 May, Sir Edwin Sandys spoke of how Henri IV of France had used impositions, and Thomas Wentworth pointed out that Henri had been 'killed like a calf', a remark that prompted a formal complaint from the French ambassador, and led to Wentworth's examination by the Privy Council.[63] On 3 June John Hoskins made an impassioned speech. This Parliament was called a Parliament of Love, but the arguments made, he pointed out, were of fear. We are no base people, and we know the King to be royal and gracious: was it then a suitable way to obtain a supply to say the Commons would not be heard on the subject of impositions? The King must be moved to suppress 'this haven of impositions' and better care must be taken in the sale of his lands. As it was, 'we have nothing but ill examples of all riot and dissoluteness'. Hoskins left no doubt as to the origin of this riot and dissoluteness. Wise princes sent strangers (foreigners) away, he claimed: Canute sent back all the Danes when he decided to stay in England; and 'the Palsgrave had lately dismissed all the English that were about the Lady Elizabeth'. And then he made a reference to the Sicilian Vespers, which one parliamentary journalist 'understood not'. But for those who knew their history, the reference was clear. In 1282, at the signal of the bells ringing for vespers, the Sicilians had massacred all the French on the island. James understood this as a threat on the lives of his Scottish entourage, and had Hoskins imprisoned for several months.[64]

Rumours spread suggesting that the Commons had been the subject of some derogatory remarks during the Lords' debate on the matter. It was said that Bishop Neile had urged the Lords not to give their consent on the conference, since the Lower House should not be meddling in such an affair, and that in doing so they were attacking the Crown; a conference would only subject the Lords to talk of mutiny and sedition.[65] As the Commons decided to take the matter directly to the King, news came that the Lords had rejected their invitation to a conference. It was decided not to proceed in any other business until the affair was sorted. A committee was appointed, and debate continued — until another interruption arrived in the form of a letter from the King.

James wanted to know what they meant by 'forbearance of proceeding in all other business' — surely he, not they, called an end to proceedings? The Commons managed to assuage the King on this point, but on Friday 3 June he let it be known that unless they dealt with his supply immediately, he would dissolve Parliament on the following Thursday.[66] James asked his preferred counsellors for advice: one faction begged him only to prorogue the Parliament; their opponents encouraged him towards dissolution. When the Commons prevaricated, James raised the stakes, informing them on Monday that since he 'did not intend to infringe the liberties of the House so as to set us a fixed time for any one certain business', that he was now resolved 'to dissolve it tomorrow'.[67] The Parliament, known to posterity as the Addled Parliament, was dissolved on Tuesday 7 June 1614, after only two months, without passing a single measure.

James seemed to have felt himself more than ever alone after the fiasco of the Addled Parliament. Over the last year, he had been secretly treating with the French King Louis XIII, in a bid to marry Charles to Louis's sister Christiana. But now he needed a stronger ally. In 1614, a new Spanish ambassador, Diego Sarmiento de Acuña, had arrived in London. James was quickly taken with the ambassador's urbane charms: Sarmiento, it was said, was 'full of conceits, and would speak false Latin on purpose in his merry fits to please the King; telling the King plainly that he spoke Latin like a pedant, but I speak it like a gentleman'. The Venetian ambassador reported that Sarmiento won James's admiration on hunting trips, by matching the King's delight in 'putting his hands in the blood of bucks and stags'. Sarmiento filled James's ears with tales of Spanish power and wealth and the security that friendship between the two nations would guarantee. He complimented him by relaying King Philip's private wish that he and James might live as brothers.[68] Now, in early June, Sarmiento was the trusted ally to whom James, miserably unhappy by the fate of the Parliament, naturally turned. Could he rely on Philip of Spain as a friend, he asked, if he cut off relations with the Commons. Sarmiento was diplomatically vague, but made enough assurance that he 'helped greatly to induce the King to break with the Puritans, contrary to the advice which he received from many'. James had a request: that the ambassador tell King Philip the story of the Addled Parliament as it actually was — that the Commons was a body with no head, that its members voted without rule or order, drowned out in confused cries and shouting. He could not believe that Elizabeth had tolerated it, but what could he do? It was already there when he came to England, and he was not able to do without it. As his mood turned gloomy, recalling what had gone before, James was reminded by Sarmiento that it lay in the King's power to call and dissolve Parliament at his will. This cheered James, who exclaimed that yes, without his consent the Acts of his Commons were nothing.[69] And if King Philip was his friend, then perhaps he could fulfil his dream, to have his son and heir Charles marry Philip's daughter, the Infanta Maria of Spain.

CHAPTER SIXTEEN

Infinite Privacy

I N 1607, JAMES fell in love.[1] At the tilt to celebrate the anniversary of his accession, Sir James Hay employed a young Scot to present his shield and device to the King. Robert Carr was twenty-three years old, handsome and a fine horseman, but that day his skill failed him, and his horse threw him, breaking his leg. James was immediately concerned, and more so when he recalled that Carr had been one of the young men he had brought down from Scotland to run alongside his coach, only to lay them off when he found that in England the vogue for running footmen had passed.[2] Arrangements were made to tend to Carr in court, with the King's own medical experts to attend him. Carr had spent the intervening years in France where he had acquired enough of a veneer of culture to impress James during his frequent visits to Carr's sickbed. Though the King 'found no great depth of literature or experience', Carr presented 'such a smooth and calm outside' that James persuaded himself that 'there might be good anchorage, and a fit harbour for his most retired thoughts'.[3]

Carr was not of course the first young man to receive such attentions from James.[4] Before his marriage, the King had taken Alexander Lindsay as his constant bedfellow, leading to Lindsay being dubbed 'the King's only minion and conceit';[5] he raised Lindsay to become Lord Spynie, and arranged a lucrative marriage for him. The hero of the Gowrie debacle, John Ramsay, had occupied a similar position from 1600. Philip Herbert, younger brother of the Earl of Pembroke, had been a favourite for a couple of years from James's accession in 1603. James had married Philip to Susan de Vere, daughter to the Earl of Oxford and niece of Sir Robert Cecil, in a lavish court wedding in December 1604, and in the following year Herbert was created a baron and then Earl of Montgomery.[6] Each in turn had receded from the King's attention, and a new, younger man had taken his place. James's intimacy with these men seems to have been taken for granted by contemporary court observers — and not given too much attention. While the King was undoubtedly overly generous to his favourites, freely showering them with gifts and titles, he made no attempt to push any of them into high office or to give them a place at the Privy Council table. Robert Carr, however, was to be different.

With Carr, James cast himself in one of his favourite roles, the kindly schoolmaster, and gave his student Latin lessons every morning, prompting Lord Thomas Howard to quip that 'I think some one should teach him English too, for, as he is a Scottish lad he hath much need of better language.' Howard's comment is typical of the jealous reactions Carr's rise occasioned among English courtiers, but even he could see why the Scottish lad had done so well so fast. 'This fellow is straight-limbed, well-favoured, strong-shouldered, and smooth-faced, with some sort of cunning and show of modesty; though, God wot, he well knoweth when to show his impudence.'[7] His looks were more fully described by Arthur Wilson who wrote that Carr was 'rather well compacted than tall; his features and favour comely, and handsome, rather than beautiful; the hair of his head flaxen, that of his face tinctured with yellow, of the Sycambrian colour: in his own nature, of a gentle mind, and affable disposition'.[8] A natural charmer of the ladies, Howard continued, Carr was now 'most likely to win the Prince's [James's] affection, and doth it wondrously in a little time. The Prince leaneth on his arm, pinches his cheek, smoothes his ruffled garment, and, when he looketh at Carr, directeth discourse to divers others. This young man doth much study all art and device; he hath changed his tailors and tiremen many times, and all to please the Prince, who laugheth at the long grown fashion of our young courtiers, and wisheth for change every day.' James had turned down many suits, and just discharged eighteen courtiers, Howard went on, just because they didn't meet his new Carr-inspired tastes in couture. Any prospective suitor would be well advised to be 'well trimmed; get a new jerkin well bordered, and not too short; the King saith, he liketh a flowing garment; be sure it be not all of one sort, but diversely coloured, the collar falling somewhat down, and your ruff well stiffened and bushy'.[9] It was not long before James's infatuation with Carr was a source of open mockery. To get on at court now meant being able to praise the new favourite. 'Will you say the moon shineth all the summer? That the stars are bright jewels fit for Carr's ears? That the roan jennet surpasseth Bucephalus, and is worthy to be bestridden by Alexander? That his eyes are fire, his tail is Berenice's locks, and a few more such fancies worthy your noticing? We are almost worn out in our endeavours to keep pace with this fellow in our duty and labour to gain favour, but all in vain; where it endeth I cannot guess, but honours are talked of speedily for him.'[10]

Honours came speedily indeed. By the end of the year, James had knighted Carr and made him one of his Gentlemen of the Bedchamber, ensuring that he would be on hand at all times; on 30 December, John Chamberlain wrote of him as a 'new favourite'.[11] In March 1608, James presented him with 'a tablet of gold set with diamonds, and the King's picture', a token more often given between lovers than master and servant.[12] The following January, Carr received estates at Sherborne that had been seized from Sir Walter Ralegh. In March 1611, James created Carr Viscount Rochester, which placed him in the House of Lords, the first Scot to achieve this accolade; James also specified that he was to have precedence over all barons.[13] A month later, Carr was made Knight of the Garter, replacing Sir George Home of Spott, Earl of Dunbar, who had died in January 1611, and in 1612 he became a Privy Councillor. But it was with the death of Salisbury that the new Viscount Rochester's career really took off. James decided not to replace Salisbury immediately as his Principal Secretary. As Viscount Fenton reported in June 1612, 'For the office of Secretary, his Majesty does still reserve that for himself.' Despatches came in to Sir Thomas Lake, who delivered them to Rochester, and he to James; they were returned to Rochester, who replied following directions from the King – and Rochester sealed them with the signet.[14] In his casual bestowing of high administrative office to an intimate favourite, James was following in his mother's footsteps: many of the complaints about Rochester as *de facto* Secretary were the same as those made of David Riccio half a century earlier.

There was a short period when it was noted that 'Viscount Rochester has been in some disgrace', but 'his tender attentions to the King' during an illness ensured that the disgrace was short lived.[15] In his first years with James, Carr was canny enough or lazy enough to rely on the King's direct favour to maintain his position, rather than aligning himself to any court faction, claiming that he'd move nowhere 'save where the King had his interest'. But Carr was soon to be forced into battle, when he fell in love with a married woman who occupied a very particular position in the factional life of English politics. Lady Frances Howard was the daughter of the Earl of Suffolk, and been married in 1606 to Robert Devereux, the third Earl of Essex, then only fifteen years old. The match had been one of James's pet projects: by marrying the scion of the Essex family to a young beauty of the Suffolk camp, he hoped to defuse a potential court antago-nism. Instead, he seems only to have pushed that antagonism into the marriage itself. The young husband and wife never shared a home, and Essex soon went off to the Continent. By the time he returned in the last months of 1609, Frances and Carr were lovers. For three years, the affair continued until Lady Frances tired of the pretence, and decided to rid herself of her husband. Plotting with her father Suffolk and her great-uncle Henry Howard, Earl of Northampton, Frances determined to divorce Essex on grounds of his impotence, and marry her lover. But, understandably, Essex refused to play along by declaring to the world that he was impotent, and instead Frances was forced to allege that Essex had been bewitched, and that he was impotent only in relations with her.[16] Neatly forgetting that he had encouraged the Essex marriage, James threw all his weight behind Frances's divorce suit; his loyalties now lay firmly with Rochester.

Facilitating Rochester's marriage was one thing; watching his friend-ship with another man was less easy for the King. The Viscount came with an intimate friend, Sir Thomas Overbury, whom he had met in Scotland in 1601. Literate and urbane, it was Overbury who had given Rochester the veneer of sophistication that James hoped promised greater intellectual and emotional depths. Now Overbury took on much of the work that was delegated to the favourite, including allegedly receiving most diplomatic despatches from James's ambassa-dors abroad, often bypassing both Rochester and the King. He soon began to develop a 'very insolent' attitude, not least by claiming publicly that it was all due to him that Rochester had done so well. As part of his secretarial duties, Overbury was happy enough to write Rochester's love letters to the Countess of Essex, but when Rochester started to talk of marriage, he lost patience. Overbury, as Bishop Goodman writes, 'did much abuse the family of the Howards', and he knew his position with his friend would be untenable if Rochester married into the Howard family – a fact that became apparent even to Rochester.

James's antipathy towards Overbury was soon obvious to the public. John Chamberlain reported that James 'hath long had a desire to remove him from about the Lord of Rochester, as thinking it a dishonour to him that the world should have an opinion that Rochester ruled him and Overbury ruled Rochester'. James decided that Overbury would be much better off in a continental diplomatic appointment – perhaps to the Archduke, or in France, or better still Muscovy. Ellesmere and Pembroke were despatched to inform Overbury of his good fortune, but Sir Thomas turned down the post, citing his lack of languages. They replied that he was young enough to pick up the native tongue quickly, but he declined again, citing his 'indisposition of body and want of health', as he was troubled with 'the spleen'. A change of air might be a good remedy, they persisted. Now Overbury refused 'stiffly', saying 'that he was not willing to forsake his country' and that 'he hoped that the King neither in law nor justice could compel him to leave his country'. James, 'incensed' at this refusal, imprisoned Overbury in the Tower in April 1613, and insisted to the Privy Council that this act should not be construed as any form of attack on Rochester: 'he had and still did take more delight in his company and conversation than in any man's living'.[17] Rochester went through the motions of trying to secure Overbury's release, but he understood that this state of affairs was better for him.[18] In early August, it was rumoured that Overbury would submit to the King, and 'have leave to travel, with a private intimation not to return until his Majesty's pleasure be further known'. He would be getting off lightly since there had been 'much ado' to keep Overbury from suffering 'a public censure of banishment and loss of office, such a rooted hatred lieth in the King's heart towards him'.[19]

Meanwhile, Frances's bizarre claim that her husband's impotence was specific only to their marriage, and was caused by bewitchment, was referred to a specially appointed commission, comprising four bishops, four doctors of the Civil Law, and two Privy Councillors – until James realised that the commission was likely to vote against the divorce. Then he and Suffolk employed strong-arm tactics, arranging private conversations with the more tractable members of the commission, and 'persuading' them to see the case for the divorce. Bishops Neile and Andrewes, and councillor Sir Thomas Parry had their judgement 'reformed' in this way. But he was less successful with his Archbishop of Canterbury, George Abbot. Abbot had been a surprise choice to replace Bancroft as Archbishop in 1611. It was widely assumed that James would pick Lancelot Andrewes, his favourite preacher, in the same manner that he notoriously promoted his chaplain Robert Abbot and his editor James Montagu to bishoprics. Instead, he chose Abbot, an academic and, worse, a Calvinist. James let Abbot know that he had been advanced not for any learning, wisdom or sincerity but through the recommendation of the late Earl of Dunbar, 'whose suit he cannot forget nor will suffer to lose his intention';[20] Abbot had been Dunbar's chaplain, and a visitor to Scotland, where he attempted to promulgate James's ecclesiastical polity. Now James may have regretted his loyalty to Dunbar. Abbot withstood several private discussions with the King. 'What a strange and fearful thing it was,' he later wrote, 'that his Majesty should be so far engaged in that business, that he should profess that himself had set the matter in that course of judgement; that the judges should be dealt with beforehand, and in a sort, directed what they should determine.' Finally, James summoned the commission to Windsor and spent three hours explaining to them the merits of the case: Abbot fell on to his knees and pleaded tearfully to be taken off the commission. James refused.

The tears and kneeling having failed, Abbot appealed to James's intellectual vanity. He wrote to the King arguing that witchcraft-induced impotency was discussed in neither the Scriptures, nor in the writings of the Church Fathers, nor in the records of councils of the primitive Church. It may have existed under the rule of the Roman Church, but now, in enlightened post-Reformation days, it had disappeared. The Essexes should turn to prayer or medicine to solve their marital woes. James rose to the challenge with a wonderfully imaginative response. Abbot could not expect the Scriptures, the Fathers or the councils to provide an *exact* answer, he claimed, but those sources said nothing that would make such a divorce impossible. In those early days the Devil had probably not discovered impotency through witchcraft, but had invented it during the papist years. 'Look [at] my *Daemonologie*,' James advised. The Reformation had not broken Satan's power – indeed, was not this case before them vivid proof of that? Abbot was merely prejudiced against the Countess of Essex, a dangerous thing in a judge; he should recall how Christ had admonished us not to judge others. James, on the other hand, was completely impartial; now he called on Abbot 'to have a kind of faith implicit in my judgement, as well in respect of some skill I have in divinity'. The best thankfulness that Abbot, 'you that are so far my creature', could use towards the King was 'to reverence and follow my judgement and not to contradict it, except when you can demonstrate unto me that I am mistaken or wrong informed'. Failing to win Abbot over, James finally proved the uprighteousness of his conscience by fiddling the figures: realising that he had five commissioners for and five against, he merely added two more amenable bishops to the list, and gained a seven to five victory on 25 September.[21] Rochester was now free to marry his Frances. In October 1613, despite his residence in England, Rochester became Lord Treasurer of Scotland, and, for the marriage, James created Rochester Earl of Somerset, so that the erstwhile Countess of Essex could remain a Countess.[22]

The marriage took place on St Stephen's Day, 26 December 1613, in the Chapel Royal.[23] The King footed the bill – even though Crown lands worth £10,000 had to be sold off just to provide jewels for the bride. He also gave away the Countess, who was 'married in her hair', her free-flowing tresses symbolising her virginity, even though some observers felt that the date, place and minister of the marriage were unfortunately chosen: as Chamberlain pointed out, it 'fell out somewhat strangely that the same man, should marry the same person, in the same place, upon the self-same day' when the first husband was 'yet living'. Despite James's expenditure, Chamberlain was not impressed by the occasion: 'Speech and expectation goes far beyond the matter,' he commented, since the marriage had taken place 'without any such bravery as was looked for.'[24] The wedding day was capped with a masque composed by Thomas Campion in which married love between a man and a woman was piquantly evaluated against male–male friendship:

> Some friendship between man and man prefer,
> But I th'affection between man and wife.

What good can be in life,
Whereof no fruits appear? . . .
How can man perpetual be
But in his own posterity?[25]

The feasting and revels lasted right through the holiday period until Twelfth Night, when they were capped by a second, rival wedding, at 'Queen's Court', Somerset House, as another Robert Ker, the Earl of Roxburgh, married one of Anna's favourites, Jane Drummond. By the time the celebrations drew to a close, James was tired, and made a speedy retreat to Newmarket.[26]

Somerset's continued ascent was remarkable. By now he was also wealthy: in the year before his marriage he was said to have got through some £90,000,[27] and in April 1613 he even offered to lend £22,000 to help out the King.[28] In politics, the Earl's *modus operandi* was praised by the Spanish ambassador Sarmiento, who noted that at the Council table, Somerset 'showeth much temper and modesty, without seeming to press and sway anything. But afterwards the King resolveth all business with him alone, both those that pass in Council and many others wherewith he never maketh them acquainted.'[29] John Chamberlain complained that 'there is no man (but one) so near that knows any thing of secret, but all things are carried *in scrinio pectoris* [in the secret space of their hearts] between them two'.[30] When James opened Parliament in April 1614, Sarmiento noted that it was Somerset who led a horse to the right of the King as he processed, acting as Master of the Horse, even though that post belonged to the Earl of Worcester.[31]

In the months following the marriage, the Howards consolidated their status. As 1614's Addled Parliament drew to its untidy close, the elder Howard statesman, the Earl of Northampton, became seriously ill. Surgeons operated on a tumour in his thigh but, as with so many invasive operations of the period, infection set in and, within a week, Northampton was dead of gangrene.[32] This blow to the Howards was tempered when James bestowed on Somerset the dead Earl's offices of Lord Privy Seal and Warden of the Cinque Ports. In July, James made two further key appointments, naming Somerset's father-in-law Suffolk as Lord Treasurer, 'with many good words, as that he had made choice of him not for his learning in Greek and Latin, or for that he could make epigrams and orations, but for his approved fidelity and integrity', another glancing blow at the memory of Salisbury. Suffolk's fidelity and integrity would prove to be no remedy for James's financial woes: soon even the victuallers providing the court's food were being forced to allow the King credit; within a few months, James was openly selling titles. At the same time, Somerset was named as Lord Chamberlain, at the head of James's household, thus sealing his control on the King's intimate life; James commented that 'no man should marvel that he bestowed a place so near himself at his friend, whom he loved above all men living'.[33]

It was the pinnacle of Somerset's career – and it was shortlived. On 3 August 1614, during the summer progress, James visited Sir Anthony Mildmay's Northamptonshire seat of Apethorpe to hunt.[34] There his attention was diverted by a new face among the usual entourage, belonging to an exceptionally handsome and charming young man of twenty-one, named George Villiers. Like the young Robert Carr, he was extremely handsome although not mannish: Bishop Goodman recalled him as 'the handsomest-bodied in England; his limbs so well compacted and his conversation so pleasing and of so sweet a disposition', and Simonds D'Ewes found 'everything in him full of delicacy and handsome features; yea, his hands and face seemed to me especially effeminate and curious'.[35]

Even within the month, news of a new favourite was becoming passé. Viscount Fenton wrote to tell the Earl of Mar but assumed 'I think your Lordship has heard before this time of a youth, his name is Villiers, a Northamptonshire man; he begins to be in favour with his Majesty.' Fenton was sure that this would not affect Somerset's supremacy: 'yet all things are absolutely done by one man [i.e. Somerset] and he more absolute than ever he was. Neither his father-in-law, with whom he keeps good quarter, nor any man else dare touch him.'[36] But Somerset knew that George Villiers spelled the end of his dominance. When, in November 1614, Sir James Graham promoted Villiers as a potential Gentleman of the Bedchamber, Somerset stepped in immediately to object. 'The fortune of Villiers, the new favourite,' wrote Chamberlain, 'seems to be at a stand, or at least not to go very fast forward; for when it was expected he should be made of the

Bedchamber, one Carr, a bastard kinsman of the Lord Chamberlain [Somerset] is stepped in, and admitted to the place.' But Chamberlain was not convinced that Somerset really had the upper hand: 'and yet most men do not believe that the world goes altogether so well on that side as it was wont.'[37]

Indeed, relations between Somerset and the King were deteriorating. James, shaken by a bad fall while riding when his horse crashed down on top of him,[38] was first upset and then indignant at Somerset's increasingly difficult behaviour. He laid bare all his anger and regret in a remarkably passionate and unguarded letter to the Earl.[39] Somerset had forced the King, he wrote, to 'turn his countenance' from Villiers's sponsor Sir James Graham, 'the like whereof I never did to any man without a known offence' – the entire incident being 'done in a needless bravery of [show of opposition to] the Queen'. Since 'this strange frenzy took you', James objected, the Earl's merits had been 'powdered and mixed' with 'strange streams of unquietness, passion, fury, and insolent pride, and (which is worst of all) with a settled kind of induced obstinacy'. James conceded that the 'trust and privacy' between them allowed Somerset 'an infinitely great liberty and freedom of speech unto me', but 'to invent a new art of railing upon me, me, nay to borrow the tongue of the devil . . . that cannot come within the compass of any liberty of friendship'. This 'strange frenzy' of 'fiery boutades [outbursts]' coupled with 'a continual dogged sullen behaviour towards me', was made much worse by being deliberately expressed at night, 'bereaving me of my rest'. Worst of all, Somerset was now refusing to sleep with the King: 'I leave out of this reckoning your long creeping back and withdrawing yourself from lying in my chamber, notwithstanding my many hundred times earnest soliciting you to the contrary, accounting that but as a point of unkindness.'

'What can or ever could thus trouble your mind?' James demanded. Somerset and Suffolk had it sewn up. Did not all court graces and place come through him as Lord Chamberlain, and rewards through Suffolk as Lord Treasurer? Had not James placed Somerset's nephew in his Bedchamber, and another kinsman in Charles's Bedchamber, in addition to Somerset's 'own infinite privacy with me'? This should be enough to silence 'these news-bringers and makers of fray'. Somerset must know that no man could come as close to James as he did. 'I must ingenuously confess ye have deserved more trust and confidence of me than ever man did: in secrecy above all flesh, in feeling and unpartial respect, as well to my honour in every degree as to my profit . . . And in those points I confess I never saw any come towards your merit: I mean in the points of an inwardly trusty friend and servant.'

James swore that he had borne this grief ('and as never grief since my birth seized so heavily upon me') as well as he could. He pleaded with Somerset not to be 'the occasion of the hastening of his death, through grief, who was not only your creator under God but hath many a time prayed for you, which I never did for no subject alive but for you'. It was now imperative that Somerset change, because his 'furious assaults' and 'cross discourse' with the King were beginning to be noticed, as well as Somerset's 'long being with me at unseasonable hours, loud speaking on both parts, and their observation of my sadness after your parting, and want of rest'; now 'there must be some exterior signs of the amendment of your behaviour towards me'.

He made a plea to Somerset. 'All I crave is that in all the words and actions of your life ye may ever make it appear to me that ye never think to hold grip of me but out of my mere love, and not one hair by fear.' All Somerset's being 'except your breathing and soul' came from the King; 'I told you twice or thrice that ye might lead me by the heart and not by the nose.' But if Somerset ever tried to provoke fear in James, then 'all the violence of my love will in that instant be changed in[to] as violent a hatred. God is my judge my love hath been infinite towards you; and the only strength of my affection towards you hath made me bear with these things in you and bridle my passions to the uttermost of my ability. Let me be met then with your entire heart, but softened with humility. Let me never apprehend that ye disdain my person and undervalue my qualities, nor let it not appear that any part of your former affection is cooled towards me.' Somerset's 'good and heartily humble behaviour may wash quite out of my heart your bypast errors', but James would 'carry that cross to the grave with me, for raising a man so high as might make one to presume to pierce my ears with such speeches'.

'Love and heartily humble obedience' were the only merits that would value Somerset to James. When anyone pleaded to him for favour to a Puritan minister because of his 'rare gifts', James had a stock response: 'that I had rather have a conformable man with but ordinary parts than the rarest men in the world that will not be obedient, for that leaven of pride sours the whole loaf. Thus have I now sent down unto you what I would say if I were to make my testament,' he concluded. 'It lies in your hand to make of me what you please, either the best master and truest friend or, if you force me once to call you ingrate, which the God of Heaven forbid, no so great earthly plague can light upon you. In a word, ye may procure me to delight to give daily more and more demonstrations of my favours towards you, if the fault be not in yourself.'

If Somerset paid attention to James's passionate warning, any good intentions were quickly dissipated by the reality of the rise of George Villiers. Sir James Graham was still pushing hard for Villiers's advancement. Money was raised to buy him a new wardrobe, and heavyweight lobbying led to Villiers's appointment as Cupbearer, which allowed him to attend on James at table every alternate month. This allowed James to speak to him, and praise his conversation.[40] In December 1614, it had been rumoured that James had given £1,500 towards the masque to be performed on Twelfth Night, just for 'the gracing of young Villiers and to bring him on the stage'.[41] Although James was no great lover of masques, the sight of Villiers dancing was enough for him to order it to be restaged two days later. Portraits of Villiers emphasise his long, slim legs, and Arthur Wilson testified that 'No one dances better, no man runs or jumps better. Indeed,' he quipped, 'he jumped higher than ever Englishman did in so short a time, from a private gentleman to a dukedom.' The jump to the dukedom was still in the future, but Villiers was already launched. In March 1615, James visited Cambridge, only to be surprised by Villiers appearing in a student play. As Roger Coke wrote, 'At this play it was so contrived that George Villiers should appear with all the advantages his mother could set him forth: and the King, so soon as he had seen him, full of admiration of him, so as he became confounded between his admiration of Villiers and the pleasure of the play . . . This set the heads of the courtiers at work, how to get Somerset out of favour, and to bring Villiers in.'[42]

It was one of the leaders of the anti-Howard faction, the Archbishop of Canterbury, George Abbot, who proved to be instrumental in bringing a group of lords together to persuade the Queen to back

Villiers's suit to join the King's Bedchamber. This was a necessity: in order for a new favourite to be allowed into the intimate circle of the King, Anna had to request it. This was strategic: if she were later to 'complain of this *dear one*, he might make his answer, "It is long of yourself, for you were the party that commended him unto me".' Anna at first declined to help. 'My lord,' she told Abbot, 'you and the rest of your friends know not what you do. I know your master better than you all, for if this young man be once brought in, the first persons that he will plague must be you that labour for him. Yea, I shall have my part also. The King will teach him to despise and hardly entreat us all, that he may seem to be beholden to none but himself.' But 'upon importunity', the Queen agreed to do her part.

On St George's Day, 23 April 1615, Anna was visited by James and Prince Charles. She took the opportunity to beseech her husband 'to do her that special favour as to knight this noble gentleman, whose name was George, for the honour of St George, whose feast he now kept'. James allegedly 'at first seemed to be afeard that the Queen should come to him with a naked sword', but she 'so pressed it with the King', wrote Abbot, 'that he assented' being 'so stricken while the iron was hot that in the Queen's bedchamber the King knighted him with the rapier which the Prince did wear'. Somerset made a last plea that Villiers should be made only a groom and not a Gentleman of the Bedchamber, but Abbot got a message to Anna that she 'would perfect her work' if he were made a Gentleman. When Villiers, now a Gentleman of the Bedchamber with a £1,000 per annum pension, emerged from the Queen's chamber, he threw himself at the Archbishop's feet, protesting 'that he was so infinitely bound unto me that all his life long he must honour me as his father'.[43]

It was a body blow to Somerset. He knew that now he could not expect always to be first in James's affections, nor first to receive his protection. In July, evidently concerned that enemies might bring some past misdemeanour to light, Somerset asked the King to grant him a formal pardon under the Great Seal to indemnify him against prosecution for all past offences in his life.[44] The Venetian ambassador believed this was a pre-emptive strike against the rumour that Somerset was 'said to have appropriated a considerable quantity of the Crown jewels'.[45] Whatever the motive, James acquiesced, and signed a pardon, but this time he was stymied by his Lord Chancellor, Lord Ellesmere, who refused to put the Great Seal to it, claiming the pardon was unconstitutional. James conferred with Somerset and gave him instructions to stage a performance at the end of the Privy Council meeting on 20 August. As planned, the Earl rose and alleged 'that the malice of his enemies had forced him to ask for a pardon', and asked James to order Ellesmere, 'if he knew anything against him, to say it there'. James instead 'spoke at length in praise of Somerset, concluding by saying that he had done very well in asking for a pardon, and that he had granted it to him with great pleasure, not because he would have any need of it in his own days, for during his life he was quite safe' – a clear message to the Council that Somerset remained in favour – 'but because he wished that the Prince', and here James put his hand on his son Charles, 'may not be able to undo that which I have done. And so, my Lord Chancellor, seal the pardon immediately, for that is my will.'

Ellesmere fell on his knees, asking the King to understand that there was no precedent for such a warrant. Since James had made Somerset Lord Chamberlain, 'guardian and keeper of his palace', did he intend to 'give him the jewels, the hangings, and the tapestry, and everything that was in the palace, since it was in the pardon that no account was to be taken of him for anything'? If the King wanted him to put his seal to the pardon, then Ellesmere required a formal indemnity for his 'fault and offence' in doing so. James 'grew very angry, saying that he ordered him to pass it, and that he was to pass it', and stormed out of the Council chamber. Somerset immediately set about finding precedents for such a pardon, employing the scholarly talents of the great manuscript collector, Sir Robert Cotton, but to no avail. The Council chamber exchange had been reported to the Queen, who went to see her husband, along with several others of the anti-Somerset camp. 'She and the enemies of Somerset were so busy with him and perplexed him so' that the Lord Chancellor got his way: neither the original pardon nor Cotton's second attempt to procure one were ever sealed.[46]

Despite James's highly theatrical support for Somerset, the Earl's influence was clearly waning. Sarmiento reported that even in the Bedchamber, where the Earl had authority, 'there are persons who will neither speak to him nor take off their hats to him', giving 'the greatest trouble and embarrassment' not only to Somerset but to the King himself.[47] There is evidence of James's increasing exasperation with his erstwhile favourite. Somerset now tried to influence James in his appointments, promoting Thomas Bilson, the Bishop of Winchester, for a major post (perhaps Lord Privy Seal or Warden of the Cinque Ports), and worse, suggesting that Bilson go to Theobalds to beg the King for it. James was mightily irritated at such importunity, and dashed off another letter, complaining about being 'needlessly troubled this day with your desperate letters', and berating Somerset for sending the Bishop.[48] James received Bilson 'with good words', said that 'he thought well of him, and perhaps meant to bestow the place upon him, but he would take his own time and not do it at other men's instance, so that he should do well to go home, and when there were use of him he would send for him'.[49]

The Bilson affair was a major rebuff for Somerset, and damaged further his relationship with James. But perhaps, as Villiers's biographer Roger Lockyer has argued, the fatal blow came at the end of August 1615. James, returning from his summer progress, spent a few days at Farnham Castle. 'It was there,' claims Lockyer, 'that Villiers played the trump card which ensured his victory over Somerset.' Somerset had withdrawn from sharing a bed with James, and it seems that Villiers may have spent the night at Farnham with the King. Years later, writing to thank James for an enjoyable court visit, Villiers related how he had spent all the journey home asking himself 'whether you loved me now . . . better than at the time which I shall never forget at Farnham, where the bed's head could not be found between the master and his dog'.[50]

In September 1615, news reached Sir Ralph Winwood that was to send Somerset crashing down. It was reported that his friend Sir Thomas Overbury, who had died in the Tower of London two years earlier, had been the victim of poison.[51] The Lieutenant of the Tower, Sir Gervase Elwes, was summoned, and admitted that he had managed to thwart attempts by the Deputy Keeper Richard Weston to poison Overbury, but that ultimately Sir Thomas had fallen victim to an arsenic-laden enema, administered by an apothecary's boy, which 'produced sixty or more stools till he expired'.[52] Elwes had not spoken of this because he was afraid of impeaching 'great persons': he did not mention the Somersets, but he did not need to. James was informed, and immediately placed the matter before the Privy Council. He 'made in the Council a great protestation before God of his desire to see justice done, and that neither his favourite, nor his son himself, nor anything else in the world should hinder him', resolving 'to use all lawful courses that the foulness of this fault be sounded to the depth, that for the discharge of our duty both to God and man, the innocent may be cleared, and the nocent may severely be punished'.[53]

At this point, James may have suspected that 'wicked persons of mean condition' might have invented the story in order to 'alienate his mind' from Somerset. Reading Elwes's confession, James wrote a memorandum that if the Deputy Keeper's allegations were not proved true, 'then there must be a foul conspiracy . . . for the finding out no pains is to be spared . . . When innocency is not clearly tried, the scar of calumny can never be clearly cured.'[54] The Deputy Keeper, Weston, was first to be arrested and interrogated, and by the end of September he had implicated a woman named Mrs Turner and, through her, the Countess of Somerset. It seems that the Countess, disliking Overbury's hold on her husband, and well aware of his personal antipathy to her, had decided to get rid of him by poison.

By now the investigators felt they had enough evidence, and their leader, Sir Edward Coke, set off for Royston to apprise the King of developments. Somerset, who was with James as usual, had already heard of the inquiry, and set off for London, meeting Coke en route and begging him to return to the capital; the Lord Chief Justice naturally refused, and Somerset knew he could hardly return to Royston with Coke, since this would 'make much of the business'. Instead he continued on his way but returned early the following morning, once again passing Coke on his way, although this time 'they passed one another with nothing more than a mutual salute'.[55] When he met James again, Somerset realised that events had moved on and he needed to return to London to clear his name. In the courtier Anthony Weldon's account, the parting of the King and his favourite was highly charged. 'The King hung about his neck, slabbering his cheeks, saying, "For God's sake, when shall I see thee again? On my soul, I shall neither eat nor sleep until you come again." The Earl told him on Monday.

"For God's sake, let me," said the King, "Shall I, shall I?" then lolled about his neck. In the same manner at the stair's head, at the middle of the stairs, and at the stair's foot. Yet as the Earl entered his coach James said: "I shall never see his face more."'[56]

From London, Somerset wrote to James, charging him of being 'too faint in not resisting the superb judges' wilfulness' in ordering an investigation. James had no regrets. He had only to look to his conscience before God, and his reputation in the eyes of the world. 'I confess I ever was and will be faint in resisting to the trial of murder, and as bold and earnest in prosecuting the trial thereof.' He complained that 'from the beginning of this business' both Somerset and Suffolk had consistently behaved 'quite contrary to the form that men that wish the trial of the verity ever did in such a case'. James rejected Somerset's claim that such a commission was unlawful and his suggestion that the unsympathetic Ellesmere should be replaced on the commission, and reproached the Earl for his 'so much scribbling and railing covertly against me and avowedly against the Chancellor'. 'I never had the occasion to show the uprightness and sincerity that is required by a supreme judge as I have in this,' he protested. 'If the delation [accusation] prove false, God so deal with my soul as no man among you shall so much rejoice at it as I, nor never shall spare, I vow to God, one grain of rigour that can be stretched against the conspirators. If otherwise (as God forbid), none of you shall more heartily sorrow for it; and never king used that clemency that I will do in such a case.' If, by serving his conscience, 'I shall lose the hands of that family, I will never care to lose the hearts of any for justice sake.' The reference to 'that family', the Howards, was not incidental. 'Fail not to show this letter to your father-in-law,' concluded the King, 'and that both of you read it twice at least; and God so favour me as I have no respect in this turn but to please Him in whose throne I sit.'[57]

On Sunday 15 October, the commissioners appointed to put the case together – Coke, Ellesmere, Lennox and Lord Zouch – met for the first time to discuss what action they could take against the Earl and Countess. By the time of their second meeting on the following Tuesday, Somerset had made their job a lot easier. The previous day, using his official powers, he had sent a pursuivant, a constable and a locksmith to the house of Weston's son with a warrant to search the premises; they confiscated some letters dealing with Mrs Turner. When the commission heard this, they ordered that the Somersets be restrained in their chambers.[58] A day later, the Earl was removed to an effective house arrest at the Dean of Westminster's residence. Now Somerset begged to have access to the King's person, claiming that he had state secrets to tell him. James rebuffed him, saying that the trials must take place, but if the Somersets were truly innocent, then they would be cleared. If, however, they proved to be guilty, they should confess now and ask for mercy, since James would 'follow the example of Almighty God who does not forgive sins until they be confessed and sorrowed for, no more can I show mercy where innocency is stood upon and the offence not made known by confession unto me'. James was aware a confession was to be preferred because, although the case against the Countess was very strong, Somerset had no known contact with some of the key players in the poisoning.

At the Countess's request, James sent two Chamber servants, Viscount Fenton and the Earl of Montgomery, to see her on New Year's Day 1616. There she confessed her part in Overbury's murder, portraying herself as 'a girl aggrieved and offended by the most unworthy things which he had said about her person'. But she also alleged that Somerset – who, as she pointed out, 'at that time was not yet her husband' – 'neither knew anything about it, nor took any part in it'. She had kept the secret from him, knowing that he was 'a very true friend of Overbury'.[59] Indeed, Sarmiento reported on 20 January that there was very little provable against the Earl, except that he used the King's name to recover papers just before he was arrested, and that he had entrusted papers of importance and jewels to a friend, hoping, in vain, that they would not be found. Among these were some of James's own papers: an embarrassment to the King, which meant that 'he now discharges all his anger against the Earl', claiming that Somerset had failed to show him some papers from his ambassador Sir John Digby in Spain; other papers, from Northampton to Somerset, showed clearly the Earl's sympathy for the Spanish and Catholic causes in England. From the jewels, James took 'a very good chain of diamonds', which he gave to Anna; the Queen passed it on to Villiers, who wore it constantly.[60]

James wanted Somerset to confess because a confession would have the added benefit of preventing one of Somerset's outbursts in a packed court. As the date of the arraignment approached in May 1616, James made increasingly frantic attempts to persuade Somerset to talk – although, given the circumstances, the King was forced to resort to a series of confidential messengers and secret letters. First, he sent a personal messenger to Somerset in the Tower 'with such directions unto him, as, if there be a spark of grace left in him, I hope they shall work a god effect'. He asked the new Lieutenant of the Tower, Sir George More, to allow him into Somerset's presence 'in such secrety [sic] none living may know of it and that, after his speaking with him in private, he may be returned back again as secretly'.[61] When that attempt failed, James wrote to engage More's services to persuade Somerset to do 'that which is both most honourable for me and his own best'. More was to assure him, in James's name, that if Somerset confessed his guilt to the commissioners before the trial, James would not only perform what he had promised through his previous messenger, but would 'enlarge it'. More should remind Somerset that last winter he had confessed to Coke that 'his cause was so evil likely as he knew no jury could acquit him'; that it was feared that the Countess would plead only 'weakly for his innocency'; that the commissioners have 'some secret assurance that in the end she will confess of him' – all the while keeping James's involvement secret. To More, James noted that he did not mean that Somerset should confess if he were innocent, 'but ye know how evil likely that is'.[62]

Even with the 'enlarged' promises, More's efforts failed, prompting a third letter from the King, lamenting Somerset's recalcitrance, which was harming not only himself but James too. 'God knows it is only a trick of his idle brain, hoping thereby to shift his trial. But it is easy to be seen that he would threaten me with laying an aspersion upon me of being, in some sort, accessory to his crime.' Somerset should write or send a message to James 'concerning this poisoning' – but it must not be a private letter: 'I cannot hear a private message from him without laying an aspersion upon myself of being an accessory to his crime.' He asked More 'to urge him, by reason, that I refuse him no favour which I can grant him without taking upon me the suspicion of being guilty of that crime whereof he is accused'.[63] As the trial grew nearer, Somerset's behaviour became more bizarre until, in a 'strange fit', he refused point blank to attend the trial. James insisted that unless he was 'either apparently sick or distracted of his wits' the trial was not to be delayed; if he was, then the trial would be adjourned for a few days, in which time 'if his sickness or madness be counterfeited it will manifestly appear'.[64]

On 17 May, Lennox and Hay visited the Countess on James's behalf, attempting in vain to push her to betray her husband's involvement. They then moved on to the Earl, telling him how his wife's confession had gained her 'much merit' and therefore 'good hope of her life', urging him to follow suit. Somerset was in no mood to bargain. 'He had nothing to say,' it was reported, 'except that he complained that he had been so badly treated without any cause, and that he hoped so much from the prudence of the King and of those who counselled him, as that they would not permit so great an error to be committed as to bring him to trial, for if they took him there, since he knew that it would only be done that he might die there, he would say that which he knew in his own defence, without the King being able to complain of it, since he was the cause of it.' Three hours of cajoling and threats that afternoon failed to move the Earl, as did a return visit by Hay the following Thursday, the day before the trial was due to start.[65]

The Countess was tried on 24 May 1616 in a packed Westminster Hall before an audience that included her ex-husband, the Earl of Essex.[66] She pleaded guilty, making the prosecution's task easy, and very remorsefully begged for the King's mercy. The Earl's arraignment the following day excited even more attention than that of his wife. 'I was there at six o'clock in the morning,' wrote John Chamberlain, 'and for ten shillings had a reasonable place.'[67] Attorney General Sir Francis Bacon laid out the case against Somerset, focusing on the Earl's friendship with Sir Thomas Overbury, claiming it tipped perilously into communication of state secrets. Somerset, acting as Secretary, routinely acquainted Overbury with foreign correspondence to the King: 'packets were sent, sometimes opened by my Lord, sometimes unbroken, unto Overbury, who perused them, copied them, registered them, made tables of them as he thought good.' Indeed, Bacon argued, there was a time 'when Overbury knew more of the secrets of state than the Council table did'. From these common secrets grew 'common dangers'. Somerset and Overbury had such an intimate 'inwardness' that 'they made a play of all the world besides themselves', suspiciously giving codenames ('ciphers and jargons') to the King, Queen and other leading personalities, usually the domain of 'such as work and practice against, or at least upon princes'. He did not charge Somerset with 'any disloyalty', however, 'only I lay this for a foundation, that there was a great communication of secrets between you and Overbury, and that it had relation to matters of estate, and the greatest causes of the kingdom'. Theirs was 'a friendship of ill men; which may be truly termed conspiracy and not friendship'.

Bacon related the history of events. Overbury was opposed to his master's planned marriage, since he was likely to lose Somerset, so he tried to dissuade the Earl from the match. Finding him determined, however, Overbury turned to 'stronger remedies', threatening to expose 'secrets of all natures'. Bacon identified Somerset's 'root of bitterness, a mortal malice or hatred, mixed with deep and bottomless fears' as proceeding from a 'fear of discovering secrets; secrets (I say) of a high and dangerous nature'.

Finally, seven hours after the opening of proceedings, Bacon finished presenting the prosecution case. At 5 p.m. Somerset answered the case against him, at length, but 'very confusedly, insisting most upon those particulars which were least material'. One onlooker commented that his answers 'were so poor and idle as many of the Lords his peers shook their heads and blushed to hear such slender excuses come away from him, of whom much better was expected'.[68] Given Somerset's ineptitude, Bacon did not even bother to sum up.[69] After an hour's deliberation, the peers returned a unanimous guilty verdict. Now Somerset chose to speak, saying to the Lords that 'his case might be any of theirs hereafter, desired them to consider that it was but the testimony of two women of bad condition that had condemned him, protested upon his salvation that he never saw Weston's face, and that he was innocent of that he was condemned'.[70] John Chamberlain thought Somerset's response strange: the sentence 'did so little appal him that when he was asked what he could say why sentence should not be pronounced, he stood still upon his innocence, and could hardly be brought to refer himself to the King's mercy'.[71] Indeed, it was reported that when the sentence condemning him to death was read out, Somerset 'kissed his hand and made a reverence with a look such as he might have had if he had been much favoured', and he 'took off from his neck and his leg the insignia of the Order of St George and the Garter'.[72]

While Somerset was being tried on 25 May, James was at Greenwich, 'so extreme sad and discontented, as he did retire himself from all company, and did forbear both dinner and supper until he had heard what answer the Earl had made'.[73] Anthony Weldon later alleged that James had spent the entire day in 'restless motion', 'sending to every boat he saw landing at the bridge, cursing all that came without tidings'; to Weldon this was evidence that 'all was not right, and there had been some grounds for his fears of Somerset's boldness'.[74] James still feared that Somerset might be prone to an outburst in court. 'It seemed something was feared should in passion have broken from him,' wrote Edward Sherburn, 'but when his Majesty had heard that nothing had escaped him more than what he was forced to answer to the business then in hand, his Majesty's countenance soon changed, and he hath ever since continued in a good disposition.'[75] Whatever secrets about James Somerset knew, he had not spilled them, and he escaped with his life: both the Earl and Countess were held in the Tower until January 1622, after which they were permitted to reside at fixed places and ultimately granted formal pardons. Somerset never regained James's affection and died in relative obscurity in July 1645.

Although the Earl did not damage the King directly during the trial, in the longer term the affair proved detrimental to James's reputation. The bizarre murder of Overbury and the precipitous fall of the Earl fuelled public speculation about the precise nature of James's relations with his male favourites.[76] A teasing example of such speculation can be found in the diary of Simonds D'Ewes, a legal student at London's Middle Temple, who recorded a conversation he had on 22 August 1622 with an old friend from his Cambridge days. D'Ewes told his friend about a letter found by Sir Edward Coke in Somerset's casket, 'for which since the King never loved him'. This odd titbit came at the end of a discussion about sodomy. 'Of things I discoursed with him that were secret as of the sin of sodomy, how frequent it was in this wicked city, and if God did not provide some wonderful blessing against it, we could not but expect some horrible punishment for it.' This was particularly likely since it was, 'as we had probable cause to fear, a sin in the prince [James] as well as the people'. To back up his claim, D'Ewes related to his friend a 'true story' of a French usher in London 'who had buggered a knight's son and was brought into the Guildhall' for trial. He would undoubtedly have received the death penalty, since sodomy was a capital felony, if Lord Chief Justice Montague had not intervened to save him – sent 'by the King, as 'twas thought'.[77]

This foreign 'familiar' talk of James's sodomy was alluded to once again in D'Ewes diary, on 2 October 1622, when he discussed a book that he described as 'terrible and wholly against the King himself, accusing him of atheism, sodomy, etc . . .'.[78] In 1615 there appeared in print what appeared to be yet another panegyric to James, entitled *Corona Regia*, supposedly written by the recently deceased Isaac Casaubon, who had spent his final years at the English court, and bearing the imprint of the King's own printer, John Bill.[79] In fact, both the authorial ascription and the printing house were fictitious: the publication was only a thinly veiled attack on James, written tongue in cheek – perhaps the most elaborated libel the King had had to face. What was regarded as the most damning passage is suggested by a copy of the book now in the British Library, in which a leaf has been torn out and a short passage on the bottom of the preceding page heavily scored.[80] From another copy, we find that the censored passage gives a remarkably informed account of how James promoted a series of young, beautiful men – John Ramsay, who allegedly saved his life during the 'Gowrie Conspiracy' of 1600; Philip Herbert, who rose to become Earl of Montgomery; Robert Carr, later Earl of Somerset, and the latest favourite, George Villiers – only to drop each one when a younger, more beautiful man came along. In keeping with the text's form of eulogy, however, the passage praises James's policy of 'advancing the beautiful', because, after all, isn't that only 'exalting the good'?[81]

James reacted to this libel more passionately than to any other, launching an international search for its author, printer and publisher, assuming that the book originated in the Anglo-Catholic stronghold at Douai[82] – as late as 1639 a Brussels bookseller named Jean de Perriet was claiming a reward for his identification of the guilty party.[83] While the English court may have accepted the fact that James would always have a beautiful young man in his Bedchamber, it seems that James himself was far from happy to have the news broadcasted in print across Europe.

With Somerset out of the picture, George Villiers became the undisputed focus of court life. While the old favourite waited for his trial in January 1616, the Earl of Worcester handed over to Villiers the post Somerset had coveted for himself: that of Master of the Horse. In April, he was appointed to the Order of the Garter, being installed in July, and in August he was elevated to the peerage as Baron Whaddon, Viscount Villiers. He was helped in this rise by a self-appointed adviser, Sir Francis Bacon: over the next few years Villiers and Bacon were to support each other in their careers, with Villiers providing Bacon with unparalleled access – albeit at one remove – to the King's ear.[84] To James, Villiers was 'Steenie', his St Stephen, because all who looked on the saint saw 'his face as it had been the face of an angel'. The King, now fifty years old, was not shy of showing his affection for the young man. At a Twelfth Night revels, James was tiring of the conceited masque and shouted 'Why don't they dance? What did they make me come here for? Devil take you all! Dance!' Villiers got up and 'cut capers', to the delight of the court. As the Venetian ambassdor said: 'none came up to the exquisite manner' of Villiers who 'rendered himself the admiration and delight of everybody'. James suddenly regained his temper, patted Villiers's face, kissed him and embraced him 'with marks of extraordinary affection'.[85]

James's affection for Villiers provoked some tension between the favourite and Prince Charles. In March 1616 Charles saw a ring on the favourite's hand, and took it for himself. When Villiers asked for it back the following day, Charles claimed that he could not find it. Villiers was upset and told the King, who sent for his son and 'used such bitter language to him as forced His Highness to shed tears'. Two months later, when Charles 'in jest' turned a waterspout on Villiers in the garden at Greenwich, James, in a rare display of violence, boxed his ears.[86] Over the next few months, however, Charles began to emerge from the too-long shadow of his beloved dead brother, Henry. He spent the end of 1617 in the country with his father, and one observer noted that Charles was making inroads into James's affections, which might be 'a danger for some other great person', meaning Villiers.[87] In time, though, Charles and Villiers became friends, and, in the summer of 1618, at the Prince's suggestion held a 'friends' feast' to seal their relationship. From then on the King, the Prince and the favourite became a firm triumvirate, often referring to each other by familiar, and familial, nicknames: Baby Charles, dear Dad.

By rights, if the author of *Corona Regia* is to be believed, James should have tired of Villiers sometime in 1618, and moved on, as was his wont, to a younger man. Evidently believing this to be likely, the Howards attempted to seize the King's attention by pushing into his purview a young man named Sir William Monson. As John Chamberlain told the story, the Howards tried 'to raise and recover their fortunes by setting up this new idol, and took great pains in tricking and pranking him up, besides washing his face every day with posset-curd', presumably in an attempt to soften his skin. James, perhaps repelled by the olfactory side-effects of this curdled milk and ale concoction, was not taken by Monson, and very soon sent him a message to the effect that 'the King did not like of his forwardness, and presenting himself continually about him'. In fact, Monson should absent himself from the royal presence – and preferably from the court. According to Chamberlain, this hit home not only with Monson, but with several other young pretenders, who promptly took off to the country: 'most of our young court gallants are vanished like mushrooms'. It was also a 'shrewd reprimand and crossblow' to the Howards,[88] but they didn't give up hope.

The Monson incident was a salutary reminder to Villiers that his preeminence was far from assured,[89] but his continued rise suggested otherwise. James appointed him Earl of Buckingham at Whitehall in January 1617, and the following month the new Earl was sworn into the Privy Council. James expressed his feelings for 'Steenie' in a speech to the other councillors: 'I, James, am neither a god nor an angel, but a man like any other. Therefore I act like a man, and confess to loving those dear to me more than other men. You may be sure that I love the Earl of Buckingham more than anyone else, and more than you who are here assembled. I wish to speak in my own behalf and not to have it thought to be a defect, for Jesus Christ did the same and therefore I cannot be blamed. Christ had his John, and I have my George.'[90] Although not a frequent attender at the Council table, Buckingham was perhaps preeminent in terms of real influence in the Jacobean court, for, like Somerset before him, he attended on James's person constantly – which meant, in the summer of 1617, that Buckingham was the man closest to the King when James went home to Scotland.

CHAPTER SEVENTEEN

A Salmonlike Instinct

I T WAS NOW thirteen long years since James had proclaimed to his people in Edinburgh in April 1603 that he would visit them 'every three year at the least, or ofter [more often], as I shall occasion'. He'd written this in the *Basilikon Doron*, he continued, 'and it were a shame to me not to perform that thing which I have written.'[1] James's promise to go home had not once been honoured. Scotland had, of course, known that James would be an absentee King, and from the outset James had taken measures to allow the country to function in his absence. James's signature on a stamp was given to Sir Patrick Murray, and the Privy Council was given special power to take certain actions (such as the granting of passports, and the auditing of Exchequer accounts) that usually required royal approval. A police guard of forty men was raised to keep the peace in the King's absence. The Scottish Privy Council were given full control of the Borders, both in Scotland and England. A system of postmasters was put in place to ensure the smooth running of the postal system between London and Edinburgh. In his own phrase, James 'governed by pen' from London, while leaving much of the daily business in the hands of his chief ministers in Edinburgh, first the Earl of Dunbar (until his death in 1611) and then Lord Chancellor Sir John Seton, Prince Charles's guardian, who had been raised to become Earl of Dunfermline. The situation was never truly happy, and James was constantly urged to consider a trip home but it was not until April 1616 that his Lord Chancellor, Dunfermline, brought back from England a firm assurance that the King was planning to visit his homeland the following year.[2]

Within weeks, the Scottish Privy Council had authorised repairs to the King's palaces at Holyroodhouse, Falkland and Stirling.[3] Since 'the place of his first rendezvous and longest abode during his stay in this kingdom' would be at Holyroodhouse, it followed naturally that the nobility and his entire retinue 'mon [must] be lodged within the Burgh of Edinburgh, the Canongate, and suburbs of the said burgh'. Lodgings and stables had to be found for five thousand men, and five thousand horse. A survey was undertaken to ensure that everything was in order for the King's reception, and, importantly, would prove 'seemly in the eyes of the many English nobles and gentlemen who will be in his train'. Edinburgh knew that the English were going to be scrutinising her: 'the strangers and others that are to accompany his Majesty here will be so much the more careful narrowly to remark and espy the carriage and conversation of the inhabitants of the said burgh, the form of their entertainment and lodging.' Therefore, strangers were to be given priority. Lodgings were to be 'furnished with honest and clean bedding, and well washin and well smelled napry and other linens, and with a sufficient number and quantity of good vessels, clean and clear, and of sufficient largeness.' Acts were passed for removing all the cattle in the King's Park of Holyrood, so that it could be stocked in good time with wethers to be fattened for his arrival. Stables were to be well provided with corn, straw and hay. The streets must be clean, so that 'no filth nor middens be seen upon the same'. The 'idle beggars and vagabonds still swarming' Edinburgh, Canongate and Leith, blithely unaware of the previous acts passed against them, were to be sent back to their own parishes. Since the time they didn't spend 'in all kind of riot and filthy and beastly lechery and whoredom to the offence and displeasure of God', they devoted to importuning the King's nobility, counsellors and subjects 'with most shameful exclamations and outcries', it was to be feared that 'they will follow his Majesty's Court, to the great discredit and disgrace of the country'.[4] Knowing the bibulous nature of James's retinue, large amounts of wine were imported from France – although for once afterwards there proved to be a surplus which had to be sold off cheap, much to the anguish of Scottish wine merchants.[5]

In making James feel at home, hunting was naturally made a matter of priority. It was solemnly proclaimed at the Mercat Cross that, since 'his Majesty mon [must] sometime have his recreation, exercise, and pastime in the fields', it was necessary 'that the moorfowl, partridges, and pouttis [young fowl], within ten miles of the places of his Majesty's abode here shall be preserved and carefully haynit for his Majesty's pastime and game'. Therefore, it was now illegal 'to slay any moorfowl, partridges, or pouttis, within ten miles of the Burgh of Edinburgh and other parts of his Majesty's abode in this kingdom, during the time of his Majesty's being within the same': the heinous crime carried a penalty of one hundred pounds.[6] Another proclamation banned 'the slaying of his Majesty's bucks' in Falkland Park, with even greater penalties: an Earl would be liable to a five hundred marks' fine.[7]

By the end of 1616 the Scottish Privy Council realised that, as ever, the funds available would not stretch to cover all the grandiose plans. James had to call a convention of estates in Scotland, which met in March 1617 to vote an extra tax the promise of which could be used as security to raise funds immediately.[8] But by now suspicions about the King's reasons for coming north were being openly voiced. Although the English Parliament had scuppered any immediate prospect of Union between England and Scotland, James remained resolved to do what he could to expedite the process. He believed that the single biggest stumbling block was the difference between the Church of England and the Scottish Kirk. Over recent months, he had made certain moves that the Kirk found ominous. When in May 1615 the Archbishop of St Andrews Gledstanes died, for example, James had replaced him with the compliant Archbishop Spottiswoode. Together in England, the King and Spottiswoode planned how the Kirk might be brought into line with Anglican practice. A memorandum, written in Spottiswoode's hand only a month after Gledstanes's death, detailed some proposals: these included a new form of service, which would eliminate spontaneous and 'impertinent' prayer; a new Confession of Faith 'agreeing so near as can be with the Confession of the English Church'; the introduction of a new order for choosing archbishops and bishops (and in the meantime, if required, the order used 'here in England' should be employed); a uniform order for the electing of ministers; and the alteration of the forms of baptism, communion and marriage, along with the introduction of confirmation. This would have to be 'advised and agreed upon', of course, through a General Assembly, but the Assembly 'must be drawn to the form of a Convocation House here in England'.[9] Throughout the memorandum, the dominant theme was enforced compliance with the Anglican model. With Spottiswoode's forceful guidance, much of this was pushed through at the August 1616 meeting of the General Assembly in Aberdeen, but there remained to be implemented important innovations that James insisted on, namely kneeling while receiving communion; observing some holy days dedicated to Christ (Christmas, Good Friday, Easter Day, Ascension and Whitsunday); episcopal confirmation, or 'bishoping'; private baptism; and private communion to sick persons — demands which became known as the 'five articles of Perth'. James agreed to put off the question of the five articles until his visit to Scotland — as a result many believed that his return home was little more than an excuse to force the Kirk into submission.[10]

To combat the rumours, in December 1616 James wrote to his Privy Council in Scotland outlining the reasoning behind his proposed visit.[11] Reminiscent in some ways of his missive to the same Council in 1589, making the case for his imminent departure for Denmark, the letter's defensive tone reveals much of James's true concerns about the possibility, whether real or imagined, of attacks on him. He was alarmed, he wrote, that on his arrival in Scotland he would meet with 'any unwelcome coldness of a number of our good subjects in that country', deriving from 'a prejudged opinion in many of our people's hearts grounded upon false rumours, either maliciously or foolishly spread, anent [concerning] the causes and errands of our intention to repair thither at this time'. He wanted to take this opportunity to present 'an ingenuous and sincere profession unto you of the motives inducing us to resolve upon our journey'. The 'main and principal motive' he declared, 'we are not ashamed to confess' was 'that we have had these many years a great and natural longing to see our native soil and of our birth and breeding. And this salmonlike instinct of our mind restlessly, both when we are awake, and many times in our sleep, so stirred up our thoughts and bended our desires to make a journey thither that we can never rest satisfied till it shall please God we may accomplish it.' This desire was joined to the practical opportunity to 'discharge our kingly office the time we are there' by hearing and resolving suits that required his presence.

Only then did James come to the crux of his letter, concerning fears that he would make 'alterations or reformations' of his government 'either ecclesiastical or civil'. He asked his subjects to 'have that settled confidence in our honesty and discretion that we will not so much as wish anything to be done there which shall not tend to the glory of God and the weal of that commonwealth and all our good subjects therein'. They should 'not only for your own parts harbour no prejudged conceit of our intentions upon the grounds of these idle rumours, but also make this our sincere declaration come to the ears of our other good subjects, that we may have comfort of such a joyful meeting there with our people as we for our part shall ever deserve'. Anxious to show their gratitude, the Scottish Privy Council decided that the letter should be placed in the Council's Register Books, 'there to remain as a perpetual remembrance of his Majesty's love, kindness, and affection to this country'.

James and his retinue set out north in mid-March 1617, travelling between ten and twenty-one miles a day, with stops of one or two nights at estates up the east coast.[12] Leaving English government largely in the hands of Sir Francis Bacon, now Lord Keeper of the Great Seal, James took with him some of his most trusted servants: the Duke of Lennox, the Earls of Arundel, Southampton, Pembroke, Montgomery, and, of course, Buckingham; John Murray of Lochmaben, and Viscount Fenton. The sizeable train included a clutch of bishops and ministers, including the Bishops of Ely, Lincoln and Winchester and the up-and-coming William Laud, on hand to push the King's ecclesiastical reforms.[13] Each venue welcomed the King with the usual celebrations, and provided the requisite hunting ground. There were other occasional treats: an Easter Sunday sermon by Andrewes at Durham Cathedral, a horse race, and a 'cocking' (cock-fight), where the King 'appointed four cocks to be put on the pit together, which made his Majesty very merry'. James, in return, performed his kingly duties. On Sunday 30 March, at Lincoln Minster, he reportedly healed fifty people of 'the King's Evil', scrofula, by the laying on of hands, and fifty-three more on Tuesday 1 April at St Catherine's.[14] Despite suffering from a bad back after another riding accident, James was in high good humour, as Buckingham reported back to Bacon in London: 'his Majesty, God be thanked, is in very good health, and so well pleased with his journey, that I never saw him better, nor merrier.'[15]

On Tuesday 13 May, James crossed the Tweed and entered his motherland for the first time in over fourteen years.[16] Travelling via Dunglass, Seton and Leith, he made his entry into Edinburgh on the afternoon of 16 May to great acclaim. It seemed that his years in England had finally taught him some skills in relating to his people: as David Calderwood noted, 'he made his entry on horseback, that he might the better be seen by the people; whereas before, he rode in the coach all the way'.[17] Seeing their King, John Hay claimed in his speech of welcome, 'our eyes behold the greatest human felicity our hearts could wish, which is to feed upon the royal countenance of our true Phoenix, the bright star of our northern firmament, the ornament of our age'.[18] The somewhat numbing succession of speeches, eulogies, poems and celebrations, in multiple languages, was captured for posterity in a handsome folio memorial volume entitled *The Muses' Welcome*.[19]

Not everyone was impressed by Scotland. One English courtier, Anthony Weldon, summed up his feelings. 'First, for the country I must confess it is too good for those that possess it, and too bad for others to be at the charge to conquer it. The air might be wholesome but for the stinking people that inhabit it, the ground might be fruitful had they the will to manure it. Their beasts be generally small, women only excepted, of which sort there are none greater in all the world.' There might well be 'great store of deer', Weldon admitted, but he was yet to see any: 'I confess all the deer I met withal was dear lodgings, dear horsemeat, dear tobacco and English beer.' The efforts of the Edinburgh magistrates went largely unappreciated by Weldon – 'there is great store of fowl, as foul houses, foul sheets and shorts, foul linen, foul dishes and pots, foul trenchers and napkins' – with one exceptional success: 'corn is reasonable plentiful at this time, for since they heard of the King's coming, it hath been as unlawful for the common people to eat wheat, as it was in the old time for any but the priests to eat the shew-bread; they prayed much for his coming, and long fasted for his welfare'.[20] But another anonymous English courtier was impressed by the Scots' efforts, as he reported to Bacon in London: 'The country affords more profit and better contentment than I could even promise myself by reading of it. The King was never more cheerful in both body and mind, never so well pleased; and so are the English of all conditions. The entertainment very honourable, very general, and very full; every day feasts and invitations. I know not who paid for it. They strive, by direction, to give us all fair contentment, that we may know that the country is not so contemptible but that it is worth the cherishing.'[21]

It was not only the English who were carefully scrutinising the meeting of the two countries. The Scottish ministers were on their guard for signs of James's intentions towards the Kirk. They did not have to wait for long. On 17 May, according to David Calderwood, by now a leading figure in the Kirk, 'the English service was begun in the Chapel Royal, with singing of choristers, surplices, and playing on organs'.[22] The Whitsun communion service on 8 June at Holyroodhouse, where James was staying, was celebrated according to the English fashion, with most of the bishops and several courtiers following the King's lead by celebrating communion kneeling. Those who did not follow suit were soon officially ordered to conform, and by the following Tuesday, the Edinburgh minister William Struthers preached in Holyrood chapel before James, 'and observed the English form in his prayer and behaviour'.[23] Shortly after, a scandal was provoked when one of the Guard who had died was buried 'after the English fashion' by the Dean of St Paul's, Valentine Carey. Carey asked all those assembled to recommend with him the soul of their deceased brother unto Almighty God. This, reported the newsgatherer John Chamberlain, 'was so ill taken, that he was driven to retract it openly, and to confess he did it in a kind of civility rather than according to the perfect rule of divinity'. When the corpse was about to be laid in the ground, William Laud donned a surplice, again causing outrage among the Presbyterians. When it came time for communion, one Scottish bishop, Chamberlain continued, refused to take it while Laud remained kneeling.[24] On 13 June, a diocesan synod held at Edinburgh appointed commissioners to declare to James that they 'could not descend' to the five articles proposed by the King.[25] They stressed the danger to the General Assembly: in England, during Parliament, there was no national Assembly, as there was in Scotland: 'there meeteth only a certain number of the inferior clergy, who sits below in the House of Convocation, like ciphers, giving naked consent of obedience to these things which are decreed by the bishops in the over house.'[26]

James avoided these tensions for a while by taking a couple of hunting trips, but he had to face the music when Parliament opened in Edinburgh on 17 June, with the King 'riding in pomp' from the Palace of Holyroodhouse to the Tolbooth; Buckingham, who had recently become the first Englishman to be admitted on to the Scottish Privy Council (five more were to follow during the visit), was singled out as the only English peer to ride with the King.[27] For once, James made a speech that avoided most of the bones of contention, and did not mention religious doctrine at all. But James still offended his Scottish audience by doing 'England and Englishmen much honour and grace'. There was nothing he 'studied' harder for, both 'sleeping and waking', as to 'reduce the barbarity', as he put it, of Scotland to 'the sweet civility' of England. He hoped that his Scottish subjects would now be as 'docible' to the good features of English culture as they were 'teachable to limp after' its bad elements, namely 'to drink healths, to wear coaches and gay clothes, to take tobacco, and to speak neither Scottish nor English!'[28] James attended Parliament every day of its three weeks' tenure. An English observer, reporting to Bacon in London, told of how James 'doth strive to shape the frame of this Kingdom to the method and degrees of the government of England'. Despite 'a momentary opposition (for his countrymen will speak boldly to him)', his campaign had 'in part been profitable'. While total success was elusive, James had 'won ground in most things, and hath gained Acts of Parliament to authorize particular Commissioners to set down orders for the Church and churchmen, and to treat with Sheriffs for their offices by way of composition.' But James would not trust those commissions. Everything was to have 'an inseparable reference to his Majesty. If any prove unreasonably and undutifully refractory, his Majesty hath declared himself, that he will proceed against him by the warrant of the law, and by the strength of his royal power.'[29]

These were James's last days in his birthplace, and there, on 19 June, he celebrated his fifty-first birthday.[30] Over the next few weeks he toured the country. James visited the celebrated coalworks at Culross belonging to Sir George Bruce, younger brother of the Earl of Kinross. The coalworks extended to an area which, at high tide, was under the sea. James, determined to see the works below ground but unfortunately ignorant of this detail, emerged from the coalpit on to a loading platform to find himself apparently surrounded by the sea, in the middle of the Forth. He was reportedly 'seized by an immediate apprehension of some plot against his liberty or life' and yelled out 'Treason!'

His guide quickly reassured the King that he was perfectly safe, and the royal party made a hasty retreat to dry land.[31]

The King moved on to Stirling on 30 June, where he was greeted by the Commissar Robert Murray with a eulogy to both James and Stirling, as the place of his nurture:

> This town, though she may justly vaunt of her natural beauty and impregnable situation, the one occasioned by the labyrinths of the delightsome Forth, with the deliciousness of her valleys, and the herds of deer in her park: the other by the stately rock on which she is raised; though she may esteem herself famous by worthy founders, re-edifiers, and the enlargers of her many privileges, – Agricola (who in the days of Galdus fortified her), Kenneth the Second (who here encamped and raised the Picts), Malcolm the Second, Alexander the First, William the Lion; yet doth she esteem this her only glory and worthiest praise, that she was the place of your Majesty's education, that these sacred brows, which now bear the weighty diadems of three invincible nations, were empalled with their first hair. And that this day the only man of Kings, and the worthiest King of men, on whom the eye of heaven glanceth, deigns (a just reward of all those cares and toils which followed your cradle) to visit her.[32]

Another happy moment came on 19 July at Stirling when in the Chapel Royal he received a deputation from Edinburgh University, which was alarmed by rumours that 'all colleges were to be laid waste, except St Andrews and Glasgow'.[33] They debated on such themes as 'Ought sheriffs and other inferior magistrates to be hereditary'; 'On the nature of local motion'; and 'Concerning the origin of fountains or springs'. After supper, the King sent for the learned disputants: John Adamson, James Fairlie, Patrick Sands, Andrew Young, James Reid and William King. Perhaps relaxed by the supper's wine, James decided to play with the scholars' names, starting with Adamson as 'Adam's Son', and ending with King who 'disputed very kingly, and of a kingly purpose concerning the royal supremacy of reason above anger and all passions'. 'I am so well satisfied with this day's exercise,' he told the academics, 'that I will be godfather to the College of Edinburgh, and have it called the College of King James, for after its founding it stopped sundry years in my minority; after I came to knowledge, I held to it, and caused it to be established; and although I see many look upon it with an evil eye, yet I will have them know that, having given it my name, I have espoused its quarrel, and at a proper time will give it a royal God-bairn gift, to enlarge its revenues.' James was so proud of his wit that he commissioned a sonnet to immortalise it, whose last couplet memorialised the tangible benefit of the exchange:

> To their deserved praise have I thus played upon their names,
> And will their college hence be *The College of King James.*

The sonnet was then rendered in Latin three times for inclusion in *The Muses' Welcome*.[34] From Stirling, James travelled to Perth, where a speech by the merchant and burgess John Stewart reminded him of the Gowrie Plot, when God 'did give you out of the bloody hands of these two unnatural traitors within this town'.[35]

The trouble with the Kirk would not go away, however. At St Andrews, James sat with the Court of High Commission as three ministers were tried on 12 July for their involvement with the recent clerical protest against the proposed innovations. There James came to blows with the man who was ironically one of the most devoted documenters of his reign, David Calderwood. Calderwood took the King to task over the question of the authority of the General Assembly. When James insisted on obedience, Calderwood equivocated by talking of active and passive obedience, namely that 'we will rather suffer than practice'. James was incensed. 'I will tell thee, man, what is obedience. The centurion, what he said to his servants, to this man, Go, and he goeth, to that man, Come, and he cometh, that is obedience.' For 'carrying himself unrevently, and braking forth into speeches not becoming a subject', Calderwood was committed to prison.[36]

The following day, still smarting from the encounter, James met with a group of thirty-six ministers in the chapel of St Andrews Castle and angrily demanded to know what 'causeless jealousies' there could be to his proposed five articles. The churchmen fell to their knees, and after being allowed to confer, begged that a General Assembly might be called to approve the articles. When James asked what assurance he could have that the Assembly would consent, the ministers replied that they could see no reason why the Assembly would not consent 'to any reasonable thing demanded by his Majesty'. 'But if it fall out otherwise,' James persisted, 'and that the Articles be refused, my difficulty will be greater; and, when I shall use my authority in establishing them, they shall call me a tyrant and persecutor.' The ministers cried out that no one would be so mad as to say that. 'Yet experience tells me it may be so,' replied James wearily, 'therefore unless I be made sure, I will not give way to an Assembly.' At length, however, James was mollified by the ministers' insistent assurances that the articles would be passed by the General Assembly, and agreed to hold one in late November.[37] His work was almost done. At Glasgow on 27 July James attended his final meeting of the Scottish Privy Council. Travelling through south-west Scotland via Hamilton, Sanquhar, Drumlanrig and Dumfries, by 4 August he was in Carlisle.[38] Regaining his good humour, James was even prevailed upon by Robert Hay, a Gentleman of his Bedchamber, to allow Calderwood bail on 28 July, although ultimately the minister was banished from Scotland.[39]

Once back in London, however, James resumed his antipathy towards the Kirk in which he had been raised. The General Assembly which he had reluctantly called was sparsely attended, and little headway was made in pushing through the proposed reforms. The conduct of his bishops was 'a disgrace', James raged by letter, threatening to impose financial penalties on dissenting ministers. 'Since your Scottish Church hath so far contemned my clemency,' he added in his own hand as a postscript to the Archbishops of St Andrews and Glasgow, 'they shall now find what it is to draw the anger of a King upon them.'[40] As he had previously hinted, what he could not achieve through the ministers' acquiescence, James now imposed by law, ordering the Privy Council in January 1618 to issue a proclamation forcing the observance of religious holy days.[41] Insult was added to injury when, on 24 May, James issued a proclamation that claimed that sports and games were lawful on Sundays and other holy days.[42] Amid rumours that more punitive measures were to come, the final General Assembly of James's reign met at Perth on 25 August 1618. A difficult, tense affair, it seemed at first as if no progress would be possible, especially on the question of kneeling at communion. To help matters, James had sent a letter which was read out twice 'to move the Assembly partly with allurements, partly with persuasions', as Calderwood put it.[43] But at last, thanks mainly to the stage management of Archbishop Spottiswoode, the General Assembly approved James's five articles.[44] To what extent the articles were effectively imposed is another matter: James's insistence in March 1620 that the punishment for disobeying the articles should be extended to laymen suggests that their success was far from wholesale.[45] But the 'salmonlike' return to Scotland in 1617 was to be a rare last chance for James to indulge himself in domestic policy. From now on, his concerns would be on an international stage.

CHAPTER EIGHTEEN

The Peacemaker

E VER SINCE PHILIP III of Spain had sent Diego Sarmiento de
Acuña to London in 1614, James had been obsessed with the
idea of marrying Prince Charles to the Spanish Infanta. While
James was thrilled by the idea of Spain's power, wealth and prestige,
Philip saw the benefit of having England on side against a possible
threat from France. During 1615, Sarmiento and other Spanish envoys
elaborated the articles for a marriage treaty. In order for Charles to
marry the Infanta, Spain would require some concessions to English
Roman Catholics: first, an agreement not to enforce the laws against
them, and, eventually, the permission for them to practise their religion. The Infanta's household would be Spanish and Roman Catholic,
and would be able to worship publicly, and be buried in Catholic
graves. Her priests would be allowed to wear their robes in public.
The Infanta would have to keep control over the education of her
children, who would be baptised according to Roman Catholic rites,
and given Catholic wet nurses. The children of the marriage would
be allowed to choose their religion, but the choice to be a Catholic
would not automatically bar them from the throne. James's first reaction to these articles was hostile, but he did not throw them out altogether – much to the horror of the anti-Spanish faction that had
emerged at court, led by Secretary of State Sir Ralph Winwood, the
Archbishop of Canterbury George Abbot, and the Earl of Pembroke.
These men called instead for war against Spain, and urged James to
call a Parliament to fund it. He, of course, refused.[1]

James did, however, give in to another petition from Winwood,
Pembroke and Abbot. It was gold that tempted the always inpecu-
nious King. In 1595, lured by tales of the legendary Indian city El
Dorado, the famed courtier and explorer Sir Walter Ralegh had reached
Orinoco, and claimed it as English. But after being imprisoned by
James in 1603, Ralegh had been unable to persuade the English government to allow him to capitalise on his discoveries, and Spain had
made considerable inroads in the region. Now the anti-Spanish faction,
led by Abbot, Pembroke and Winwood pressured James to free Ralegh

from the Tower and allow him to sail to the Orinoco River, to reclaim it and its rumoured wealth for England. In March 1616 James finally relented, and Ralegh was released, in order to begin preparations for the venture. Ralegh was permitted to sail heavily armed, but only after solemnly undertaking that he would not attack any Spanish subject, on pain of death. Sarmiento protested, but James reassured him by saying that on his faith, his hand and his word, he would send Sir Walter bound hand and foot directly to Spain should he injure a single Spaniard; any Spanish gold would be returned to King Philip, and Ralegh would be delivered for hanging in Madrid.[2]

Ralegh's mission was a catastrophe. Battered by gales, hurricanes and fever on board, the fleet was horribly weakened by the time it reached the mouth of the Orinoco. With Sir Walter too ill to go further, a group of boats was led up the river by Keymis and Ralegh's nephew, George. Coming close to the Spanish settlement of San Thomé, the Englishmen were fired on during the night; in the battle that followed, Ralegh's son Walter was killed, and the English captured the town, only to fall under siege from the Spanish. After twenty-nine days, Keymis admitted defeat, returned to tell Ralegh of his failure and then committed suicide. Unable to attempt another push up river and without the force necessary to launch an assault on any other settlement, Ralegh returned home with the dregs of his men via Newfoundland, arriving at Portsmouth on 21 June 1618. He was promptly arrested, and put back in the Tower.[3]

Ralegh had broken every promise he had made to the King. Sarmiento (now elevated as Count de Gondomar) insisted that James must fulfil his promise to send Ralegh to Madrid for his due punishment. According to Secretary of State Sir Thomas Lake, James was 'very disposed and determined against Ralegh and will join the King of Spain in ruining him'; Gondomar reported home that 'The King promises that he will do whatever we like to remedy and redress it.'[4] On 21 June, the Privy Council objected as best they could without criticising the King directly: Gondomar was insolent, they said, to insist that Ralegh be hanged in Madrid, as though England were nothing more than a tributary to Spain.[5] The following day, James put it to Gondomar that in fact Keymis was the guilty party, but the Spaniard was not impressed. James, he declared, could not act as judge of the case, because he himself had given Ralegh his commission, and he was surrounded on his Privy Council by Ralegh's friends. Gondomar, sadly, had no power to punish Sir Walter himself: instead, he could only point out that Ralegh remained unhanged, and his friends on the Council were still at liberty. For once, James grew angry at Gondomar: he pulled his hat off and threw it on the floor, and, clutching his hair, screamed that this might be justice in Spain, but it was not justice in England. He would not punish a man unheard – even if an assassin were to kill the Prince of Wales, he had to be tried before he could be punished. Gondomar pressed home the case against Ralegh and at length James admitted that Sir Walter's crimes were scarlet, and formally promised to send Ralegh to Spain for execution. When the Privy Council protested at this development, James declared that he was King, and would take whatever course he desired, 'without following the advice of fools and of designing persons'.[6]

In the end, though, some degree of compromise had to be allowed to creep in. A commission of Privy Councillors was appointed to examine the case, and concluded that Ralegh planned to plunder Spanish holdings in America, contrary to his undertaking. This, they decided, demanded the death penalty. However, since Ralegh already had a death penalty hanging over him and was thus legally dead, he could not be tried on the new charge. A special commission was appointed to hear the case; it was found that the death sentence imposed for his original crime could still be carried out; Ralegh was executed; and Bacon was set to work drafting a *Declaration* justifying the King's course of action in the case.[7] James had won the day – but at great personal cost. To many of his subjects, it seemed that he had kowtowed to Spanish pressure and put to death an English national hero.

He soon had a chance to win back popular support. James was on his 1618 summer progress when a plea for help reached him from Bohemia. By 1617, the Hapsburg Emperor Matthias, hereditary Archduke of Austria, Holy Roman Emperor, and King of Bohemia and Hungary by election, was bedridden with gout, and concerned about his successor. He had persuaded Bohemia and Hungary to accept his cousin and heir apparent, Archduke Ferdinand of Styria, as his successor. But Ferdinand was an ardent Roman Catholic, and Bohemia, a religiously pluralistic state with a sturdy Protestant element, had good reason over time to reconsider her decision. In May 1618, a group of Protestant Bohemian nobles broke into the palace in Prague and threw two leading officials out of the window, violently marking the end of their support for Ferdinand's claim. Imperial armies were soon despatched to quash the rebellion, but the Bohemians were saved by mercenary forces financed by the Duke of Savoy and by Frederick, Elector Palatine, husband of James's daughter Elizabeth.

The Bohemians looked to other Protestant princes for military and financial support with less success. They approached James with their grievances, asking for his 'aid and favour'. But James failed to reply, 'either by writing or by word'.[8] He was tempted instead by an alternative suggestion from King Philip III of Spain that James should 'interpose himself for the accommodating of the business of Bohemia',[9] that is, function as an intermediary arbitrator. James immediately took a fancy to this new role of international peacemaker. Before long a tract was published entitled *The Peace-Maker: or Great Brittaines Blessing*, which, although anonymous (and probably penned by playwright Thomas Middleton), was directed in a style very like James's own 'To all our true loving, and peace-embracing subjects.' The pamphlet presented England not only as the home of peace – '*Insula pacis*. The Land of Peace, under the King of Peace' – but as the source of all peace. 'Nay, what Christian kingdom that knows the blessing of peace, has not desired and tasted this our blessing from us? Come they not hither as to the fountain from whence it springs? Here sits Solomon, and hither come the tribes for judgements: oh happy moderator, blessed father, not father of thy country alone, but father of all thy neighbour countries about thee.' In making its case for peace as the perfect state, it attacked as unmanly and irrational the current fashion among young English gentlemen for duelling, which it linked to James's two other *bêtes noires*, witchcraft and tobacco[10] – James had already taken action a few years earlier to discourage the voguish bloodsport which he regarded with understandable horror.[11] As Gondomar reported, 'The vanity of the present King of England is so great that he will always think it of great importance that peace should be made by his means, so that his authority will be increased.' The English envoy in Spain, Francis Cottington, told King Philip that James 'was resolved to use his utmost endeavours and to interpose his best credit and authority for compounding the difference, if he should find the same disposition and inclination' in Philip.[12] In England, Buckingham assured Gondomar that James would 'do all that he can and that lies in his power, and to finish the business peaceably and quietly, if the Bohemians will listen to him, and are willing to have his advice'. But should the Bohemians prove 'obstinate and pertinacious' he would persuade his son-in-law and the other German princes to refrain from giving them any aid.[13]

Historians have long derided James for his arrogance and naivety in this matter. 'The Spanish suggestion was, of course, a bit of trickery,' writes D.H. Willson, typically. 'The King accepted it so quickly, without caution or reservation, that he all but invited the Spaniards to cheat him.'[14] But, in truth, the battle lines were not well drawn. Spain by no means immediately committed herself to the embattled Austrians. As Cottington reported, when news first reached Madrid of the rebellion the Spaniards were 'not a little troubled', not least for financial reasons: they 'already groan under the excessive charge and expense which they are daily at for the subsistence of those Princes of Austria, and especially this King of Bohemia', Matthias.[15] Moreover, the Twelve Years' Truce between the Spanish and the Dutch had only three years to run: once that expired, and if they were to engage in this new conflict, Spain could very easily find herself fighting in both Bohemia and the Low Countries. James still withheld his reply from the Bohemians, instead allowing Buckingham to act on his behalf. Buckingham's ascent had continued unabated. After his successes in Scotland, he was created Marquis of Buckingham on New Year's Day 1618, and the following day the new Marquis threw a great feast for James and Charles in the Cockpit at Whitehall. While supper was still in progress, James stood up and took his son by the hand. Walking to the other table, he toasted Buckingham. 'My lords, I drink to you all and I know we are all welcome to my George. And he that doth not pledge it with all his heart, I would the Devil had him for my part.'[16] Now the personal favour was translated directly into political influence on the international stage.

Buckingham forwarded the Bohemians' declaration of grievances to Madrid, to ascertain Philip's verdict. At the same time, he told the English ambassador in Spain, Cottington, James was 'very glad that the winter is so far advanced that there is hope that both parties may be hindered from engaging with one another any further by way of arms'.[17] The Venetian ambassador in London commented wisely that although James loved to pass himself off as 'the chief of a great union in Europe', the English were likely to 'resolve upon nothing, and by offering a league as they have so often done, wish to bind others without binding themselves, or with little idea of carrying it into effect'.[18] But as winter drew on, peace seemed less possible. Cottington reported from Madrid that 200,000 ducats had finally been sent from Spain to support Matthias's troops in Bohemia, and provision made for the future payment of the army there; he also expressed concern at reports that 'the Prince Palatine doth therein no good offices' and Philip 'was much assured he observed not the orders given him' by James.[19]

For the first time in his lengthy reign, James was dangerously implicated in what promised to be a major international crisis, but his attention was suddenly absorbed by matters closer to home. On 2 March 1619 Queen Anna died at Hampton Court after a lengthy illness. On her instructions, her faithful Danish maid Anna Roos had refused to let anyone visit her until her final hours, when the Queen lost her sight, and Roos called Charles to be with his mother as she died. An inquest found the Queen to be 'much wasted within, specially her liver'. James was not with his wife in her final days nor did he attend her funeral, which was postponed for several weeks due, it was rumoured, to the King's unwillingness to commit the necessary cash. But the image of a callous, indifferent husband is misplaced. As Anna lay dying, James was himself sick at Newmarket with a combination of arthritis, gout and 'a shrewd fit of the stone'.[20] The news of his wife's death sent him spiralling down into a serious melancholy. After the Queen's death, his physician Theodore de Mayerne observed 'pain in his joints and nephritis with thick sand'. Moving to Royston, James suffered from 'continued fever, bilious diarrhoea, watery and profuse throughout the illness. Hiccoughs for several days. Aphthae all over mouth and fauces, and even the oesophagus. Fermentation of bitter humours boiling in his stomach which, effervescing by froth out of his mouth, led to ulceration of his lips and chin. Fainting, sighing, dread, incredible sadness, intermittent pulse' – this last a frequent symptom in the King – and a continuation of nephritis 'from which, without any remedy having been administered, he execreted a friable calculus, as was his wont. The force of this, the most dangerous illness the King ever had, lasted for eight days.' In the process he had voided three stones, and the pain had caused such violent vomiting that his life seemed to be in danger.[21]

Charles, Buckingham and the leading Privy Councillors were summoned from London to hear James's deathbed speech. According to John Williams, Bishop of Lincoln, there was 'not a syllable in all the same, but deserves to be written in letters of gold. How powerfully did he charge him with the care of religion and justice, the two pillars (as he termed them) of his future throne? How did he recommend unto his love, the nobility, the clergy, and the commonalty in the general? How did he thrust, as it were into his inward bosom, his bishops, his judges, his near servants; and that disciple of his whom he so loved in particular?' In Williams's account, James was still looking forward to a great Catholic marriage for his heir, concluding 'with that heavenly advice, to his son, concerning that great act of his future marriage, to marry like himself, and marry where he would. But if he did marry the daughter of that King, he should marry her person, but he should not marry her religion.'[22] More practically, James recommended to Charles that when he became king he should take as his principal counsellors Lennox, Arundel, Pembroke and especially Hamilton and Buckingham. But the good advice was not needed: within days James began to recover, although he remained extremely weak for some time to come. In April he moved to Theobalds, borne in a litter and in a portable chair carried on his men's shoulders; arriving at his favourite estate, 'weak and weary as he was', he 'would not settle within doors till he had his deer brought to make a muster before him'.[23] Still too frail to attend his wife's funeral on 13 May, it was not until June that James felt strong enough to make a solemn entry into Whitehall.[24] Later in the summer he was observed trying one of his own cures: 'On Saturday last the King killed a buck in Eltham Park and so soon as it was opened stood in the belly of it and bathed his bare feet and legs with the warm blood; since which time he has been so nimble that he thinketh this the only remedy for the gout.'[25]

The King's return to health, celebrated in sermons up and down the country, provided only a momentary boost to his waning popularity at home. By the time an English embassy of a hundred and fifty men, headed by James Hay, now Viscount Doncaster, left for Bohemia in April 1619, Emperor Matthias was already dead. Londoners were abuzz with the possibilities of what they called these German 'combustions': it was even rumoured (on no grounds whatsoever) that Matthias would be succeeded as Emperor by the Elector Frederick.[26] In August, Archduke Ferdinand was elected Emperor at Frankfurt; in Prague, at the same time, the Bohemians deposed Ferdinand as their King and offered the throne of Bohemia instead to the Elector Frederick. Frederick, unsure what to do, sent to James for advice, and his wife Elizabeth wrote to Buckingham to point out that her father 'hath now a good occasion to manifest to the world the love he hath ever professed to the Prince here. I earnestly entreat you to use your best means in persuading his Majesty to show himself now, in his helping of the Prince here, a true loving father to us both.'[27] The King's answer was not immediately forthcoming. To James, the fact that Frederick could keep the Bohemian throne Protestant was irrelevant: this was not a matter of religion, but of kingship. 'What hath religion to do to decrown a king?' he asked. 'Leave that opinion to the Devil and to the Jesuits, authors of it and brands of sedition. For may subjects rebel against their prince in quarrel of religion? Christ came into the world to teach subjects obedience to the king, and not rebellion!'[28] But by the time James's response, urging caution, was delivered to his son-in-law's hands, Frederick had already accepted the throne. 'He wrote to me to know my mind if he should take that crown,' James later complained, 'but within three days after; and before I could return answer, he put it on.'[29] It was said that it was Elizabeth who had persuaded Frederick: she wrote to him that as God directed all things, He had undoubtedly sent this; if Frederick felt it advisable to accept, she would be ready to follow the divine call, to suffer whatever God should ordain — if necessary to pledge her jewels and whatever else she had in the world.[30]

Frederick and Elizabeth entered Prague in late October 1619 to scenes of unalloyed joy. Then eight months pregnant, Elizabeth had insisted (against general advice) on accompanying her husband on his journey. The royal couple's popularity was only enhanced when Elizabeth gave birth to another son, Rupert, in December, who was immediately proclaimed as Duke of Lusatia. Britain shared in the popular rejoicing, which soon transmuted into a widespread call for action against Spain, on the streets and in the pulpits, as the Archbishop of Canterbury preached that the Book of Revelation was about to be realised as Roman Catholic power was toppled. Prince Charles wrote to assure the Elector Palatine that 'I will be glad not only to assist him with my countenance but also with my person, if the King my father would give me leave',[31] a formulation that suggests only too clearly how James and Charles were not in agreement on this point. At the Privy Council table, a hawkish pro-war faction emerged, headed by Buckingham. With Buckingham aboard, surely now the King would fall into line? The Earl of Pembroke seemed sure enough. 'It is true that the King will be very unwilling to be engaged in a war,' he admitted. 'And yet I am confident, when the necessity of the cause of religion, his son's preservation, and his own honour call upon him, that he will perform whatsoever belongs to the Defender of the Faith, a kind father-in-law, and one careful of that honour which I must confess by a kind of misfortune hath long lain in suspense.'[32]

But James remained adamant and angry. In his eyes, the Bohemians had rebelled against their natural leader, and, by accepting the throne, Frederick had endorsed the rebellion, and effectively usurped the kingdom, threatening 'to set all Christendom by the ears'. James turned his scholarly attention to poring over Bohemian public law to ascertain whether or not Frederick's election was legal. He held long, aimless conferences with ambassadors. He refused to let the Privy Council express its opinion – since he knew they wanted to help Frederick. But James had his weaknesses. Frederick instructed his five-year-old son, Frederick Henry, to write a letter to his grandfather, appealing for help: James, fancying himself the family man, was deeply touched. To the new Spanish ambassador Father Diego Lafuente (known as Padre Maestro) James deplored how he had been put 'in a great strait, being drawn to one side by his children and grand-children, his own flesh and blood, and to the other side by the truth and by his friendship to Philip and to the House of Austria' – but Lafuente noted that the equation placed the 'truth' with Philip rather than with the

King's flesh and blood. Nevertheless James's paternal pride could not but be stirred by the fact that he now had a King for a son-in-law – and, more important, a Queen for a daughter. As the Venetian envoy Piero Antonio Marioni wrote, 'those who converse familiarly with his Majesty tête à tête easily perceive his delight at this new royal title for his son-in-law and daughter'.[33] Cracks appeared in his friendship for Spain: occasionally he would blurt out that they were playing with him, and pined for the company of Gondomar, who had returned to Spain the previous year.[34] At other times, he became afraid that it would be thought he had plotted for Frederick's election, and blurted out, on his word as a Christian Prince, that he was innocent. Foreign observers lost patience with these mixed messages and even began to doubt that James was in full control of his faculties. The French ambassador Count Leveneur de Tillières wrote home that 'It seems to me that the intelligence of this King has diminished. Not that he cannot act firmly and well at times and particularly when the peace of the kingdom is involved. But such efforts are not so continual as they once were. His mind uses its powers only for a short time, but in the long run he is cowardly. His timidity increases day by day as old age carries him into apprehension and vices diminish his intelligence.'[35]

Meanwhile, Catholic powers on the Continent were plotting. Maximilian of Bavaria, the leader of the Catholic League, offered to provide assistance to the ousted Ferdinand on the condition that on defeating Frederick he, Maximilian, would inherit the title of Elector Palatine, and a good proportion of his estates. In secret, Ferdinand agreed to the deal; Philip of Spain was let in on the pact, and agreed with some reluctance to provide a diversion by attacking the Palatinate from the Netherlands.[36] Preparations for this attack from Spain became evident to observers in early 1620, but James refused to believe it. If the Princes of the Union were in any danger, it was self-inflicted, brought on by their plotting in Bohemia. His alliance with them was purely defensive, and he would not assist them in what he saw as offensive attacks.

Finally, in the spring of 1620, Gondomar made his return to James's court. Now James found himself placating the ambassador, asking for his patience, and swearing that he was doing all he could to avoid giving offence to Spain, though he was surrounded by anti-Spanish zealots and must not be squeezed. 'I give you my word, as a king, as a gentleman, as a Christian, and as an honest man, that I have no wish to marry my son to anyone except your master's daughter, and that I desire no alliance but that of Spain,'[37] he exclaimed heatedly, taking off his hat, and wiping his head with a hankerchief. He looked to Gondomar for the answers. 'All that is needed,' James said, 'is that we two should talk over these matters together.' Would the Emperor attack the Palatinate? he asked. 'What would you do,' replied Gondomar tartly, 'if anyone had taken London from you?' James had no answer. He hoped that God would arrange matters for the best.[38] James fell to secret scheming with Gondomar. In public, he contradicted himself daily, with promises that he would send armies to the Palatinate and grand pledges of support to the Princes of the Union, followed almost immediately by querulous excuses that he did not have the funds. Finally, he allowed volunteers to be raised in England (four thousand signed up), a strategy that allowed Englishmen to fight for the Palatinate, but let him off the hook.

When news came in April 1620 that Frederick was considering an alliance with the Turks to pursue his causes, James finally lost sympathy. At table – and therefore in public – the King declared that even if the Turk 'moved against Christendom in force, even in favour of his son-in-law, he would use all the forces of these realms to oppose him, and would not stand even at fighting against his own daughter'.[39] To Gondomar, he declared: 'The Palatine is a godless man and a usurper. I will give him no help. It is much more reasonable that he, young as he is, should listen to an old man like me, and do what is right by surrendering Bohemia, than that I should be involved in a bad cause. The Princes of the Union want my help; but I give you my word that they shall not have it.'[40] The bond with Gondomar was tightened when news arrived in May of Dutch attacks against English merchants in the Spice Islands. James and Buckingham took their complaints to Gondomar, and plotted with him to launch an attack on Holland; Gondomar was allowed to convey it to Spain as a serious, royally sanctioned proposition. He reported home that it was now safe for the Palatinate to be invaded: England would not go to war to save it.

On 28 July 1620, James set off on his annual summer progress, visibly relieved to be leaving this complex international power-brokering behind. The Venetian envoy reported that he started 'with so much the more satisfaction as in leaving the city behind he throws off the weight of negotiations and removes himself from the annoyance of ministers and ambassadors, from whom he is naturally always ready to remove himself and of whom he wishes to be rid, especially in these days of trouble and involved affairs, and to get as far off as possible'.[41] The King, he added in cipher, 'seemed utterly weary of the affairs that are taking place all over the world at this time, and he hates being obliged every day to spend time over unpleasant matters and listen to nothing but requests and incitements to move in every direction, and to meddle with everything. He remarked: "I am not God Almighty."'[42]

But even deep in the English countryside, James could not escape events on the Continent. In August, as planned, a Spanish army in the Low Countries led by Spinola invaded the Palatinate while Emperor Ferdinand moved against Prague. James refused to admit what was happening. The Venetian ambassador reported that 'When any one reminds his Majesty that Spinola is on the march and proceeding towards the Palatinate, he says, "What do you know? You are ignorant. I know quite well what I am about. All these troubles will settle themselves, you will see that very soon. I know what I am talking about."' James refused to make any new decisions, declaring that 'he does not know what more he can do, since he wishes to procure peace in any event and he does not wish to weaken the force of his mediation by any stronger declarations. He says: "I allow them to levy as many men as they wish from these kingdoms, I leave my subjects free, and even exhort them to give help in money, I perform all the good offices which are opportune with all the powers. What can I do more?"' Although his ambassadors were told to reiterate that while James would not let the Palatinate 'fall in any circumstances', there was evidently only 'slight disposition to do more'; and indeed he could not do more without summoning a Parliament, an option that after the disasters of 1610 and 1614 was 'very far from the King's thoughts'.[43]

It was only in the early autumn of 1620 that James started to accept that Spain had duped him. At Hampton Court on 24 September, he angrily accused Gondomar of deceiving him, declaring that he would not allow his children nor his religion to perish – even if it meant going himself to defend the Palatinate. Gondomar pointed out that he had never actually promised that the Palatinate would not be invaded. James knew this to be true; he burst into tears. To the Privy Council, he made a formal declaration that he would defend the Palatinate. Having made the decision, James finally seemed happy, throwing a banquet, letting wine flow freely around the court, and drinking toasts to his children. But he soon started listening again to Gondomar, who assured him that, in fact, this invasion was the beginnings of peace. All Frederick had to do was renounce his claim to Bohemia, and his Palatinate would be restored to him. Gaining ground, Gondomar asserted his influence, forcing James to admit formally that Spain had not broken any promise about the Palatinate. The court was outraged at James's acquiescence to Gondomar – it was 'as if all our councillors were petty companions in respect of him, the great ambassador (as he calls himself) of the great King of Spain'.[44] As the French ambassador put it, Gondomar was 'not only an ambassador, but one of the first councillors of State of this kingdom, being day and night at the Palace of Whitehall, where the most secret counsels are confided to him and where they listen to his advices and follow them almost to the letter'.[45]

James was increasingly isolated from public opinion, which was virulently stirred up against Spain – often personalised in the form of Gondomar – by the sermons and writings of preachers. Most prolific among these was the Reverend Thomas Scott, who penned a series of tracts, starting with *Vox Populi*, a supposed translation of a report by Gondomar to the Spanish Council, gloating of his success in bringing England into the Spanish fold.[46] On reading it, the Venetian ambassador reported, Gondomar 'foams with wrath in every direction'.[47] Simonds D'Ewes recorded that James 'was much incensed at the sight of it' and ordered the arrest of the anonymous author, who escaped to the Low Countries; meanwhile, the pamphlet enraged the English against Gondomar who had his Holborn residence 'secured by a guard of men'.[48] James was heard to remark that his people were becoming too republican, and issued a proclamation banning all speech on matters of state. While many of his counsellors urged him to call a Parliament, Buckingham and Gondomar persuaded him otherwise.

Then, in November, word reached England that on the 8th Maximilian of Bavaria had routed the Bohemian troops at the battle of the White Hill outside Prague. After just a year in power, Frederick and Elizabeth had been forced to flee the city, ignominiously, at night, and to head north. In England, there was an outpouring of grief for 'the beloved Queen, who in her flight never had a helping hand from her father to protect and accompany her'. Now, reported Girolamo Lando, 'tears, sighs and loud expressions of wrath are seen and heard in every direction. They have even found letters scattered in the streets, against the King, threatening that if his Majesty does not do what is expected of him, the people will assuredly display unmistakably their feelings and their wrath.'[49] James, hunting hare at Newmarket, was shattered. 'Very sad and grieved', abandoning the chase, he 'remained constantly shut up in his room in great sadness and dejection, forbidding the courtiers any kind of game or recreation.' In December, the Bishop of London summoned his clergy and instructed them, in the King's name, 'not to meddle in their sermons with the Spanish match nor any other matter of state'. But by now feelings were too high, and the very next Sunday, a preacher at Paul's Cross 'spake very freely' on the matter.[50] Over the next three months, at least three clerics were imprisoned for speaking out against Spain: Ralph Clayton for expatiating on the dangers of importing a Spanish ewe, a thinly veiled reference to James's plans to marry Charles to the Infanta; Dr John Everard, a reader at St Martin's in the Fields, a stone's throw from Whitehall Palace, was gaoled twice, also for preaching against the Spanish match; and Samuel Ward of Ipswich for caricaturing Gondomar in writing.[51]

At times James remarked 'that he never wished to meddle in the affairs of Bohemia, and he clearly foresaw these disasters'. But skilled observers thought that now for the first time they saw 'various signs that he really means to help the Palatinate and is steadily determined to listen no more to words or to the singing of deceitful sirens'.[52] They were proved right when the King finally decided to call a Parliament, nearly seven years after the collapse of his last. James rode to Westminster on 30 January 1621 to make his usual opening speech but, to the consternation of many, had to be carried into the House of Lords in a chair, 'being so weak in his legs and feet that it is doubted he will find little use in them hereafter, but be altogether *perdus* [lost] that way'.[53] He would speak only briefly, he declared, since he had found that his former speeches had been turned against him (in the event he spoke for an hour). He reminded the members that Parliament was called to make laws and reform abuses. While he was ready to defend the religion of his people by pen and person, he preferred persuasion to martyrdoms. The proposed marriage with Spain would not lead to toleration of the Roman Catholic religion, nor would it encourage popery. He also had to call Parliament for his own necessities. No king, he declared, had reigned for so long, received so little, and spent so much for the public good. Despite this, he had been accused of giving away too much. Over the last two years, he had looked into and reduced his expenditure – here he gave thanks to the assistance of his 'young Admiral', Buckingham. And then there was the miserable state of Christendom. He might not have supported his son-in-law's claim to the Bohemian throne, but he had spent immense sums in defending the Palatinate and in diplomatic embassies – and he would spend his own and his son's blood to restore the Palatinate. Finally, he declared his willingness to reform all real grievances, but not to hunt after pretended ones. This Parliament had been long looked for; he hoped it would prove a happy one.[54]

At first it seemed that a happy Parliament was possible, as two subsidies were agreed on 15 February, as a 'present of love' to the King. But in return, the Commons took up Sir Edward Coke's suggestion that such generosity entitled them 'to appoint two days every week to hear grievances'.[55] A slew of controversial monopolies was put under scrutiny, and, more pertinently, the men who sanctioned them: the 'referees'. Sir Giles Mompesson, a relative of Buckingham's by marriage, and Sir Francis Bacon (now Viscount St Albans) were both investigated on these grounds, and then, on 14 March, two charges of accepting bribes as Lord Chancellor were presented against Bacon. The Lord Chancellor appealed to his patron Buckingham and directly to the King, but to no effect: on 3 May Bacon was found guilty, fined £40,000, imprisoned at the King's pleasure in the Tower, held 'uncapable of any office, place or employment in the state or commonwealth', evicted from Parliament, and required to remain twelve miles away from court. There were many who believed that Buckingham had sacrificed Bacon to save himself; some even alleged that James himself was under threat. One of Bacon's servants alleged that the Lord Chancellor told the King that 'Those that will strike at your Chancellor, it's much to be feared, will strike at your crown.'[56] One observer in Paris even reported that there was talk that Bacon's fall would lead to the deposing of King James himself, in favour of the Prince of Wales.[57]

In February 1621, while Parliament was proceeding, the Council of War gave its report on a plan for intervention to help the Palatinate. It estimated that an army of 30,000 men would be needed, costing over £200,000 to raise, and almost one million pounds a year to maintain in action. James was horrified at the sums, and doctored them for public consumption. He asked Parliament for £500,000 and at the end of the first parliamentary session, in June 1621, the Commons passed a resolution stating that if the King's attempts to mediate failed, they would 'be ready to the utmost of their powers, both with their lives and fortunes, to assist him, so as by the divine help of Almighty God . . . he may be able to do that with his sword which by a peaceable course shall not be effected'.[58] In fact the Commons voted for only two subsidies, which brought in some £160,000.

James, however, made no military preparations. Wanting to believe that he had Philip of Spain's promise that the Palatinate would be restored if Frederick renounced Bohemia, he convinced himself that this was the case. He determined that he would offer to Emperor Ferdinand Frederick's renunciation of Bohemia, with a promise of good behaviour in the future. If Ferdinand were not moved, then James would simply call in his promise from Spain. If Spain refused . . . well, then and only then he would have to abandon hopes of an alliance with Spain and resort to force. 'I am a King who loves peace,' he declared. 'I do not delight in shedding blood and therefore I strain every nerve to avert it if possible. But if notwithstanding my great dexterity and his promises, the King of Spain will not do his duty and fulfil them, I shall then have every reason and justice to take up arms against him and his, hoping with God's help, in so righteous a cause, to make him repent of having roused a pacific lion.'[59]

In May 1621, Sir John Digby was despatched to the Emperor in

Vienna to present the English terms, but James had reckoned without his son-in-law. Despite his losses, Frederick had no intention of giving up the fight, and called on his Protestant brothers for help. His general Ernst von Mansfeld was driven into the Upper Palatinate, where his growing army, subsisting off the local peasantry, became a menace. Digby did manage to bring about a truce, but its impact was hardly felt: Maximilian invaded the Upper Palatinate from Bavaria, driving Mansfeld towards the Rhine; at the same time, the Spanish forces gained the upper hand in the Lower Palatinate. Finally, military preparations began in England. Parliament, which had been prorogued until the following February, was called into session on 20 November. Money was forwarded to Frederick, along with pleas that he should renounce his claims to the Bohemian throne, while heading his own troops in the Palatinate. And then, suddenly, the momentum was broken. Before Parliament opened, James left London with Buckingham for Royston then Newmarket, where the Villiers ladies were in attendance, and did not return.

D.H. Willson writes of James's 'criminal folly': 'His absence from London was sheer indulgence, proof that he had sunk lower in his love of ease, of Buckingham, and of Bacchus.'[60] But it might have been a canny strategy to focus Parliament's minds on raising the finance to support Frederick's troops: with James so publicly absent, the usual parading of grievances would have little impact. Fired by some passionate anti-Spanish and anti-Catholic rhetoric, Parliament voted one subsidy to aid the Palatinate, and framed a petition asking for the enforcement of existing anti-Catholic laws and urging that Charles should be found a Protestant wife. James was furious – 'God give me patience' – and refused to receive the petition. He wrote angrily to the Speaker of the House, protesting that his absence had given some fiery and popular spirits the boldness to debate matters that were far beyond their reach and capacity, matters moreover, 'tending to our high dishonour and breach of prerogative royal'. He commanded that in future no member of Parliament should meddle with his government nor the *arcana imperii*, nor 'deal with our dearest son's match with the daughter of Spain, nor touch the honour of that King'. 'We think ourselves very free and able to punish any man's misdemeanours in Parliament,' he warned, 'as well during their sitting as after; which we mean not to spare henceforth.' Gondomar was outraged. He wrote to the King threatening to leave England if James did not give him an assurance that the Commons would be punished; if they were not, then James had ceased to be King.

But the Commons were not to be easily quashed. Twelve MPs brought a second, slightly gentler petition to Newmarket, asking the King to ignore misreporting of their debates, to receive their first petition and to confirm their privileges. In a display of kingly condescension, James was Grace incarnate, calling for stools for the MPs to sit on, and assuring them that he, of all kings, was the freest from trusting to idle reports. 'We,' after all, 'are an old and experienced King, needing no such lessons'. The Commons, however, had usurped his prerogative, no matter that they claimed they hadn't meant to. How could they presume to discuss the Prince's marriage without committing high treason: indeed, 'What have you left unattempted in the highest point of sovereignty in that petition of yours?' He could not permit the Commons to call their privilege an undoubted, inherited right. As long as they kept within the limits of their duty, then he would protect their lawful liberties; but if they trenched upon his prerogative then he – or any king – would reduce the privilege of those who dared pluck the flowers of his Crown. The MPs immediately drew up a protestation. They would stop quarrelling, they guaranteed, but a statement of rights had to be set down. The Commons' privileges *were* their ancient and undoubted birthright and inheritance, they insisted; the weightest matters of state should be debated in Parliament, and every MP had the freedom of speech and the freedom from arrest.

Christmas arrived, and the Commons retired for the festivities. James was in a quandary. All his instincts told him to dissolve Parliament: 'The plain truth is we cannot with patience endure our subjects to use such anti-monarchical words to us concerning their liberties, except they had subjoined that they were granted unto them by the grace and favour of our predecessors.' But if he dissolved Parliament, then he would lose the money. Gondomar, meanwhile, was urging him that, while Parliament was in session, negotiations with Spain were impossible; if James was to be secure on his throne, Parliament must be dissolved. Gondomar had Buckingham's support here: Tillières complained that the Marquis scarcely acted as if he were English. In the final days of 1621, James came to a decision. He came to the Council chamber and demanded that the Clerk of Parliament produce the Commons' Journal Book, in which the protestation had been recorded. He was offended with the protestation, he announced to the Council. It had ignored his repeated declarations that he wished to preserve all the Commons' liberties. It had been written just as he was receiving a deputation with them – and, moreover, agreeing to their adjournment. It had been voted on at six o'clock at night, when only a third of members were in the House. It contained words that invaded most of the prerogatives of the Crown. There was only one thing to be done: 'His Majesty erased it from the Journal Book with his own hand, and ordered an Act of Council to be entered thereof.'[61]

James kept the Parliament 'full ten days in suspense', and then suddenly dissolved it by proclamation, making a speedy escape to Theobalds, 'not intending, as the speech is, to return till towards Easter'. Gondomar applauded him, saying that the dissolution of Parliament was the best thing that had happened in the last century. But James's troubles were not over. After dining at Theobalds, he decided to go out riding, and his horse stumbled in a ditch, throwing the King into the New River, 'where the ice brake; he fell in so that nothing but his boots were seen'. Sir Richard Young went into the water to pull him out, and 'there came much water out of his mouth and body'. The King was strong enough to ride back to Theobalds and a warm bed.[62] Despite the gravity of the incident – 'if he had not been rescued promptly he would have drowned' – some listeners found it amusing. The French ambassador Tillières joked that the only ill effect of his immersion was that it had 'put much water into his wine'.[63]

Soon afterwards, James was back with the hunting crew at Newmarket, and more especially with Buckingham. Many believed that Buckingham's show of love for the King was far from altruistic. His enemies pointed angrily to the inexorable social and financial rise of Buckingham's relatives, especially his mother and his brothers, one of whom was openly spoken of as insane. Once again, James found himself the target of libels. Now he was cast as Jove, King of the

Gods, with Buckingham as his young lover Ganymede, 'his white-faced boy'.[64] Buckingham was parodied as the King's false idol:

> Come, offer up your daughters and fair wives,
>   No trental nor no dirge
> Will open good King James his eyes,
>   But sacrifice to St George.[65]

But the relationship between King and favourite seemed almost to be strengthened by adverse public opinion. In 1620, James had arranged a fine marriage for Buckingham, to Lady Catherine Manners, the only daughter of the Earl of Rutland. James absorbed 'Kate' into his family vision: 'My only sweet and dear child, Thy dear dad sends thee his blessing this morning, and also to his daughter. The Lord of Heaven send you a sweet and blithe wakening, all kind of comfort in your sanctified bed, and bless the fruits thereof, that I may have sweet bedchamber boys to play me with.'[66] When the marriage did indeed bear fruit, James revelled in playing with the children – a remarkable change of heart, it was observed, for a man who had shown no real affection for his own offspring in their infancy. As even the satirists had to admit, albeit with sarcasm, it was a happy family:

> Heaven bless King James our joy,
>   And Charles his baby
> Great George our brave viceroy,
>   And his fair lady.[67]

Compared to the passion and violence of James's relations with Somerset, his love for Buckingham was a gentle, fulfilling thing indeed.

CHAPTER NINETEEN

Of Jack, and Tom

B Y 1622, JAMES had been negotiating with Spain for eight years to win Charles his bride. Now he had to balance his desire to see the Infanta married to his son with the popular English call for aid to the Palatinate, but how? Philip III had died in 1620, to be succeeded by his son, the young Philip IV. Through the year, negotiations continued as usual, constantly crippled by rumours and false starts. The Infanta was about to be handed over, it was said; Lord Admiral Buckingham was raising funds to build a suitably grand fleet to go and collect her the next spring, accompanied by the Prince of Wales. In October, Endymion Porter, a Buckingham protégé and Groom of the Bedchamber to Charles, was sent to Spain to push affairs along. But the impatient bridegroom had other ideas. When Porter returned from Spain in December, Charles stepped up his campaign, demanding that Secretary of State Sir George Calvert, accelerate negotiations with Spain and the Pope. He pestered James's current ambassador in Madrid, Sir John Digby, now Earl of Bristol, as to when it would be acceptable to start sending love letters; he took up Spanish lessons, a nice touch to put his new bride at her ease when she arrived in England. But the language classes had a more immediate purpose, as he had confided to Gondomar as early as May of 1622: once the Spanish ambassador returned to Spain, he should send instructions for Charles to go and place himself in the hands of King Philip, and Charles would make the trip to Madrid 'incognito and only accompanied by two servants'.[1]

Charles later declared that 'that heroic thought started out of his own brain, to visit the court of Madrid'.[2] At some point, the Prince confided in Buckingham, winning his support and, according to their own later testimonies, Buckingham and Charles together then persuaded James to agree: the Prince 'being of fit age and ripeness for marriage', recalled James, 'urged me to know the certainty in a matter of so great weight'. James's response was to insist on a travelling companion: 'I only sent the man whom I most trusted,

Buckingham, commanding him never to leave him nor to return home without him.'[3] But then the King got cold feet, and called in to give his advice Sir Francis Cottington, Charles's own secretary, and a previous ambassador to Spain. When Cottington argued against the plan, James reportedly 'threw himself upon his bed', crying 'I told you this before', lamenting passionately 'that he was undone, and should lose Baby Charles'. Buckingham then attacked Cottington 'with all possible bitterness of words' and berated the King, saying that if he did not allow Charles to go nobody could accept his word on anything: 'It would be such a disobligation upon the Prince, who had set his heart now upon the journey after his Majesty's approbation, that he could never forget it, nor forgive any man who had been the cause of it.'[4]

Buckingham's vehement support won the day for the Prince, and the plan was put into commission in February 1623. On Monday 17th, Charles and Buckingham were with James at Theobalds. That day, the King departed for Royston, but Charles and Buckingham headed instead for Buckingham's estate at New Hall. As they took their parting from the King, James said he expected them to 'be with me upon Friday night'. 'Sir,' replied Buckingham, 'if we should stay a day or two longer I hope your Majesty would pardon us.' 'Well, well,' replied James. The little exchange was for the benefit of onlookers, because the King was well aware of their plans. After a night at New Hall, Charles and Buckingham rode to Gravesend calling themselves Thomas and John, or Tom and Jack Smith, accompanied only by Buckingham's Gentleman of the Horse, Richard Greames.[5]

Despite his reservations, and his very real concern for the wellbeing of his son and favourite, James could not help but be struck by the romance of the plot. In his many letters written and sent during the time of the escapade, Charles and Buckingham became 'My sweet boys and dear venturous knights, worthy to be put in a new romance.'[6] He was even struck with the Muse long enough to pen an eight-stanza poem entitled 'Of Jack, and Tom' that saw the quest for the Infanta as an echo of his grandfather's and his own advances to French and Danish princesses:

Love is a world of many Spains,
Where coldest hills, and hottest plains
With barren rocks, and fertile fields,
By turn despair, and comfort yields.
 But who can doubt of prosperous luck
 Where love, and fortune, doth conduct?
Thy grandsire great, thy father too
Were thine examples, this to do;
Whose brave attempts, in heat of love,
Both France and Denmark, did approve.
 So Jack and Tom do nothing new
 When love and fortune they pursue.
Kind shepherds, that have loved them long
Be not so rash, in censuring wrong
Correct your fears, leave off to mourn,
The heavens will favour their return.
 Remit the care, to royal Pan
 Of Jack his son, and Tom, his man.[7]

But as chivalric heroes, Tom and Jack were almost farcically inept. Their choice of supposed disguise, 'fair riding coats and false beards' immediately 'gave suspicion they were no such manner of men'. While they were crossing the Thames at Gravesend, one of their beards fell off, and, to make matters worse, they used a gold piece to pay the ferryman who within minutes had raised the town officers, forcing them to escape by some energetic riding. Their bad luck continued. Near Rochester, they bumped into the train of the ambassador of the Holy Roman Emperor, finishing its long journey to London — and, to avoid it, leapt over a hedge into the fields. Sir Lewis Lewkener, in attendance on the ambassador, took the two 'for suspicious persons' and sent word to the Mayor of Canterbury. They managed to evade capture at Rochester, but a horseman was despatched to follow them, and overtook them near Sittingbourne. By the time they reached Canterbury, the Mayor was waiting for these two antic men, and Buckingham was forced to reveal his identity, and claim that he was paying a secret visit to the fleet in his capacity as Lord Admiral before they were allowed to proceed. Even at Dover they were stopped again until they gave 'some secret satisfaction'. In Dover, Endymion Porter, Sir Francis Cottington, James Leviston (one of the Prince's Bedchamber) and a Scot named Kirk joined them, and they set sail for Dieppe on Wednesday morning.[8]

The same day, news of their flight broke, and was soon, according to John Chamberlain, 'in every man's mouth, but few believed it at first, because they could not apprehend the reasons of so strange a resolution as being a mystery of state beyond common capacities'. On Thursday, James wrote to the Privy Council explaining that he had not told them because 'secrecy was the life of the business'. It was 'the Prince's own desire', he continued, and Buckingham 'had no hand in it but only by his [the King's] commandment'. 'The world talks somewhat freely,' reported Chamberlain, 'as if it were done', that the Prince was planning to be married at a Catholic Mass in Madrid, to avoid the trouble it would cause at home. Whatever the cause, Chamberlain concluded, 'all concur that it is a very costly and hazardous experiment'.[9]

Although James was undoubtedly privy to the planning of the posting to Spain, it is less certain to what extent Buckingham and Charles involved him from the moment they left France. It seems that they did not write to him until they had passed the border into Spain, so presumably James was dependent on the same news networks that informed the likes of John Chamberlain, who marvelled that messengers between Madrid and London 'go up and down like a well with two buckets'. Yet even Chamberlain admitted on 8 March that 'we have little certainty of the Prince's journey'. On the Sunday after their flight, St Paul's Cross had been packed, in expectation of news during the sermon, but the preacher merely prayed 'for the Prince's prosperous journey and safe return'. After landing on French soil on Wednesday, Charles and Buckingham arrived in Paris on Friday, and left again on Sunday: some had it that in Paris 'they saw the King at supper, and the Queen practising a ball with divers other ladies', but others pointed out that this was unlikely on the first Saturday in Lent. Word had it that they had been stopped again, or had passed Bayonne, or that Gondomar and Digby were waiting for them at the border. Now, others were planning to join them, following a list left by the Prince, with the addition (by James) of physician Dr John Craig, and two chaplains, Leonard Mawe and Matthew Wren 'that were forgotten'.[10]

The sweet boys' letters home to Dad were determinedly upbeat. Crossing the border into Spain, they met Walsingham Gresley, bearing the post from James's ambassador Digby to London, and 'saucily opened' the letters directed to King James, discovering 'your business so slowly advanced, that we think ourselves happy that we have begun it so soon'; it appeared that no marriage articles had been concluded, since the negotiators were waiting until a papal dispensation arrived, 'which may be God knows when'.[11] This lack of progress, neatly if tacitly ascribed to Digby, would make their unexpected arrival all the more welcome. Arriving in Madrid, Buckingham made sure James knew 'how we like your daughter, his wife, and my lady mistress', that is, the Infanta, 'without flattery, I think there is not a sweeter creature in the world. Baby Charles himself is so touched at the heart, that he confesses all he ever yet saw, is nothing to her, and swears if that he want her, there shall be blows. I shall lose no time in hastening their conjunction.' He also vouched for the 'kind carefulness' shown by his opposite number, King Philip's chief counsellor the Condé de Olivares, towards Charles.[12]

They had hoped to keep secret Charles's presence in Madrid, but they were soon forced to change plans; Buckingham knew that with so many posts 'making such haste after us', Charles could not be kept hidden. In Buckingham's narrative, their reception in Madrid was remarkably smooth. He sent for Gondomar, who went to Olivares, who obtained for Buckingham a private audience with the King; Olivares properly insisted on saluting the Prince in Philip's name. The next day, sitting in 'an invisible coach', they were treated to 'a private visit of the King, the Queen, the Infanta, Don Carlos, and the Cardinal' as they passed by three times. Then Olivares came into their coach and took them to their lodgings, telling them that King Philip 'longed and died for want of a nearer sight of our wooer'. Olivares and Buckingham encountered Philip 'walking in the streets, with his cloak thrown over his face, and a sword and buckler by his side'; the King leapt into their coach, and was brought to meet Charles; 'much kindness and compliment' passed between the two young men. 'You may judge by this,' Buckingham assured James, 'how sensible this King is of your son's journey; and if we can either judge by outward shows, or general speeches, we have reason to condemn your ambassadors for rather writing too sparingly than too much.' He urged James to write 'the kindest letter of thanks and acknowledgment you can' to Olivares, and concluded by quoting Olivares's latest come-on: 'he said no later unto us than this morning, that if the Pope would not give a dispensation for a wife, they would give the Infanta to thy son's Baby, as his wench.' While the Spaniards were open, the Pope's nuncio 'works as maliciously, and as actively as he can against us, but receives such rude answers, that he hopes he will be soon weary on't'. Charles and Buckingham inferred from this that the Pope was unlikely to grant a dispensation, and therefore asked for James's directions as to 'how far we may engage you in the acknowledgement of the Pope's spiritual power, for we almost find, if you will be contented to acknowledge the Pope, chief head under Christ, that the match will be made without him'.[13]

This negative account of the papal nuncio was squeezed into the last paragraph of the letter, but James was not fooled, and singled out Buckingham's 'cooling card' concerning 'the nuncio's averseness to this business' for special attention. It was for this very reason that he had sent two of Charles's chaplains 'fittest for this purpose', Leonard Mawe and Matthew Wren. He had, he wrote, fully instructed the clerics so that their 'behaviour and service' should at once conform to the 'purity of the primitive [Anglican] church' while getting 'as near the Roman form as can lawfully be done, for it hath ever been my way to go with the Church of Rome *usque ad aras*', literally, even unto the altars.[14] But in truth James had very firm ideas about just how far he would go. He reminded Buckingham that Spain had never raised the possibility that the dispensation would not be granted; that Spain had set down the spiritual conditions, which he had then signed, and Spain had sent them to Rome, where the *consulto* opined that 'the Pope might, nay ought, for the weal of Christendom grant a dispensation upon these conditions'. But, he continued, 'I know not what ye mean by my acknowledging the Pope's spiritual supremacy. I am sure ye would not have me to renounce my religion for all the world. But all I can guess at your meaning is that it may be ye have an allusion to a passage in my book against Bellarmine' (his 1609 *Monitory-Preface*) 'where I offer, if the Pope would quit his godhead and usurping over kings, to acknowledge him for the chief bishop, to whom all appeals of churchmen ought to lie *en dernier resort*'. In case Buckingham and Charles did not have his complete works to hand, he enclosed a copy of 'the very words'. That, he concluded, 'is the furthest that my conscience will permit me to go upon this point; for I am not a monsieur who can shift his religion as easily as he can shift his shirt when he cometh from tennis' – a sly dig at the once Huguenot, then Catholic Henri IV of France.[15] Charles and Buckingham hurriedly wrote to James 'to assure you, that neither in spiritual nor temporal things, there is any thing pressed upon us more than is already agreed upon'. Although the Spanish had tried to capitalise on their friendly relations, the Englishmen had outmanoeuvred them with 'many forcible arguments'. The Spanish were also, they revealed, 'in hope of a conversion of us both, but now excuses are more studied than reasons for it, though the⌊y⌋ say their loves shall ever make them wish it. To conclude: we never saw the business in a better way than now it is. Therefore we humbly beseech you, lose no time in hastening the ships . . .'[16]

Buckingham's confident assertion that the Spaniards realised that their conversion to the Roman Catholic faith was unlikely to happen was completely disingenuous. Even as he wrote the letter, he and Charles were under immense pressure to consider the possibility, and during Holy Week in April Buckingham agreed to a discussion with Father Francisco de Jesus at the monastery of San Geronimo. Later in the month, Charles submitted to a similar session with Philip IV's confessor, and was apparently shaken by his arguments for papal supremacy – much to Buckingham's annoyance: the Marquis was seen to leave, and go 'down to a place where he could be alone, in order to show his extreme indignation, going so far as to pull off his hat and to trample it under feet'. Buckingham forbade any future sessions.[17]

On 27 April, the Prince and the favourite reported that the papal dispensation had arrived 'clogged' with conditions that were forwarded for James to consider; the boys urged the King to comfort himself with the thought that it 'will not be long before we get forth of this labyrinth, wherein we have been entangled these many years'. Assuring him they would 'yield to nothing', they begged James to keep the conditions secret: 'if you should not keep them so, it will beget disputes, censures, and conclusions there to our prejudice.'[18] But it became clear that they could not afford to wait for James's authority to clear every little detail, and Charles asked his father for a formal written commitment to support whatever Charles agreed to in his name. 'I confess that this is an ample trust that I desire,' wrote the Prince, 'and if it were not mere necessity I should not be so bold. Yet I hope your Majesty shall never repent you of any trust ye put upon your Majesty's humble and obedient son and servant.' On 11 May, James forwarded his commitment: 'I now send you, my baby, here enclosed the power you desire. It were a strange trust that I would refuse to put upon my only son and upon my best servant. I know such two as ye are will never promise in my name but what may stand with my conscience, honour, and safety, and all these I do fully trust with any one of you two.'[19] As if to prove his trust, on 18 May James made Buckingham a Duke, raising him above all other English peers except the Duke of Lennox, who was now also created Duke of Richmond.[20]

As one problem was solved, another appeared. Now it transpired that the dispensation could not be delivered until Philip had sworn an oath that James and Charles would carry out the new conditions of the marriage treaty. The 'conditions' turned out to be a demand that James, subsequently endorsed by the Privy Council and Parliament, would allow English Catholics to worship freely and openly, and that the Spaniards would continue their attempts at conversion – in support of which the Pope wrote himself to James, arguing that even the fact of these current marriage negotiations was the silent word of the Holy Spirit telling him that he was right to embrace his mother's faith.[21] The result was another round of talks in early May to thrash out the new amendments, and especially the matter of allowing English Catholics to worship freely. Worship was one thing – Charles quite promptly gave his father's word that laws against recusants would be suspended and their repeal put before Parliament – but free worship was quite another. James would tolerate private Roman worship in the worshippers' own houses, and even secret worship at the Infanta's chapel, but he would never agree to the public toleration of open worship at the chapel.[22]

The Spanish were split on the issue. The Council of State was quite willing to allow the marriage to proceed, even without any assurance from James. But Philip's theological advisers, along with Olivares, demanded proof of sincere change on the part of the English King before any marriage could take place – and Olivares had no realistic expectation that the change could or would take place. From a good start, relations deteriorated between Olivares and Buckingham, as the latter believed that it was his opposite number who was blocking the process.[23] It could be argued that Buckingham was scarcely more cooperative: when the papal nuncio informed the Duke that he could not look beyond his orders from Rome, Buckingham retorted 'I assure you that if this marriage is not concluded, what little remains of Catholicism in that kingdom [England] will be utterly rooted out, and they will proceed against the Catholics with the utmost rigour.'[24] To Buckingham's eyes, the only way to negotiate in future was, he declared, with a sword drawn over the heads of the papists.[25] At the same time, Charles, though still enamoured of the Infanta, was having second thoughts. His conscience was piqued by the plight of his sister Elizabeth, who was said to be 'in a pitiful case, almost distracted' at news of the possibility of her brother marrying the Infanta. In early May, Charles sent word to Elizabeth that he would not consent to marry without first obtaining her permission. In Madrid, he tried to bring the Palatinate question into the negotiations, but Philip refused to consider the question until after the marriage – once that were done, Frederick 'should be restored to all without any treaty – to lands, honours, and dignities'.[26]

Still the negotiations continued. According to Olivares, Charles had two options. Either he could send an agent to the Pope asking him to modify the articles, or send a messenger to James pleading with him to agree to the Pope's terms. Neither appealed to Charles. Buckling under the Duke's persuasions, he announced that he would go home, and fixed 13 May as his departure date. Buckingham told Father Francisco de Jesus that the Prince was experiencing a 'great sinking at the heart' at this unhappy conclusion, and that they were 'much dissatisfied at having to go away after . . . failing to obtain that which they had hitherto looked forward to as sure and certain'. Although Buckingham insisted that he and the Prince 'wished that there might be no change in the friendship between them' he was clearly angry. Francisco recorded that the Duke 'looked upon all plain dealing as an injury to himself'. But negotiations were not at an end. Gondomar rushed to beg Charles on Philip's behalf 'to be so good as to refrain from taking any resolution in opposition to the plans which had been proposed'. Charles reluctantly agreed, and a secret messenger was sent to inform James of the latest complications. (Charles changed his mind a few days later, and sent Cottington to ask Olivares if he might be discharged from his promise to stay, but Philip refused.)[27]

While in Spanish eyes Buckingham was a resented obstacle, to many Englishmen that position was utterly laudable. Sir Henry Rich, Viscount Kensington, praised Buckingham as 'so brave, so judicious and religious as not only his master has reason to put honour upon him, but also our nation hath cause to reverence and admire him, so careful hath he been to serve, and nobly to serve, his King and country with offices of a true and religious heart, giving way to nothing but what wisdom and honour directs him'. The Duke's stand had lost him favour at the Spanish court precisely because 'those great and powerful persons here . . . would have pressed unfit and unlooked-for conditions upon us'. Sir George Goring declared that Buckingham had given 'such proof of his courage, judgement, religion and true English heart, with such resolution of stability in all these, as the like, I believe, were never met with in any one person'.[28] Capitalising on Buckingham's dislike of James's resident ambassador Bristol, whom he considered dangerously 'hispaniolized', they suggested that the Duke return to England, and leave the resident ambassador to negotiate; that manoeuvre was effectively countered by James, who sent a message saying that Bristol should leave all negotiation to Buckingham.[29] But by June, Buckingham's intransigence had begun to annoy even Charles. According to the Venetian ambassador in Madrid, the Prince 'blamed the Duke for harshness in his methods', and Buckingham was forced to soften his tone and allow Bristol back into the negotiations. Charles, it was rumoured, was growing increasingly dissatisfied by what he perceived as Buckingham's lack of respect for him.[30]

Cottington was despatched back to England with the unwelcome news that negotiations were at an impasse, and that the 'sweet boys' would not be coming home soon. James received the news on 14 June at Greenwich; for the first time, his emotions overflowed: 'Your letter by Cottington hath strucken me dead. I fear it shall very much shorten my days.' How could he satisfy 'the people's expection here'? How would he explain to the Privy Council that the fleet, already delayed a fortnight by ill winds, now had to be held back longer. As for 'advice and directions', he was clear: if 'they will not alter their decree it is, in a word, to come speedily away if ye can get leave, and give over all treaty' whatever is offered. If not,

> ye never look to see your old dad again, whom I fear ye shall never
> see, if ye see him not before winter. Alas, I now repent me sore
> that ever I suffered you to go away. I care for match nor nothing,
> so I may once have you in my arms again. God grant it! God grant
> it! God grant it! Amen, amen, amen. I protest ye shall be as heartily
> welcome as if ye had done all things ye went for, so that I may
> once have you in my arms again. And so God bless you both, my
> only sweet son and my only best sweet servant, and let me hear
> from you quickly with all speed, as ye love my life. And so God
> send you a happy and joyful meeting in the arms of your dear
> dad.[31]

Realising that the Spanish theologians would not be budged and that they had nothing to lose, Buckingham drew up a long letter to Philip, putting Charles's case in the strongest terms. The marriage must take place soon, he urged. Just by coming to Spain, Charles had made himself vulnerable; now there was the possibility that if he were to depart, and 'leave his wife behind him in pawn', his honour would be impugned. The whole affair was a question of trust, and should be resolved through friendship rather than bonds and 'securities'. Matters had progressed so far that, if Philip insisted on postponing the marriage in this way, Charles would have no alternative but to believe there must exist 'some disesteem of his person'.[32] But the theologians remained adamant. The consummation of the marriage could not happen a single day sooner.

Charles could finally see the writing on the wall. The Spanish clearly intended to stall for as long as possible, and in the meantime he was trapped in Madrid. In late June, he wrote secretly to his father asking for his permission 'to depart from Madrid as secretly as he came thither', if Philip refused to give him formal permission to leave. And if this plan didn't work, he urged James to turn his attention elsewhere: 'reflect . . . upon the good of his sister and the safety of his own kingdoms.'[33] James was only too happy to provide the permission. At the same time, Buckingham played his last hand with Olivares. Leaking to him a draft of a declaration Charles was supposedly about to make to Philip, Buckingham let Olivares know that it contained a complaint against Olivares, who had originally assured Charles that, if the Pope were not willing to give the Infanta as a wife, Philip would give her to him as a mistress. Now, however, Olivares had changed his mind, and risked 'the breach of the business of most consequence in Christendom'. Olivares came back promptly with new, final terms from the King: Charles and the Infanta would be betrothed as soon as news was received that James had sworn to accept the amended articles. A formal marriage ceremony would then take place at Christmas, and the Infanta would sail to England when weather permitted the following spring.[34]

The terms were still unappealing, but Charles agreed to them. It seemed that the negotiations were done. For four nights, Madrid celebrated, and Buckingham wrote to Lord Treasurer Middlesex on 8 July that 'our business here is at an end, all points concluded'.[35] In London, on 20 July, James and the Privy Council formally swore to the articles of the marriage treaty, although, according to Simonds D'Ewes, hearing the unfavourable terms caused the King to start shaking.[36] In the month between Charles's agreement, and news of James's swearing reaching Madrid, Buckingham continued to barter around the terms, suggesting that Charles would stay until September if the Infanta then accompanied him back to England; Philip suggested that if Charles stayed until Christmas, the marriage could be consummated before he left. But the theologians blocked each suggestion, and Buckingham fixed on 29 August as a departure date, urging James to send them 'preemptory commands to come away, and with all possible speed', just in case they had need of it, and Charles might then 'press his coming away, under the colour of your command, without appearing an ill lover'.[37]

There was to be one final red herring. On 12 August, Olivares brought another scenario to the Council of State, proposing that the son of the ex-Elector Frederick (James's grandson) should marry the Emperor's daughter, and be raised a Catholic in the imperial court at Vienna. When the Duke of Bavaria died, he could become Elector Palatine, thus restoring title and lands to his father's family. James, thought Olivares, would be in favour of this, since he would understand the advantages of having Catholic rather than Puritan grandchildren. But Olivares miscalculated. James refused to have any grandchild raised as a Catholic, and insisted that some restoration, albeit token, should be made now to Frederick. Charles took up his brother-in-law's cause with Olivares, urging first the restoration of the Palatinate, which Olivares refused, and then an assurance that – as had been promised to Bristol – Spain would allow its troops to join with English soldiers to clear the Palatinate and restore it. When Olivares made it clear that Spain would under no circumstances agree to bear arms against any Hapsburg, Charles became angry. He later claimed to have told the Spanish minister that 'if you hold yourself to that, there is an end of all; for without this you may not rely upon either marriage or friendship'.[38] This outburst may well be an invention of hindsight, however, since Charles appears to have spent most of August still furthering his marriage plans. On one occasion he was said to have leapt over a garden wall the better to see his Infanta; and the Venetian ambassador wrote of how the Prince 'longingly expecteth the nuptial day when the business so long in treaty is to be consummated in the bed'.[39]

It was time to go. Now their departure was delayed only by Buckingham's illness, a fever which had left him weak and unable to walk. To James, though, he maintained his good spirits: 'Sir, my heart and very soul dances for joy, for the change will be no less than to leap from trouble to ease, from sadness to mirth – nay, from hell to heaven.'[40] On 28 August 1623, first Charles and Philip, and then their chief ministers, swore solemnly that they would see through the articles of the marriage treaty. Buckingham swore a particular oath that he would refrain from executing any law against an English Roman Catholic. Charles put his signature to a document authorising his marriage by proxy when the papal dispensation arrived, an arrangement that would expire at Christmas. And then, after the ritual exchange of gifts, the Prince and the favourite finally started on their journey home, travelling from Madrid to the Escorial palace, and then on via Segovia to Santander. One final piece of business occurred on this journey. Charles sent Buckingham's man Edward Clerke back to Madrid, ordering him to stay in Bristol's household until the papal dispensation arrived. At that moment, he would produce an undated letter from Charles instructing Bristol not to proceed with the proxy marriage until another condition was met: a promise that the Infanta would not carry out her oft-mentioned threat to go into a convent. While not rescinding his oath, it would buy time, and perhaps allow negotiations about the Palatinate to reopen (en route, Charles and Buckingham had met Elizabeth's envoy Sir Francis Nethersole, carrying her plea not to conclude the marriage without new assurances about the future of the Palatinate).[41]

Sailing from Santander, the English party reached Plymouth harbour on 5 October. Charles, Buckingham and a small party rode to London, attempting to disguise their identities, but once again blowing their cover by paying a tavern bill in Spanish coin.[42] Reaching London early on the 6th, they found that the celebrations had already started: 355 bonfires, fireworks, and the roof of St Paul's decorated with torches, one for each year of the Prince's life. Leaving York House later in the day to ride to his father at Royston, Charles had to drive his coach up Charing Cross Road rather than through the City because the streets were blocked by bonfires that 'seemed to turn the City into one flame'.[43] John Chamberlain wrote: 'I have not heard of more demonstrations of public joy than were here and everywhere from the highest to the lowest, such spreading of tables in the streets with all manner of provisions, setting out whole hogsheads of wine and butts of sack, but specially such numbers of bonfires both here and all along as he went, as is almost incredible . . . At Blackheath there was fourteen load of wood in one fire, and the people were so mad with excess of joy that if they met with any cart loaden with wood they would take out the horses and set cart and all on fire.' Condemned prisoners on the way to the gallows at Tyburn were reprieved; and in a solemn service at St Paul's, Psalm 114 became 'a new anthem': 'when Israel came out of Egypt, and the house of Jacob from among the barbarous people.'[44]

Later that day, Charles and Buckingham reached Royston. As they went up the steps to the King, he was already on his way down; 'the sweet boys fell to their knees, James fell on their necks and they all wept'.[45]

CHAPTER TWENTY

Solomon Slept

FOR A WHILE it seemed to be business as usual: 'The Prince and my Lord of Buckingham spend most of their hours with his Majesty, with the same freedom, liberty and kindness as they were wont.'[1] But the signs of dissent soon became evident to court observers. Despite the rapturous public acclaim on his homecoming, Charles was mortified by his failure to bring home the Infanta, and, encouraged by Buckingham, was easily won to the idea that the only honourable course was to go to war against Spain. James, pathologically opposed to war, declared himself convinced, despite all evidence to the contrary, that the Spanish might be trusted. He continued to carry on negotiations with Philip, and during October and November 1623, a succession of not altogether consistent instructions reached an increasingly bewildered Earl of Bristol in Madrid, as James attempted yet again to win assurances about the Palatinate. But then in early November, James fell ill again with gout and retired to Royston and Theobalds, attended by Buckingham. This had happened countless times before, and customarily government business slowed to a trickle until the King's attention could be gained again. But his experiences in Madrid had given the Prince of Wales a new resolve, and commentators soon observed that in his father's absence Charles was 'entering into command of affairs . . . and all men address themselves unto him'.[2]

The Prince's new confidence extended to relations with his father. In late November Charles finally told James in no uncertain terms that the Spaniards had deceived him, and would continue to deceive him if he allowed it. In the account of the Elector Frederick's ambassador Johan van Rusdorf, James, with tears in his eyes, asked his son, 'Do you want me to go to war, in my twilight years, and force me to break with Spain?'[3] It spelled the end of many cherished dreams for the self-styled Peacemaker. Bowing to insistent pressure from Charles and Buckingham he recalled Bristol from Madrid. Charles and Buckingham knew that the next step to forward their war policy was to turn to Parliament. The Commons had shown their zeal for military intervention in the Parliament of 1621, and now the momentum of the glorious return from Spain should guarantee that their policy would be carried. James raged and called them fools, but they, and he, now realised that he could have little effect on their actions. On 28 December James agreed with great reluctance to call a Parliament. Together, the Prince and the Duke launched a campaign to ensure their success, exploiting their influence to select sympathetic MPs to fill the Commons, and giving lurid accounts of their time in Spain.

As he waited for Parliament to open, James received surprising new proposals via Spain's ambassador the Marquis de Inojosa, offering to send the Infanta in March and to return the Lower Palatinate by August 1624 and agreeing to all James's demands concerning military cooperation. Charles and Buckingham were momentarily winded by this unexpected move, but managed to interpret it as a response to their hardline approach, and continued to press ahead with their campaign. They had serious opposition: the Venetian ambassador reported home in cipher that he was afraid that 'these two young men, without good advisers and without supporting props, may come off badly in opposing the obstinate will of a very crafty King and the powerful arts of the most sagacious Spaniards'.[4] But Charles's new confidence was real, and at the end of January 1624 he informed his father that he would not tolerate any alliance or even agreement of friendship with Spain. James realised that for the first time Charles would not be moved, and decided not to force the issue.

Charles now chaired meetings of the Privy Council while James did as he had done so often – stayed in the country with Buckingham. 'The balance of affairs leans to the side of the Prince,' observed the Venetian ambassador; 'while Buckingham remains at Newmarket to prevent any harm, he stays here [in London] to achieve the good. Thus they both cooperate towards the same end, although with different functions, yet with a good understanding.' Buckingham watched the King 'like a sentinel' and wisely so: 'at the present moment one may say that he needs watching as closely as the Spaniards themselves, as he is as willing to be deceived as they are to deceive him. They therefore watch him with great jealousy, and as though he were in a state of siege they keep away from him those whom they consider suspect.'[5] At the end of January, the Council followed the Prince's lead, and sent the King the advice that he should break off negotiations with Spain.[6]

Diplomatic reports from this period testify to a sharp decline in James's health, both physical and mental. The Venetian ambassador wrote home that James seemed 'practically lost; he comes to various decisions and inclines to his usual negotiations; he does not care to fall in with the wishes of his son-in-law and the favourite. He now protests, now weeps, but finally gives in.' It was reported that the King had become obsessed with importing Spanish asses from the Low Countries, 'making great estimation of those asses, since he finds himself so well served with the mules to his litter'. Tillières, the French ambassador, wrote sadly that 'the King descends deeper and deeper into folly every day, sometime swearing and calling upon God, heaven and the angels, at other times weeping, then laughing, and finally pretending illness in order to play upon the pity of those who urge him to generous actions and to show them that sickness renders him incapable of deciding anything, demanding only repose and, indeed, the tomb'.[7]

On 16 February 1624, Parliament was 'expected to have begun, the King ready to have gone, thousands of people gathered to see him, the Lords in their robes' — until news reached James of the sudden death of the Duke of Lennox, early that morning of apoplexy.[8] The opening was postponed for three days, and Lennox was buried the following day at Westminster in the Chapel of Henry VII, with Bishop Williams officiating; on 19 April he was afforded a splendid funeral, 'celebrated with great pomp, his portraiture being drawn in a chariot from Ely House . . . to Westminster'.[9] James opened Parliament on Monday 19 February with a meandering and defensive opening speech.[10] He had always tried to rule well, he claimed, and he deserved the love of his people. Now he needed the advice of his Parliament. How could the treaties with Spain be dealt with in such a way as to advance religion and the common good, and to restore the Palatinate to Frederick? He knew that there was talk that in negotiating with Spain he had sacrificed religion to political expediency, 'But, as God shall judge me, I never thought or meant it, nor ever in a word expressed anything that savoured of it.'[11] 'Never soldiers marching the deserts and dry sands of Arabia where there is no water, could more thirst in hot weather for drink, than I do now for a happy end of this our meeting. And now I hope that after the miscarriage of three Parliaments this will prove happy . . . Consider with yourselves the state of Christendom, my children and this my own kingdom. Consider of these, and upon all give me your advice . . . you that are the representative body of this kingdom . . . [be] my true glasses to show me the hearts of my people.'[12]

Five days later, in Whitehall's Banqueting House, Buckingham met with a joint meeting of Lords and Commons to give the details of the past year's relations between England and Spain, pointing up the duplicity of the Spanish at every opportunity. The Spanish ambassadors objected to James about the Duke's characterisation of their King, but Buckingham's was precisely the message the parliamentarians had been waiting to hear: he was cleared by both Houses of any blame in his dealings in Madrid. Buoyed by this account, the Commons and a small group of lords decided to petition the King to break off nego tiations with Spain. But while Buckingham was back in Westminster, James had been in contact with the Spanish ambassadors, and was being tempted back towards negotiations with Philip.[13] He seems to have attacked Buckingham, since the Duke wrote angrily to the King, complaining of the 'unfavourable interpretation I find made of a thankful and loyal heart in calling my words crude Catonic [severe] words', and the suspicion that he was prone 'to look more to the rising sun', Charles, 'than my maker', the King. James had cried off a meeting with him, giving as an excuse the 'fierce rheum and cough' he had caught while hunting that afternoon; 'notwithstanding of your cold,' Buckingham wrote bitterly, 'you were able to speak with the King of Spain's instruments, though not with your own subjects.'[14]

Buckingham rode to Theobalds on 4 March to defuse the situation. James, mollified by this display of apparent humility, agreed to receive the proposed parliamentary deputation, although he still refused to commit himself to accept their advice. On 11 March, the Commons came to the resolution that only when there was a formal assurance that all negotiations between the King and Spain had ended, would they be ready 'to assist His Majesty with both our persons and abilities in a Parliamentary course'.[15] James demanded on 14 March a specific vote of five subsidies and ten fifteenths to cover the 'great business' of the military effort, plus one subsidy and two fifteenths annually until his debts were covered – a total of some half a million pounds.[16] On hearing the King's demands, which Parliament was sure to reject, Charles and Buckingham 'turned pale', according to the Venetian ambassador, 'and the Prince never uttered a word the whole day'.[17] It was left to Buckingham to act as an intermediary between King and Parliament; he persuaded James to reword his response according to Parliament's modifications, and on 17 March informed the Houses that the King had accepted their terms, dropping his call for annual payments, and asking for six subsidies and twelve fifteenths for war expenses, some £780,000. James promised to accept Parliament's advice and to break off the treaties with Spain.[18] Parliament offered three subsidies and three fifteenths, about half of what was required; Buckingham took the draft declaration to James, who insisted on only a few amendments. A few days later, a delegation from both Houses met the King at Whitehall; there James accepted their advice to break off the treaties, but clarified that he would only be committed to war to the extent that Parliament fulfilled their promise to assist him. He expected more than the three subsidies: this would do 'at least to make a good beginning of the war' but 'when the end will be, God knows'. Conduct of war was his own affair: 'I desire you to understand, I must have a faithful and secret council of war that must not be ordered by a multitude, for so my designs might be discovered beforehand. A penny of this money shall not be bestowed but in the sight of your own committees. But whether I shall send twenty thousand or ten thousand, whether by sea or by land, east or west, by diversion or otherwise, by invasion upon the Bavarian or the Emperor – you must leave that to the King.'[19]

Buckingham's display of political *savoir faire* had come as a shock to the Spanish ambassadors in England, who had (like many others) dismissed him as a mere favourite. Now they attempted to turn James against him. In early April, they told James that he was 'a prisoner, or at leastwise besieged, so as no man could be admitted to come at him', that the Duke had made strategic alliances with 'all the popular men of the state', as part of his masterplan to assume government himself. Buckingham had 'oftentimes bragged openly in Parliament, that he had made the King yield to this and that', they continued;

Britain was 'not now governed by a monarchy, but by a triumviri, whereof Buckingham was the first and chiefest, the Prince the second, and the King the last; and that all look towards *solem orientem* [the rising sun, Charles]'. To combat this, they urged that James must show himself to be 'as he was reputed, the oldest and wisest King in Europe' by freeing himself from his captivity and danger, by 'cutting off so dangerous and ungrateful an affector of greatness and popularity as the Duke was'. According to the Spaniards, this touched a nerve with James who admitted that recently he had had 'good cause to suspect' Buckingham, and especially his influence over Prince Charles. When his son rode to Madrid, James continued, 'he was as well affected to that nation as heart could desire, and as well disposed as any son in Europe; but now he was strangely carried away with rash and youthful counsels and followed the humour of Buckingham, who had he knew not how many devils within him since that journey'.[20]

Buckingham's troubles did not all stem from the Spanish. At the same time, the court was buzzing about the news of the return from France to England of Arthur Brett, a young kinsman of Lord Treasurer Middlesex who had tried before to inveigle his way into James's affections. The Venetian ambassador saw Brett's return as part of a scheme by Middlesex to oust Buckingham,[21] and the Duke, it seems, had similar apprehensions. Middlesex, a blunt-speaking man, had had the nerve to tell the Prince in a Council meeting in 1622 that public good outweighed private feeling in the case of royal marriages, and that 'he ought to submit his private distaste therein to the general good and honour of the kingdom'. Charles had retorted sharply that the Lord Treasurer should 'judge of his merchandises, if he would, for he was no arbiter in points of honour'. Now Middlesex had emerged as perhaps the most vocal opponent of the pro-war policy. Buckingham decided that the time had come to act and on 5 April one of his protégés, Sir Miles Fleetwood, brought charges against Middlesex in the Lower House, and Middlesex was shortly after impeached on charges of financial corruption.[22]

As the case progressed, James sounded out various peers and realised that 'most did love to warm themselves in the light of the rising sun', that they supported Charles. He urged the Prince and Duke to abandon the impeachment, telling Charles 'that he should not take part with a faction in either House, but to reserve himself, that both sides might seek him; and chiefly to take heed, how he bandied to pluck down a peer of the realm by the arm of the Lower House, for the Lords were the hedge between himself and the people; and a breach made in that hedge, might in time perhaps lay himself open'.[23] When the Duke refused to abandon the impeachment, James raged at him: 'By God, Steenie, you are a fool and will shortly repent this folly and will find that in this fit of popularity you are making a rod with which you will be scourged yourself.' Charles, he declared with wonderful foresight, 'would live to have his bellyful of Parliaments, and that when he should be dead, he would have too much cause to remember how much he had contributed to the weakening of the Crown by this precedent he was now so found of.'[24] As it became clear that the Lord Treasurer would indeed sink, James called Bishop Williams to Greenwich to give his advice. Williams, who had himself been vocal in the hearings against Middlesex, was candid: 'Sir, I must deal faithfully. Your son, the Prince, is the main champion that encounters the Treasurer; whom, if you save, you foil yourself. For though matters are carried by the whole vote of Parliament, and are driven on by the Duke, yet they that walk in Westminster Hall, call this the Prince's undertaking, whom you will blast in his bud, to the opinion of all your subjects, if you suffer not your old, and perhaps innocent servant to be plucked from the sanctuary of your mercy. Necessity must excuse you from inconstancy, or cruelty.'[25] Realising that to fight for the Lord Treasurer would be to fight against his son, heir and the next King, James admitted defeat. Middlesex was found guilty by the Lords, deprived of the office of Lord Treasurer, imprisoned in the Tower, and fined £50,000.

Buckingham missed the fall of Middlesex. On the very day that the Lord Treasurer was charged in the Commons, the Duke, perhaps worn down by the constant travelling and negotiation, fell ill and had to retire to his estate at New Hall. But his enemies took advantage of even this brief absence to push further their case with the King. The current Spanish ambassador, Father Diego Lafuente (Padre Maestro), alleged to James that Buckingham had deliberately sabotaged the marriage to the Infanta as part of a deal with the Elector Frederick. Buckingham had designs to marry his daughter to Frederick's son; by keeping Charles childless, Buckingham's hypothetical grandson would one day gain the British thrones. It was a far-fetched, and presumably baseless, accusation, but it served to unnerve James.[26] A few days later Inojosa alleged further that Buckingham had been negotiating with various lords, and they had concluded that if James 'would not accommodate himself to their counsels, they would give him a house of pleasure, whither he might retire himself to his sports', and Charles would take the reins of government.[27]

This last possibility stung James – no doubt because it was horribly close to the state of affairs in which he had so long luxuriated. Leaving St James's for Windsor for the annual St George's Day Garter ceremonies, James sent Buckingham on 'a slight errand' just as he was about to join the King and Prince in their coach; Buckingham burst into tears, and asked to know what he had done to offend his master. James also wept, crying out that he was the unhappiest alive, to be forsaken by those dearest to him, before driving off to Windsor with Charles. Buckingham took to his couch at Wallingford House, refusing to see anybody until, at the insistence of Lord Keeper John Williams, he followed the King to Windsor and begged for a reconciliation, becoming as 'inseparable as his shadow'. James accepted him, but was still committed to the idea of an investigation.[28] By the time the two men returned to London on 5 May, Buckingham was still ill, and took to his bed at Wallingford House. By 10 May, it was said that his survival was uncertain, and James came to spend three hours by his bedside. As Buckingham convalesced, James sent him regular gifts of cherries, and 'the eyes, the tongue and the dowsets [testicles] of the deer he killed in Eltham Park'. When the press of suitors threatened a relapse, James placed a guard on Buckingham's lodgings, giving rise to Spanish rumours that the Duke had gone insane, as his brother had done, or that the King did not trust him.[29] But James's regained love for Buckingham seemed genuine. On his final visit to Wallingford House he had prayed on his knees alongside the Duke's bed, calling on God to cure his beloved Steenie or to give him the sickness. Nor would he now permit the Spanish ambassador into his presence: 'If I admit Maestro,' he said, 'it will kill the Duke with grief.'[30]

After a brief period of convalescence with the King in the fresh air of Greenwich, Buckingham fell ill with fever again and retired to

New Hall. James sent him and Kate gifts of 'excellent melons, pears, sugared beans', strawberries, raspberries and 'assurance of better fruit planted in your bosom than ever grew in paradise'. Their correspondence from this period is passionate: James's letters, wrote Buckingham, had 'more care than servants have of masters, than physicians have of their patients . . . Of more tenderness than fathers have of children, or more friendship than between equals; of more affection than between lovers in the best kind, man and wife.' James was 'my purveyor, my goodfellow, my physician, my make, my friend, my father, my all'.[31] But, as ever, Buckingham could not feel secure. There were rumours that James was talking to the Spanish ambassadors, and that he had met with the Earl of Bristol on his return from Madrid, and was planning to be lenient at his trial. There was also the more easily confirmed news that Middlesex was already out of gaol, and Arthur Brett was back at court.[32]

On 29 May 1624, James prorogued Parliament, promising to recall it 'towards the winter'. The session ended with another display of royal anger, as James launched into a tirade against the Commons and, more problematically, refused to give his assent to a number of bills. James had claimed that the restitution of the Palatinate was the only valid reason to declare war and insisted that this be included in the preamble to the subsidy bill. Seeing that the Commons had refused to do so, James asserted his right to 'alter it and set his marginal note upon it'.[33] On the day Parliament was prorogued, James dined, as he did frequently, with Lancelot Andrewes, now Bishop of Winchester, and Neile, Bishop of Durham, on hand to provide learned discourse. Parliament's intransigency was playing on James's mind. He asked whether or not he could take the money of his subjects without parliamentary sanction. Neile replied 'readily': 'God forbid, Sir, but you should; you are the breath of our nostrils.'

Andrewes was more equivocal. 'Sir, I have no skill to judge of Parliament.'

'No put-offs, my lord,' exclaimed the King, 'answer me presently.'

'Then, Sir,' replied Andrewes, 'I think it's lawful for you to take my brother Neile's money, for he offers it.' The bishop's rejoinder provoked laughter, but not from the King, who realised the wisdom behind the wit.[34]

Parliament had granted three subsidies, designed first to strengthen naval forces for a war which, it was assumed, would be fought at sea, and second, to provide support for the Dutch against Spain. Together the subsidies amounted to £253, 139, 12 shillings and tuppence three farthings. Charles and Buckingham ignored the figures. Over the next few months, they budgeted £720,000 for military preparations, not including the navy; £240,000 to Ernst von Mansfeld to pay for the levying of more English soldiers to fight in the Protestant cause (the last of the 1619 volunteers had recently surrendered); and another £360,000 to the King of Denmark to finance his entry into the Thirty Years' War. They envisaged leading a huge European alliance against Spain, and committed themselves recklessly, with no financial under-pinning. On only one matter did they come to an agreement with James: that Charles should pursue a marriage with Henrietta Maria, the sister of King Louis XIII of France.

These negotiations made real headway when Buckingham returned to court in mid-June. The French had caveats. They did not want to alienate Spain. They worried about the treatment of Roman Catholics in England. James had assured the Commons that no marriage treaty would include concessions to English Catholics. When France demanded a marriage settlement on a par with that negotiated with Spain, James lost interest, saying it was impossible. Buckingham disagreed, and set out to isolate James by winning over first Charles and then a new French ambassador, the Marquis d'Effiat, who arrived in late June. He certainly made a favourable impact on d'Effiat, who wrote back to Louis claiming that the Duke 'was the unchallenged ruler of England. The King . . . loved him so deeply that he let him do what he liked and saw everything through his eyes. The Prince looked on him as the sole source of his happiness and contentment. And as for the ministers, they were all Buckingham's creatures and held their places only during his good pleasure.'[35]

Buckingham had regained his confidence, and celebrated by throwing a great feast at Burley-on-the-Hill; James made a public endorsement of the Duke by accepting an invitation as guest of honour. In a last ditch attempt to undo Buckingham, Arthur Brett was persuaded that now was the moment to return to court. In July he suddenly appeared before the King while he was hunting in Waltham

Forest, grabbing hold of the King's bridle (or stirrup, in some accounts), begging to plead his case. James was reportedly 'much offended' at the intrusion, and galloped away, ordering the Earl of Warwick to forbid Brett from coming into his presence again (he was later arrested), and sending word that Middlesex should move away from the court, as his sentence required.[36]

During August, Buckingham and d'Effiat put pressure on James to submit to the terms of the marriage, and James agreed to order the suspension of all prosecutions of recusants. But then a new chief minister was appointed in France: Cardinal Richlieu. Richlieu insisted that James should sign a formal written undertaking, a demand that deeply offended the King. James despatched a harshly worded response to France, and Buckingham (who had again been ill and away from court) was forced to intercept the letter and smooth things over with d'Effiat. Observers watched the King carefully for signs of his relative goodwill to France and Spain, but many, including even the highly experienced John Chamberlain, remained mystified.[37] By the end of September 1624 James agreed to promise in writing that English Catholics would be freed from persecution. On Sunday 21 November, the French match was concluded, and Thomas Carey, 'a privado of the Prince's Bedchamber' was sent into France 'with a love letter and some rich and rare jewel' for the Princess; in London, the organ in St Paul's was played for two hours 'on their loudest pipes', followed by bells, bonfires, and 'a great peal of ordnance at the Tower'.[38] This had been very much the doing of James, Charles, Buckingham and to some extent Secretary of State Sir Edward Conway. It was reported that some other Privy Councillors had to be told what was being celebrated by the bonfires they saw in late November; the Archbishop of Canterbury quipped that there were now two Privy Councils in England, and that of the two, 'that of Newmarket was the higher'.[39]

The French ambassadors followed James to Theobalds, Royston and then to Cambridge where James received them on 10 December. James was 'so ill troubled with a universal pain in shoulders, elbows, knees and feet' that he was forced to leave the entertaining of his guests to the Prince. The articles were agreed and signed with only the King, Prince, the two ambassadors, Buckingham and Secretary

Conway in attendance, deliberately excluding the lords of the Privy Council who were also in the King's retinue; this was to reduce the number of men who knew that James and Charles had also signed a separate *ecrit particulier*, in which they gave their undertaking to free Roman Catholics from prosecution.[40]

James was increasingly frail. When he came to sign the treaty, his hand was too afflicted with arthritis, and he had to use a stamp. A planned comedy was cancelled as he felt himself too ill to attend. James took to his bed, once again leaving the entertainment of his visitors to his son, the Lord Keeper, and the Earl of Warwick, and was still there on the 18th, 'pained with the gout in his hands and arms'.[41] It may have been after this encounter that James wrote a strange letter to Buckingham, begging him to come to him quickly with his family:

Notwithstanding of your desiring me to write yesterday yet had I written in the evening, if at my coming in out of the park such a drowsiness had not comed [sic] upon me, as I was forced to sit and sleep in my chair half an hour. And yet I cannot content myself without sending you this billet, praying God that I may have a joyful and comfortable meeting with you, and that we may make at this Christenmass a new marriage, ever to be kept hereafter; for God so love me, as I desire only to live in this world for your sake, and that I had rather live banished in any part of the earth with you, than live a sorrowful widow-life without you. And so God bless you, my sweet child and wife, and grant that ye may ever be a comfort to your dear dad and husband.
My only sweet and dear child,

James R.[42]

James went to Whitehall for the holiday festivities but 'kept his chamber all this Christmas, not coming once to the chapel or to any of the plays'.[43] On Christmas Day, he heard Lancelot Andrewes preach on Psalm 2. 7, the seventeenth and last Christmas sermon by Andrewes he was to attend. Occasionally, 'in fair weather' he went out in his letter 'to see some flights at the brook'.[44] The Twelfth Night masque,

Ben Jonson's *The Fortunate Isles and their Union*, was put off until 9 January, when James attended it seated with the French and Venetian ambassadors and agents from the King of Spain and the Archduchess.[45]

Early in the New Year, he made his usual journey to his favourite haunts of Theobalds, Royston and Newmarket, this time with Charles in attendance while Buckingham remained in control in London. In late January, the Duke fell ill again. Charles forwarded a message from the King: 'he commands me to tell you [that] he is extremely sorry for your late sickness & likkwise for your delay of coming hither, but he assures himself that ye will not lose an hour of time of coming away out of that filthy town as soon as your pressing occasions will permit you, & that ye may see how mischiefs come by planets & never one single, he has commanded me to tell you, that he is as ill tormented at this time in his right elbow and knee, as he was at Cambridge, but he hopes that your coming merrily hither with the counts [i.e. the Villiers women] in your company to be his nurses will make him a whole man again.'[46] The 'pressing occasions' keeping Buckingham in London concerned the English army commanded by Mansfeld. Buckingham had wanted to land the army in France, but King Louis refused. According to Charles, James was convinced that 'this juggling proceeds from the importunity of the Jesuits and Spanish faction with that King',[47] and he was easily persuaded to follow Buckingham's suggestion to allow Mansfeld to go directly to Holland instead, and the ships set sail on 31 January. But their fate was miserable. Some men were put ashore at Walcheren, but the others were forced to sail to Gertruidenburg; there, frost made it impossible for them to land, and they were left to the mercy of a virulent infection that killed hundreds, their bloated corpses pushed overboard to pollute the beaches. When the survivors eventually landed, they starved to death. In England, the terrible news was met with public outrage – and the finger of blame was pointed not at Mansfeld, but at Buckingham.[48]

In February, news reached Paris that the papal dispensation for the marriage of Charles and Henrietta Maria had been issued, but it demanded changes to the articles signed by Louis and James. But then Buckingham heard from his friend Lord Nithsdale in the Vatican that the dispensation was 'free and unclogged' – suggesting that the French were lying to force further concessions from England. James was unsurprised. 'Where is your glorious match with France?', he demanded of Buckingham, 'and your royal frank *Monsieurs?*' Buckingham was himself disgusted at the French 'shitten mouths'. He urged James to 'roundly let the ambassador know you so much prize your honour that neither in a circumstance nor form will you make any alteration'. James needed no encourgement to follow that advice and when he met with d'Effiat (without Buckingham in attendance), despite giving in on a few details, it was France who had to climb down.[49] In mid-March Buckingham sent his coaches to Dover in preparation for his journey to Paris to bring back Charles's new bride. But his plans were to be altered.

On 28 February, at Royston, James knighted Sir Richard Bettenson of Essex — a routine occurrence, but this was to be his last knight.[50] It was at Theobalds in the early days of March 1625 that he fell ill with the 'tertian', a malaria-like fever characterised by paroxysms every two or three days. At first no one was too worried: the Countess of Bedford wrote to a friend that 'there was no more doubt of his safety than of every man's that hath an ordinary tertian ague',[51] and John Chamberlain reported that the King was in no 'manner of danger if he would suffer himself to be ordered and governed by physical rules', that is, by the rules of physicians.[52] But characteristically, James delighted in ignoring medical advice, trying instead to allay his fever by holding his hands in cold water, and drinking prodigious amounts of small beer.[53] When his fever abated temporarily, he tormented his doctors by demanding of them where they thought his ague had gone. Buckingham rushed to be by the King's bedside, but by the time of his 'seventh fit' on 16 March, they had become 'less intemperate' and Secretary Conway reported that it had 'left more clearness and cheerfulness in his looks than the former'.[54] Recovery seemed to be indicated on the 23rd as convulsions were reported to grow 'less and less',[55] but suddenly James started to deteriorate, and the convulsions became more violent. News came that another of his favourites, Hamilton, had died, and James was plunged into a depression. 'I shall never see London again', he realised.[56]

Buckingham was at his King's bedside throughout. A week into the illness, the Duke and his mother remembered that, during a recent illness, Buckingham had been relieved by the remedies of one Dr John

Remington, a country practitioner from Dunmow in Essex. He sent for Remington's medicines, and mother and son administered plasters (poultices) without the knowledge of the royal physicians. One plaster 'eat down into his belly without the least hurt of disturbance of nature', but, shortly afterwards, James took a turn for the worse, and the physicians protested that their work had been undermined. They refused to give James any more physic until the plasters had been taken off, which was done; and the next three fits were said to be 'easier'. But then on Monday 21st, the plasters were applied once again, and James 'grew worse and worse', and his surgeon Mr Hayes had to be wakened to take them off. Then one of Buckingham's servants named Baker made a julip, which the Duke brought to James himself; James took two draughts, but refused a third. After his death, it was claimed, the physicians were presented with a bill to sign, affirming that the plasters and the julip were safe, but most refused to do so, pointing out that they had no idea what the ingredients of either were.

Buckingham was now in control, and had one of the physicians, the Scot John Craig, dismissed.[57] But another, George Eglisham, took his revenge a year later when he published at Frankfurt a Latin tract with a sensational story. Buckingham, he claimed, had given the King a white powder that made him extremely ill. The physicians declared that the King had been poisoned, but Buckingham expelled them violently from the sickroom, threatening to draw his sword. Buckingham's mother then knelt before the King and craved justice against these accusations that she and her son had poisoned him. 'Poisoned me?' said the King, 'and with that, turning himself, swooned.'[58]

One source claims that, while he was still lucid, James had three hours' private talk with Charles, sending all his attendants two or three rooms away, 'to be out of hearing'.[59] If true, he had grasped his last chance for a proper conversation. 'Late at night' on the 24th, Conway wrote to the Earl of Carlisle:

> This last night was the tenth night of his Majesty's fever, which exercised such illness on a weak body, which, being reverenced and loved with so much cause as his Majesty hath given, struck much

sense and fear into the hearts of his servants that looked upon him. Yet to deliver to you the state clearly, this day his Majesty hath taken broths, hath had large benefit of nature, and slept well. And, more to your comfort, his Majesty did, with life and cheerfulness, receive the Sacrament in the presence of the Prince, the Duke, and many others, and admitted many to take it with him; and in the action and the circumstances of it, did deliver himself so answerable to his writings, and his wise and pious professions, as did justly produce mixed tears between comfort and grief; and this day, and now this night, he recovers temper, rests, in appearance to us, strength, appetite, and digestion; which gives us great hope of his amendment, grounded not only upon desire, but upon the method of judicious observation.[60]

On the night of Friday 25th, a stroke loosened the King's face muscles, so that his jaw dropped. His swollen tongue, combined with huge quantities of phlegm, constantly threatened to suffocate him: it was said that 'his tongue was swollen so big in his mouth, that either he could not speak at all, or not be understood'.[61] He was also afflicted with severe dysentery, suffering, it was reported, 'in filth and misery'.

Sensing he was near death, he called for his trusted Andrewes, but Andrewes was himself ill with 'a sore fit of the stone and gout'.[62] Instead Lord Keeper John Williams and George Abbot came. After failing to engage the King with cheerful conversation, Williams knelt beside the bed and told the King that the end was near. James asked to partake of the Communion, repeated the Creed, declared himself in love and charity with his neighbours, and received the Sacrament, according to Williams, 'with that zeal and devotion as if he had not been a frail man but a cherubim clothed with flesh and blood'. Conway wrote how James ended the Creed by saying 'There is no other belief, no other hope!' and when Williams asked him whether he would have the absolution read, answered 'As it is practised in the English Church I ever approved it; but in the dark way of the Church of Rome, I do defy it.'[63]

On Saturday afternoon, his physician Sir William Paddy told him 'that there was nothing left for me to do but to pray for his soul'.[64] The King called for his son Charles and tried to speak to him, 'but nature being exhausted he had no strength to express his intention'. Williams prayed with the King, and read out forty-one 'sentences', short devotional phrases that James attempted to repeat, 'but his soul began to retreat more inward and so by degrees he took less notice of external things'. The end came on Sunday 27 March 1625, just before noon, when with 'lords and servants kneeling on one side, his archbishops, bishops and other of his chaplains on the other side of his bed, without pangs or convulsions at all, Solomon slept'.[65]

On the night of Monday 28 March, the corpse of King James was brought from Theobalds back to London, travelling through Smithfield, Holborn, Chancery Lane, and down the Strand to Queen Anna's old residence, Denmark House, to lie in state until 10 April. As he had been twenty-two years earlier, James was welcomed to the capital 'by all the nobility about the town, the pensioners, officers, and household servants, besides the Lord Mayor and aldermen', but according to John Chamberlain the solemnity was lost: 'it was marred by foul weather, so that there was nothing to be seen but coaches and torches'.[66]

From the outset, the accession of King Charles was hailed as a fresh new start for British royalty. To the public, the twenty-four-year-old was already a dashing figure, due to his romantic exploits in Madrid and his committed military stance against Spain; to the Commons, he seemed to be well informed and receptive to their point of view. By the end of his reign, in stark contrast, James had become a distant, aloof monarch; his occasional forays into public life were hopelessly compromised by an innate distaste for crowds and an almost instinctive knack for putting his most offensive thoughts into words. Twenty-two years of what many perceived as negligent government, a grossly lavish lifestyle, and an unsavoury parade of pretty young favourites, was at an end, and not before time.

Immediate reactions to the new King focused on the destruction of James's corrupt Bedchamber. Already James's men, sent to Denmark House to attend on the late King's body, were worried, 'apprehensive that by their absence they might be dispossessed of their places and lodgings'. They were right to be concerned: they had been quietly ousted, and Charles's smaller personal retinue had moved into lodgings next to his own at Whitehall.[67] The Countess of Bedford reported on 12 April that Charles was showing all the right signs of being his own man: 'for ought anybody yet can discover, he makes his own determinations, and is very stiff in them'. Already, the Countess wrote, he had 'changed the whole face of the court very near to the same form it had in Queen Elizabeth's time', cutting down on his personal retinue, letting the Privy Council go no further than the Privy Gallery, and permitting only the Gentlemen of his Bedchamber to go beyond. The new King was pious, never failing, 'morning and evening', to come to prayers in his closet, and listening attentively to sermons: 'so as there is all good signs that God hath set him over this kingdom for a blessing'.[68]

John Chamberlain confirmed that 'The King shows himself every way very gracious and affable, but the court is kept more strait and private than in the former time. He is very attentive and devout at prayers and sermons gracing the preachers and assembly with amiable and cheerful countenance, which gives much satisfaction, and there is great hope conceived that the world will every way amend, if the necessity of the time constrain not the contrary now at the first.'[69] The Venetian ambassador Zuane Pesaro was similarly impressed. 'The King's reputation increases day by day. He professes constancy in religion, sincerity in action and that he will not have recourse to subterfuges in his dealings. His attention to those things renders him more popular, and he conducts himself with every propriety.' Charles was seen to spend many hours of his day reading a book, which was thought to be a manuscript collection of edifying maxims. Well briefed on matters of state, Charles made a point of appearing in the Privy Chamber every morning, 'in the presence of all the lords and officials of that apartment. He detains some in conversation and salutes the others and leaves them all happy and devoted.'[70] The finishing touches were put to the picture when Charles married Henrietta Maria by proxy on 1 May, and six weeks later welcomed his bride at Canterbury.

And yet this same gilded youth was to become the most despised of kings, the man who pushed the country into Civil War, was forced from his throne, tried for treachery, and died on the scaffold on 30 January 1649, in front of what had been his own Whitehall Palace. Why Charles should have fallen so precipitously has exercised the minds of historians, politicians and biographers for three and a half centuries, and no critical consensus has been reached. But some of the most rooted causes may lie not in his reign, but in that of his father. For Charles's accession in March 1625 was not the clean start so lauded by contemporaries. James left many legacies, not all of them good. Even as he lay dying, his most recent foreign policy decisions were proving themselves murderously disastrous on the ground. His finances were hopelessly compromised. A series of scandals — the Overbury murder, the fall of Bacon and Middlesex — had shaken public confidence in government. His series of fraught encounters with the English Commons had left the Crown constantly on the defensive.

Another successor might have avoided some of these unwanted bequests, but Charles was already too implicated. Unlike James, who had consistently distanced himself from government, for the past five years Charles had shown himself keenly interested, a regular attender at Privy Council meetings and in Parliament. And Charles made one decision that was to prove highly damaging: he followed James by keeping Buckingham as his confidant and chief counsellor. Buckingham had reacted to the death of his self-styled maker by publicly wallowing in grief, falling seriously ill once again ('much troubled with an impostume that brake in his head' reported Chamberlain), and having to be carried to the funeral in a chair.[71] Charles immediately adopted him: 'I have lost a good father and you a good master,' he said, 'but comfort yourself, you have found another that will no less cherish you.' Buckingham joined Charles's own Bedchamber, and was confirmed in all his offices — Charles even gave him a golden key as a symbol of his right to enter any royal residence at any time of day or night.

But within months, Buckingham was a liability, despised by the public, and vilified by the House of Commons. Much of the opprobrium was a reaction to his foreign policy failures: various much-vaunted attempts at an alliance with France fell through, and a 1627 mission to save the Huguenots of La Rochelle ended in an ignominious siege on the Isle of Ré, leaving the Duke as the object of widespread ridicule. In 1626 Dr George Eglisham implicated Buckingham of malpractice in the deaths of the Duke of Lennox, the Earl of Southampton, the Marquis of Hamilton, as well as that of King

James himself.[72] Charges were brought against Buckingham, claiming that he had acted improperly when he caused an empirical medicine to be administered to the King, and a parliamentary inquiry was held in April, hearing evidence from the royal physicians, including William Harvey. The Duke was formally criticised but not condemned for his actions.[73] Buckingham's immediate influence came to an abrupt end on 23 August 1628, when he was stabbed to death by a discharged officer named John Felton. But Charles would never fully rid himself of the accusation that he owed his throne to murder. In February 1648, when a list of offences was being drawn up against the deposed and doomed King Charles, alongside the charges of violating the privileges of the kingdom, of causing the present Civil War, Parliament dredged up 'old and almost forgotten charges, that his Majesty hastened the death of his father by poison, or that Buckingham attempted it with his consent . . .'.[74]

It is perhaps fitting that the death of King James aroused such speculation and innuendo. After all, his mother, it was said, had murdered his father. James himself, some had claimed, had connived at the death of his eldest son. And his father, many had claimed, had killed David Riccio precisely in order to ensure that Mary's child would never be born alive. James, it seems, had not come so far from the bloody nest. As his life drew to a close, the attacks on him continued to multiply, many of them harshly *ad hominem*. When a libel entitled 'The Commons' Tears' was dropped in court, James responded with a verse that opened 'The wiper of the people's tears | the drier up of doubts and fears'. Much of it was a typically uncompromising declaration of James's superiority over the reader – 'Kings walk the milky heavenly way | but you by bye-paths gad astray' – but it did, however, contain an uncharacteristic admission of his own fallibility.

> Tis true I am a cradle king
>   yet do remember every thing
> That I have heretofore put out
>   and yet begin not for to doubt.[75]

It is only a passing stumble before James resumes his tirade – 'O how gross is your device . . .' – but in these four lines of doggerel rhyme, there is a rare hint of self-knowledge. For James was indeed a 'cradle king', crowned when barely a year old; by the time he came to respond to 'The Commons' Tears' he was approaching sixty, and had over five decades of kingly experience on which to draw, all of which, as he here declared, he could still remember. But there is something telling in James's expression here. Despite his age, despite his many years on two great thrones, he still uses the present tense – 'Tis true I *am* a cradle king' – as if, even now, he remains an infant, an innocent for whom the harsh realities of kingship are still unimaginable.

Notes

The following abbreviations are used in the notes.

PERSONAL ABBREVIATIONS

A	Anna of Denmark
C	Charles, later Prince of Wales
DC	Dudley Carleton
E	Elizabeth I of England
FW	Francis Walsingham
GV	George Villiers, later Duke of Buckingham
H	Henry Stuart, Lord Darnley, later King of Scots
J	James VI and I
JC	John Chamberlain
M	Mary, Queen of Scots
PC	Privy Council
RCa	Robert Carr, later Viscount Rochester, Earl of Somerset
RCe	Robert Cecil, later Viscount Cranborne, Earl of Salisbury
TR	Thomas Randolph
WC	Sir William Cecil, later Lord Burghley

FREQUENTLY CITED SOURCES

APC	*Acts of Privy Council*
Akrigg	*Letters of King James VI and I*, ed. G.P.V. Akrigg
Barlow	William Barlow, *The summe and substance of the conference*
Bergeron	David M. Bergeron, *King James and Letters of Homoerotic Desire*
BL	British Library
Border Papers	Joseph Bain ed., *The Border Papers*
Calderwood	David Calderwood, *History of the Kirk of Scotland*, ed. Thomas Thomson

CJ	*Journal of the House of Commons*
CSPD	*Calendar of State Papers — Domestic*
CSPF	*Calendar of State Papers — Foreign*
CSPSc	*Calendar of State Papers — Scotland*
CSPSp	*Calendar of State Papers — Spain*
CSPV	*Calendar of State Papers — Venice*
CSP Simancas	*Calendar of Letters and State Papers relating to English affairs preserved in . . . the archives of Simancas*
Dalrymple	David Dalrymple ed., *Secret Correspondence of Sir Robert Cecil with James VI. King of Scotland*
'Danish Account'	'Danish Account' in David Stevenson, *Scotland's Last Royal Wedding*
Diurnal	*A Diurnal of Remarkable Occurants*, ed. Thomson
DNB	*Dictionary of National Biography*
FSL	Folger Shakespeare Library
Gardiner	Samuel Rawson Gardiner, 'On certain Letters of Diego Sarmiento de Acuña, Count of Gondomar'
HMC	Historical Manuscripts Commission
HMCD	HMC, *Report on the Manuscripts of Lord L'isle & Dudley*
HMCS	HMC, *Calendar of the Manuscripts of . . . the Marquess of Salisbury*
LJ	*Journals of the House of Lords*
McClure	*The Letters of John Chamberlain*, ed. Norman Egbert McClure
Nichols	Nichols, John ed., *The Progresses, Processions, and Magnificent Festivities of King James the First*
Normand & Roberts	Lawrence Normand and Gareth Roberts eds, *Witchcraft in Early Modern Scotland*
PRO	Public Record Office
Rait & Cameron	Robert S. Rait and Annie L. Cameron, *King James's Secret*
RPCS	*Registers of the Privy Council of Scotland*
SHR	*Scottish Historical Review*
Sommerville	James VI and I, *Political Writings*, ed. Johann P. Sommerville
SP	State Papers

Stevenson David Stevenson, *Scotland's Last Royal Wedding*
Willson D.H. Willson, *King James VI and I*

NOTES TO INTRODUCTION

1. Oglander, *A Royalist's Notebook*, 193–8. The dating is Oglander's.
2. *His Majesties Speach in This Last Session of Parliament*; Sommerville 147–8.

NOTES TO CHAPTER ONE

1. Mauvissière to Charles IX, cit. Strickland, *Lives of the Queens of Scotland*, 4: 207.
2. For Mary, see esp. Fraser, *Mary Queen of Scots*; Wormald, *Mary Queen of Scots*. For Henry, see Bingham, *Darnley*.
3. TR to Leicester, 3 July 1565, cit. Fraser, *The Lennox*, 1: 480–81.
4. Keith, *History of the Church and State*, 2: 347.
5. On Scottish political and religious history of this period, see Tytler, *History of Scotland*; Reid, *Kirk and Nation*; McMillan, *Worship of the Scottish Reformed Church*; Donaldson, *Scotland*; Donaldson, 'The Scottish Church'; Wormald, *Court, Kirk and Community*. On Knox, see Ridley, *John Knox*.
6. TR to WC, 8 May 1565. *CSPSc* 2: 156. *DNB* s.v. Stewart, Lord James, Earl of Mar, and afterwards Earl of Moray (1531?–1570).
7. *DNB* s.v. Hamilton, James, second Earl of Arran and Duke of Châtelhérault (d. 1575).
8. Reid, *Kirk and Nation*, 40.
9. Melvill, *Autobiography and Diary*, 1: 33.
10. Knox, *A Sermon preached . . . vpon Sonday, the 19. of August. 1565*; Knox, *History of the Reformation*, 332.
11. Fraser, *Mary Queen of Scots*, 282; Bingham, *Darnley*, 112–13.
12. Knox, *History of the Reformation*, 334.
13. Bingham, *Darnley*, 124.
14. *DNB* s.v. Hepburn, James, fourth Earl of Bothwell (1536?–1578); Bingham, *Darnley*, 117.
15. Herries, *Historical Memoirs*, 80.
16. Bingham, *Darnley*, 117–18.

17. TR to WC, 25 December 1565, Edinburgh. *CSPF 1564–1568*, 541.
18. TR to WC, 25 December 1565. *CSPSc* 2: 248.
19. Herries, *Historical Memoirs*, 74.
20. Herries, *Historical Memoirs*, 75.
21. Blackwood, *History of Mary Queen of Scots*, 9–10.
22. *Lennox Narrative*, para. III in Mahon, *Mary Queen of Scots*, 121.
23. Herries, *Historical Memoirs*, 75.
24. Fraser, *Mary Queen of Scots*, 289–90.
25. Blackwood, *History of Mary Queen of Scots*, 10–11.
26. Melville, *Memoirs*, 51.
27. Ruthven, 'Relation', 16–18; Bingham, *Darnley*, 133.
28. Ruthven, 'Relation', 17–18.
29. TR to Leicester, 13 February 1566; Keith, *History of the Church and State*, 402n.
30. Melville, *Memoirs*, 49; Bingham, *Darnley*, 134.
31. Accounts by: M to the Archbishop of Glasgow [after 9 March 1566]. Mary, Queen of Scots, *Letters*, ed. Strickland, 1: 22–5; Ruthven, 'Relation', 12–35, also in Keith, *History of the Church and State*, 3: 260–78; TR and Bedford to WC, 27 March, 1566. Mumby, *Fall of Mary Stuart*, 48–56; Knox, *History of the Reformation*, 34.
32. Herries, *Historical Memoirs*, 76–7.
33. Cit. Bingham, *Darnley*, 139–40.
34. Nau, *History of Mary Stewart*, 4, 7.
35. Melville, *Memoirs*, 52.
36. Keith, *History of the Church and State*, 3: 276–7.
37. Nau, *History of Mary Stewart*, 16.
38. M to E, 15 March 1566, Dunbar Castle. *CSPSc* 2: 268.
39. TR to WC, 21 March 1566. *CSPSc* 2: 269.
40. Bingham, *Darnley*, 143.
41. Wormald, *Mary Queen of Scots*, 159; TR to WC, 21 March 1566, *CSPSc* 2: 269–70.
42. Bingham, *Darnley*, 148–9.
43. TR to WC, 4 April 1566, *CSPSc* 2: 274, mentioned again, TR to WC, 25 April 1566, *CSPSc* 2: 276.
44. *English and Scottish Popular Ballads*, ed. Sayer and Kitteredge, no. 174, 'Lord Bothwell', 423–4.

45. M to E, 4 April 1566, Edinburgh. *CSPSc* 2: 275.
46. TR to WC, 25 April 1566, Berwick. *CSPSc* 2: 276.
47. TR to WC, 26 May 1566, Berwick. *CSPSc* 2: 281. For *Maister Randolphes Phantasey*, see Cranstoun ed., *Satirical Poems*.
48. TR to WC, 7 June 1566, Berwick. *CSPSc* 2: 283.
49. Killigrew to WC, 28 June 1566, Edinburgh. *CSPSc* 2: 290.
50. Robertson ed., *Inventaires*, xxxi–xxxii, cit. Bingham, *Darnley*, 149–50.
51. TR to WC, 14 June 1566, Berwick. *CSPSc* 2: 286.
52. *Diurnal*, 100; Sir William Drury to WC, 24 June 1566, Berwick. *CSPF 1566–1568*, 93.
53. Herries, *Historical Memoris*, 79.
54. Killigrew to WC, 24 June 1566, Edinburgh, *CSPSc* 2: 290.
55. *Lennox Narrative*, para. V in Mahon, *Mary Queen of Scots*, 122–3.
56. Bedford to WC, 3 August 1566. Stevenson, *Selection of Unpublished Manuscripts*, 165.
57. Nau, *History of Mary Stewart*, 28.
58. Bingham, *Darnley*, 155.
59. Bedford to WC, 8 August 1566, Berwick. *CSPF 1566–1568*, 114. See also 'Advertisements out of Scotland', [15] August 1566. *CSPF 1566–1568*, 118.
60. Herries, *Historical Memoirs*, 80–81.
61. Sir John Forster to WC, 8 September 1566. *CSPF 1566–1568*, 128.
62. 'Advertisements out of Scotland', [15] August 1566. *CSPF 1566–1568*, 118.
63. Hume, *Love Affairs of Mary Queen of Scots*, 318.
64. Lords of Council to Catherine, 8 October 1566, cit. Mumby, *Fall of Mary Stuart*, 116; Keith 2: 455.
65. Bingley, *Darnley*, 157–8: Mumby 117, 121, 122; Keith, *History of the Church and State*, 2: 450, 451, 456.
66. *Diurnal*, 101. See also Maitland to WC, 24 October 1566, Jedburgh. *CSPSc 1563–1568*, 301. Maitland to WC, 26 October 1566, Jedburgh, reports a crisis on 25 October 1566 after a brief reprieve. *CSPSc 1563–1568*, 302.
67. *Diurnal*, 101–2.
68. Lethington to Beaton, 24 October 1566. Mumby, *Fall of Mary Stuart*, 127.
69. Fraser, *Mary Queen of Scots*, 274.

70. Herries, *Historical Memoirs*, 81.
71. Herries, *Historical Memoirs*, 82–3.

NOTES TO CHAPTER TWO

1. Adamson, *Genethliacum*, title page. See *DNB* s.v. Adamson, Patrick; E to Bedford, 13 November 1566. *CSPF 1566–1568*, 146; Bedford to WC, 17 November 1566, Garendon. *CSPF 1566–1568*, 148.
2. Giovanni Correr to the Signory of Venice, 13/23 January 1567, Paris. *CSPV* 7: 386–7.
3. Bedford to WC, 25 November 1566. *CSPF 1566–1568*, 151.
4. Le Croc to the Archbishop of Glasgow, 23 December 1566, Stirling. Keith, *History of the Church and State*, 1: xcvii.
5. James VI and I, *Apologie*, (e3)ʳ.
6. Keith, *History of the Church and State*, 2: 486–7; *Diurnal*, 104.
7. Instructions to Bedford, 7 November 1566. Keith, *History of the Church and State*, 2: 477–83.
8. *Diurnal*, 103.
9. Melville, *Memoirs*, 171.
10. Melville, *Memoirs*, 171–2.
11. Nau, *History of Mary Stuart*, cxlvii–cxlviii.
12. Le Croc to Glasgow, 23 December 1566, Stirling. Keith, *History of the Church and State*, 1: xcvii–xcviii.
13. Le Croc to Glasgow, 23 December 1566, Stirling. Keith, *History of the Church and State*, 1: xcviii.
14. Herries, *Historical Memoirs*, 81.
15. Fleming, *Mary Queen of Scots*, 540.
16. M to Beaton, 20 January 1567, Edinburgh. Mumby, *Fall of Mary Stuart*, 154.
17. *Diurnal*, 105.
18. *Lennox Narrative*, para. VIII, in Mahon, *Mary Queen of Scots*, 125.
19. Melville, *Memoirs*, 179.
20. H to Lennox, 7 February 1567, Edinburgh. *Lennox Narrative*, para. XI, in Mahon, *Mary Queen of Scots*, 127.
21. Herries, *Historical Memoirs*, 84.
22. Herries, *Historical Memoirs*, 84.

23. Herries, *Historical Memoirs*, 84.
24. Fraser, *Mary Queen of Scots*, 305–6.
25. Killigrew to WC, 8 March 1567, Edinburgh. *CSPSc* 2: 317.
26. E to M, 24 February 1567, Westminster. *CSPSc* 2: 316.
27. Killigrew to WC, 8 March 1567, Edinburgh. *CSPSc* 2: 317.
28. Herries, *Historical Memoirs*, 85.
29. Herries, *Historical Memoirs*, 85.
30. M to Mar, 29 March 1567, Edinburgh. HMC Mar & Kellie 16–17.
31. Herries, *Historical Memoirs*, 87.
32. Answers to Bothwell's cartel, April 1567. *CSPSc* 2: 320–21.
33. William Kirkcaldy of Grange to Bedford, 20 April 1567. *CSPF 1566–1568*, 212.
34. Drury to WC, 24 April 1567. *CSPF 1566–1568*, 213.
35. Drury to WC, 25 April 1567, Berwick. *CSPF 1566–1568*, 215.
36. Drury to WC, 27 April 1567. *CSPF 1566–1568*, 216.
37. Calderwood 2: 365; Drury to WC, 27 April 1567, *CSPF 1566–1568*, 216.
38. Drury to WC, 20 May 1567, Berwick. *CSPF 1566–1568*, 235.
39. Calderwood 2: 355–6.
40. Melville, *Memoirs*, 64.
41. Bingham, *Darnley*, 188.
42. Kirkaldy of Grange to Bedford, 8 May 1867. *CSPSc* 2: 237.
43. Bingham, *Darnley*, 189.
44. Fraser, *Mary Queen of Scots*, 343; Nau, *History of Mary Stewart*.
45. Bingham, *Darnley*, 190.
46. 'Coronation Ja 6 in Castro Striuelensi 29 Julii 1567', in Dalyell, *Fragments of Scottish History*, Appendix XIII.
47. Bingham, *Darnley*, 190–91.
48. Reid, *Kirk and Nation*, 40.
49. Bingham, *Darnley*, 191. Donaldson, *First Trial*, 67.
50. Melville, *Memoirs*, 200.
51. Bingham, *Darnley*, 191.

NOTES TO CHAPTER THREE

1. Hewitt, *Scotland Under Morton*.
2. 10 March 1568, Stirling. HMC Mar & Kellie 18–20.

3. E to the Countess of Mar, 7 February 1572, Westminster. HMC Mar & Kellie, 28.

4. Moore, *History of the Study of Medicine*, 97, 162.

5. Moray [10 March 1568, Stirling]. HMC Mar & Kellie, 20–21.

6. Moray to Mar, 1 May 1568, Glasgow. HMC Mar & Kellie, 21.

7. Mar to E, 28 January 1570, Stirling Castle. *CSPF 1569–1571*, 176.

8. Act of PC for safety of the King. Signed by Lennox, 12 October 1570, Edinburgh. HMC Mar & Kellie 22–3.

9. Bannatyne, *Journal of Transactions*, 246–7.

10. *Historie and Life of King James the Sext*, 143. Bannatyne has the hole in the ceiling of the Tolbooth: see *Journal of Transactions*, 257.

11. *Historie and Life of King James the Sext*, 143–4.

12. J to the Parliament [28 August 1571], Tolbooth. *Calendar of the State Papers relating to Scotland and Mary Queen of Scots 1547–1603*, ed. William K. Boyd, vol. III, *A.D. 1569–1571* (Edinburgh: H.M. General Register House, 1903); for another version see Bannatyne, *Journal of Transactions*, 256–7. John Case to Drury, 2 September 1571, Stirling. *CSPSc* 3: 677–9 at 678.

13. E to Mar, 2 October 1571, Richmond. HMC Mar & Kellie 24–5.

14. Melville, *Memoirs*, 96.

15. Melville, *Memoirs*, 101.

16. Moore, *History of the Study of Medicine*, 100, 99, 98.

17. In the Act of Caution, 1572. HMC Mar & Kellie 30.

18. Certainly by 30 July 1570, Buchanan was in place: Regent Lennox signed a precept to allow 'Mr George Munro, servant to Mr George Buchanan, into the King's household, and to give him his daily allowance'. Lennox to Master and Steward of the King's Household, 30 July 1570, Stirling. HMC Mar & Kellie 22. On Buchanan, see McFarlane, *Buchanan*.

19. Rait & Cameron, *King James's Secret*, 2.

20. BL Add. MS 34, 275 discussed in Warner, 'The Library of James VI. 1573–1583'.

21. Warner, 'Library of James VI', xviii.

22. Smith, *Vitae Quorundam Eruditissimorum et Illustrium Virorum*, Fff 2ᵛ, in his life of Petrus Junius [Peter Young].

23. BL Add. MS 34, 275 fo. 1ᵛ; Warner, 'Library of James VI', lxxii.

24. BL Add. MS 34, 275 fo. 2ʳ; Warner, 'Library of James VI', lxxiii.

25. BL Add. MS 34, 275 fo. 1ʳ; Warner, 'Library of James VI', lxxii–lxxiii.

26. Killigrew to FW, 30 June 1574, Edinburgh. *CSPSc* 5: 13–14.

27. Killigrew to FW, 30 June 1574, Edinburgh. *CSPSc* 5: 13–14.

28. J to the Countess of Mar [mid-1570s]. Akrigg 41.

29. J to George Buchanan [mid-1570s]. Akrigg 42.

30. *RPCS* 2: 181 (28 January 1572–3); 689 (3 May 1578).

31. Row, *History of the Kirk of Scotland*, 33–5.

32. Bèze, *Icones*; idem, *Beza's 'Icones': Contemporary Portraits of Reformers of Religion and Letters*, ed. McCrie.

33. Mackenzie, 'Life of Buchanan', 180.

34. Mackenzie, 'Life of Buchanan', 179–80.

35. Melville, *Memoirs*, 262.

36. Osborn, *Advice to a Son*, B7ʳ.

37. Melville, *Memoirs*, 262; for the whipping boy, see Rait & Cameron 3.

38. Melville, *Memoirs*, 262.

39. Chytraeus, *Collectanea*, A7ʳ⁻ᵛ. This rendering and translation is Ian McFarlane's: see *Buchanan*, 448–9.

40. Buchanan to J, November 1576, Stirling. Buchanan, *Baptistes*, A.ijᵛ; trans. Baldwin, *Shakspere's Small Latin*, 1: 544–5.

41. Crauford, *Memoirs*, 81–7, cit. Grant, *Story of the University of Edinburgh*, 1: 174.

42. *Ben Jonson*, ed. Herford & Simpson I: 148.

43. Melvill, *Autobiography and Diary*, 68.

44. *RPCS* 2: 164.

45. The *Historie of King James the Sext* gives a precise date of 15 September 1577; other accounts give 4 March 1578. It is possible that the earlier date is correct, but the later date allows for a more dramatic story; or that chroniclers have confused two incidents. Other accounts have Morton writing to James rather than visiting him.

46. *Historie of King James the Sext*, 260–61.

47. BL Add. MS 34, 275 fo. 2r; Warner, 'Library of James VI', lxxiv.

48. *Historie of King James the Sext*, 260–61.

49. *Historie of King James the Sext*, 263–4.

50. See *DNB* s.v. Erskine, John, second or seventh Earl of Mar (1558–1634).

51. *RPCS* 3: 3–4.
52. Calderwood 3: 417, 419, 425.
53. *RPCS* 3: 105, 112–14.
54. *Historie of King James the Sext*, 174.
55. Donaldson, *Scotland*, 172–3; Bingham, *James VI*, 48.

NOTES TO CHAPTER FOUR

1. On d'Aubigny see Cust, *Stuarts of Aubigny*, 85–97; Willson 32–47; Donaldson, *Scotland*, 172–80; Bingham, *James VI*, 50–66; Normand, 'Edward II and James VI'; Bergeron, *King James and Letters of Homoerotic Desire*, 32–64.
2. Moysie, *Memoirs*, 25.
3. Johnston, *Historie of Scotland*, 114.
4. Calderwood 3: 456, 460–61.
5. Melvill, *Autobiography and Diary*, 76–7.
6. Calderwood 3: 456–8; Bingham, *James VI*, 52.
7. Calderwood 3: 457–9.
8. Woddryngton to FW, 4 May 1582, Berwick. *Border Papers* 1: 82.
9. Moysie, *Memoirs*, 27.
10. Hacket, *Scrinia Reserata*, 39. For the theft accusation see Aubrey, *Brief Lives*, 150–51.
11. Bingham, *James VI*, 144.
12. Calderwood 3: 461.
13. 'Memoriall of the present state of Scotland', 31 December 1579. *CSPSc* 2: 370–72.
14. Calderwood 3: 460, 461; Donaldson, *Scotland*, 173; Willson 37.
15. Cuddy, 'Revival of the Entourage', 180.
16. Willson 33.
17. Calderwood 3: 462.
18. Melvill, *Autobiography and Diary*, 81–2.
19. Lennox to the Kirk, 14 July 1580, St Andrews. Calderwood 3: 468–9.
20. Calderwood 3: 468, 472, 474, 477.
21. Calderwood 3: 480, 583.
22. See *DNB*; s.v. Stewart, James, of Bothwellmuir, Earl of Arran (d. 1596); *RPCS* 3: 323.

23. Calderwood 3: 480–85.
24. Donaldson, *Scotland*, 173.
25. Melvill, *Autobiography and Diary*, 119–20.
26. Melvill, *Autobiography and Diary*, 133.
27. Calderwood 3: 473.
28. Calderwood 3: 486.
29. Cit. Willson 34.
30. Calderwood 3: 486–7.
31. Calderwood 3: 488–95.
32. Calderwood 3: 507–10.
33. See 'Reasons for which the King of Scots is unacceptable to the people of England'. *HMCS* 3: 210. Willson 34.
34. J to E, 19 June 1582, Stirling Castle. Akrigg 48–9.
35. Calderwood 3: 557–8, 569, 559, 575; Bingham, *James VI*, 58–9.
36. Calderwood 3: 576.
37. See Shire, *Song, Dance and Poetry*; *Poems by James*, ed. Craigie, introduction; Hudson, *Historie of Judith*, ed. Craigie, introduction; *DNB* s.v. Montgomerie, Alexander.
38. Hudson, *Historie of Ivdith*, A ij^r–A iij^v.
39. Hudson, *Historie of Ivdith*; James VI, *Essayes of a Prentise*; James VI, *His Majesties Poeticall Exercises*.
40. J to M, 28 May 1582, Dalkeith. Akrigg 46.
41. J to M, 29 January 1581, Edinburgh. Akrigg 45.
42. Calderwood 3: 592, 592–3, 594. See also J to M, 28 May 1582, Dalkeith. Akrigg 46.
43. Calderwood 3: 593, 595–6.
44. Kirk's supplication to J, 23 August 1582. Calderwood 3: 637–8.
45. Calderwood lists Mar, Gowrie, the Master of Glamis, the Master of Oliphant, young Lochleven, the Laird of Cleish, the Laird of Easter Wemes, Sir Lewes Bellenden (Justice Clerk) the Lord Boyd, the Lord Lindsay, the Abbot of Dunfermline (Secretary), the Abbots of Cambuskenneth, Dryburgh and Paisley, the Prior of Pittenweeme and the Constable of Dundee. Calderwood 3: 637.
46. A 'tulchan' bishop was a titular bishop, most of whose see's income went to the layman who appointed him. 'Tulchan' is the Scots word for the stuffed calfskin placed beside a cow to induce it to give milk. Reid, *Kirk and Nation*, 45.

47. Calderwood 3: 640–42.
48. Calderwood 3: 643.
49. Statement of offences committed by Lennox [17 September 1582]. *CSPSc* 6: 171–4.
50. Melville, *Memoirs*, 133–4.
51. Lennox's proclamation, 20 September 1582, Dumbarton Castle. Calderwood 3: 665–8. Answer to 'the declaration of the dissembled innocency' of Lennox. Calderwood 3: 668–73.
52. Calderwood 3: 673, 689.
53. Calderwood 3: 689–93.
54. Lennox to J, 16 December 1582. *CSPSc* 6: 222–3; Bergeron 47–8.
55. Lennox to J, 18 December 1582, Dumbarton. *CSPSc* 6: 223–4; Bergeron 49–50.
56. Bowes to FW, 1 May 1583 and 29 May 1583. *CSPSc* 6: 439, 475.
57. Calderwood 8: 243.
58. Spottiswoode, *History* (1677 edn), 298.
59. Melville, *Memoirs*, 134.
60. Cobham to FW, 9 June 1583. *CSPF* 17: 394.
61. James VI, 'A Tragedie called Phoenix' in *Essayes of a Prentise*; see also *Poems of James VI*, ed. Craigie 1: 40–59; Bergeron 220–29. For discussions see Bingham, *James VI*, 63–5; Akrigg, 'Literary Achievement of King James I'; Goldberg, *James I*; McClure, '"O Phoenix Escossois"'; Bergeron 54–63.
62. As suggested by Bergeron 60.
63. Melville, *Memoirs*, 134.
64. 'A Tragedie called Phoenix', in James VI, *Essayes of a Prentise*.
65. Woddryngton to FW, 21 November 1583, Berwick. *Border Papers* 1: 116–17.

NOTES TO CHAPTER FIVE

1. Calderwood 3: 645.
2. Melville, *Memoirs*, 110–11.
3. Melville, *Memoirs*, 287.
4. *Historie of King James the Sext*, 198.
5. Hoby to WC, 15 August 1584. Tytler, *History of Scotland*, 3: 164; Melville, *Memoirs*, 109.

6. *RPCS* 3: 626.
7. FW to E, 11 September 1583. *CSPSc* 6: 603.
8. Calderwood 4: 25.
9. Melville, *Memoirs*, 326; Calderwood 4: 32.
10. Davison to FW, 27 May 1584. *CSPSc* 7: 155.
11. Reid, *Kirk and Nation*, 52; Donaldson, *Scotland*, 181.
12. Fontenay to Nau, 15 August 1584, Edinburgh. *CSPSc* 7: 274–5.
13. James later declared that he had no further 'intelligence with my mother sen [since] the Master of Gray's being in England'. Gray's mission started in October 1584. See J to Leicester, 15 December 1586, Holyroodhouse. Rait & Cameron 101–2. See also Rait & Cameron 10.
14. Fontenay to Nau. 15 August 1584. *CSPSc* 7: 275.
15. Lee, *Maitland of Thirlestane*, 86; Bingham, *James VI*, 80–81.
16. 'Articles of a treaty', 31 July 1585, and response. *CSPSc* 8: 44, 45.
17. 'The League', June 1586. *CSPSc* 8: 491.
18. Bingham, *James VI*, 84–5.
19. Courcelles to Henri III, 4 October 1586. Bell, *Despatches of Courcelles*, 4.
20. Moysie, *Memoirs*, 152.
21. Gray to Douglas, [1] October 1586, Dumfries. HMCS 3: 178; the dating here follows Rait & Cameron 25.
22. J to Douglas, 20 October 1586. *Warrender Papers* 1: 235–6.
23. Mary, Queen of Scots, *Lettres, Instructions et Mémoires de Marie, Reine d'Ecosse*, 7: 36. See also Scott, *Tragedy of Fotheringhay*, 31.
24. [Douglas] to [Gray], [21 September 1586]. HMCS 13: 308–9.
25. Douglas to Gray, 22 November 1586. *Warrender Papers* 1: 236–7.
26. Courcelles to Henri III, 4 October 1586. Bell, *Despatches of Courcelles*, 6–7.
27. See Courcelles to Henri III, 31 October 1586. Bell, *Despatches of Courcelles*, 12–13.
28. Gray to Douglas, 23 November 1586, Holyroodhouse. HMCS 3: 196.
29. Courcelles to Henri III, 30 November 1586. Bell, *Despatches of Courcelles*, 18–19.
30. J to Keith, 27 November 1586. Rait & Cameron 60–62, who pluralise 'bedfellow'. I follow Bingham here, who reads it in the singular.

31. Douglas to J, 8 December 1586. Rait & Cameron 72–82; Keith to [Maitland], 8 December 1586. *Warrender Papers* 1: 245.
32. Instructions by J to Gray, [17 December 1586]. *Warrender Papers*, 250–1.
33. J to [Leicester], 15 December 1586, Holyroodhouse. Rait & Cameron 101; *Warrender Papers* 1: 248–9.
34. Young to Maitland, 10 January 1587. *Warrender Papers* 1: 255–8.
35. Gray to J, 12 January 1587, London. Warrender ed., *Illustrations of Scottish History*, 19–25.
36. Courcelles to Henri III, 10 February 1587. Bell, *Despatches of Courcelles*, 31–2.
37. Courcelles to Henri III, 10 February 1587. Bell, *Despatches of Courcelles*, 28–9.
38. 'Reasons for which the King of Scots is unacceptable to the people of England' [1586]. HMCS 3: 210–11.
39. Teulet, *Relations politiques*, 4: 166–7.

NOTES TO CHAPTER SIX

1. Moysie, *Memoirs*, 60.
2. Lord Scrope to [FW], 21 February 1587, Carlisle. *CSPSc* 9: 300.
3. Ogilvy of Powrie to Douglas, 2 March 1587, Edinburgh. HMCS 13: 334.
4. Calderwood 4: 611.
5. Moysie, *Memoirs*, 60.
6. Courcelles to Henri III, 8 March 1587. Bell, *Despatches of Courcelles*, 40–41.
7. Woddryngton to FW, 25 February 1587. *Border Papers*, 1: 247.
8. Robert Carvell to FW, 6 March 1587. *CSPSc* 9: 330.
9. J's instructions to Mrs Carmichael, 10 March 1587. *CSPSc* 9: 332.
10. E to J, 14 February 1587. Rait & Cameron 194.
11. Carey to J, [*c.* 14 March 1587]. Rait & Cameron 195.
12. J to E, [late February 1587]. Akrigg 84–5.
13. [WC] to Sir Robert Carey, 3 April 1587. *CSPSc* 9: 394. See also the similar [WC] to Hunsdon, 6 April 1587. *CSPSc* 9: 398–400.
14. FW to [Maitland], March 1587. *CSPSc* 9: 388–92.
15. WC to Douglas, 2 March 1587. Warrender ed., *Illustrations of Scottish History*, ep. 11.

16. See *Border Papers*.
17. Instructions for Richard Douglas [to be communicated to Archibald Douglas], 8 July 1587, Falkland. HMCS 3: 267–8.
18. Bingham, *James VI*, 103.
19. Carvylle to FW, 3 August 1587, Berwick. *Border Papers* 1: 265.
20. Justice Clerk Bellenden to Archibald Douglas, 24 October 1587. *CSPSc* 9: 491–4. 'Answer of the PC to the Scottish Ambassador', [25 October 1587]. *CSPSc* 9: 495. 'Discoures between Elizabeth and Mr Archibald Douglas', [October 1587]. *CSPSc* 9: 496–502.
21. See Hunsdon's despatches in *Border Papers* 1: 280–98.
22. See Bell, *Despatches of Courcelles*, 53–4.
23. M to Mendoza, 20 May 1586. Mary, Queen of Scots, *Lettres, Instructions, et Mémoires*, ed. Labanhoff 6: 309; Mackie, 'Will of Mary Stuart'; Bingham, *James VI*, 102. Spottiswoode, *History of the Church of Scotland*, 2: 387; Mackie, 'Scotland and the Spanish Armada'.
24. Philip II to Olivares, 11 February 1587. *CSP Simancas* 4: 16.
25. Robert Bowes to WC, November 1596, Edinburgh. *CSPSc* 12: 359–60; and Aston to Bowes, 31 October 1596. *CSPSc* 12: 354. See the perceptive discussion in Goldberg, *James I*, 1–17.
26. James to the Dean of Peterborough, 20 September 1613. Bodl. Ashmole MS 836 fo. 277, as cit. Goldberg, *James I*, 14.
27. *DNB* s.v. Gray, Patrick, sixth Lord Gray.
28. Cit. Grant, 'Brig o' Dee Affair', 93.
29. John, Bishop of Ross, to Cardinal de Como, 10/20 June 1579, Paris. Forbes-Leith ed., *Narratives of Scottish Catholics*, 139.
30. Calderwood 4: 632.
31. Councillors at the Scottish Parliament, [13 July 1587] and Mar to [?], 17 July 1587. *CSPSc* 9: 451; 452–3.
32. [?] to [FW], 13 August 1587, Edinburgh. *CSPSc* 9: 475–7 at 476.
33. Ogilvy to FW, [August] 1587. *CSPSc* 9: 480–81 at 481.
34. *RPCS* 4: 103.
35. Barroll, *Anna of Denmark*, 76.
36. Fowler to [WC], 14 March 1589, Edinburgh. *CSPSc* 10: 3.
37. Grant, 'Brig o' Dee Affair', 99–100.
38. Melvill, *Autobiography and Diary*, 260.
39. James VI, *A Fruitful Meditation*; James VI and I, *Workes*. The *Workes* opens with 'A Paraphrase vpon the Reuelation', and then 'Two

Meditations', on Revelation 20: 7–10 and 1 Chronicles 15: 25–9.

40. William Asheby to FW, 21 July 1588, Berwick. *CSPSc* 9: 583.

41. Bellenden to Archibald Douglas, 24 October 1587, Holyrood-house. *CSPSc* 9: 491. Mendoza to Philip II, 5 April 1588, Paris. *CSP Simancas* 4: 260 and enclosure, 4: 260–1.

42. [John Selby] to [FW], 5 May 1588, Berwick. *CSPSc* 9: 558.

43. Bowes to FW, 8 and 26 May 1588, Berwick. *CSPSc* 9: 559, 560.

44. Bingham, *James VI*, 106–7.

45. J to E, 1 August 1588, Edinburgh. *CSPSc* 9: 588–9.

46. Asheby to FW, 12 August 1588, Edinburgh. *CSPSc* 9: 596.

47. Gray to Douglas, 14 December 1588. *CSPSc* 9: 649.

48. Calderwood 5: 2, 7, letters at 8–13.

49. *Warrender Papers* 2: 93–4.

50. Lee, *Maitland*, 182; Law, 'Robert Bruce'.

51. Calderwood 5: 7–8.

52. Calderwood 5: 36; Fowler to FW, 1 March 1589, Edinburgh. *CSPSc* 9: 701.

53. Asheby to WC, 14 March 1589, Edinburgh. *CSPSc* 10: 1; Grant, 'Brig o' Dee Affair', 104.

54. Fowler to FW, 6 March 1589, Edinburgh. *CSPSc* 9: 704.

55. Fowler to [WC], 14 March 1589, Edinburgh. *CSPSc* 10: 3–4.

56. Fowler to WC, 14 March 1589, *CSPSc* 10: 3–4.

57. Calderwood 5: 37.

58. Asheby to [WC], 14 March 1589, *CSPSc* 10: 2; Fowler to FW, 14 March 1589, Edinburgh. *CSPSc* 10: 4–5; Asheby to [FW], 15 March 1589, Edinburgh. *CSPSc* 10: 6–7; Ashton to Hudson, 15 March 1589, *CSPSc* 10: 7–8; Fowler to FW, 18 March 1589, Edinburgh. *CSPSc* 10: 10. Woddryngton to WC, 18 March 1589, *Border Papers* 1: 335–6; Calderwood 5: 37; Grant, 'Brig o' Dee Affair', 104.

59. Calderwood 5: 52–4.

60. Colville to Asheby, 12 April 1589, Stirling. Colville, *Letters*, 90.

61. Huntly to J, [April 1589] cit. Grant, 'Brig o' Dee Affair', 104–5.

62. J to Huntly, [1589]. Akrigg, *Letters*, 89–91. The correct line in the Vulgate is 'Peccavi in caelum, et coram te' [I have sinned against heaven and before you]. Akrigg and Grant date this letter to February 1589, immediately after the interception of the Spanish letters, but I propose that its content suggests a date after the military action.

63. Colville to WC, 18 April 1589, Aberdeen. Colville, *Letters*, 91.
64. Fowler to [FW], 23 April 1589, Aberdeen. *CSPSc* 10: 44–5.
65. Calderwood 5: 55.
66. Calderwood 5: 56–7; Fowler to WC, 11 May 1589, *CSPSc* 10: 69–70.
67. Calderwood 5: 56–9.

NOTES TO CHAPTER SEVEN

1. Sir John Gilbert to Bedford, 25 December 1583, Exeter. *CSPD 1581–1590*, 139. FW to Davison, 6 October 1584, Barn Elms. *CSPD 1581–1590*, 205. Anon., secret advertisments, to FW, March 1585. *CSPD 1581–1590*, 233.
2. 'Articles to be ministered to Don Pedro de Valdez and his associates.' *CSPD 1581–1590*, 523.
3. Woddryngton to FW, 11 April 1582. *CSPSc* 6: 112.
4. William Davison to FW, 8 October 1586, Windsor. *CSPD 1581–1590*, 361.
5. Calderwood 4: 612.
6. R. Lemacon de la Fonteine to Buchanan, 14 March and 7 May 1580, London. Buchanan, *Opera Omnia*, ed. Ruddimann, 2: G2^r, G2^v-H^r (epp. XXX and XXXII).
7. Melville, *Memoirs*, 364.
8. J to Catherine de Bourbon, [c. September 1588]. *Warrender Papers* 2: 80–81.
9. Catherine de Bourbon to J, [c. December 1588]. *Warrender Papers* 2: 92–3.
10. Fowler to FW, 23 May 1589, Edinburgh. *CSPSc* 10: 82.
11. Cit. Stafford, *James VI of Scotland*, 52.
12. Melville, *Memoirs*, 365.
13. See Fowler to WC, 28 [May] 1589. *CSPSc* 10: 87–8; Melville, *Memoirs*, 368. Lee, *John Maitland*, 193.
14. J to Henri de Navarre, [c. July, 1589]. *Warrender Papers* 2: 107–8.
15. Calderwood 5: 59; for the making of the treaty see 'Danish Account' in Stevenson 79–86.
16. Calderwood 5: 60–63.
17. Cit. Normand & Roberts 31; Calderwood 5: 59–60.
18. Moysie, *Memoirs*, 79.

19. Melville, *Memoirs*, 369.

20. *RPCS* 4: 423n.

21. Calderwood 5: 59; Moysie, *Memoirs*, 79.

22. J to A, [c. 2 October 1589]. *Warrender Papers* 2: 109–10; trans. Bingham *James VI*, 117.

23. Craigie, *Poems*, 68–73.

24. Asheby to FW, 24 September 1589. *CSPSc* 10: 157.

25. Riis, *Should Auld Acquaintance*, 1: 264–5 (based on Niel Krag's journal); 'Danish Account', 86–8; Calderwood 5: 60, 64.

26. J to the people of Scotland, [22? October 1589]. Akrigg 97–100.

27. *RPCS* 4: 423; Calderwood 5: 67.

28. J to the people of Scotland, [22? October 1589]. Akrigg 97–100.

29. Calderwood 3: 486–7; see ch. 4.

30. [Woddryngton] to FW, 30 April 1588, Berwick. *CSPSc* 9: 557–8.

31. 'Danish Account' 87, 90.

32. William Hunter to Asheby, 3 November 1589, 'Fleckra'. *CSPSc* 11: 187.

33. Melvill, *Autobiography and Diary*, 277.

34. Melvill, *Autobiography and Diary*, 277; 'Danish Account' 90–92 and 138 n. 19.

35. Moysie, *Memoirs*, 80–81.

36. Hunter to Asheby, 29 November 1589, 'Houslo'. *CSPSc* 11: 188; 'Danish Account' 91.

37. 'Danish Account' 92.

38. David Lindsay to eldership of Edinburgh, 28 November 1589, Upslaw, cit. Calderwood 5: 68. For the sermon see 'Danish Account' 92–4.

39. 'Danish Account' 94.

40. Hunter to Asheby, 29 November 1589, 'Houslo'. *CSPSc* 11: 188.

41. Mortenson, 'Anders Sørensen Vedel', 276, 280; Ekrem, 'Historiography in Norway', 247; Ekrem, 'Jens Nielssøn', 224.

42. On 3 December. 'Danish Account' 95–6.

43. For the journey see 'Danish Account' 96–9.

44. 'Danish Account' 96.

45. Calderwood 5: 70.

46. 'Danish Account' 96–7.

47. Calderwood 5: 72; Spottiswoode 2: 405.

48. Kirby, *Northern Europe*, 95, 70; Stevenson, *Scotland's Last Royal Wedding*, 47.

49. Melville, *Memoirs*, 277.

50. 'Danish Account' 99.

51. 'Danish Account' 99; Marryat, *Residence in Jutland*, 1: 120; Bowes to WC, 24 April 1590, Edinburgh. *CSPSc 10*: 281.

52. Thirlestane's Accounts, f. 11r, cit. Stevenson, *Scotland's Last Royal Wedding*, 50.

53. Brahe, *Opera omnia*, 81–95; Thoren, *Lord of Uraniborg*, 334.

54. See McFarlane, *Buchanan*, 360–62; Riis, *Should Auld Acquaintance*, 1: 121.

55. Brahe, *Opera omnia*, 6: 309; Dreyer, *Tycho Brahe*, 203; Thoren, *Lord of Uraniborg*, 334–5.

56. Brahe, *Opera omnia*, 2: 11; Thoren, *Lord of Uraniborg*, 315–16.

57. Brahe, *Opera omnia*, 2: 11, trans. Stevenson, *Scotland's Last Royal Wedding*, 51.

58. See James VI and I, *Poems*, ed. Craigie, 100–102.

59. Quoted in Dreyer, *Tycho Brahe*, 204.

60. Marryat, *Residence in Jutland*, 1: 306–7 n.+; Bingham, *James VI*, 127.

61. Brahe, *His Astronomicall Coniectur*, A4^r. The Latin verse reads: 'QVam temerè est ausus Phaëton, vel prastat Apollo | Qui regit ignivomos Æthere anhelus equos. | Plus TYCHO; cuncta astra regis: tibi cedit Apollo | Charus & Vraniæ es hospes, alumnus, amor.' Ibid., A4^r.

62. Christianson, *On Tycho's Island*, 140–41. For Maitland's poetry see 'Ioannis Metallani Thirlistonii Domini, Scotiae quondam Cancellarii, Epigrammata' in Johnston ed., *Delitiae poetarvm Scotorvm*, 2: F9^v–F11^v; and Maitland, *The Poems of Sir Richard Maitland*.

63. Brahe, *Opera omnia*, 2: 12, 9: 83, trans. in Brahe, *His Astronmicall Coniecture*; Christianson, *On Tycho's Island*, 141.

64. J to Bruce, 19 February 1590, Kronborg Castle; Calderwood 5: 81–2.

65. Hunter to Asheby, 29 November 1589, 'Houslo'. *CSPSc 11*: 188. 'Danish Account' 95.

66. Maitland to Bruce, 12 February 1590, Kronborg Castle. Calderwood 5: 83–6.

67. Bowes to WC and FW, 16 March 1590, Edinburgh, and Bowes to WC, 16 April 1590, Edinburgh. *CSPSc* 10: 252, 276.
68. Dreyer, *Tycho Brahe*, 205.
69. *Papers Relative* has the oration in Latin, no pagination.
70. Calderwood 5: 94–5.
71. Calderwood 5: 95; Bingham, *James VI*, 123.
72. See Calderwood 5: 96.
73. Williams, *Anne of Denmark*, 30.
74. *Papers Relative*, 54.
75. Melvill, Στεφανισκιον, rpt in *Papers Relative*, no pagination. See also Calderwood 5: 96–8 although Calderwood has this as part of Anna's entry celebrations; *Papers Relative* places it at the coronation (p. 55).
76. Calderwood 5: 95–6.
77. Russell, *Verba . . . pro senatv popvloque Edinbvrgensi habita*, rpt in *Papers Relative*, no pagination.
78. Another account has Justice, Temperance, Prudence, Fortitude; *Papers Relative*, 41.
79. Riis, *Should Auld Acquaintance*, 1: 265–6.
80. Calderwood 5: 99.
81. Calderwood 5: 98; Riis, *Should Auld Acquaintance*, 1: 265.
82. Calderwood 5: 99.
83. Meikle, 'Anna of Denmark', 129; Nichols 3: 531, 549, 541, cit. Meikle, '"Oeconomicall rule"', 105.
84. Melville, *Memoirs*, 393–5.
85. Calderwood 5: 98.
86. Calderwood 5: 99.
87. Calderwood 5: 105–6.

NOTES TO CHAPTER EIGHT

1. Riis, *Should Auld Acquaintance*, 1: 267.
2. See Larner, 'James VI and Witchcraft'; Larner, *Enemies of God*; Cowan, 'Darker Vision of the Scottish Renaissance'; and especially Normand & Roberts.
3. Larner, 'James VI and Witchcraft', 74–5.
4. Kirby, *Northern Europe*, 95.

5. Riis, *Should Auld Acquaintance*, 1: 267.
6. Larner, 'James VI and Witchcraft', 79; see also Black, *Calendar of Cases of Witchcraft*, 21–3; Stafford, 'Notes on Scottish Witchcraft Cases'.
7. *News from Scotland*; Normand & Roberts 316.
8. Melville, *Memoirs*, 395.
9. Normand & Roberts 159.
10. Melville, *Memoirs*, 397.
11. Robert Bowes to WC, 17 April 1591, Edinburgh. *CSPSc* 10: 504.
12. Bothwell's declaration, 7 February 1592. *CSPSc* 11: 61–4.
13. R[alph?] Carr to William Jennison, 4 May 1591, Pierce Bridge, co. Durham. *CSPSc* 10: 514.
14. *RPCS* 4: 643–4.
15. 'To the Nobility' [June–July? 1591]. *Warrender Papers* 2: 154–64.
16. Calderwood 5: 129.
17. J to Maitland, April 1591. *CSPSc* 10: 510.
18. Cit. Larner, 'James VI and Witchcraft', 83.
19. *Daemonologie*; Normand & Roberts.
20. *Daemonologie*; Normand & Roberts.
21. See Willson, 'James VI and his literary assistants'.
22. Bodl. MS Bodley 165 nos 17 and 18.
23. FSL MS V.a.185.
24. The suggestion is by Dunlap, 'King James and Some Witches', 43.
25. FSL MS V.a.185; *Daemonologie*.
26. Larner, 'James VI and Witchcraft', 86–7.
27. Willson 106; Bingham, *James VI*, 132.
28. See Bowes to WC, 1 August 1590, Edinburgh. *CSPSc* 10: 371.
29. Meikle, 'Anna of Denmark', 130.
30. Bowes to WC, 14 July 1591, Edinburgh. *CSPSc* 10: 543.
31. Meikle, 'Anna of Denmark', 130–31.
32. Melville, *Memoirs*, 403.
33. Bowes to WC, 26 January 1592, Holyroodhouse. *CSPSc* 10: 626–7.
34. Bowes to WC, 6 June 1592, Edinburgh. *CSPSc* 10: 687; News from Scotland, [August 1592]. *CSPSc* 10: 755; Meikle, 'Anna of Denmark', 131.
35. Craigie, *Poems of James VI*, 106. See also 'An epitaphe on John Shaw': Craigie, *Poems of James VI*, 106.

36. Calderwood 5: 140–42.
37. Calderwood 5: 142–3.
38. Calderwood 5: 143–4.
39. Bingham, *James VI*, 133.
40. For Moray's murder see Roger Aston to James Hudson, 9 February 1592, Edinburgh. *CSPSc* 10: 633–4; and Aston to Bowes, 8 February 1592, Edinburgh. *CSPSc* 10: 635–6.
41. Calderwood 5: 144–5.
42. Willson 108–9; Bingham, *James VI*, 135.
43. Bowes to WC, 12 August 1592, Edinburgh. *CSPSc* 10: 752–4.
44. News from Scotland, [August 1592]. *CSPSc* 10: 755.
45. Lee, *Maitland of Thirlestane*, 254.
46. For the Spanish blanks affair see Law, 'The Spanish Blanks'; Stafford, *James VI*, 74–123.
47. Burgh to WC, 5 March 1593, Edinburgh. *CSPSc* 11: 66.
48. Calderwood 5: 255–6.
49. J to Lord Burgh, [late March 1593]. Akrigg 120–21.
50. Quoted in Willson 112.
51. For Bothwell's attack see Thomson, *Historie and Life of James the Sext*, 270–2; Calderwood 5: 256.
52. Craigie, *Poems*, 2: 111.
53. Lee, *Maitland of Thirlestane*, 262–7.
54. E to J, [November 1593]. Bruce ed., *Letters of Elizabeth and James*, 98 n.*.
55. Calderwood 5: 296.
56. See *DNB* s.v. Gordon, George, sixth Earl and first Marquis of Huntly (1562–1636).
57. Grant, 'Brig o' Dee Affair', 108, 109.

NOTES TO CHAPTER NINE

1. Worcester to WC, 15 June 1590, Edinburgh. *CSPSc* 10: 324–5.
2. Advertisements from an Englishman in Berwick, 30 September 1591. *CSPSc* 10: 574. For a false rumour of Anna's pregnancy see Robert Bowes to WC, 21 November 1591, Berwick. *CSPSc* 10: 591.
3. Calderwood 5: 171.
4. Chambers, *Elizabethan Stage*, 3: 351; *New Poems*, ed. Westcott, lviii.

5. HMC Mar & Kellie 1: 40.
6. Colville, *Letters*, 163–77; Calderwood 5: 365–6.
7. Roger Aston to Bowes, 22 March and 30 May 1595, Holyroodhouse. *CSPSc* 11: 554, 602.
8. Nicholson to Bowes, 15 July 1595. *CSPSc* 11: 640.
9. J to Mar, 24 July 1595. HMC Mar & Kellie 1: 43–4.
10. Aston to Bowes, 31 July 1595, Edinburgh. *CSPSc* 11: 662–3.
11. Colville to Bowes, 20 August 1595. *CSPSc* 11: 683.
12. Craigie, *Poems*, 107.
13. George Nicolson to Bowes, 8 October 1595, Edinburgh. *CSPSc* 12: 41.
14. The Octavians were Walter Stewart, Prior of Blantyre (a fellow student with James); Alexander Seton, Lord Urquhart; John Lindsay, the parson of Menmuir; James Elphinstone; Thomas Hamilton ('Tam o' the Cowgate'); and Pluscardine.
15. Meikle, '"Oeconomicall rule"', 108–9; Willson 121–2.
16. Bowes to E, 24 February 1596, Edinburgh. *CSPSc* 12: 149–51. This account is based on Barroll, *Anna of Denmark*, 25.
17. Melvill, *Autobiography and Diary*, 2: 369–70.
18. Calderwood 5: 510–14.
19. Melvill quoted in Willson 125.
20. Calderwood 5: 681; Bingham, *James VI*, 139–40.
21. Calderwood 6: 96.
22. James VI, *Daemonologie, in forme of a Dialogue*. See Willson, 'James VI and his literary assistants'; Dunlap, 'King James and Some Witches'.
23. See, for example, Gentili, *Regales disputationes tres*, 18–19.
24. *Trew Law of Free Monarchies*; Sommerville 62, 63, 71.
25. *Trew Law of Free Monarchies*; Sommerville 64.
26. As BL Royal MS 18. B. xv.
27. *Basilikon Doron*, Sommerville 1.
28. *Basilikon Doron*, Sommerville 2.
29. *Basilikon Doron*, Sommerville 9–10.
30. *Basilikon Doron*, Sommerville 3.
31. Buchanan, *De ivre regni apvd Scotos*, A.2.ᵛ; trans. Arrowood, *Powers of the Crown in Scotland*, 37–8.
32. *Basilikon Doron*, Sommerville 41.

33. *Basilikon Doron*, Sommerville 46.
34. *Basilikon Doron*, Sommerville 25–6.
35. Calderwood 5: 744; Willson 126.
36. This summary is based on Craigie 2: 6–17.
37. By Peter Blayney, as quoted in Wormald, 'James, *Basilikon Doron* and *Trew Law*', 51.

NOTES TO CHAPTER TEN

1. On the Gowrie conspiracy see Bisset, 'Sir Walter Scott'; Lang, *James VI and the Gowrie Mystery*; Barbé, *Tragedy of Gowrie House*.
2. Calderwood 6: 45–6.
3. Calderwood 6: 46.
4. Melvill, *Autobiography and Diary*, 326 n.*.
5. Calderwood 6: 49–50.
6. Calderwood 6: 50.
7. Calderwood 6: 47.
8. Nicolson to RCe, 14 August 1600, Edinburgh. *CSPSc* 13: 684. Calderwood 6: 50–51.
9. Calderwood 6: 51–2.
10. Calderwood 6: 52, 53, 55.
11. Calderwood 6: 56.
12. Calderwood 6: 56, 49.
13. Nicolson to RCe, 11 August 1600, Edinburgh. *CSPSc* 13: 681–3.
14. Brouncker to RCe, 30 August 1600, Berwick. *CSPSc* 13: 693.
15. Calderwood 6: 68–70.
16. Calderwood 6: 46.
17. Calderwood 5: 57–8.
18. Calderwood 6: 85.
19. Calderwood 5: 58–9; Melvill, *Autobiography and Diary*, 326.
20. Nicolson to RCe, 6 August 1600, Edinburgh. *CSPSc* 13: 679.
21. *DNB* s.v. Ruthven, John, third Earl of Gowrie (1578?–1600); *DNB* s.v. Ramsay, Sir John, Viscount Haddington and Earl of Holderness (1580?–1626).
22. J to Christian IV, 11 November 1605, Westminster. Akrigg 276.
23. J to C and GV, 5 August [1623]. Akrigg 421.
24. Nicolson to RCe, 11 August 1600, Edinburgh, *CSPSc* 13: 682. For

Anna and the Ruthvens see Barroll, *Anna of Denmark*, 25–7.

25. Nicolson to RCe, 6 August 1600, Edinburgh. *CSPSc* 13: 679.
26. Nicolson to RCe, 21 August 1600, Edinburgh. *CSPSc* 13: 691.
27. Aston to RCe, 1 November 1600, Berwick. *CSPSc* 13: 723.
28. Sir Robert Carey to RCe, 21 October 1600, Woodrington. *Border Papers* 2: 698.
29. Neville to Winwood, 15 November 1600, London. Sawyer, *Memorials*, 1: 274.
30. Gray to RCe, 31 October 1600, Chillingham. *CSPSc* 13: 721.
31. Cit. Meikle, 'Anna of Denmark', 139.
32. Nicolson to RCe, 20 November 1600, Edinburgh. *CSPSc* 13: 737.
33. Hudson to RCe, [December 1602]. *CSPSc* 13: 1092.
34. Nicolson to RCe, 1 January 1603, Edinburgh. *CSPSc* 13: 1095–6.
35. Aston to RCe, 6 February 1603, Edinburgh. *CSPSc* 13: 1110.
36. Bruce, *Letters of Elizabeth and James*, vii–ix.
37. For the Adamson affair see PRO SP 12/41/28; Neale, *Elizabeth I and Her Parliaments 1559–1581*, 158–60; Hartley, *Proceedings in the Parliament*, 1: 121, 158–9, 163.
38. Stafford, *James VI of Scotland*, 200–201.
39. J to Essex, 31 October 1592, cit. Stafford, *James VI of Scotland*, 203.
40. See for example J to Essex, 13 April 1594, Edinburgh. Birch, *Memoirs*, 1: 175.
41. Lambeth Palace Library MSS 647–62; for Anthony Bacon, see Jardine and Stewart, *Hostage to Fortune*.
42. Stafford, *James VI of Scotland*, 200–201.
43. See Nicolson to RCe, 14 October 1598. HMCS 9: 307–10.
44. Sir Charles Davers's confession, 22 February 1601. Birch, *Memoirs*, 2: 470–2.
45. Bacon, *Letters and Life*, 2: 336–7, 359.
46. 7 [Essex] to J, 17 May [1600?]. Birch, *Memoirs*, 1: 176.
47. Essex to J, 25 December 1600. Stafford, *James VI of Scotland*, 214–15.
48. J to Mar and Kinloss, [early February 1601]. Akrigg 169–70.
49. J to Mar and Kinloss, [mid-February 1601]. Akrigg 170.
50. RCe to Nicolson, 23 May 1601. HMCS 10: 155–6 (misdated).
51. Mar and Kinloss to [RCe], 29 April 1601. Stafford, *James VI of Scotland*, 251.
52. RCe to Gray, 14 May 1601. HMCS 14: 176.

53. Bruce, *Letters of Elizabeth and James*, 134–8.
54. E to J, 11 May 1601. Stafford, *James VI of Scotland*, 253.
55. On Howard and Essex, see Peck, *Northampton*, 13–18.
56. Rowland Whyte to Sir Robert Sidney, 30 September 1599. HMCD 2: 397; Peck, *Northampton*, 17.
57. Whyte to Sidney, 30 August 1600. HMCD 2: 481; Peck, *Northampton*, 17.
58. J to 10 [RCe], first letter [April? 1601]. Akrigg 178–80.
59. J to 10 [RCe], second letter [June? 1601]. Akrigg 181.
60. See Stafford, *James VI of Scotland*, 256–7.
61. Howard to Bruce. Dalrymple 202–3.
62. RCe to J, first letter [March? 1601]. Bruce, *Letters of Elizabeth and James*, 3–8.
63. J to RCe, second letter [1601]. Bruce, *Letters of Elizabeth and James*, 10–11.
64. RCe to J, second letter, 4 October 1601. Bruce, *Letters of Elizabeth and James*, 13.
65. RCe to J, third letter, [February 1602]. Bruce, *Letters of Elizabeth and James*, 17.
66. J to RCe, [Autumn 1602?]. Akrigg 198–9.
67. Stafford, *James VI of Scotland*, 288.
68. Beaumont to Henri, 2 October 1602. Teulet, *Relations Politiques*, 4: 165.
69. Indernyty to J, 9 February 1603 cit. Stafford, *James VI of Scotland*, 288.
70. J to RCe, [December 1602?]. Akrigg 201.

NOTES TO CHAPTER ELEVEN

1. Calderwood 6: 215–16.
2. RCe to PC, 18 April 1603, York. HMCS 15: 52.
3. J to Henry, [April 1603]. Akrigg 211–12.
4. Calderwood 6: 223.
5. Wilbraham, *Journal*, 55–7. cit.
6. Nichols 1: 107–10.
7. Nichols 1: 113–14, 139–40.
8. Wilbraham, *Journal*, 56.

9. J to Mar, 24 July 1595, Stirling. Crawfurd, *Lives and Characters*, 403.

10. James, Marquis of Hamilton, James Cunningham, seventh Earl of Glencairn, Alexander Livingston, Earl of Linlithgow, Alexander, fourth Lord Elphinstone and John, Master of Orkney. See also *RPCS* 6: 571–2 for another list. Barroll notes that Hamilton and Glencairne were Protestants, but not politically active; Linlithgow and Elphinstone Roman Catholic. Anderson, *Letters and State Papers*, 333–53. Barroll, *Anna of Denmark*, 179–80 n. 40.

11. Scaramelli to the Doge and Senate of Venice, 18/28 May 1603, London. *CSPV* 10: 40.

12. Calderwood 6: 231.

13. J to A, [May? 1603]. Akrigg 214.

14. Calderwood 6: 231.

15. Calderwood 6: 231–2.

16. Fyvie to James, 30 May 1603, Edinburgh. Maidment, *Letters and State Papers*, 55.

17. Wilbraham, *Journal*, 60; Scaramelli to the Doge and Senate of Venice, 14/24 April and 18/28 May 1603, London. *CSPV* 10: 9, 39.

18. Bacon to Northumberland [April 1603]. Bacon, *Letters and Life*, 3: 77.

19. See Nichols 1: 329–401; Bergeron, 'Harrison, Jonson, and Dekker'; Bergeron, *English Civil Pageantry*, 61–89.

20. Dekker, *Dramatic Works*, 2: 258.

21. See Harrison, *Arches of Triumph*; Jonson, *Ben Jonson*, ed. Herford and Simpson, vol. 7; Dekker, *Dramatic Works*, 2: 231–52; Wickham, 'Contributions de Jonson et de Dekker'.

22. Dekker, *Dramatic Works*, 2: 258.

23. Wilson, *History of Great Britain*, 12–13.

24. Beaumont to Villeroy, 17 May 1603, PRO SP 31/3/35, cit. Cuddy, 'Revival', 193.

25. Cuddy, 'Revival'.

26. Cuddy, 'Revival'.

27. Holles, *Memorials of the Holles Family*, 94.

28. HMC Portland 9: 113, cit. Cuddy, 'Revival', 205.

29. Nottingham University Library, Portland MS PwV92, art. 17

(fo. 7v), cit. Cuddy, 'Revival', 192.

30. Scaramelli to the Doge and Senate of Venice, 12/22 May 1603. *CSPV* 10: 33.

31. Thomas Wilson to Sir Thomas Parry, 22 June 1603, Greenwich. Nichols 1: 188.

32. Giovanni Carlo Scaramelli to the Doge and Senate of Venice, 25 August/4 September 1603, Sunbury. *CSPV* 10: 90.

33. *Basilikon Doron*; Sommerville 56.

34. Assheton, *Journal*, 40 (entry for 12 August 1617).

35. DC to JC, 21 September 1604, Syon. *CSPD 1603–1610*, 151.

36. Scaramelli to the Doge and Senate of Venice, 25 August/4 September 1603, Sunbury. *CSPV* 10: 90.

37. Cuddy, 'Revival', 193.

38. Nicolo Molin, 'Report on England', 1607. *CSPV* 10: 513.

39. JC to Ralph Winwood, 26 January 1605. McClure 1: 201.

40. Molin to the Doge and Senate of Venice, 31 January/10 February 1605, London. *CSPV* 10: 218.

41. J to RCe, n.d. Salisbury MS 134/48.

42. Worcester to Cranborne, 3 May 1605, Thetford. Lodge, *Illustrations of British History*, 3: 137–8.

43. Worcester to Shrewsbury, 4 December 1604, Royston. Lodge, *Illustrations of British History*, 3: 110.

44. RCe to Sir John Harington, [1603]. Harington, *Nugae Antiquae*, 1: 345.

45. Edmund Lascelles to Shrewsbury, 4 December 1604. Lodge, *Illustrations of British History*, 3: 108.

46. Molin to the Doge and Senate of Venice, 31 January/10 February 1605, London. *CSPV* 10: 218–19.

47. Zorzi Guistinian to Doge and Senate of Venice, 21/31 May 1606, London. *CSPV* 10: 353.

48. 'Since that time neither that king nor any of his successors have visited the town.' Martin, *History of the Town of Thetford*, 57.

49. Samuel Calvert to Winwood, 6 April 1605, London. Sawyer, *Memorials*, 2: 57.

50. Molin to the Doge and Senate of Venice, 30 October/9 November 1605, London. *CSPV* 10: 285.

51. Goodman, *The Fall of Man*, L2^{r-v}.

52. Matthew [Hutton], Archbishop of York, to Cecil, 18 December

1604, Bishop Throp. BL Harley MS 677 f. 45^v.

53. Worcester to RCe, 25 February 1605, Royston. HMCS 17: 70.

54. RCe to Hutton, BL Harley MS 677 ff. 47^v–48^r.

55. J, 'A carteill or challenge to a trinite of knaues', n.d. Salisbury MS 134/66.

56. J to RCe, March 1605. Salisbury MS 134/71. J to RCe, 1610. Salisbury MS 134/145.

57. Hyde, *History of the Rebellion*, 1: 74.

58. See Marcham, 'James I of England and the Little Beagle Letters'; and the discussion of the term in Stewart, 'Government by Beagle'.

59. J to RCe, various dates. Salisbury MS 134/49, 48, 79, 66, cit. Marcham, 'James I', 320.

60. J to RCe, March 1605, Salisbury MS 134/66.

61. Worcester to RCe, 22 July 1609, Windsor, and 24 July 1609, Farnham. Nichols 2: 261, and 2: 262.

62. Worcester to RCe, 22 July 1609, Windsor, and 24 July 1609, Farnham. Nichols 2: 261, 262.

63. RCe to Lake, 16 April 1607. *CSPD 1603–1610*, 355.

64. Weldon, 'The Character of King James', in Scott ed., *Secret History*, 2: 5–6; Goodman, *Court of King James*, 1: 168.

65. J to RCe, [1605–1608]. Akrigg 286–7. The letter mentions 'Dunbar' so must date from between the creation of George Hume as Earl of Dunbar on 3 July 1605, and his death in 1608. See also A to RCe [1605–1608]. Akrigg 287 n. 1, on the same matter.

66. Molin, 'Report on England', 1607. *CSPV* 10: 513.

67. Barroll, *Anna of Denmark*, 38–9, 47, 57–8; Strong, *Henry*, 88–92. For Anna's household see Lodge, *Illustrations*, 3: 65.

68. JC to DC, 3 February 1621, London. McClure 2: 339. See also Jardine and Stewart, *Hostage to Fortune*, 437–9.

69. Nichols 1: 193–4.

70. Nichols 1: 416.

71. De la Boderie, 31 October 1606, cit. Birch, *Prince Henry*, 75–6.

72. De la Boderie, 31 October 1606, cit. Birch, *Prince Henry*, 75–6.

73. Cornwallis, *Account of Prince Henry*, 22.

74. De la Boderie, 31 October 1606, cit Birch, *Prince Henry*, 75–6.

1. Calderwood 6: 222.
2. Calderwood 6: 220–21.
3. See Collinson, *Religion of Protestants*; Collinson, *Birthpangs of Protestant England*; Lake, *Anglicans and Puritans?*.
4. Walton, 'Life of Hooker', 212–13.
5. See Tyacke, *Anti-Calvinists*.
6. Willson 198–9.
7. Quoted in Willson 200.
8. Proclamation, 24 October 1603, Wilton. Wilkins, *Concilia*, 4: 371–2.
9. J to Whitgift, 29 October 1603, Wilton. Akrigg 217.
10. Sir John Harington to Sir Amias Paulet, [December 1603?]. Harington, *Letters and Epigrams*, ed. McClure, 109–11.
11. Osborn, *Miscellany of Sundry Essayes*, B10^{r-v}.
12. Hacket, *Scrinia Reserata*, 38.
13. Quoted in Willson 203.
14. On the Hampton Court Conference see Barlow; Curtis, 'The Hampton Court Conference and its Aftermath'.
15. Barlow M2^{r-v}. The reference is to Eunapius' characterisation of Longinus.
16. Barlow B2^{v}.
17. Barlow B2^{v}–B3^{v}.
18. Barlow B3^{v}–C^{v}.
19. Barlow C^{v}–D^{r}.
20. Barlow D2^{r-v}.
21. *DNB* s.v. 'Rainoldes or Reynolds, John (1549–1607)'.
22. Barlow D3^{r}–E2^{v}.
23. Barlow I^{r}.
24. Barlow F^{r}–F4^{v}.
25. Barlow G4^{r-v}.
26. J to Whitgift, 29 October 1603, Wilton. BL Harley MS 677 f. 107; Akrigg 216.
27. Barlow H2^{r}–H3^{r}.
28. Barlow K^{v}–K2^{v}.
29. Barlow K3^{v}–K4^{r}.
30. Barlow L2^{r-v}, L2^{v}, L2^{v}–L3^{r}, K4^{v}–L^{r}.

31. Barlow K4^v–L^r.
32. Barlow L3^v–L4^v.
33. Barlow L4–M2^r.
34. Barlow O3^r–O4^r.
35. Harington, 'Breefe Notes and Remembraunces.' Harington, *Nugae Antiquae*, 1: 181–2.
36. J to Northampton, [January 1604]. Ellis, *Original Letters*, 3rd ser., 4: 162.
37. On the King James Bible, see Daiches, *The King James Version*; Opfell, *The King James Bible Translators*.
38. Barlow G3^r.
39. Spottiswoode, *History*, 3: 98.
40. 'Their disobedience herein was lawful, but their dissembling evil.' *Geneva Bible*, ed. Berry, Exodus 1: 19, marginal note (f. iiij.^{v}).
41. 'Herein he showed that he lacked zeal: for she ought to have died both by the covenant, and by the law of God: but he gave place to foolish pity, and would also seem after a sort to satisfy the Law.' *Geneva Bible*, ed. Berry, 2 Chronicles 15: 16 (Dd.i.^{r}).
42. Barlow G4^{r-v}.
43. See J to Bancroft, 22 July 1604, Wesminster Palace. Wilkins, *Concilia*, 4: 407–8. 'An order set down by king James the first, for the translating of the Bible' [1604]. Wilkins, *Concilia*, 4: 432–3.
44. James VI, *Poeticall Exercises*, 3^v; Craigie, *Poems*, 1: 100.
45. Spottiswoode, *History*, 3: 98–9.
46. For the discussion of metre see Alexander to Drummond, 4 February 1617, Newmarket, quoted in Rogers, *Memoirs of . . . the House of Alexander*, 50. For his answer ('When Britain's monarch, in true greatness great') to James's sonnet ('How cruelly these catives do conspire') see ibid., 50.
47. Alexander to Drummond, 18 April 1620. Rogers, *Memoirs of . . . the House of Alexander*, 53–4.
48. Rogers, *Memoirs of . . . the House of Alexander*, 81, 142–4.
49. Willson 209.
50. J to RCe, [22? November 1605]. Akrigg 236. On the Royston Petition see Quintrell, 'The Royal Hunt and the Puritans'.
51. J to RCe [February 1604]. Akrigg 255.
52. JC to Winwood, 26 January 1605, London. McClure 1: 201.

NOTES TO CHAPTER THIRTEEN

1. See Doelman, *King James I*, 1–2; Stewart, 'Boys' Buttocks Revisited'.
2. *Basilikon Doron*; Sommerville 27.
3. Eedes, *Six Learned and Godly Sermons*; see also King, *A Sermon at Paules Crosse*, 42.
4. Sempill, *Sacrilege sacredly Handled*.
5. *Covnter-Blaste to Tobacco*, B^v, C4$^{r–v}$, D2^r.
6. *Covnter-Blaste to Tobacco*, A3$^{r–v}$.
7. *Covnter-Blaste to Tobacco*, A3^v–A4^r.
8. Lee, *Government by Pen*, 6; *Basilikon Doron*, Sommerville 21.
9. On the Union see Galloway, *Union of England and Scotland*.
10. J to the PC of Scotland, 12 January 1604, Hampton Court. *Letters of King James the Sixth*, lv.
11. J to Parliament, 19 March 1604. Sommerville 134–7.
12. *CJ* 1: 150, 154–7.
13. *CJ* 1: 154–7.
14. *CJ* 1: 157–8.
15. *CJ* 1: 166.
16. *CJ* 1: 171.
17. *CJ* 1: 180.
18. J to Parliament, 1 May 1604. *CJ* 1: 193.
19. Notestein, *House of Commons*, 84–5.
20. Willson 253.
21. Stow, *Annales*, 856.
22. *CJ* 1: 332.
23. *CJ* 1: 333–6.
24. Willson 255–6.
25. Howell, *Annales*, 2: 559–75; *CJ* 1: 366–8.
26. Cit. Strong, *Henry Prince of Wales*, 46.
27. Molin 'Report on England', 1607. *CSPV* 10: 513–14.
28. Correr to the Doge and Senate of Venice, 16/26 December 1608, London. *CSPV* 11: 206.
29. Coke, *Detection of the Court and State*, 1: 61.
30. Goodman, *Court of King James* 1: 250–51.

1. On the Gunpowder Plot see Nicholls, *Investigating Gunpowder Plot*; Haynes, *Gunpowder Plot*; Fraser, *Gunpowder Plot*.
2. *His Majesties Speach in This Last Session of Parliament*; Sommerville 149.
3. Plowden, *Stuart Princesses*, 12–13.
4. Nicholls, *Investigating Gunpowder Plot*, 41.
5. Quoted in Akrigg, *Jacobean Pageant*, 72–3.
6. J to [PC?], [6 November 1605]. Akrigg 274–5.
7. Lee, *Government by Pen*, 36–7.
8. Plowden, *Stuart Princesses*, 13–14.
9. *His Majesties Speach in This Last Session of Parliament*; Sommerville 147–8.
10. *His Majesties Speach in This Last Session of Parliament*; Sommerville 150–51.
11. *Discourse of the Maner of the Discovery; Workes*.
12. Plowden, *Stuart Princesses*, 14.
13. Molin to the Doge and Senate of Venice, 11/12 November 1605, London. *CSPV* 10: 293.
14. *Copie of a Letter written from Master T.M. . . .*, A3^r, B^r and passim.
15. *His Majesties Speach in This Last Session of Parliament*; Sommerville 150, 152.
16. 3 & 4 Jac.I c. 5. For the wording of the 'Oath' see Tanner ed., *Constitutional Documents of the Reign of James I*, 90–91.
17. Molin to the Doge and Senate of Venice, 27 December/6 January 1605/6, London. *CSPV* 10: 308.
18. James VI and I, *Workes*, d2^{r-v}.
19. Giustinian to Doge and Senate of Venice, 29 September/9 October 1608, London. *CSPV* 11: 178.
20. James VI and I, *Workes*, d2^v.
21. De la Boderie to Puisieux, 22 December 1607/1 January 1608, de la Boderie, *Ambassades*, 3: 5. See also Giustinian to the Doge and Senate of Venice, 9/19 December 1607, London. *CSPV* 11: 74.
22. Hacket, *Scrinia Reserata*, 1: 221.
23. De la Boderie to Villeroy, 12 March 1608, London. De la Boderie, *Ambassades*, 3: 164.
24. James VI and I, *Workes*, d2^v–d3^r.

25. De la Boderie to Puisieux, 16/26 March 1608, London. De la Boderie, *Ambassades*, 3: 190–91.

26. Tortus, *Responsio . . . ad librvm inscriptvm, Triplici nodo triplex cvnevs*; Parsons, *Judgement of a Catholicke Englishman*.

27. De la Boderie to Puisieux, 22 September/2 October 1608, Richmond. De la Boderie, *Ambassades*, 4: 17.

28. James to Henri IV, 15/25 May 1609, n.p. *Fortescue Papers*, ed. Gardiner, 3–6 at 4.

29. Tortus, *Responsio*, D3^v–D4^r.

30. J to RCe, [October 1608]. Akrigg 309.

31. See also Andrewes, *Tortvra Torti*, Z3^r–Bb4^r (181–99) with Balmerino's confession at Aa4^r–Bb^v (191–4).

32. Willson, 'James I and His Literary Assistants', 43–4.

33. James VI and I, *Workes*, d3^v.

34. Corner to the Doge and Senate of Venice, 18/28 November 1608, London. *CSPV* 11: 193.

35. De la Boderie to Puisieux, 4/14 March 1609, London. De la Boderie, *Ambassades*, 4: 266–74 at 271.

36. Lake to RCe, 3 December 1608. *CSPD 1603–1610*, 472.

37. De la Boderie to Puisieux, 26 April/6 May 1609, Chelsea. De la Boderie, *Ambassades*, 4: 318–21 at 318.

38. JC to DC, 26 April 1609, Ware Park. McClure 2: 291.

39. *Apologie* (1609 edn), (a 2)$^{r-v}$.

40. *Apologie* (1609 edn), (f)^v, (f 3)^r, (f 4)^r.

41. See J to RCe, [12? September 1609]. Akrigg 312–13.

42. Wotton to James, 14 August 1609 n.s., Venice. Pearsall Smith, *Wotton*, 1: 465–7, and 101–2.

43. Casaubon to Charles Labbé, November 1611, cit. Pattison, *Isaac Casaubon*, 286–7.

44. Hobbes, *Leviathan*, ch. 19, final para.; Locke, *Two Treatises of Government*, 2nd treatise, section 200; quoted by Sommerville xv.

NOTES TO CHAPTER FIFTEEN

1. See Usher, 'James I and Sir Edward Coke'.

2. J to RCe, [19? October 1607]. Akrigg 294–5.

3. Wilbraham to PC, 11 October 1607. HMCS 19: 275.

4. *State Trials* 2: 131–59.
5. Coke, *Twelfth part of the Reports*, J4ᵛ.
6. J to RCe, [18 October 1605]. HMCS 17: 457.
7. Harington to Barlow, [July 1606, Theobalds]. Harington, *Letters and Epigrams*, 119–21.
8. For the celebrations, see Anon., *The King of Denmarkes welcome*; 'The Monarchs meeting' in Anon., *Honor Trivmphant*, E4ʳ–F3ᵛ; Robarts, *The Most royall and Honourable entertainement*; Nichols 1: 319–423 and 4: 1074–5; Bergeron, *English Civil Pageantry*, 91–2.
9. Anon., *The King of Denmarkes welcome*, Bᵛ–B2ʳ.
10. Harington to Barlow, [July 1606, Theobalds]. Harington, *Letters and Epigrams*, 119–21.
11. J to PC, [19? October 1607]. Akrigg 291–3. The dating is Akrigg's.
12. Dietz, *English Public Finance*, 100–126.
13. Gardiner, *Parliamentary Debates in 1610*, ix–xx; Dietz, *English Public Finance*, 100–126.
14. Gardiner, *Parliamentary Debates in 1610*, 1–9, 13–14.
15. James VI and I, 'A Speech to the Lords and Commons of the Parliament at White-Hall, on Wednesday the XXI. of March. Anno 1609', *Workes*, 527–48; see also the account in Inner Temple, Petit MS 537/14, ff. 172ʳ–176ʳ, printed in Foster, *Proceedings in Parliament 1610*, 59–63.
16. BL Add. MS 4210, printed in Gardiner, *Parliamentary Debates in 1610*, at 34–6; and PRO SP 14/54/65, printed in ibid., 34–6 n.a.
17. JC to DC, 24 May 1610, London. McClure 1: 301.
18. BL Harley MS 777 ff. 53ʳ–54ʳ; Sir Roger Aston to [unknown], 24 July 1610. PRO SP 14/56/42, both printed in Foster, *Proceedings in Parliament 1610*, 283–4, and 284–6 at 285.
19. Quoted in Willson 266.
20. Sir Thomas Lake to RCe, 21 October 1608, Newmarket. PRO SP 14/37/23.
21. J to RCe, [6? December 1610]. Akrigg 317. See also Lake to [Salisbury], 27 November 1610, Royston. *CSPD 1603–1610*, 647.
22. BL Add. MS 48119 fo. 213ʳ, printed in Foster, *Proceedings in Parliament 1610*, 348.
23. J to PC, 7 December 1610. HMCS 21: 266.

24. RCe to J, [3 December 1610]. HMCS 21: 264.

25. J to RCe, [6? December 1610]. Akrigg 316–17.

26. RCe to J, 9 December [1610]. HMCS 21: 267.

27. RCe to Lake, 9 December 1610. HMCS 21: 268.

28. John More to Winwood, 17 February 1612, London. Nichols 2: 437.

29. BL Add. MS 25548 fo. 9v and BL Egerton 2230 fo. 34, quoted in Croft, 'Reputation of Robert Cecil', 55.

30. Northampton to RCe, 26 May 1612. PRO SP 14/69/56; *CSPD* 1611–1618, 133.

31. JC to DC, 27 May 1612, London. McClure 1: 351.

32. Cit. Strong, *Henry*, 144–5.

33. Landesbibliothek Kassle, MS Hass. 68, ff. 61v–62, cit. Strong, *Henry*, 211–12.

34. Garganò, *Scapigliatura*, 68–9, cit. Strong, *Henry*, 211.

35. Salisbury to Newton, n.d. BL Harley MS 7002 ff. 95–96v, cit. Strong, *Henry*, 74.

36. Plowden, *Stuart Princesses*, 18–20.

37. Plowden, *Stuart Princesses*, 20–21.

38. JC to Winwood, 3 November 1612, London. McClure 1: 384.

39. On H's decline, see Cornwallis, *Account*, 26–32.

40. JC to DC, 12 November 1612, London. McClure 1: 388–90.

41. Cornwallis, *Account*, 44.

42. JC to DC, 12 November 1612, London.

43. Moore, *History of the Study of Medicine*, 96–7; MacAlpine and Hunter, *George III and the Mad Business*, 209–10.

44. Osborne, *Traditional Memoirs*, in Scott ed., *Secret History of the Court*, 1: 267–8.

45. JC to DC, 12 November 1612, London. McClure 1: 390.

46. Foscarini to the Doge and Senate of Venice, 1/11 April 1613, London. *CSPV* 12: 521.

47. JC to DC, 8 February 1617, London. McClure 2: 52.

48. For a list see Nichols 2: 504–12.

49. Cit. *DNB* s.v. Henry Frederick, Prince of Wales.

50. Greville, *Five Years of King James*, D[v].

51. Osborne, *Traditional Memoirs*, in Scott ed., *Secret History of the Court*, 1: 261–2.

52. Most persuasively in Strong, *Henry Prince of Wales*.
53. JC to Winwood, 9 January 1613, and JC to DC, 31 December 1612, London. McClure 1: 403, 399.
54. JC to Alice Carleton, 18 February 1613, London. McClure 1: 423–6.
55. JC to DC, 11 March 1613, London. McClure 1: 436–7.
56. Plowden, *Stuart Princesses*, 27.
57. Trumbull to Winwood, 25 June 1613, Brussels. Sawyer, *Memorials*, 3: 407.
58. Plowden, *Stuart Princesses*, 30.
59. Willson, *Privy Councillors*, 130–46.
60. 'Memorial of some points'. Bacon, *Letters and Life*, 5: 24–30.
61. J's speech to Parliament, 5 April 1614. Bodl. MS Carte 77 ff. 145–6, printed in Jansson, *Proceedings*, 13–19. Gondomar to Philip III [April 1614]. Jansson 7–9.
62. J's speech to Parliament, 9 April 1614. Bodl. MS Carte 77 ff. 142ᵛ–143ᵛ, printed in Jansson, *Proceedings*, 43–6.
63. Wotton to Sir Edmund Bacon. Wotton, *Letters*, 32; Jansson, *Proceedings*, 313 n. 19.
64. Anonymous diary, entry for 3 June 1614. Kenneth Spencer Research Library MS E237 printed Jansson, *Proceedings*, 422–3. JC to DC, 14 July 1614, London. McClure 1: 548. See also Jansson, *Proceedings*, 423 n. 33.
65. *CJ* 1: 496.
66. *CJ* 1: 505; *LJ* 1: 716.
67. Anonymous diary, entry for 6 June 1614. Kenneth Spencer Research Library MS E237 printed Jansson, *Proceedings*, 427.
68. Willson 363–4.
69. Francisco de Jesus, *Hecho*, 286–8.

NOTES TO CHAPTER SIXTEEN

1. On Somerset see Willson, ch. 18; Seddon, 'Robert Carr'; Bergeron, *King James and Letters of Homosexual Desire*, ch. 3.
2. See Greville, *Five Years of King James*, A4ᵛ–Bʳ.
3. Wilson, *History of Great Britain*, H3ᵛ–H4ʳ.
4. For treatment of James's relations with men, see especially Bergeron; Young, *James VI and I*.

5. [Woddryngton] to FW, 30 April 1588, Berwick. *CSPSc* 9: 557–8. See *infra*, chapter 7.

6. Barroll, *Anna of Denmark*, 131–2.

7. Lord Thomas Howard to Sir John Harington, [1607?] Harington, *Nugae Antiquae*, 390–97. Harington dates this letter to 1611, but it clearly derives from a period earlier in Carr's ascent before he had been given any title, possibly even before being knighted.

8. Wilson, *History of Great Britain*, M2^r.

9. Howard to Harington, [1607?] Harington, *Nugae Antiquae*, 390–97.

10. Howard to Harington, [1607?] Harington, *Nugae Antiquae*, 390–97.

11. JC to DC, 30 December 1607, London. McClure 1: 249.

12. Warrant to Henryck van Hulfen, 22 March 1608. *CSPD 1603–1610*, 417.

13. Correr to the Doge and Senate of Venice, 11/21 April and 4 May 1611, London. *CSPV* 12: 135–6, 142.

14. Fenton to Mar, 22 June 1612, Greenwich. HMC Mar & Kellie 2: 40–41.

15. Isaac Wake to DC, 17 December 1612, cit. Bergeron 71.

16. Somerset, *Unnatural Murder*, ch. 3.

17. JC to DC, 29 April 1613, London. McClure 1: 443–4. See also JC to DC, 6 May 1613, London. McClure 1: 448.

18. See Fenton to Mar, 20 May 1613 and [c. June 1613]. HMC Mar & Kellie 2: 51 and 52.

19. Southampton to Winwood, 6 August 1613, n.p. Sawyer, *Memorials*, 3: 475.

20. Somerset, *Unnatural Murder*, 139–69.

21. Cobbett, *State Trials* 2: 794–820, 860–62. The original commission comprised Bishops Abbot, Andrewes, King and Neile; civilians Sir Daniel Donne, Sir John Bennet, Dr James and Dr Edwards; councillors Sir Thomas Parry and Sir Julius Caesar. The two extra bishops were Bilson and John Buckridge.

22. JC to DC, 27 October 1613 and 11 November 1613, London. McClure 1: 481, 485. James made Lennox Earl of Richmond before making Rochester Earl of Somerset, to ensure his cousin's precedence. See Lee, *Government by Pen*, 150 n. 29.

23. See Nichols 2: 704–45.

24. JC to DC, 30 December 1613, London. McClure 1: 495–7. See 25

November 1613, London. McClure 1: 487; 9 December 1613, London. McClure 1: 490–91; 30 December 1613, London. McClure 1: 498–9.

25. Campion, *The Description of a Maske*, in Nichols 2: 707–14 at 713.
26. Willson 343.
27. JC to DC, 14 October 1613, London. McClure 1: 480.
28. Gardiner, *History of England*, 2: 199–201, 227–8; Dietz, *English Public Finance*, 149–58.
29. Cit. Willson 343.
30. JC to DC, 3 March 1614, London. McClure 1: 515.
31. Gondomar to Philip III, [April 1614]. Jansson, *Proceedings*, 5.
32. Edward Reynoldes to Francis Mills, 9 July 1614, London. PRO SP 14/77/59.
33. JC to DC, 14 July 1614, London. McClure 1: 548.
34. For the progress see Nichols 3: 10–24.
35. Goodman, *Court of King James*, 1: 225–6; D'Ewes, *Autobiography*, 166–7.
36. Fenton to Mar, 2 November 1614. HMC Mar & Kellie 2: 56.
37. JC to DC, 24 November 1614. McClure 1: 559.
38. See PC to J, [20 November 1614]. PRO SP 14/78/58.
39. James to RCa [1615]. Akrigg 335–44; Bergeron 80–84.
40. Lockyer, *Buckingham*, 16.
41. JC to DC, 1 December 1614, London. McClure 1: 561.
42. Coke, *Detection of the Court and State of England*, 82.
43. Rushworth, *Historical Collections*, 1: 456; Goodman, *Court of King James the First* (1839), 1: 22. Lockyer, *Buckingham*, 18–20.
44. Sarmiento to the Duke of Lerma, 20/30 October 1615. Gardiner 166–8.
45. Foscarini and Barbarigo to the Doge of Venice, 28 October/7 November 1615. Gardiner 175.
46. Sarmiento to the Duke of Lerma, 20/30 October 1615. Gardiner 166–8. See also Foscarini and Barbarigo to the Doge of Venice, 28 October/7 November 1615. Gardiner 175–6. For the second pardon see Gardiner 176 n.a.
47. Sarmiento to the Duke of Lerma, 7/17 November and 20/30 October 1615. Gardiner 177, 168.
48. J to RCa, [July? 1615]. Akrigg 341–2; Bergeron 87–8.

49. JC to DC, 20 July 1615, London. McClure 1: 609.
50. Lockyer, *Buckingham*, 22.
51. On the Overbury affair, see Spedding, 'Review of the evidence'; Somerset, *Unnatural Murder*; for a sensational near-contemporary account see Greville, *Five Years of King James*.
52. Sarmiento to Lerma, 20/30 October 1615. Gardiner 170.
53. Willson 353.
54. Bodl. Smith 17, fo. 30; SP 14/81/88 fo. 149r–v cit. Somerset, *Unnatural Murder*, 293.
55. Sarmiento to Lerma, 20/30 October 1615. Gardiner 171.
56. Weldon, *Court and Character of King James*, in Scott ed., *Secret History of the Court of James the First*, 1: 411.
57. J to RCa, [October 1615]. Akrigg 343–5; Bergeron 88–90.
58. Sarmiento to Lerma, 20/30 October 1615. Gardiner 171–4.
59. Sarmiento to Philip III, 20/30 January 1616. Gardiner 177–9.
60. Sarmiento to Philip III, 20/30 January 1616. Gardiner 179–80.
61. J to Sir George More, [May 1616]. Akrigg 350–51.
62. J to More, [May 1616]. Akrigg 351–2.
63. J to More, [May 1616]. Akrigg 352–3.
64. J to More, [May 1616]. Akrigg 353–4.
65. Sarmiento to Philip III, 31 May/10 June 1616. Gardiner 182–4.
66. See Jardine and Stewart, *Hostage to Fortune*, 377–80; Stewart, 'The Body Archival'.
67. JC to DC, 8 June 1616, London. McClure 2: 6.
68. Edward Sherburn to DC, 25 May 1616. PRO SP 14/87/29; *CSPD 1611–1618*, 368.
69. Howell, *State Trials*, 2: 996.
70. Bacon, *Letters and Life*, 5: 334.
71. JC to DC, 8 June 1616, London. McClure 2: 6.
72. Sarmiento to Philip III, 31 May/10 June 1616. Gardiner 185.
73. Sherburn to DC, 31 May 1616, London. PRO SP 14/87/40 cit. Spedding, 'Review', 111. Sarmiento claims that James called for him that day, and he 'was a long time with him'. See Sarmiento to Philip III, 31 May/10 June 1616. Gardiner 181.
74. Weldon, in Scott, *Secret History*, 1: 411–12, 424.
75. Sherburn to DC, 31 May 1616, London. PRO SP 14/87/40, cit. Spedding, 'Review', 111–12.

76. For this see Stewart, 'Homosexuals in History'.
77. BL Harley MS 481 ff. 16ᵛ–17ʳ. D'Ewes, *Diary*, ed. Bourcier, 92–3 [entry for 22 August 1622].
78. BL Harley MS 481 f. 20ᵛ. D'Ewes, *Diary*, ed. Bourcier, 100 [entry for 2 October 1622].
79. 'Casaubon', *Corona Regia*.
80. BL shelfmark 292.a.42.
81. 'Casaubon', *Corona Regia*, D9ᵛ–D10ᵛ.
82. For correspondence relating to this hunt, see BL Stowe MS 176, f. 170; BL Egerton MS 2592 f. 37b; BL Egerton MS 2593 ff. 17, 28; BL Egerton MS 2594 f. 19; BL Egerton MS 2595 f. 197.
83. Pattison, *Isaac Casaubon*, 483.
84. See Jardine and Stewart, *Hostage to Fortune*, chs. 13–15.
85. 'Anglipotrida', 14/24 January 1618, London. *CSPV* 15: 113–14.
86. Sherburn to DC, 31 May 1616, London. *CSPD 1611–1618*, 370. PRO SP 14/86/95, 14/87/40, cit. Lockyer, *Buckingham*, 33–4.
87. Salvetti Correspondence in HMC 11th Report, Appendix, Part I, Henry Duncan Skrine (1887) 14 Nov. 1617. Archivio Mediceo 4192, cit. Lockyer, *Buckingham*, 34.
88. JC to DC, 28 February 1618, London. McClure 2: 144. This episode is discussed in Young, *James VI and I*, 76.
89. See Lockyer, *Buckingham*, 35–6.
90. Quoted in Williamson, *George Villiers*, 68.

NOTES TO CHAPTER SEVENTEEN

1. For a full account of Scotland from 1603 see Lee, *Government by Pen*, here at 27–30 and passim.
2. For Dunfermline's news, see Lee, *Government by Pen*, 155.
3. Nichols 3: 308–9.
4. Various proclamations, *RPCS* 10: 681–4.
5. Lee, *Government by Pen*, 155.
6. 'Proclamatioun aganis the slaughter of Murefoule', Nichols 3: 315.
7. 'Proclamation againis the slaying of his Majestie's Buckis', 14 January 1617. Nichols 3: 327–8.

8. Lee, *Government by Pen*, 155.
9. 'Articles required for the service of the Church of Scotland'. Laing, *Original Letters*, 2: 445–6.
10. Lee, *Government by Pen*, 159–60.
11. J to PC of Scotland, 15 December 1616, Newmarket. *RPCS* 10: 684–6.
12. For the itinerary, see Nichols 3: 257.
13. Calderwood 7: 245.
14. Nichols 3: 279, 264, 263–4.
15. GV to Bacon, 23 April 1617. Nichols 3: 280–21.
16. Nichols 3: 300.
17. Calderwood 7: 245.
18. On James's entry into Edinburgh, see Calderwood 7: 245–6; Nichols 3: 317–28, here at 319.
19. *The Muses' Welcome*.
20. Anthony Weldon, quoted in Nichols 3: 338–9.
21. [Anonymous] to Bacon, 28 June 1617, Edinburgh. PRO SP 14/92, no. 75 quoted Nichols 3: 347.
22. Calderwood 7: 246.
23. Calderwood 7: 246–7; *RPCS* 11: 137.
24. JC to DC, 21 June 1617, London. McClure 2: 82.
25. Calderwood 7: 249.
26. 'Reasons to dissuade ministers from assisting to bishops at Parliament'. Calderwood 2: 247–9 at 248.
27. Lee, *Government by Pen*, 164.
28. [Anonymous] to Bacon, 28 June 1617, Edinburgh. PRO SP 14/92, no. 75 quoted Nichols 3: 345–8.
29. [Anonymous] to Bacon, 28 June 1617, Edinburgh. PRO SP 14/92, no. 75 quoted Nichols 3: 345–8.
30. Nichols 3: 337–8.
31. Forsyth, *Beauties of Scotland*, 4: 293–4.
32. Adamson, *The Muses' Welcome*, Gg^r.
33. Calderwood 7: 246.
34. Adamson, *The Muses' Welcome*, Vu5$^{r–v}$; Nichols 3: 370–71; Chambers, *Domestic Annals of Scotland*, 1: 483–5; *RPCS* 11: 196–8 n.1.
35. Adamson, *The Muses' Welcome*, Ii^v.
36. Calderwood 7: 261–83; Spottiswoode, *Historie*, 3: 247.

37. Spottiswoode, *Historie*, 3: 245–7.
38. Nichols 3: 372, 382, 385–9; Lee, *Government by Pen*, 170.
39. Calderwood 7: 273–4.
40. J to the Archbishops of St Andrews and Glasgow, 6 December 1617, Newmarket. Laing, *Original Letters*, 524.
41. *RPCS* 11: 296–7.
42. Calderwood 7: 298–301.
43. James to the PC and the Bishops, 10 July 1618, Theobalds. Calderwood 7: 308–11.
44. Calderwood 7: 304–39; Lee, *Government by Pen*, 174–6.
45. Lee, *Government by Pen*, 179.

NOTES TO CHAPTER EIGHTEEN

1. For the marriage negotiations from the Spanish point of view, see Francisco de Jesús, *Hecho, passim*.
2. Gardiner, *History of England*, 3: 39–43; Willson 369–70.
3. Gardiner, *History of England*, 3: 113–26; Quinn, *Ralegh and the British Empire*, 240–67.
4. Willson 374–5.
5. Gondomar to Philip III, 5/15 July 1618 cit. Willson 374–5; Gardiner, *History of England*, 3: 132–3.
6. Gardiner, *History of England*, 3: 132–4.
7. Gardiner, *History of England*, 3: 141–51.
8. See GV to Cottington, [?November 1618]. BL Add MS 14,015 f. 75; trans. Gardiner, *Letters*, 1: 24–5 at 24.
9. Gardiner, *Letters*, 1: 4 n.a.
10. *The Peace-Maker*, A3ʳ, A4ʳ, Bᵛ; see also discussion in Young, *James VI and I*, 86–7.
11. See Stewart, 'Purging Troubled Humours'.
12. Cottington to Sir Robert Naunton, 17/27 September 1618, Madrid; Gardiner, *Letters*, 1: 9–12 at 10.
13. GV to Gondomar, 30 September/10 October 1618; Gardiner, *Letters*, 1: 13.
14. Willson 409–10.

15. Cottington to Sir Thomas Lake, 25 June/5 July 1618, Madrid; Gardiner, *Letters*, 1: 3–4.

16. PRO SP 14/95/6 discussed in Lockyer, *Buckingham*, 32–3.

17. GV to Cottington, [?November 1618]. BL Add. MS 14,015 f. 75; trans. Gardiner, *Letters*, 1: 24–5.

18. Antonio Donato to the Doge and Senate of Venice, 14/24 January 1619, London. *CSPV* 15: 444.

19. Cottington to Naunton, 3/13 December 1618, Madrid. Gardiner, *Letters*, 1: 25–6 at 26.

20. JC to DC, 6 March 1619, London. McClure 2: 219–20. See also JC to DC, 19 March 1619, London. McClure 2: 222.

21. Moore, *History of the Study of Medicine*, 101–2; 166–7. See also JC to DC, 24 April 1619, London. McClure 2: 232.

22. Williams, *Great Britains Salomon*, I3ᵛ.

23. JC to DC, 24 April 1619, London. McClure 2: 232.

24. JC to DC, 5 June 1619, London. McClure 2: 242–3.

25. Cit. Willson 405.

26. Plowden, *Stuart Princesses*, 34.

27. Gardiner, *History of England*, 2: 2, cit. Plowden, *Stuart Princesses*, 34.

28. Notestein, *Commons Debates 1621*, 6: 370.

29. Notestein, *Commons Debates 1621*, 6: 370.

30. Plowden, *Stuart Princesses*, 35.

31. C to Doncaster, 27 June 1619. Cit. Plowden, *Stuart Princesses*, 36.

32. Willson 411.

33. Piero Antonio Marioni to Doge and Senate of Venice, 22 November 1619, London. *CSPV* 16: 53.

34. Willson 411–12.

35. Cit. Willson 412.

36. Willson 412–13.

37. Gardiner, *History of England*, 3: 338.

38. Gardiner, *History of England*, 3: 336–8.

39. Lando to Doge and Senate, 24 April 1620, London. *CSPV* 16: 239. See also Lando to Doge and Senate, 9 July 1620, London. *CSPV* 16: 308–10.

40. Tillières, 26 May/5 June 1620, quoted in Gardiner, *History of England*, 3: 350.

41. Lando to Doge and Senate, 23 July 1620, London. *CSPV* 16: 327.

42. Lando to Doge and Senate, 14 August 1620, London. *CSPV* 16: 363.
43. Lando to Doge and Senate, 27 August 1620, London. *CSPV* 16: 377.
44. Gardiner, *History of England*, 3: 370–7; Willson 415–16.
45. Quoted in Willson 416.
46. *Vox Populi*; on Scott see Wright, 'Propaganda Against James'.
47. Lando to Doge and Senate, 4 December 1620. *CSPV* 16: 491.
48. D'Ewes, *Autobiography*, 1: 158–9.
49. Lando to Doge and Senate of Venice, 11 December 1620, London. *CSPV* 16: 496.
50. JC to DC, 22 December 1620. McClure 2: 331. See Davies, 'English Political Sermons'.
51. JC to DC, 10 March 1621, London. McClure 2: 350; Wright, 'Propaganda Against James', 154–5.
52. Lando to Doge and Senate, 11 December 1620, London. *CSPV* 16: 495–7 at 496.
53. JC to DC, 3 February 1621, London. McClure 2: 338. On the 1621 Parliament see *LJ* 3; Nicholas, *Proceedings and Debates*; Notestein et al., *Commons Debates 1621*; Zaller, *Parliament of 1621*; Russell, *Parliaments and English Politics*.
54. J's speech to Parliament, [30] January 1621. PRO SP 14/119/47; *CSPD 1619–21*, 217.
55. Notestein, *Commons Debates 1621*, 2: 92–3.
56. Bushell, *Abridgment*, A3^r. On Bacon's fall see Jardine and Stewart, *Hostage to Fortune*, ch. 16.
57. Peiresc to Barclay, 21 April 1621, Paris. *Lettres de Peiresc*, 7: 456.
58. Rushworth, *Historical Collections*, 1: 36.
59. Lando to the Doge and Senate of Venice, 8/18 June 1621, London. *CSPV* 17: 68.
60. Willson 420.
61. Account of J's coming to PC, [30 December 1621]. PRO SP 14/124/83; *CSPD 1619–2?*, 326–7.
62. Joseph Meade to Sir Martin Stuteville, 11 January 1622, London. Ellis, *Original Letters*. 1st ser., 3: 116–17.
63. Tillières to Puisieux, 24 January 1622. Quoted in Willson 462 n.19.
64. 'The Warre of the Gods', BL Add. MS 22603, f. 33r. On these libels see Farmer, 'Poems from a Seventeenth-Century

Manuscript'; Knowles, '"To scourge the arse"'.

65. 'As I went to Walsingham'. Salisbury MS 140/125.

66. J to GV, [17 May 1620]. BL Harley MS 6987 f. 180; Akrigg 374.

67. 'Heaven Bless King James our Joy'.

NOTES TO CHAPTER NINETEEN

1. Cit. Lockyer, *Buckingham*, 135.

2. Hacket, *Scrinia Reserata*, 1: 114.

3. *LJ* 209.

4. Hyde, *History*, 1: 20–21.

5. Chamberlain believed that Cottington rode with them from New Hall to Dover, and that Greames joined them at Dover, but it was the other way around. JC to DC, [22 February 1623, London]. McClure 2: 480.

6. J to C and GV [27 February 1623] BL Harley MS 6987 f. 13; Bergeron 151.

7. BL Harley MS 837 ff. 72v–73r; James VI and I, *Poems*, ed. Craigie, 193.

8. JC to DC, [22 February 1623, London]. McClure 2: 480.

9. JC to DC, [22 February 1623, London]. McClure 2: 480–81.

10. JC to DC, [8 March 1623, London]. McClure 2: 482.

11. GV and C to J, [March 1623]. BL Harley MS 6987 f. 19; Bergeron 185.

12. GV to J, [early March 1623]. BL Harley MS 6987 f. 23; Bergeron 186.

13. GV to J, 10 March 1623, Madrid. BL Harley MS 6987 f. 212; Bergeron 166–8.

14. J to C and GV, 17 March [1623], Newmarket. BL Harley MS 6987 f. 29; Akrigg 397.

15. J to C and GV, 25 March [1623]. BL Harley MS 6987 f. 41; Akrigg 400–401.

16. C and GV to J, 27 March 1623, Madrid. BL Harley MS 6987 f. 46; Bergeron 189–90.

17. Lockyer, *Buckingham*, 145–6.

18. GV to C to J, 27 April 1623, Madrid. BL Harley MS 6987 ff. 88–9; Bergeron 190.

19. J to C and GV, 11 May [1623], Greenwich. BL Harley MS 6987 f. 94; Bergeron 166.

20. Lockyer, *Buckingham*, 154–5.

21. Francisco de Jesus, *Hecho*, 214.

22. Francisco de Jesus, *Hecho*, 216–17; Lockyer. *Buckingham*, 146–7.

23. Francisco de Jesus, *Hecho*, 220–23; Lockyer, *Buckingham*, 147–8.

24. Lockyer, *Buckingham*, 148–9.

25. Francisco de Jesus, *Hecho*, 228–30.

26. Lockyer, *Buckingham*, 162. In early April, James had authorised Buckingham to raise the issue of the Palatinate. See Goodman 2: 273–5.

27. Francisco de Jesus, *Hecho*, 230–33, 241; Rushworth, *Historical Collections*, 122; Lockyer, *Buckingham*, 149–50.

28. Quoted in Lockyer, *Buckingham*, 151.

29. Lockyer, *Buckingham*, 151.

30. Correr to the Doge and Senate of Venice, 21 June/1 July 1623, Madrid. *CSPV* 18: 53.

31. J to C and GV, 14 June [1623], Greenwich. BL Harley MS 6987 f. 100; Bergeron 167–8.

32. Lockyer, *Buckingham*, 157.

33. Francisco de Jesus, *Hecho*, 243–4; BL Harley MS 6987 f. 107; Hacket, *Scrinia Reserata*, 1: 137, 145; Lockyer, *Buckingham*, 157.

34. Lockyer, *Buckingham*, 158.

35. GV to Middlesex, 8 July 1623. Quoted in Lockyer, Buckingham, 158.

36. D'Ewes, *Diary*, 147–8.

37. C and GV to J, 29 July [1623], Madrid. BL Harley MS 6987 ff. 126–7; Bergeron 194.

38. Lockyer, *Buckingham*, 161–2.

39. Correr to the Doge and Senate of Venice, 3/13 June and 18/28 August 1623, Madrid. *CSPV* 18: 37, 101.

40. Lockyer, *Buckingham*, 162.

41. Lockyer, *Buckingham*, 163–4.

42. D'Ewes, *Diary*, 162–3.

43. Cogswell, *Blessed Revolution*, 6–7.

44. JC to DC, 11 October 1623, London. McClure 2: 515–16.

45. Finett, *Finetti Philoxenis*, 121; Pett, *Autobiography*, 128–9; JC to DC, 11 October 1623; London. McClure 2: 516.

NOTES TO CHAPTER TWENTY

1. [Conway] to DC, 9 October 1623, Royston. *CSPD 1623–1625*, 91.
2. Dudley Carleton (Clerk of the Council) to DC, 10 November 1623, London. PRO SP 14/154/19, quoted in Lockyer, *Buckingham*, 171.
3. Rusdorf, *Mémoires*, 1: 147; my translation.
4. Alvise Valaresso to the Doge and Senate of Venice, 23 January/2 February 1624, London. *CSPV* 18: 207, 208.
5. Valaresso to Doge and Senate, 16/26 January 1624 and 23 January/2 February, London. *CSPV* 18: 207, 208, 201.
6. Lockyer, *Buckingham*, 180.
7. Quoted in Willson 441–2.
8. D'Ewes, *Diary*, 181 [entry for 16 February 1624].
9. D'Ewes, *Diary*, 192 n. 408.
10. On the 1624 Parliament see Ruigh, *Parliament of 1624*; Russell, *Parliaments and English Politics*.
11. Fuller, *Church History*, 3: 328.
12. BL Harley MS 159, ff. 10–12; cit. Ruigh, *Parliament of 1624*, 154–6.
13. Ruigh, *Parliament of 1624*, 189; Weldon, *Court and Character*, 155; Lockyer, *Buckingham*, 185.
14. GV to J, [2 March 1624]. BL Harley MS 6987 ff. 196^{r-v}.
15. Harvard University, Houghton Library, MS English 980 [Sir William Spring: Proceedings in the Commons 19 February – 27 May 1624]: 11 March 1624, quoted in Lockyer, *Buckingham*, 185.
16. *LJ* 266.
17. Valaresso to the Doge and Senate of Venice, 19/29 March 1624, London. *CSPV* 18: 254.
18. Ruigh, *Parliament of 1624*, 213–16; Lockyer, *Buckingham*, 186.
19. *LJ* 282, 275, 283; Lockyer, *Buckingham*, 187.
20. 'The Heads of that Discourse which fell from Don Francisco, 7. Die Aprilis, 1624.' *Cabala* 275–6. For similar accusations, see Eglisham, *Fore-runner*, B3^{v}–B4^{r}.
21. Valaresso to Doge and Senate, 12 April 1624, London. *CSPV* 18: 268.
22. Gardiner, *History of England*, 5: 229. For Middlesex, see Prestwich, *Cranfield*.

23. Hacket, *Scrinia Reserata*, 1: 189–90.

24. Hyde, *History of the Rebellion*, 1: 28.

25. Hacket, *Scrinia Reserata*, 1: 190.

26. Ruigh, *Parliament of 1624*, 279–81; Lockyer, *Buckingham*, 194.

27. 'A Memorial to the King of Spain by Sir Walter Aston, Ambassadour in Spain'. *Cabala* 13.

28. Hacket, *Scrinia Reserata*, 1: 196–7.

29. JC to DC, 13 May 1624, London. McClure 2: 558; John Coke to Lord Brooke, 19 May 1624, Greenwich. HMC, *Manuscripts of the Earl Cowper*, 1: 163.

30. Lockyer, *Buckingham*, 197.

31. GV to J, n.d.. Bergeron 180; Lockyer, *Buckingham*, 197–8.

32. Pesaro to the Doge and Senate of Venice, 4/14 June 1624, London. *CSPV* 18: 343–4; C to GV, n.d.. BL Harley MS 6987 f. 207^r.

33. Ruigh, *Parliament of 1624*, 384–5.

34. *Life of Waller*, quoted in Nichols 4: 976–7.

35. PRO 31/4 (Crisp Transcripts), 2. 14v–15 as rendered in Lockyer, *Buckingham*, 200.

36. Maidstone, Kent Archive Office, Sackville MS ON.245 as cit. Lockyer, *Buckingham*, 201–2; JC to DC, 24 July 1624, London. McClure 2: 571.

37. See for example JC to DC, 9 October 1624, London. McClure 2: 581.

38. JC to DC, 4 December 1624, London. McClure 2: 588–9.

39. Lockyer, *Buckingham*, 209.

40. See Kellie to Mar, 15 December 1624, Cambridge. HMC Mar & Kellie 216. JC to DC, 18 December 1624, London. McClure 2: 591.

41. JC to DC, 18 December 1624, London. McClure 2: 591–2.

42. J to GV, [December 1624?]. Halliwell, *Letters*, 2: 236.

43. JC to DC, 8 January 1625, London. McClure 2: 594, 596.

44. Nichols 4: 1010.

45. Finet, *Finetti Philoxenis*, cit. Nichols 4: 1011; JC to DC, 8 January 1625, London. McClure 2: 594–7 at 594, 596. The masque is printed in Nichols 4: 1012–26.

46. C to GV, 24 January 1625. BL Harley 6987 ff. 203^v–204^r.

47. C to GV, 24 January 1625. BL Harley 6987 f. 203^r.

48. Lockyer, *Buckingham*, 227–9.
49. GV to J, [January 1625?]. Bergeron 216–17.
50. Nichols 4: 1028.
51. Countess of Bedford to Jane Lady Cornwallis, 23 March 1625 [writing of the early stages of the illness], More Lodge. Cornwallis, *Correspondence*, 120.
52. JC to DC, 12 March 1625, London. McClure 2: 604–6 at 606.
53. On James's 'impatience and irregularities' and 'excess in drinking' during his illness, see Zuane Pesaro to Doge and Senate of Venice, 18/28 March and 25 March/4 April 1625, London. *CSPV 1623–1625*, 620, 623.
54. Conway to Carlisle, 23 March 1625, Theobalds. Yorke, *Miscellaneous State Papers*, 1: 562.
55. Conway to Carlisle, 23 March 1625, Theobalds. Yorke, *Miscellaneous State Papers*, 1: 564.
56. Quoted in Willson 445.
57. HMC, *Manuscripts of the Earl of Lonsdale*: 'Notes in Parliament', 2–3, 4–6, 8–9, 13, 18, 28; Harley, 'Political Post-Mortems', 9–10.
58. See Eglisham, *Prodromvs Vindictæ*; Eglisham, *The Fore-Runner of Revenge*.
59. Meade to Stuteville, [March 1625], cit. Nichols, *Progresses*, 4: 1032.
60. Conway to Carlisle, 24 March 1625, Theobalds. Yorke, *Miscellaneous State Papers* 1: 566, cit. Nichols, *Progresses*, 4: 1029.
61. Meade to Stuteville, [March 1625] cit. Nichols, *Progresses*, 4: 1032.
62. JC to DC, 9 April 1625. McClure 2: 608.
63. Conway to DC, March 1625. Collet, *Relics of Literature*, cit. Nichols, *Progresses*, 4: 1029.
64. Paddy's memorandum, cit. Nichols, *Progresses*, 4: 1031–2.
65. Williams, *Great Britains Salomon*, K^v-K2^r.
66. JC to DC, 9 April 1625, London. McClure 2: 609.
67. JC to DC, 9 April 1625, London. McClure 2: 609.
68. Countess of Bedford to Jane Lady Cornwallis, 12 April [1625], More Lodge. Cornwallis, *Correspondence*, 125–6.
69. JC to DC, 9 April 1625, London. McClure 2: 609.
70. Zuane Pesaro to Doge and Senate, 22 April/2 May 1625, London. *CSPV* 19: 26–7.
71. JC to DC 9 April 1625, London. McClure 2: 609. *Fortescue Papers*, ed. Gardiner (1871), 213–14; Birch, *Charles*, 4. Lockyer 234.

72. JC to DC 9 April 1625, London. McClure 2: 609.
73. HMC, *Manuscripts of the Earl of Lonsdale*: 'Notes in Parliament', 2–3, 4–6, 8–9, 13, 18, 28; Harley, 'Political Post-Mortems', 10.
74. Advices from London, 3/13 February 1648. *CSPV* 28: 44.
75. James VI and I, *Poems*, ed. Craigie, 2: 182–91 and notes at 2: 262–5.

Bibliography

1. WORKS BY JAMES VI AND I
(IN CHRONOLOGICAL ORDER OF PUBLICATION)

The Essayes of a Prentise, in the Divine Art of Poesie (Edinburgh: Thomas Vautrollier, 1584)

Ane Frvitfvll Meditatioun contening ane plane and facill expositioun of ye 7.8.9 and 10 versis of the 20 Chap. of the Reuelatioun in forme of ane sermone (Edinburgh: Henrie Charteris, 1588)

Ane Meditatiovn vpon the xxv, xxvi, xxvii, xxviii, and xxix verses of the xv. chapt. of the first buke of the Chronicles of the Kingis (Edinburgh: Henrie Charteris, 1589)

His Maiesties Poeticall Exercises at vacant houres (Edinburgh: Robert Waldegrave, 1591)

Daemonologie, in forme of a Dialogue (Edinburgh: R. Walde-graue, 1597)

A Covnter-blaste to Tobacco (London: R.B., 1604)

His Majesties Speech in this last Session of Parliament, as neere his very words as could be gathered at the instant. Together with a discourse of the maner of the discovery of this late intended treason, joyned with the examination of some of the prisoners (London: Robert Barker, 1605)

Triplici nodo triplex cuneus. Sive Apologia pro ivramento fidelitatis, Aduersus duo Breuia P. Pavli Qvinti, & Epistolam Cardinalis Bellarmini, ad G. Blackvellvm Archipresbyterum nuper scriptam (London: Robert Barker, 1607)

An Apologie for the Oath of Allegiance. First set foorth withovt a name: And now acknowledged by the Author, the Right High and Mightie Prince, Iames . . . Together with a Premotion of his Maiesties, to all most Mightie Monarches, Kings, free Princes and States of Christendome (London: Robert Barker, 1609)

The Workes of the most high and mighty Prince, Iames . . . Printed by Iames, Bishop of Winton & Deane of his Ma[jes]t[ie]s Chapell Royal (London: Robert Barker and John Bill, 1616 [i.e. 1617])

New Poems by James I of England, ed. Allan F. Westcott (New York: Columbia University Press, 1911)

The Basilicon Doron of King James VI, ed. James Craigie, 2 vols (Edinburgh: William Blackwood, 1944–1950)

Letters of King James VI & I, ed. G.P.V. Akrigg (Berkeley: University of California Press, 1984)

Political Writings, ed. Johann P. Sommerville (Cambridge: Cambridge University Press, 1994)

2. MANUSCRIPT SOURCES CONSULTED

British Library
Additional MS 34, 275
Cotton Titus C.vi
Harley 159, 389, 677, 6986
Hatfield House
Salisbury MSS [consulted on microfilm]
Public Record Office
State Papers Domestic James I 14
State Papers Scotland 53

3. EARLY PRINTED SOURCES
(TO 1700) AND LATER EDITIONS OF EARLY WORKS

Anonymous, *The Copie of a Letter written from Master T.M. neer Salisbury, to Master H.A. at London, concerning the proceeding at Winchester* . . . (London: R.B., 1603)

Anonymous, *Honor Trivmphant. Or The Peeres Challenge . . . Also The Monarches meeting: or The King of Denmarkes welcome into England* (London: Francis Burne, 1606)

Anonymous, *The King of Denmarkes welcome* (London: Edward Allde, 1606)

Adamson, John ed., *The Mvses Welcome to the High and Mightie Prince Iames* . . . (Edinburgh: T. Finlason 1618)

Adamson, Patrick, *Serenissimi ac Nobilissimi Scotiae, Angliae, Hyberniae Principis, Henrici Stuardi inuictissimi herois, ac Mariae Reginae amplissimae filij Genethliacum* (Paris: Carolus Perier, 1566)

Bacon, Francis, *Works*, ed. James Spedding, Robert Leslie Ellis and Douglas Denon Heath, 7 vols (London: Longman et al., 1857–1859)

Bancroft, Richard, *A Sermon preached at Paules Crosse the 9. of Februarie, being the first Sunday in the Parleament, Anno. 1588* (London: E.B. for Gregorie Seton, 1588)

Barlow, William, *The summe and substance of the conference, which, it pleased his majestie to have with the lords, bishops, and other clergie, at Hampton Court* (London: John Law, 1604)

Bèze, Théodore de, *Icones, id est Verae imagines virorvm doctrina simvl et pietate illvstrivm* . . . (Geneva: Jean de Laon, 1580)

Bèze, Théodore de, *Beza's 'Icones': Contemporary Portraits of Reformers of Religion and Letters*, ed. C.G. McCrie (London: The Religious Tract Society, 1906)

Bible, *The Geneva Bible: A facsimile of the 1560 edition*, ed. Lloyd E. Berry (Madison: University of Wisconsin Press, 1969)

Bizari, Pietro, *Historia . . . Della guerra fatta in Vngheria dall'inuittissimo Imperatore de Christiani, contra quello de Turchi* (Lyon: appresso Gvilel. Rovillio, 1569)

Brahe, Tycho, *Opera omnia*, ed. I.L.E. Dreyer, 15 vols (Hauniæ: Gyldendaliana, 1913–1929)

Buchanan, George, *Baptistes, sive calvmna, tragoedia* (London: Thomas Vautrollier, 1577)

Buchanan, George, *De ivre regni apvd Scotos, dialogvs* (Edinburgh: apud Iohannem Rosseum, pro Henrico Charteris, 1579)

Buchanan, George, *Opera Omnia*, ed. Thomas Ruddimann, 2 vols (Edinburgh: Robert Freebairn, 1715)

Buchanan, George, *The Powers of the Crown in Scotland*, trans. Charles Flinn Arrowood (Austin: The University of Texas Press, 1949)

Bushell, Thomas, *Mr Bushell's Abridgment of the Lord Chancellor Bacon's Philosophical Theory in Mineral Prosecutions* (London, 1659)

Cabala: sive Scrinia Sacra. Mysteries of State & Government: in Letters (London: G. Bedel and T. Collins, 1654)

'Casaubon, Isaac', *Is. Casavboni Corona Regia. Id est Panegyricvs cvivsdam vere Avrei, Quem Iacobo I. Magnae Britanniae, &c. Regi* ('London': 'John Bill', 1615)

Chytraeus, Nathan, ed., *In Georgii Bvchanani paraphrasin psalmorvm Collectanea* (Herbonæ: Christopher Corvin, 1600)

Coke, Edward, *The Twelfth part of the Reports of Sr Edward Coke*, 2nd edn (London: Henry Twyford and Thomas Basset, 1677)

Coke, Roger, *A Detection of the Court and State of England*, 2nd edn (London, 1696)

Copie d'vne lettre escripte a Monsievr l'Archevesqve de Glasgo, Embassadeur pour le Roy d'Escosse en France, discourant la pernicieuse & damnable conspiration faite sur la personne dudit Roy. Du 13. Aoust, 1600 (Lyon: Thibavd Ancelin, 1600)

Cornwallis, Charles, *An Account of Baptism, Life, Death and Funeral, of the Most Incomparable Prince Frederick Henry, Prince of Wales* (London: J. Freeman, 1751)

Dekker, Thomas, *The Dramatic Works of Thomas Dekker* (London: John Pearson, 1873)

The Earle of Gowries conspiracie against the Kings Maiestie of Scotland. At Saint Iohn stoun vpon Tuesday the fift of August. 1600 (London: Valentine Simmes, 1600)

Eedes, Richard, *Six Learned and Godly Sermons* (London: Edward Bishop, 1604)

Eglisham, George, *The Fore-Runner of Revenge, Being two Petitions: The one To the Kings most Excellent Majesty, the other To the most Honorurable Houses of Parliament. Wherein is expressed divers actions of the late Earle of Buckingham; especially concerning the death of King James, and the Marquesse Hamelton, supposed by Poyson* (London, 1642)

A fourme of Prayer with Thankesgiuing, to be vsed by all the Kings Maiesties louing Subiects euery yeere the fift of August: Being the day of his Highnesse happy deliuerance from the traiterous and bloody attempt of the Earle of Gowry and his brother, with their Adherents. Set foorth by Authoritie (London: Robert Barker, 1603)

Fuller, Thomas, *The Church History of Britain, from the birth of Jesus Christ until the year MDCXLVIII*, ed. James Nichols, 3rd edn, 3 vols (London: Thomas Tegg, 1842)

Gentili, Alberico, *Regales disputationes tres id est, de potestate regis absoluta. De vnione regnorvm Britanniae* (London: Thomas Vautrollier, 1605)

Goodman, Godfrey, *The Fall of Man, or the Corrvption of Natvre, proved by the light of our naturall Reason* (London: Felix Kyngston for Richard Lee, 1616)

Greville, Fulke, *The Five Years of King Iames, or, The Condition of the State of England, and the Relation it had to other Provinces* (London: W.R., 1643)

H., W., *The Trve Pictvre and Relation of Prince Henry His Noble and Vertuous disposition* . . . (Leiden: William Christian, 1634)

Hacket, John, *Scrinia Reserata: A Memorial Offer'd to the Great Deservings of John Williams, D.D.* (London: Edward Jones for Samuel Lowndes, 1693)

Harrison, Stephen, *Arches of Triumph* (London, 1604)

Hudson, Thomas, *The Historie of Ivdith in forme of a poeme. Penned in French, by the Noble Poet, G. Salust. Lord of Bartas. Englished by Tho. Hudson* (Edinburgh: Thomas Vautrollier, 1584)

Hudson, Thomas, *Historie of Judith*, ed. James Craigie (Edinburgh: Scottish Text Society, 1941)

Johnston, Arthur ed., *Delitiae poetarvm Scotorvm hujus ævi illvstrivm*, 2 vols (Amsterdam: Iohannes Blaev, 1637)

Johnston, Robert, *The Historie of Scotland during the Minority of King James*, trans. T.M. (London, 1646)

King, John, *A Sermon at Paules Crosse* (London: 1620)

Knox, John, *The History of the Reformation of Religion in Scotland*, ed. William McGavin (Glasgow: Blackie, Fullarton & Co., 1831)

Knox, John, *A Sermon preached by Iohn Knox Minister of Christ Iesus in the Publique audience of the Church of Edenbrough, within the Realme of Scotland, vpon Sonday, the 19. of August. 1565.* (Edinburgh, 1566)

M., T., *The Copie of a Letter written from Master T.M. neer Salisbury, to Master H.A. at London, concerning the proceeding at Winchester . . .* (London: R.B., 1603)

[Marcelline, George], *The Triumphs of King Iames the First, Of Great Brittaine, France, and Ireland, King; Defender of the Faith. Published vpon his Maiesties aduertisement to all the Kings, Princes, and Potentates of Christendome, and confirmed by the wonderfull Works of God, declared in his life* ('Brittaines Burse': John Budge, 1610)

Melvill, Andrew, Στεφανισκιον. *Ad Scotiae regem, habitvm in coronatione reginae* (Edinburgh: Robert Waldegrave, 1590)

Milwarde, John, *Jacobs Great Day of Trovble, and Deliverance. A Sermon Preached at Pauls Crosse, the fifth of August 1607. vpon his Maiesties deliuerance from the Earle Gowries Treason and Conspiracie* (London: Eleazar Edgar, 1610)

Osborne, Francis, *Advice to a Son. Or Directions For your better Conduct*, 6th edn (Oxford: H.H. for Tho. Robinson, 1656)

Osborne, Francis, *A Miscellany of Sundry Essayes, Paradoxes, and Problematicall Discourses, Letters and Characters* (London: John Grismond, 1659)

The Peace-Maker: or, Great Brittaines Blessing (London: Thomas Purfoot, 1619)

A Proclamation for the discovery and apprehension of William Ruthven, and Patricke Ruthven, brethren to the late Earle of Gowrie (London: Robert Barker, 1603)

Russell, John, *Verba Ioann. Rvsselli ivreconsvlti pro senatv popvloqve Edinbvrgensi habita, ad serenissimam Scotorum Reginam Anna, dum Edinburgum ingreditur 19. Maij. An. 1590* (Edinburgh: Robert Waldegrave, 1590)

Sanderson, William, *A Compleat History of The Lives and Reigns of Mary Queen of Scotland, And of Her Son and Successor, James The Sixth, King of Scotland* . . . (London: Humphrey Mosley, Richard Tomlins and George Sawbridge, 1666)

[Scott, Thomas], *The Belgicke Pismire: Stinging the slothfull Sleeper, and Awaking the Diligent to Fast, Watch, Pray; And Worke Ovt their Owne Temporall and Eternall Salvation with Feare and Trembling* (London, 1622)

Sempill, James, *Sacrilege sacredly Handled, that is, according to Scripture onely* (London: W. Jones for E. Weaver, 1619)

A Short Discovrse of the good ends of the higher prouidence, in the late attemptat against his Maiesties person ([London]: Robert Waldegraue, 1600)

Spottiswoode, John, *The History of the Church and State of Scotland*, 4th edn (London: R. Royston, 1677)

Spottiswoode, John, *The History of the Church of England*, 3 vols (Edinburgh: Bannatyne Club, 1850)

'Tortus, Matthaeus', *Responsio Matthaei Torti presbyteri, et theologi papiensis, ad librvm inscriptvm, Triplici nodo triplex cvnevs* (Coloniae Agrippinae: Bernard Gualther, 1608)

Turquet de Mayerne, Théodore, *Opera Medica* . . . ed. Joseph Browne (London: D. Browne and Rich. Smith, 1703)

Turquet de Mayerne, Théodore, *Praxeos Mayernianæ in Morbis internis præcipue Graviorius & Chronicis Syntagma* (London: Sam. Smith, 1690)

Vox Popvli. Or Newes from Spayne, translated according to the Spanish coppie. Which may serve to forwarn both England and the Vnited Provinces how farre to trust to Spanish pretences (1620)

Walton, Izaak, 'Life of Mr Richard Hooker', in *The Lives of John Donne, Sir Henry Wotton, Richard Hooker, George Herbert & Richard Sanderson*, ed. George Saintsbury (London: Oxford University Press [World's Classics], 1927), 153–249

Williams, John, *Great Britains Salomon. A Sermon Preached at the magnificent Funerall, of the most high and mighty King, Iames, the late King of Great Britaine, France, and Ireland, defender of the Faith, &c. At the Collegiat Church of Saint*

Peter at Westminister, the seuenth of May 1625 (London: John Bill, 1625)

Wilson, Arthur, *The History of Great Britain, being the Life and Reign of King James the First* (London: Richard Lownds, 1653)

Wotton, Henry, *Letters of Sir Henry Wotton to Sir Edmund Bacon* (London: R. W., 1661)

4. EDITIONS OF MANUSCRIPT SOURCES

Acts of the Privy Council of England, n.s. ed. John Roche Dasent, vol. 32, *1601–1604* (London: HMSO, 1907)

Anderson, Adam ed., *Letters and State Papers during the Reign of King James VI . . . from the MS Collections of Sir James Balfour of Denmyln* (Edinburgh: Abbotsford Club, 1838)

Assheton, Nicholas, *The Journal of Nicholas Assheton of Downham, in the County of Lancaster, esq. for part of the year 1617, and part of the year following,* ed. F.R. Raines (Manchester: Chetham Society, 1848)

Aubrey, John, *Brief Lives,* ed. Oliver Lawson Dick

Bacon, Francis, *Letters and Life,* ed. James Spedding, 7 vols (London: Longmans et al., 1861–1874)

Bannatyne, Richard, *Journal of the Transactions in Scotland, during the contest between the Adherents of Queen Mary, and those of her son* (Edinburgh: J. Ballatyne, 1806)

Bell, Robert ed., *Extract from the Despatches of M. Courcelles, French Ambassador at the Court of Scotland. M.D.LXXXVI.–M.D.LXXXVII* (Edinburgh: Bannatyne Club, 1828)

de Bethune, Maximilian, duc de Sully, *Memoirs of Maximilian de Bethune, Duke of Sully, Prime Minister to Henry the Great . . .,* 3rd edn, 3 vols, vol. 2 (London: A. Millar, 1761)

Birch, Thomas ed., *Memoirs of the Reign of Queen Elizabeth,* 2 vols (London: A. Millar, 1754)

Blackwood Adam, *History of Mary Queen of Scots; A Fragment,* trans. [from the French] anon., ed. Robert Adam (Edinburgh: Maitland Club, 1834)

The Border Papers: Calendar of Letters and Papers Relating to the Affairs of the Borders of England and Scotland, 2 vols ed. Joseph Bain (Edinburgh: HM General Register House, 1894)

Bromley, Sir George ed., *A Collection of Original Royal Letters . . .* (London: John Stockdale, 1787)

Bruce, John ed., *Correspondence of King James VI. of Scotland with Sir Robert Cecil and others in England* (London: Camden Society, 1856)

Bruce, John ed., *Letters of Queen Elizabeth and King James VI. of Scotland* (London: Camden Society, 1849)

Calderwood, David, *The History of the Kirk of Scotland*, ed. Thomas Thomson, 8 vols (Edinburgh: Wodrow Society, 1842–1849)

Calendar of State Papers, Domestic Series, of the Reign of Elizabeth, 1581–1590, ed. Mary Anne Everett Green (London: Longman et al., 1865)

Calendar of State Papers, Domestic Series of the Reign of James I: 1603–1610, 1611–1618, 1619–1623, 1623–1625 with Addenda 1603–1625, all ed. Mary Anne Everett Green (London: Longman et al., 1857–1859)

Calendar of State Papers, Foreign Series, of the Reign of Elizabeth, 1564–1565, ed. Joseph Stevenson (London: Longman and Trübner, 1870)

Calendar of State Papers, Foreign Series, of the Reign of Elizabeth, 1566–1568 and 1569–1571, ed. Allen James Crosby (London: Longman and Trübner, 1871–1874)

Calendar of the State Papers relating to Scotland and Mary, Queen of Scots 1547–1603, 13 vols, eds Joseph Bain (vols 1 and 2), William K. Boyd (3–9), Boyd and Henry W. Meikle (10), Annie I. Cameron (11), M.S. Giuseppi (12) and J. D. Mackie (13) (Edinburgh: H . M. General Register House, 1898–1969)

Calendar of Letters and State Papers relating to English affairs preserved in, or originally belonging to, the archives of Simancas, vol. 4, Elizabeth 1587–1603, ed. Martin A. S. Hume (London: HMSO, 1899)

Calendar of State Papers and Manuscripts relating to English Affairs, existing in the archives and collections of Venice, and in other libraries of Northern Italy (London: HMSO) vol. 7, ed. Rawdon Brown & G. Cavendish Bentinck (1890); vols 10–12 ed. Horatio F. Brown (1900–1905); vols 16, 18–19, 28 ed. Allen B. Hinds (1910–1927)

Cameron, Annie I. and Robert S. Rait eds, *The Warrender Papers*, 2 vols (Edinburgh: Scottish History Society, 1931–1932)

Chamberlain, John, *The Letters of John Chamberlain*, ed. Norman Egbert McClure, 2 vols (Philadelphia: American Philosophical Society, 1939)

Cobbett, William, *Cobbett's Complete Collection of State Trials and Proceedings for High Treason and other Crimes and Misdemeanors from the earliest period to the present time*, 6 vols (London: Longman & Co., 1809)

Colville, John, *Original Letters of Mr John Colville 1582–1603. To which is added, His Palinode, 1600. With a Memoir of the Author* (Edinburgh: Bannatyne Club, 1858)

Cornwallis, Jane Lady, *The Private Correspondence of Jane Lady Cornwallis 1613–1644*, ed. Richard Griffin, Lord Braybrooke (London: privately printed, 1842)

Cranstoun, James ed., *Satirical Poems of the Time of the Reformation*, 2 vols (Edinburgh: Scottish Text Society, 1893)

Dalrymple, David, Lord Hailes ed., *The Secret Correspondence of Sir Robert Cecil with James VI. King of Scotland. Now First Published* (Edinburgh: A. Millar, 1766)

D'Ewes, Simonds, *The Autobiography and Correspondence of Sir Simonds D'Ewes, Bart., During the Reigns of James I and Charles I*, ed. James O. Halliwell (London, 1845)

D'Ewes, Simonds, *The Diary of Sir Simonds D'Ewes (1622–1624): Journal d'un étudiant londonien sous le règne de Jacques 1er*, ed. Elisabeth Bourcier (Paris: Didier, 1974)

A Diurnal of Remarkable Occurrents that have passed within the country of Scotland since the death of King James the Fourth till the Year M.D.LXXV, ed. Thomas Thomson (Edinburgh: Bannatyne Club, 1833)

Elizabeth, Queen of Bohemia, *The Letters of Elizabeth Queen of Bohemia*, ed. L.M. Baker (London: The Bodley Head, 1953)

Ellis, Henry ed., *Original Letters, Illustrative of English History*, 1st ser., 3 vols (London: Harding, Triphook & Lepard, 1824)

Ellis, Henry ed., *Original Letters, Illustrative of English History*, 3rd ser., 4 vols (London: Richard Bentley, 1846)

Fabri de Peiresc, *Lettres de Peiresc*, ed. Philippe Tamizey de Larroque, vol. 7, *Lettres de Peiresc à divers, 1602–1637* (Paris: Imprimerie Nationale, 1898)

Farmer, Norman K. ed., 'Poems from a Seventeenth-Century Manuscript with the Hand of Robert Merrick', *Texas Quarterly* 16 (1973), supplement

Firth, C.H. ed., *Stuart Tracts 1603–1693* (Westminster: Archibald Constable, 1903)

Forbes-Leith, William ed., *Narratives of Scottish Catholics under Mary Stuart and James VI* (Edinburgh: William Patterson, 1885)

Francisco de Jesus, *El Hecho de los Tratados del Matrimonio pretendido por el Principe de Gales con la serenissima Infante de Espana Maria* trans./ed. Samuel Rawson Gardiner (London: Camden Society, 1869)

Gardiner, Samuel Rawson ed., *The Fortescue Papers . . . collected by John Packer* (London: Camden Society, 1871)

Gardiner, Samuel Rawson, 'On certain Letters of Diego Sarmiento de Acuña, Count of Gondomar, giving an account of the affair of the Earl of Somerset, with Remarks on the career of Somerset as a public man', *Archaeologia* 41 (1867), 151–86

Harington, Henry ed., *Nugae Angiquae: being a miscellaneous collection of original papers*, 2 vols (London: Vernor and Hood, and Cuthell & Martin, 1804)

Harington, John, *The Letters and Epigrams of Sir John Harington together with The Prayse of Private Life*, ed. Norman Egbert McClure (Philadelphia: University of Pennsylvania Press, 1930)

Herries, Lord, *Historical Memoirs of the Reign of Mary Queen of Scots and a portion of the reign of King James the Sixth*, ed. Robert Pitcairn (Edinburgh: Abbotsford Club, 1836)

Historical Manuscripts Commission, *Calendar of the Manuscripts of the Most Honourable the Marquess of Salisbury . . . Preserved at Hatfield House, Herfordshire*

Historical Manuscripts Commission, *Manuscripts of the Earl Cowper . . . Preserved at Melbourne Hall, Derbyshire*, vol. 1 (London: HMSO, 1888)

Historical Manuscripts Commission, *Report on the Manuscripts of the Earl of Mar and Kellie preserved at Alloa House, N.B.* (London: HMSO, 1904)

Historical Manuscripts Commission, *Report on the Manuscripts of Lord de L'Isle & Dudley Preserved at Penshurst Place*, 6 vols (London: HMSO, 1925–1966)

Historical Manuscripts Commission, *Supplementary Report on the Manuscripts of the Earl of Mar & Kellie preserved at Alloa House, Clacmannanshire*, ed. Henry Paton (London: HMSO, 1930)

Historical Manuscripts Commission, *Thirteenth Report, Appendix, Part VII. The Manuscripts of the Earl of Lonsdale* (London: HMSO, 1893)

Holles, Gervase, *Memorials of the Holles Family 1493–1656* (London: Camden Society [3rd ser., vol. 55], 1937)

[Hyde], Edward, Earl of Clarendon, *The History of the Rebellion and Civil Wars in England begun in the year 1641*, ed. W. Dunn Macray, 6 vols (Oxford: Clarendon Press, 1888)

Jansson, Maija ed., *Proceedings in Parliament 1614 (House of Commons)* (Philadelphia: American Philosophical Society, 1988)

Keith, Robert ed., *History of the Affairs of Church and State in Scotland, from the beginning of the Reformation to the year 1568*, 3 vols (Edinburgh: Spottiswoode Society, 1850)

Laing, David ed., *Original Letters relating to the Ecclesiastical Affairs of Scotland*, 2 vols (Edinburgh: Bannatyne Club, 1851)

Lodge, Edmund ed., *Illustrations of British History, Biography, and Manners*, 2nd edn, 3 vols (London: John Chidley, 1838)

Maidment, J. ed., *Letters and State Papers during the Reign of King James the Sixth. Chiefly from the manuscript collections of Sir James Balfour of Denmyln* (Edinburgh: Abbotsford Club, 1838)

Maitland, Richard, John Maitland, and Thomas Maitland, *The Poems of Sir Richard Maitland, of Lethingtoun, Knight. With an Appendix of Selections from the Poems of Sir John Maitland Lord Thirlestane, and of Thomas Maitland*, ed. Joseph Bain (Glasgow: Maitland Club, 1830)

Mary, Queen of Scots, *Letters of Mary, Queen of Scots*, ed. Agnes Strickland, new edn, 2 vols (London: Henry Colburn, 1844)

Mary, Queen of Scots, *Lettres, Instructions, et Mémoires de Marie, Reine d'Ecosse*, ed. Prince Labanoff [A. I. Lobanov-Rostovsky], 7 vols (London, 1844)

Melvill, James, *The Autobiography and Diary of Mr James Melvill . . . with a Continuation of the Diary*, ed. Robert Pitcairn, 2 vols (Edinburgh: Wodrow Society, 1842)

Melville of Halhill, Sir James, *Memoirs of his Own Life*, ed. T. Thomson (Edinburgh: Bannatyne Club, 1827)

Molyneux, James More ed., 'Message from King James I. to the Earl of Somerset, in the case of Sir Thomas Overbury, sent on the 29th of December, 1615, through Sir George More, Lieutenant of the Tower: communicated from the Manuscripts at Loseley', *Archaeologia* 41 (1867), 75–8

Moysie, David, *Memoirs of the Affairs of Scotland . . . M.D.LXXVII. – M.DC.III.*, ed. James Dennistoun (Edinburgh: Bannatyne Club, 1830)

Nau, Claude, *The History of Mary Stewart from the Murder of Riccio until her Flight into England*, ed. Joseph Stevenson (Edinburgh: William Paterson, 1883)

Nichols, John ed., *The Progresses, Processions, and Magnificent Festivities of King James the First*, 4 vols (London: J. B. Nichols, 1828)

Normand, Lawrence and Gareth Roberts eds, *Witchcraft in Early Modern*

Scotland: James VI's Demonology and the North Berwick Witches (Exeter: University of Exeter Press, 2000)

Notestein, Wallace, Frances Helen Relf and Hartley Simpson eds, *Commons Debates 1621*, 7 vols (New Haven: Yale University Press, 1935)

Papers Relative to the Marriage of King James the Sixth of Scotland, with the Princess Anna of Denmark; A. D. M.D.LXXXIX. And the Form and Manner of Her Majesty's Coronation at Holyroodhouse. A.D. M.D.XC., ed. J.T. Gibson Craig (Edinburgh: Bannatyne Club, 1828)

Peiresc, *Lettres de Peiresc*, ed. Philippe Tamizey de Larroque, vol. 7, *Lettres de Peiresc à divers, 1602–1637* (Paris: Imprimerie Nationale, 1898)

The Register of the Privy Council of Scotland, 1st series, 14 vols, ed. John Hill Burton (vols 1 and 2) and David Masson (3–14) (Edinburgh: H.M. General Register House, 1877–1898) *A.D. 1616–1619* (Edinburgh: H.M. General Register House, 1894)

Robertson Joseph ed., *Inventaires de la Royne Descosse, Douairière de France* (Edinburgh: Bannatyne Club, 1863)

Rogers, Charles ed., *Memorials of the Earl of Stirling and of the House of Alexander*, 2 vols (Edinburgh: William Patterson, 1877)

Rusdorf, Johan von, *Mémoires et negociations secrètes de Mr. de Rvsdorf*, ed. Ern. Guill. Cuhn, 2 vols (Leipzig: Weygand, 1739)

Ruthven, 'Relation of the Death of David Rizzio', *Miscellanea Antiqua Anglicana* (1816), 16–18

Sawyer, Edmund ed., *Memorials of Affairs of State in the Reigns of Q. Elizabeth and K. James I. Collected (chiefly) from the original papers of the right honourable Sir Ralph Winwood*, 3 vols (London: T. Ward, 1725)

Scott, Walter ed., *Secret History of the Court of James the First*, 2 vols (Edinburgh: John Ballantyne, 1811)

Tanner, J.R. ed., *Constitutional Documents of the Reign of James I A.D. 1603–1625 with an historical commentary* (Cambridge: Cambridge University Press, 1930)

Teulet, A., *Relations politiques de la France et de l'Espagne avec l'Ecosse au 16ᵉ siècle*, 5 vols (Paris, 1862)

Thomson, Thomas ed., *A Diurnal of Remarkable Occurrents that have passed within the country of Scotland since the death of King James the Fourth till the Year M.D.LXXV* (Edinburgh: Bannatyne Club, 1833)

Wilbraham, Roger, *The Journal of Sir Roger Wilbraham*, ed. Harold Spencer

Scott in *The Camden Miscellany, Volume the Tenth* (London: Camden Society, 1902)

Wotton, Henry, *The Life and Letters of Sir Henry Wotton*, ed. Logan Pearsall Smith, 2 vols (Oxford: Clarendon Press, 1907)

Yorke, Philip, Earl of Hardwicke, *Miscellaneous State Papers. From 1501 to 1726*, 2 vols (London: W. Strahan and T. Cadell, 1778)

5. LATER PRINTED SOURCES

Akrigg, G.P.V., *Jacobean Pageant* (Cambridge: Harvard University Press, 1962)

Akrigg, G.P.V., 'The Literary Achievement of King James I', *University of Toronto Quarterly* 44 (1975), 115–29

Ashton, Robert ed., *James I by his Contemporaries* (London: Hutchinson, 1969)

Baldwin, T.W., *William Shakspere's Small Latine & Lesse Greeke*, 2 vols (Urbana: University of Illinois Press, 1944)

Barbé, Louis A., *The Tragedy of Gowrie House: An Historical Study* (Paisley and London: Alexander Gardner, 1887)

Barroll, Leeds, *Anna of Denmark, Queen of England: A Cultural Biography* (Philadelphia: University of Pennsylvania Press, 2001)

Barwick, G.F., 'A Sidelight on the Mystery of Mary Stuart: Pietro Bizari's Contemporary Account of the Murders of Riccio and Darnley', *Scottish Historical Review*, 31 (1924), 115–27

Bellany, Alastair, '"Rayling Rymes and Vaunting Verse": Libellous Politics in Early Stuart England, 1603–1628', in *Culture and Politics in Early Stuart England*, ed. Kevin Sharpe and Peter Lake (Basingstoke: Macmillan, 1994), 285–310

Bergeron, David M., 'Harrison, Jonson, and Dekker: The Magnificent Entertainment for King James (1604)', *Journal of the Warburg and Courtauld Institutes*, 31 (1968), 445–8

Bergeron, David M., *English Civic Pageantry 1558–1642* (London: Edward Arnold, 1971)

Bergeron, David M., *King James and Letters of Homoerotic Desire* (Iowa City: University of Iowa Press, 1999)

Bergeron, David M., *Royal Family, Royal Lovers: King James of England and Scotland* (Columbia: University of Missouri Press, 1991)

Bingham, Caroline, *Darnley: A Life of Henry Stuart, Lord Darnley Consort of Mary Queen of Scots* (London: Constable, 1995)

Bingham, Caroline, *James I of England* (London: Weidenfeld & Nicolson, 1981)

Bingham, Caroline, *James VI of Scotland* (London: Weidenfeld & Nicolson, 1979)

Birch, Thomas, *The Life of Henry Prince of Wales, Eldest Son of King James I* (London: A. Millar, 1760)

Bisset, Andrew, 'Sir Walter Scott' in his *Essays on Historical Truth* (London: Longmans, Green & Co., 1871), 172–302

Black, F.F., *A Calendar of Cases of Witchcraft in Scotland* (New York, 1938)

Bushnell, Rebecca W., *A Culture of Teaching: Early Modern Humanism in Theory and Practice* (Ithaca: Cornell University Press, 1996)

Carter, Charles H., 'Gondomar: Ambassador to James I', *Historical Journal* 7 (1964), 189–208

Chambers, Robert, *Domestic Annals of Scotland From the Reformation to the Revolution*, 2nd edn, vol. 1 (Edinburgh and London: W. & R. Chambers, 1859)

Chambers, Robert, *The Life of King James the First*, 2 vols (Edinburgh: Constable & Co., 1830)

Christianson, John Robert, *On Tycho's Island: Tycho Brahe and his Assistants, 1570–1601* (Cambridge: Cambridge University Press, 2000)

Cogswell, Thomas, *The Blessed Revolution: English Politics and the Coming of War 1621–1624* (Cambridge: Cambridge University Press, 1989)

Collinson, Patrick, *Birthpangs of Protestant England: Religion and Cultural Change in the Sixteenth and Seventeenth Centuries* (New York: St Martin's Press, 1988)

Collinson, Patrick, *The Religion of Protestants: The Church in English Society, 1559–1625* (Oxford: Clarendon Press, 1982)

Cowan, Edward J., 'The Darker Vision of the Scottish Renaissance: The Devil and Francis Stewart', in *The Renaissance and Reformation in Scotland: Essays in honour of Gordon Donaldson* (Edinburgh, 1983), 125–31

Crawfurd, George, *The Lives and Characters of the Officers of the Crown and State in Scotland* (London: Thomas Woodman, 1736)

Croft, Pauline, 'The Reputation of Robert Cecil: libels, political opinion and popular awareness in the early seventeenth century', *Transactions of the Royal Historical Society*, 6th ser., 1 (1991), 43–69

Cuddy, Neil, 'The Revival of the Entourage: The Bedchamber of James I, 1603–1625', in David Starkey et al., *The English Court: From the Wars of the Roses to the Civil War* (London: Longman, 1987), 173–225

Curtis, Mark, 'The Hampton Court Conference and its Aftermath', *History* 46 (1961), 1–16

Cust, Lady Elizabeth, *Some Account of the Stuarts of Aubigny, in France [1422–1672]* (London: privately printed, 1891)

Daiches, David, *The King James Version of the English Bible* (Chicago: University of Chicago Press, 1941)

Davies, Godfrey, 'English Political Sermons, 1603–1640', *Huntington Library Quarterly* 3 (1939–40), 1–22

Doleman, James, *King James I and the Religious Culture of England* (Cambridge: D.S. Brewer, 2000)

Donaldson, Gordon, 'The Scottish Church, 1567–1625', in *The Reign of James VI and I*, ed. Alan G.R. Smith (New York: St Martin's Press, 1973)

Donaldson, Gordon, *Scotland, James V to James VII* (Edinburgh: Oliver and Boyd, 1965)

Dreyer, J.L.E., *Tycho Brahe: A Picture of Scientific Life and Work in the Sixteenth Century* (Edinburgh: Adam and Charles Black, 1890)

Duchein, Michel, *Le Duc de Buckingham* (Paris: Fayard, 2001)

Dunlap, Rhodes, 'James I, Bacon, Middleton, and the Making of *The Peace-Maker*', in *Studies in the English Renaissance Drama*, ed. Josephine W. Bennett et al. (New York: New York University Presss, 1959)

Dunlap, Rhodes, 'King James and Some Witches: The Date and Text of the *Daemonologie*', *Philological Quarterly*, 54 (1975), 40–46

Ekrem, Inger, 'Historiography in Norway c. 1523–1614', in *A History of Nordic Neo-Latin Literature* (Odense: Odense University Press, 1995), 240–50

Ekrem, Inger, 'Jens Nielssøn (Johannes Nicolai) 1538–1600', in *A History of Nordic Neo-Latin Literature* (Odense: Odense University Press, 1995), 219–28

Ekrem, Inger, 'Norway', in *A History of Nordic Neo-Latin Literature* (Odense: Odense University Press, 1995), 66–83

Fincham, Kenneth, *Prelate as Pastor: The Episcopate of James I* (Oxford: Clarendon Press, 1990)

Fincham, Kenneth and Peter Lake, 'The Ecclesiastical Policy of James I', *Journal of British Studies*, 24 (1985), 169–207

Fleming, David Hay, *Mary Queen of Scots: From her Birth to her Flight into England*, 2nd edn (London: Hodder and Stoughton, 1898)

Forsyth, Robert, *The Beauties of Scotland*, vol. 4 (Edinburgh: Arch. Constable et al., 1806)

Fraser, Antonia, *The Gunpowder Plot: Terror and Faith in 1605* (London: Weidenfeld & Nicolson, 1996)

Fraser, Antonia, *King James VI of Scotland, I of England* (New York: Alfred A. Knopf, 1975)

Fraser, Antonia, *Mary Queen of Scots* (London: Weidenfeld & Nicolson, 1969)

Fraser, William, *The Lennox*, 2 vols (Edinburgh: privately printed, 1874)

Galloway, Bruce, *The Union of England and Scotland, 1603–1608* (Edinburgh: John Donald, 1986)

Garbanò, G.S., *Scapigliatura italiana a Londra sotto Elisabetta e Giacomo I* (Florence: Luigi Battistelli, 1923)

Gardiner, Samuel Rawson, *History of England 1603–42*, 10 vols (London, 1883–1884)

Goldberg, Jonathan, *James I and the Politics of Literature* (Stanford: Stanford University Press, 1989)

Goodare, Julian, 'James VI's English Subsidy', in *The Reign of James VI*, ed. Goodare and Lynch, 110–25

Goodare, Julian and Michael Lynch eds, *The Reign of James VI* (East Linton: Tuckwell Press, 2000)

Grant, Alexander, *The Story of the University of Edinburgh*, 2 vols (London: Longman, Green & Co., 1884)

Grant, Ruth, 'The Brig o' Dee Affair, the sixth Earl of Huntly and the Politics of the Counter-Reformation', in *The Reign of James VI*, ed. Goodare and Lynch, 93–109

Hammer, Paul E.J., *The Polarisation of Elizabethan Politics: The Political Career of Robert Devereux, 2nd Earl of Essex, 1585–1597* (Cambridge: Cambridge University Press, 1999)

Harley, David, 'Political Post-Mortems and Morbid Anatomy in Seventeenth-Century England', *Social History of Medicine*, 7 (1994), 1–28

Haynes, Alan, *The Gunpowder Plot: Faith in Rebellion* (Stroud: Alan Sutton, 1994)

Hewitt, George R., *Scotland Under Morton 1572–80* (Edinburgh: John Donald, 1982)

Jardine, Lisa and Alan Stewart, *Hostage to Fortune: The Troubled Life of Francis Bacon 1561–1626* (London: Victor Gollancz, 1998)

Knowles, James, 'To "scourge the arse | Jove's marrow so had wasted": scurrility and the subversion of sodomy', in *Subversion and Scurrility: Popular Discourse in Europe from 1500 to the Present*, ed. Dermot Cavanagh and Tim Kirk (Aldershot: Ashgate, 2000), 74–92

Lake, Peter, *Anglicans and Puritans? Presbyterianism and English Conformist Thought from Whitgift to Hooker* (London: Unwin Hyman, 1988)

Lang, Andrew, *James VI and the Gowrie Mystery* (London: Longman, Green & Co., 1902)

Larner, Christina, *Enemies of God: The Witch-Hunt in Scotland* (London: John Donald, 1981)

Larner, Christina, 'James VI and I and Witchcraft', in *The Reign of James VI and I*, ed. Alan G.R. Smith (New York: St Martin's Press, 1973), 74–90

Law, Thomas Graves, *Collected Essays and Reviews*, ed. P. Hume Brown (Edinburgh: Edinburgh University Press, 1904)

Law, Thomas Graves, 'The Spanish Blanks and the Catholic Earls, 1592–1594', *Scottish Review* 22 (1893), 1–32

Lee, Maurice, Jr, *Government by Pen: Scotland under James VI and I* (Urbana: University of Illinois Press, 1980)

Lee, Maurice, Jr, *Great Britain's Solomon: James VI and I in his Three Kingdoms* (Urbana: University of Illinois Press, 1990)

Lee, Maurice, Jr, *John Maitland of Thirlestane and the Foundation of the Stewart Despotism in Scotland* (Princeton: Princeton University Press, 1959)

Lewalski, Barbara Kiefer, *Writing Women in Jacobean England* (Cambridge, Mass: Harvard University Press, 1993)

Lockyer, Roger, *Buckingham: The Life and Political Career of George Villiers, First Duke of Buckingham 1592–1628* (London and New York: Longman, 1981)

Lockyer, Roger, *The Early Stuarts: A Political History of England 1603–1642* (Harlow: Longman, 1989)

Lockyer, Roger, *James VI and I* (Harlow: Longman, 1998)

Lossky, Nicholas, *Lancelot Andrewes The Preacher (1555–1626): The Origins of the Mystical Theology of the Church of England*, trans. Andrew Louth

(Oxford: Clarendon Press, 1991)

Lyall, Roderick J., 'James VI and the Sixteenth-Century Cultural Crisis', in *The Reign of James VI*, ed. Goodare and Lynch, 55–70

MacAlpine, Ida, and Richard Hunter, *George III and the Mad-Business* (London: Allen Lane, 1969)

McElwee, William, *The Wisest Fool in Christendom: The Reign of James I and VI* (New York: Harcourt, Brace and Co., 1958)

McFarlane, I.D., *Buchanan* (London: Duckworth, 1981)

Mackenzie, George, 'The Life of Mr. George Buchanan', *The Lives and Characters of the most Eminent Writers of the Scots Nation*, vol. 3 (of 3) (Edinburgh: William Adams Jr., 1722), 156–83

McClure, J., '"O Phoenix Escossois": James VI as Poet', in *A Day Estivall*, ed. A. Gardner-Medwin and J. Williams (Aberdeen, 1990), 96–111

McCullough, Peter, *Sermons at Court: Politics and Religion in Elizabethan and Jacobean Preaching* (Cambridge: Cambridge University Press, 1998)

McMillan, William H., *The Worship of the Scottish Reformed Church, 1550–1638* (London: J. Clarke, 1931)

Mackie, J.D., 'Scotland and the Spanish Armada', *SHR* 12 (1915), 1–23

Mackie, J.D., 'The Will of Mary Stuart', *SHR* 11 (1914), 338–44

Mahon, R. H., *Mary Queen of Scots: A Study of the Lennox Narrative* (Cambridge: Cambridge University Press, 1924)

Marcham, Frederick George, 'James I of England and the Little Beagle Letters', in *Persecution and Liberty: Essays in honor of George Lincoln Burr* (New York: The Century Co.), 311–34

Marryat, Horace, *A Residence in Jutland, The Danish Isles, and Copenhagen*, 2 vols (London: John Murray, 1860)

Martin, Thomas, *The History of the Town of Thetford, in the Counties of Norfolk and Suffolk* (London: J. Nichols, 1779)

Mason, Roger A., 'George Buchanan, James VI and the Presbyterians', in *Scots and Britons: Scottish Political Thought and the Union of 1603*, ed. Roger A. Mason (Cambridge: Cambridge University Press, 1994)

Mathew, David, *James I* (London: Eyre & Spottiswoode, 1967)

Meikle, Maureen M., '"Holde her at the Oeconomicke rule of the House": Anna of Denmark and Scottish Court Finances, 1589–1603', in *Women in Scotland c. 1100 – c. 1750*, ed. Elizabeth Ewan and Maureen M. Meikle (Phantassie, East Linton: Tuckwell Press, 1999), 105–11

Meikle, Maureen M., 'A Meddlesome Princess: Anna of Denmark and Scottish Court Politics, 1589–1603', in *The Reign of James VI*, ed. Goodare and Lynch, 126–40

Miller, Amos C., *Sir Henry Killigrew: Elizabethan Soldier and Diplomat* (Leicester: Leicester University Press, 1963)

Moore, Norman, *The History of the Study of Medicine in the British Isles* (Oxford: Clarendon Press, 1908)

Mortensen, Lars Boje, 'Anders Sørensen Vedel: The Latin Writings of a Vernacular Humanist', in *A History of Nordic Neo-Latin Literature* (Odense: Odense University Press, 1995), 267–80

Mumby, Frank Arthur, *The Fall of Mary Stuart: A Narrative in Contemporary Letters* (London: Constable, 1921)

Nicholas, Edward, *Proceedings and Debates in the House of Commons in 1620 and 1621*, 2 vols (Oxford: Clarendon Press, 1766)

Nicholls, Mark, *Investigating Gunpowder Plot* (Manchester: Manchester University Press, 1991)

Normand, Lawrence, '"What passions call you these?": *Edward II* and James VI', in *Christopher Marlowe and English Renaissance Culture*, ed. Darryll Grantley and Peter Roberts (Aldershot: Scolar Press, 1998), 172–97

Oman, Carola, *The Winter Queen: Elizabeth of Bohemia* (London: Hodder & Stoughton, 1938)

Opfell, Olga, *The King James Bible Translators* (Jefferson: McFarland, 1982)

Orgel, Stephen, *The Illusion of Power: Political Theater in the English Renaissance* (Berkeley: University of California Press, 1975)

Orgel, Stephen and Roy Strong, *Inigo Jones: The Theatre of the Stuart Court*, 2 vols (Berkeley: University of California Press, 1973)

Patterson, W.B., *King James VI and I and the Reunion of Christendom* (Cambridge: Cambridge University Press, 1997)

Pearsall Smith, Logan, *The Life and Times of Sir Henry Wotton*, 2 vols (Oxford: Clarendon Press, 1907)

Peck, Linda Levy, *Court Patronage and Corruption in Early Stuart England* (Boston: Unwin Hyman, 1990)

Peck, Linda Levy, *Northampton: Patronage and Policy at the Court of James I* (London: George Allen & Unwin, 1982)

Perry, Curtis, *The Making of Jacobean Culture: James I and the Negotiation of Elizabethan Literary Practice* (Cambridge: Cambridge University Press,

1997)

Prestwich, Menna, *Cranfield: Politics and Profits under the Early Stuarts* (Oxford: Clarendon Press, 1966)

Questier, Michael C., *Conversion, Politics and Religion in England, 1580–1625* (Cambridge: Cambridge University Press, 1996)

Quinn, D. B., *Ralegh and the British Empire* (London: English Universities Press, 1947)

Quintrell, B.W., 'The Royal Hunt and the Puritans, 1604–1605', *Journal of Ecclesiastical History* 31 (1980), 41–59

Rait, Robert S. and Annie I. Cameron, *King James's Secret: Negotiations Between Elizabeth and James VI. Relating to the Execution of Mary Queen of Scots, From the Warrender Papers* (London: Nisbet & Co., 1927)

Ridley, J., *John Knox* (Oxford: Oxford University Press, 1968)

Riis, Thomas, *Should Auld Acquaintance Be Forgot . . .: Scottish-Danish relations c. 1450–1707*, 2 vols (Odense: Odense University Press, 1988)

Roughead, William, 'The Riddle of the Ruthvens', in *The Riddle of the Ruthvens and Other Studies* (Edinburgh: W. Green, 1919), 1–36

Ruigh, Robert E., *The Parliament of 1624: Politics and Foreign Policy* (Cambridge: Harvard University Press, 1971)

Russell, Conrad, *Parliaments and English Politics, 1621–1629* (Oxford: Clarendon Press, 1979)

Rypins, Stanley, 'The Printing of *Basilikon Doron*', *Papers of the Bibliographical Society of America* 64 (1970), 393–417

Scott, Mary Maxwell, *The Tragedy of Fotheringhay, founded on the Journal of Bourgoing and unpublished MS documents* (Edinburgh and London: Sands & Co., 1915)

Scott, Walter ed., *Secret History of the Court of James the First*, 2 vols (Edinburgh: John Ballantyne & Co., 1811)

Seddon, P.R., 'Robert Carr, Earl of Somerset', *Renaissance and Modern Studies*, 14 (1970), 48–68

Seton, W.W., 'The Early Years of Henry Frederick, Prince of Wales, and Charles, Duke of Albany', *SHR* 13 (1915–16), 366–79

Sharpe, Kevin, *The Personal Rule of Charles I* (New Haven and London: Yale University Press, 1992)

Sharpe, Kevin, *Politics and Ideas in Early Stuart England: Essays and Studies* (New York: Pinter, 1989)

Shire, Helena Mennie, *Song, Dance and Poetry of the Court of Scotland under*

King James VI (Cambridge: Cambridge University Press, 1969)

Shriver, Frederick, 'Hampton Court Re-visited: James I and the Puritans', *Journal of Ecclesiastical History*, 33 (1982), 48–71

Smith, Thomas, *Vitae Quorundam Eruditissimorum et Illustrium Virorum* (London: David Mortier, 1707)

Smout, T.C., *A History of the Scottish People 1560–1830* (London: William Collins, 1969)

Smuts, Malcolm, *Court Culture and the Origins of a Royalist Tradition in Early Stuart England* (Philadelphia: University of Pennsylvania Press, 1987)

Smuts, Malcolm, 'Cultural Diversity and Cultural Change at the Court of James I', in *The Mental World of the Jacobean Court*, ed. Linda Levy Peck (Cambridge: Cambridge University Press, 1991)

Somerset, Anne, *Unnatural Murder: Poison at the Court of James I* (London: Weidenfeld & Nicolson, 1998)

Sommerville, Johann P., 'James I and the Divine Right of Kings: English Politics and Continental Theory', in *The Mental World of the Jacobean Court*, ed. Linda Levy Peck (Cambridge: Cambridge University Press, 1991)

Spedding, James, 'Review of the evidence respecting the conduct of King James I. in the case of Sir Thomas Overbury', *Archaeologia*, 41 (1867), 79–115

Stafford, Helen Georgia, *James VI of Scotland and the Throne of England* (New York and London: D. Appelton-Century Company, 1940)

Stafford, Helen, 'Notes on Scottish Witchcraft Cases 1590–1591', in *Essays in Honour of Conyers Read* (Chicago, 1935), 96–118

Stevenson, David, *Scotland's Last Royal Wedding: The Marriage of James VI and Anne of Denmark* [with a Danish Account of the Marriage translated by Peter Graves] (Edinburgh: John Donald, 1997)

Stewart, Alan, 'The Body Archival: Re-Reading the Trial of the Earl of Somerset', in *The Body in Late Medieval and Early Modern Culture*, ed. Darryll Grantley and Nina Taunton (Basingstoke: Ashgate, 2000), 65–81

Stewart, Alan, 'Homosexuals in History: A.L. Rowse and the Queer Archive', in *Love, Sex, Friendship and Intimacy Between Men, 1550–1800*, ed. Katherine O'Donnell and Michael O'Rourke (Aldershot: Palgrave, 2003)

Stewart, Alan, 'Boys' Buttocks Revisited: James VI and I and the Myth of the Sovereign Schoolmaster', in *Sodomy in Early Modern Europe*, ed. Tom Betteridge (Manchester University Press, 2002), 131–47

Stewart, Alan, 'Purging Troubled Humours: Bacon, Northampton and the Anti-Duelling Campaign of 1613–1614', in *The Crisis of 1614 and the Addled Parliament: Literary and Historical Perspectives*, ed. Stephen Clucas and Rosalind Davies (Basingstoke: Ashgate, 2002), 84–97

Stone, Lawrence, *The Causes of the English Revolution 1529–1642* (London: Routledge & Kegan Paul, 1972)

Strickland, Agnes, *Lives of the Queens of Scotland and English Princesses connected with the Regal Succession of Great Britain*, 8 vols (Edinburgh and London: William Blackwood, 1850–1859)

Strong, Roy, *Britannia Triumphans: Inigo Jones, Rubens and Whitehall Palace* (London: Thames & Hudson, 1980)

Strong, Roy, *Henry, Prince of Wales and England's Lost Renaissance* (London: Thames & Hudson, 1986)

Thoren, Victor E. (with John R. Christianson), *The Lord of Uraniborg: A Biography of Tycho Brahe* (Cambridge: Cambridge University Press, 1990)

Tyacke, Nicholas, *Anti-Calvinists: The Rise of English Arminianism ca. 1590–1640* (Oxford: Clarendon Press, 1987)

Tytler, Patrick Fraser, *History of Scotland*, vol. 9 (Edinburgh: William Tait, 1843)

Usher, Roland G., 'James I and Sir Edward Coke', *English Historical Review*, 18 (1903), 664–75

Usher, Roland G., *The Reconstruction of the English Church*, 2 vols (New York: D. Appleton, 1910)

Warner, George F. ed., 'The Library of James VI. 1573–1583 From a Manuscript in the Hand of Peter Young, His Tutor', *Miscellany of the Scottish History Society* (Edinburgh: Edinburgh University Press for the Scottish History Society, 1893), ix–lxxv

Warrender, Margaret ed., *Illustrations of Scottish History* (Edinburgh: James Stillie, 1889)

Welsby, Paul, *George Abbot* (London: SPCK, 1962)

Wickham, Glynne, 'Contributions de Ben Jonson et de Dekker aux Fêtes du Couronnement de Jacquers Ier', in *Fêtes de la Renaissance*, ed. Jean Jacquot (Paris, 1956), 1: 279–83

Williams, Ethel Carleton, *Anne of Denmark: Wife of James VI of Scotland: James I of England* (London: Longman, 1970)

Williamson, Arthur H., 'Scotland, Antichrist and the Invention of Great Britain', in *New Perspectives on the Politics and Culture of Early Modern Scotland*, ed. John Dwyer et al. (Edinburgh: John Donald, 1980–1982), 34–58

Williamson, Arthur H., *Scottish National Consciousness in the Age of James VI* (Edinburgh: John Donald, 1979)

Williamson, Hugh Ross, *George Villiers, First Duke of Buckingham: Study for a Biography* (London: Duckworth, 1940)

Willson, David Harris, 'James I and His Literary Assistants', *Huntington Library Quaterly* 8 (1944–5), 35–57

Willson, David Harris, *King James VI and I* (London: Jonathan Cape, 1956)

Willson, David Harris, *The Privy Councillors in the House of Lords 1604–1629* (Minneapolis: University of Minnesota Press, 1940)

Wormald, Jenny, 'Ecclesiastical Vitriol: the Kirk, the Puritans, and the Future King of England', in *The Reign of Elizabeth I: Court and Culture in the Last Decade*, ed. John Guy (Cambridge: Cambridge University Press/The Folger Institute, 1995), 171–91

Wormald, Jenny, 'James VI, James I, and the Identity of Britain', in *The British Problem, c. 1534–1707*, ed. Brendan Bradshaw and John Morrill (New York: St Martin's Press, 1966)

Wormald, Jenny, 'James VI and I, *Basilikon Doron* and *The Trew Law of Free Monarchies*: The Scottish Context and the English Translation', in *The Mental World of the Jacobean Court*, ed. Linda Levy Peck (Cambridge: Cambridge University Press, 1991), 36–54

Wormald, Jenny, 'James VI and I: Two Kings or One', *History*, 68 (1983), 187–209

Wormald, Jenny, '"'Tis True I Am A Cradle King": The View from the Throne', in *The Reign of James VI*, ed. Goodare and Lynch, 241–56

Wright, Louis B., 'Propaganda against James I's "Appeasement" of Spain', *Huntington Library Quarterly*, 6: 2 (1943), 149–72

Young, Michael B., *James VI and I and the History of Homosexuality* (Basingstoke: Macmillan, 2000)

Zaller, Robert, *The Parliament of 1621: A Study in Constitutional Conflict* (Berkeley: University of California Press, 1971)

Zeeberg, Peter, 'The Inscriptions at Tycho Brahe's Uraniborg', in *A History of Nordic Neo-Latin Literature* (Odense: Odense University Press, 1995), 251–66

Index

Index

Index

Index

Henry Julius, Duke of Brunswick-Wolfenbüttel, 117–18, 246

Hepburn, James, fourth Earl of Bothwell, 5–6, 11, 14–18, 20, 23, 25, 26, 27–8, 29–30, 86; marries Mary, Queen of Scots, 30

Herbert, Sir Philip, later Earl of Montgomery, 174, 181, 257, 274, 287

Herbert, Earl of Pembroke, 217, 257, 261, 287, 295, 301, 303

Hermitage Castle, 17, 23

Herries, John, fourth Lord, see Maxwell, Sir John

Herries, Dr, 161

Hertford, Edward, Earl of, see Seymour, Edward

Hewatt, Peter, minister, 156

Hiegait, William, 23

Hobbes, Thomas, 232

Hoby, Sir Edward, 73

Holles, Gervase, 174

Holles, Sir John, 175

Holyroodhouse, Palace of, 1, 11, 12, 24, 52, 65, 68, 82, 118, 131, 133, 283, 289; Bothwell's raids on, 129–30, 135–6

Holyrood, Abbey of, 11, 30, 119

Home, Sir George, of Sprot, later Earl of Dunbar, 157, 173–4, 259, 262, 283

Hooker, Richard, 187–8, 194; *Of the Lawes of Ecclesiasticall Politie*, 187

Hoskins, John, 254

Howard, Charles, Lord Howard of Effingham, Earl of Nottingham, 98, 221

Howard, Lady Frances, later Countess of Essex, Countess of Somerset, 260, 261–3, 274, 275, 278; and murder of Overbury, 272; trial of, 276

Howard, Lord Henry, later Earl of Northampton, 164–5, 173, 200, 221, 224, 227, 244, 251, 260, 274; death of, 264

Howard, Lord Thomas, 258

Hudson, James, 34

Hudson, James, English agent, 158–9, 161

Hudson, Robert, 34, 63

Hudson, Mekill Thomas, 34, 63–4; *The Historie of Judith*, 63–4

Hudson, William, 34

Hume, Alexander, 63

Hume, Sir Patrick, of Polwarth, 63

Hume, William, 104

Hunsdon, Henry, first Lord, see Carey, Henry

hunting, 176–8, 179–81, 213, 289, 308, 313, 339–40, 341

Huntingtower [Ruthven], 157

Huntly, Earl of, see Gordon, George

Huntly, dowager Lady, 10

Hutton, Matthew, Archbishop of York, 180

Hveen (Denmark) James's visit to, 115–16

Hyde, Edward, Earl of Clarendon, 181

impositions, 238, 240, 254

Inchaffray, Lord of, 150

Indernyty, Scottish gentleman, 166

Isabella Clara Eugenia, Infanta of Spain, 93

James III, King of Scots, 44

James V, King of Scots, 1, 2, 47, 148, 316

James VI, King of Scots and I, King of England:

(1566–1583)

birth of, 12–14; guardianship of, 17; baptism, 19–22; threats of abduction, 22–3; placed at Stirling, 26–7, 28–9; Mary's last encounter with, 28–9; coronation, 31; household at Stirling, 33–5, 38–45; at 1571 Parliament, 36; death of Lennox, 36; education of, 38–45; and Buchanan, 38–45; entrusted to Erskine of Gogar, 46; meets with Morton, 47; assumes government, 47–8; Morton's attack on Stirling, 48–9; meets Esmé Stuart, 51; enters Edinburgh, 52–3; relationship with Esmé Stuart, 53–4; 1580 progress, 56; 'corrupted' by Lennox, 58–9; relations with England, 59–62; death of Morton, 62–3; Act of Association 64; Ruthven Raid, 65–7; reactions to Lennox's death, 69–71

(1583–1603)

escapes from Ruthven Raiders, 72–4; Fontenay's assessment of (1584), 74–7; negotiations over Mary, 80–7; reactions to Mary's death, 88–93; relations with Huntly, 94–6, 137–8; Spanish Armada, 97–8; treachery of Huntly, 99–102; marches against Huntly, 102–4; marriage negotiations, 105–7; resolves to collect Anna, 109–10; letter to the Privy Council, 110–11; sails for Norway, 111; marries Anna, 112; visits Denmark, 113–18; meets Tycho Brahe, 115–16; returns to Scotland, 118; appoints Melville to Anna's household, 121–2; interest in witchcraft, 125–8; dealings with Bothwell, 128–33, 135–8; murder of Moray, 131–2; 'Spanish Blanks' affair, 133–4; birth of son Henry, 140; quarrels with Anna over Henry's upbringing, 140–2; death of Maitland, 142; finances of, 142–3;

Index

Index